# THE BIOLOGY OF
# MORAL SYSTEMS

When a biologist publishes a treatise with a title like *The Biology of the Amphibia*, *The Biology of the Mountain Bluebird*, or *The Biology of the Gene*, he means "everything about the life and natural history" of the group or unit in question, as seen through the eyes of a biologist. That is precisely how the title of this book should be translated. I have tried to discuss everything about the life and natural history of moral systems, as seen through the eyes of a biologist.

# THE BIOLOGY OF MORAL SYSTEMS

## Richard D. Alexander

ALDINE DE GRUYTER
New York

# ABOUT THE AUTHOR

**Richard D. Alexander** is Donald Ward Tinkle Professor of Evolutionary Biology, Department of Biology and Curator of Insects, Museum of Zoology, The University of Michigan. A recipient of numerous awards, Dr. Alexander has been a major contributor to professional journals and edited volumes and is the author of *Darwinism and Human Affairs*.

ALDINE DE GRUYTER
A Division of Walter de Gruyter, Inc.
200 Saw Mill River Road
Hawthorne, New York 10532

**Library of Congress Cataloging-in-Publication Data**

Alexander, Richard D.
    The biology of moral systems.

    (Foundations of human behavior)
    Bibliography: p.
    Includes index.
    1. Ethics.     2. Biology—Moral and ethical aspects.
3. Arms race—Moral and ethical aspects.     I. Title.
II. Series.
BJ58.A43   1987     171'.7     86-25897
ISBN 0-202-01173-9 (lib. bdg.)
ISBN 0-202-01174-7 (pbk.)

Printed in the United States of America
10   9   8   7   6   5   4   3   2

**To my children**

**And theirs**

# FOUNDATIONS OF HUMAN BEHAVIOR
*An Aldine de Gruyter Series of Texts and Monographs*

*Edited by*
**Sarah Blaffer Hrdy,** *University of California, Davis*
**Richard W. Wrangham,** *University of Michigan*

# CONTENTS

## 2   A BIOLOGICAL VIEW OF MORALITY

## 3   MORALITY AS SEEN BY PHILOSOPHERS AND BIOLOGISTS

# LIST OF ILLUSTRATIONS

## Figures

## Tables

# PREFACE

Thoughtful people seem increasingly to agree that our society—indeed, world society as a whole—has entered into a crisis of unprecedented magnitude, and with potential consequences almost too horrible and irreversible to contemplate. This deepening crisis arises from the interaction of several contributing factors. First, is an accelerating technological alteration of the environment and, concomitantly, of our social structures and ourselves. Second, is an accelerating depletion of the world's resources, and an accompanying interest among the more powerful nations in manipulating and competing over those less powerful who possess the scarce resources they need. Third, is an elaboration and proliferation of weapons now so terrible as to assure, for the first time in history, that almost no imaginable alternative is worse than their employment. Finally, coincident with the rise of weaponry, there has been an effective shrinking of the social brain that controls it. No matter how many millions of citizens may exist in a given nation-state, no matter how hideous its weaponry, the decision regarding use of that weaponry eventually comes down to about the same small number of individuals, or even to the calculations of a single brain. At least as a final step, it takes only one finger to push a button that could bring on what might aptly be termed the ultimate holocaust. Moreover, modern nations are now so large and complex that internal differences of interests and the possibilities for deception may allow small, special-interest groups to promote the international arms race at the cost of the rest of the society, and even of the world as a whole (including, ultimately, even if inadvertently, themselves). It may be appropriate to characterize the so-called great nations of the world today as the most enormous, most awesomely weaponed, smallest-brained "dinosaurs" of all time.

Even if I have exaggerated its seriousness (the growing public clamor suggests otherwise), the crisis is undeniable. Just as undeniably, the crisis arises out of our social activities: out of the nature and consequences of our personal and group interactions around the world; out of the nature and consequences of our beliefs, individual and collective, with respect to right and wrong; out of our attitudes and actions in the realm that we call ethics and morality, whether at international, national, local, or even family levels. Discords that bear strong resemblances to one another permeate the entire hierarchy of social organization, from the smallest social groups right through to the largest. These discords are invariably centered on moral and ethical enigmas. It is difficult to avoid the impression that some common problems underlie the solutions to all of them.

During 1977–1978, I participated in a series of conferences at the Hastings Institute in New York, charged with a search for the "foundations" of ethics. These conferences, which together with an earlier series gave rise to five published volumes (Engelhardt and Callahan, 1976–1980; Callahan and Engelhardt, 1981), were organized as a result of the flood of new ethical questions arising out of technology: abortion, euthanasia, the right to reject certain kinds of technological prolongation of life, etc. The Hastings Institute itself was organized for the same general reason, in 1969, and it has become widely known for its examination of the questions involving medical ethics and bioethics. More than anything else, the Hastings conferences set me to thinking and reading about the general background of human ideas about morality. I read all of the reports published by the Hastings Institute and entered the philosophical literature on the same topics. As a result, I began to puzzle over what I saw as an incompleteness or inconclusiveness, not only of the collection of Hastings reports and the discussions in the conferences in which I had participated, but, indeed, of all general arguments on ethics. I found myself sharing the attitude expressed by the philosopher, Alasdair MacIntyre (1981a), in a question in the title of his final paper in the Hastings Center conference series: "A crisis in moral philosophy: Why is the search for the foundations of ethics so frustrating?"

Even if quick and decisive solutions to ethical and moral problems are simply not possible, I find myself thinking that in all of the arguments something is missing. Indeed, I believe that something crucial has been missing from all of the great debates of history, among philosophers, politicians, theologians, and thinkers from other and diverse backgrounds, on the issues of morality, ethics, justice, right and wrong. Why have the greatest minds throughout history left such questions seemingly as unresolved as ever? Why is it that, as MacIntyre (1981b) put it, debates about morality "apparently can find no terminus"? Why should it be that, despite our most intense and sincere efforts, we are not really prepared to deal with the crises that our own activities bring about, even though we cannot but admit that they now have the potential, incredibly, to cause the destruction of life, or at least civilization, on our planet?

Part of the answer is that those who have tried to analyze morality have failed to treat the human traits that underlie moral behavior as outcomes of evolution—as outcomes of the process, dominated by natural selection, that forms the organizing principle of modern biology.

This omission is not really the fault of those who have studied ethical and moral systems. The science of biology has been so vague about how to apply natural selection that not until the last two decades have biologists themselves been able to use it to analyze social systems.

Discussions of moral issues seem invariably to end up confronting a core of unanalyzable mystery. Sometimes this mystery is acknowledged, or dealt with, by relegating moral decisions to the supernatural—by asserting, for example, that the answers to moral questions come only from God. Sometimes the mystery is simply what is left when a philosopher or other intellectual has wrestled through an issue—like the conflict between seeking what is best for one's self and seeking to bring "the greatest good to the greatest number"—and failed to explain how the issue can be resolved by referring to the concept of morality. Sometimes the mystery seems to represent all that we do not understand about human nature or motivations.

Part of my purpose here is to see if this core of mystery can be dispelled by re-examining human striving, using new information and ideas from the discipline of biology. Although I may not have succeeded, at least I believe I have demonstrated that the undertaking is reasonable. I think I have shown that evolved human nature and morality are compatible; that morality as generally conceived, and possibly even as seen by idealists from philosophy and theology, is neither contrary to biologists' understanding of evolution by natural selection (as thought by T. H. Huxley, 1896) nor independent of selection, requiring a divine origin (as thought by Lack, 1957, 1965).

Moral problems involve the interests of people, and biology gives good reasons for expecting different individuals to behave as if their interests are unique, and thus as if interests conflict among individuals to some degree almost all of the time. Regardless of the value of insights provided by individuals, then, only the collective—directly or through representatives—is likely to serve the collective's interests. Arguments from biology support those from other sources which indicate that, for many conflicts of interest, compromises and enforceable contracts represent the only real solutions. Appeals to morality, I will argue, are simply the invoking of such compromises and contracts in particular ways. Moreover, the process of natural selection that has given rise to all forms of life, including humans, operates such that success has always been relative. One consequence is that organisms resulting from the long-term cumulative effects of selection are expected to resist efforts to reveal their interests fully to others, and also efforts to place limits on their striving or to decide for them when their interests are being "fully" satisfied.

These are all reasons why we should expect no "terminus"—ever—to debates on moral and ethical issues. But they are not reasons for supposing that the mystery underlying the concept of morality is inevitable or that practical solutions to moral questions cannot be devised that will lessen the social and political problems of the world.

Biologists do not typically talk much about morality, and I have often heard people express disappointment and frustration because biologists seem always to stop short of explaining how Darwinian evolution might help in the search for ideas on how to turn our social behavior into more positive and less terrifying channels. As a student once said to me, "What good is a theory about human behavior that cannot help us with our worst [moral and ethical] problems?" Although this is a serious and useful question, I am convinced that biology can never offer what most such people seem to expect: easy or direct answers to the questions of what is right and wrong. I explicitly reject the attitude that whatever biology tells us is so is also what ought to be (David Hume's so-called "naturalistic fallacy"), as offered by such biologist-philosophers as Julian Huxley (1947) and Wolfgang Wickler (1972). Contrary to Wickler's arguments, biologists do not have special abilities to assess what is ethical; and, contrary to the implications of Huxley, there are within biology no magic solutions to moral problems.

The opinion seems to be widespread that for evolutionary biology to be important to humans it has to provide quick and dramatic solutions to specific problems. It is not my experience that such solutions are likely. Some are possible, as in the discovery, from applying evolutionary theory, of means for telling which disease symptoms of a host aid the disease organism and which aid the host (Ewald, 1980). This approach may enable one to decide the highly practical question of which symptoms of human disease to alleviate by palliatives, and which to leave alone. Generally speaking, however, the great value of evolutionary understanding lies in its guidance in developing appropriate and useful ideas and hypotheses about human activities and tendencies. Evolutionary understanding *changes attitudes*, therefore it may affect almost anything we do, but sometimes quite indirectly and only after considerable delay. Scarcely any reasonable person exposed to Darwin's theory would deny that it has significantly altered human existence. But the exact ways in which evolutionary knowledge participates in solutions to human problems are usually subtle and difficult to evaluate. For the very reason that evolutionary understanding affects nearly everything humans think about themselves, most people would be hard-pressed to explain or summarize its effects adequately.

Biology provides a broad source of information about humans that has no substitute. It clarifies long-standing paradoxes. It shows that some things have indeed been missing from the debates about morality, and they have been missing because the process of organic evolution that gave rise to all forms of life has been left out of the discussions. Knowledge of the human background in organic evolution can provide a deeper self-understanding by an increasing proportion of the world's population; self-understanding that I believe can contribute to answering the serious questions of social living.

These are reasons why I regard it as a responsibility of biologists—in the tradition of Charles Darwin, Thomas Huxley, Sir Arthur Keith, David Lack, Theodosius Dobzhansky, George G. Simpson, and a few others—to develop a better "natural history" of moral and ethical attitudes and beliefs. They are reasons why I think it useful to examine the biology of moral systems.

This book may be regarded as continuing the arguments in my 1979 book, *Darwinism and Human Affairs*; the first chapter of that book is a useful introduction to what follows here. In the present book there are five chapters. The first takes up biological issues that underlie the theoretical positions, and deals with some concepts and problems that have in the past made it difficult for biologists, philosophers, and social and political scientists to understand one another. I do not think *all* of the biology in this first chapter is required to follow my arguments, but the more of it that is absorbed the better the reader will understand my positions.

The second chapter develops the theory and discusses its application to human actions, the human psyche, and the ontogeny of moral ideas. The third reviews arguments of moral philosophers, philosophers of biology, and biologist-philosophers on several moral issues. This review is mainly critical, trying to show how philosophers' arguments have been affected by leaving out concepts and facts essential for understanding the strivings of organisms. I have not tried to review the voluminous history of philosophical writing or even to trace the development and priority of ideas; rather, I have chosen a few prominent authors that seem representative of modern philosophical discussions of morality and discussed aspects of their writing that seem most important in illustrating my arguments.

The fourth chapter considers the consequences of applying a biological approach to morality. It includes an effort to interpret the human psyche in evolutionary terms and a review of problems associated with the international arms race. The fifth chapter briefly reviews conclusions, and the epilogue is, in part, a brief abstract of the entire book.

> I am sincerely of opinion that the views . . . propounded by Mr. Darwin may be understood hereafter as constituting an epoch in the intellectual history of the human race. They will modify the whole system of our thought and opinion, our most intimate convictions.
>
> T. H. Huxley, 1894

*Richard D. Alexander*

# ACKNOWLEDGMENTS

I thank first the members of The Entomology Department of The University of California, Davis, who successfully nominated me to deliver the Tracy and Ruth Storer Lectures in 1980. If there was dismay at learning that, innocent of the identity of my sponsors, I had selected as my topic the biology of moral systems, it was not evident during my visit there. I especially thank Karen Loeblich and Andrew McClelland for being gracious hosts who afforded me every opportunity to develop and present my lectures without difficulty.

Second, I appreciate the tolerance of the directors and staff of the Museum of Zoology of the University of Michigan during the past 15 years, when much of my time has been spent, not in curating insects, but in thinking and writing about human behavior. The Frank Ammerman Fund of the Insect Division of the Museum helped meet the expenses of library work, editing assistance, and computer time. I believe that Dr. Ammerman, an entomologist who in later years preoccupied himself with human ecology, would have approved of this project. The Collegiate Institute for Values in Science of The College of Literature, Science, and the Arts of the University of Michigan has also supported me, both financially and by the positive encouragement of its membership.

Third, I thank Bill E. Frye, formerly Vice President for Academic Affairs and Provost of the University of Michigan, now of Emory University, for having been the most significant intellectual-administrative force in providing a positive environment at the University of Michigan for evolutionary approaches to human behavior.

Fourth, I thank all the people who helped produce the manuscript: Gloria Jadwin, June OConnor, and Theresa Duda for skill and patience in typing and structuring it; Elizabeth Rockwell, Kathy Noble, and Aina Bernier for assisting with the literature searches; Marilyn Houck for much help with text editing; Darius Mehregan for assisting with the data underlying Figure 1.1; and Margaret Van Bolt for preparing the illustrations. I also thank Margaret Gruter and the editor of *Zygon* for permission to use material from my earlier published papers.

Fifth, I thank Pat Overby of the University of Michigan Department of Political Science for using her knowledge of biology, human affairs, and English to help me greatly with the manuscript.

Sixth, I thank the many who individually, and as members of organizations, have discussed morality with me as the manuscript progressed. The following are singled out for special appreciation: The Canadian

Psychological Association; The University of Michigan Research Club; The University of Michigan Society of Fellows Angus Campbell Round-table; members of the First and Second Monterey Dunes Conferences on Law, Biology, and Culture (1981, 1984); The University of Utah (Darwin Lectures, 1982); The College of Science, Pennsylvania State University (Chemerda Lectures); The Ann Arbor Huron High School Humanities Class (and David Stringer); the Coe College Social Sciences Program (and Fred Wilhoite); the students in my classes in Evolution and Human Behavior at the University of Michigan; Allen Gibbard, William Frankena, Peter Railton, and Nicholas White of the University of Michigan Philosophy Department; Jesse Chanley, Theodore H. Hubbell, Selma Isil, Gene Mesher, David Queller, and Beverly Strassmann of the University of Michigan Division of Biological Sciences; Laura Betzig and Paul Turke of the University of Michigan Museum of Zoology; Bobbi S. Low of the University of Michigan School of Natural Resources; Gordon Kane of the University of Michigan Department of Physics; Randolf M. Nesse of the Department of Psychiatry of the University of Michigan Medical School; Dierdre Bloch, Mark Flinn, Lars Rodseth, and Richard Wrangham of the University of Michigan Department of Anthropology; Warren G. Holmes of the University of Michigan Department of Psychology; William Irons of the Northwestern University Department of Anthropology; Randy and Nancy Wilmsen Thornhill of the University of New Mexico Departments of Biology and Anthropology, respectively; Donald Symons of the Anthropology Department of the University of California at Santa Barbara; Michael Ruse of the Department of Philosophy of the University of Guelph, Ontario; Douglas J. Futuyma of the Department of Ecology and Evolutionary Biology of Stonybrook State University of New York; James E. Lloyd and Thomas J. Walker of the University of Florida Department of Entomology; Victor Weisskopf of the Massachusetts Institute of Technology; Paul Sherman of Cornell University; Ann E. Pace of Minneapolis, Minnesota; Mildred Dickemann of Berkeley, California; Robert W. Smuts of Ann Arbor, Michigan; and my philosophically-minded good neighbor, Thomas Pyle. As most of these people will know, I have not followed all of their suggestions, and in some cases I may not have followed them well. The shortcomings that remain are thus my own responsibility.

Finally, and most important, I thank my wife, Lorraine Kearnes Alexander. Her loyalty, understanding, intelligence, and good sense, through the easier and the more difficult parts of our 37 years together, have more than anything else advised me of the nature and potency of confluences of interest, and of the very special effects of the unique symmetry of interests that exists within the nuclear family.

Should a traveller give an account of men who were entirely divested of avarice, ambition, or revenge; who knew no pleasure but friendship, generosity, and public spirit, we should immediately detect the falsehood and prove him a liar with the same certitude as if he had stuffed his narration with centaurs and dragons.

David Hume, 1772,
*Essays and Treatises*

A hydrogen bomb is an example of mankind's enormous capacity for friendly cooperation. Its construction requires an intricate network of human teams, all working with single-minded devotion toward a common goal. Let us pause and savor the glow of self-congratulation we deserve for belonging to such an intelligent and sociable species.

Robert S. Bigelow, 1969
*The Dawn Warriors*

The self-extinction of our species is not an act that anyone describes as sane or sensible; nevertheless, it is an act that, without quite admitting it to ourselves, we plan in certain circumstances to commit.

Jonathan Schell, 1982
*The Fate of the Earth*

# 1

# BIOLOGY AND THE BACKGROUND
# OF MORAL SYSTEMS

## The Evolutionary Approach

## INTRODUCTION

Moral systems are societies with rules. Rules are agreements or understandings about what is permitted and what is not, about what rewards and punishments are likely for specific acts, about what is right and wrong. Although moral rules are somewhat different from legal rules, or laws, the two are not unrelated and frequently overlap.

Moral behavior, in general, consists of following the rules—of not "cheating." But this is where the problems begin, rather than where they end. Few would accept that following the rules that prevail in society at any particular time is necessarily the most moral thing that one can do. Rules change. They are sometimes imposed by tyrants. There is probably no rule that everyone agrees with.

Moreover, we have come to regard morality—in the sense of concern for others—as something above and beyond rules per se, an ideal to be striven for even if there is no real hope of achieving it in its purest form. Many people believe that morality is an absolute, that there are general rules of moral behavior that are unchanging, and even that such rules are "natural laws" or God-given. I wish to examine such seeming absolutes, how they might have arisen, how hard we really strive toward them, what are the consequences of our striving, why we have failed so far, and how all of these questions are affected by an evolutionary viewpoint.

I will argue that the concepts of moral and ethical arise because of conflicts of interest, and that—at least up to now—moral systems have been designed to assist group members and explicitly not to assist the members of other competing groups. Because between-group competition and aggression are major concomitants of within-group cooperativeness, moreover, I will also argue that moral "advances" are not necessarily related to the philosophical ideal of morality as either indiscriminate or self-sacrificing beneficence or producing the greatest good for the greatest number. Although not necessarily denying the

1

feasibility of achieving or approaching such ideals, I will argue that failing to distinguish them from what has really been going on in the world has been—and still is—the main source of confusion and mystery with respect to moral and ethical considerations.

If there had been no recent discoveries in biology that provided new ways of looking at the concept of moral systems, then I would be optimistic indeed to believe that I could say much that is new. But there have been such discoveries. They are the advances in evolutionary theory developed principally by William D. Hamilton (1964), George C. Williams (1966b), and Robert L. Trivers (1971). These refinements, which were systematically reviewed in *Darwinism and Human Affairs* (Alexander, 1979a; see also Dawkins, 1976; Alcock, 1984; Chagnon and Irons, 1979; Symons, 1979) have been incorporated into the research and teaching of hundreds of young biologists active in fields like ecology, animal behavior, and population biology (e.g., see Alexander and Tinkle, 1981; Clutton-Brock and Harvey, 1978; Hunt, 1980; Krebs and Davies, 1981, 1984; Trivers, 1985; and biological journals like *The American Naturalist, Animal Behaviour, Ecology, Evolution,* and *Behavioral Ecology and Sociobiology*). They have also been used by a small group of biologists and social scientists, probably fewer than 100 so far, in renewed efforts to apply evolutionary biology to the human under-standing of humans (Alcock, 1984; Alexander, 1979a; Alexander and Tinkle, 1981; Betzig, 1986; Cavalli-Sforza and Feldman, 1981; Chagnon and Irons, 1979; Daly and Wilson, 1983; Dawkins, 1976, 1982; Hull, 1978; Lumsden and Wilson, 1981; Pulliam and Dunford, 1980; Ruse, 1979; Strate, 1982; Symons, 1979; Trivers, 1985; Wilson, 1975, 1978. See also, especially: *Ethology and Sociobiology, Current Anthropology, American Anthropologist, Journal of Social and Biological Structures, Human Ecology*).

The interpretations of different authors with regard to the recent advances in evolutionary theory often vary considerably. Aside from the pages that follow, my own views are most completely expressed in the first chapter of *Darwinism and Human Affairs*. With respect to humans my views probably coincide most closely with the general statements of Alcock (1984), Daly and Wilson (1983), Irons (1979), Symons (1979), and Trivers (1985). Otherwise, I recommend that the reader return to the original writings of Hamilton, Williams, and Trivers, which have now been reprinted many times (e.g., Clutton-Brock and Harvey, 1978; Krebs and Davies, 1981; Hunt, 1980). The central point in these writings, separated from all of its consequences and ramifications, is that natural selection has apparently been maximizing the survival by reproduction of genes, as they have been defined by evolutionists, and that, with respect to the activities of individuals, this includes effects on copies of their genes, even copies located in other individuals. In other words, we are evidently evolved not only to aid the genetic materials in our own bodies, by creating and assisting descendants, but also to assist, by nepotism, copies of our genes that reside in collateral (nondescendant) relatives.

During the past few years, I have heard several people suggest that the above-mentioned refinements of evolutionary theory represent the greatest intellectual advance of the century. I agree, in the sense that significant improvements in the theory that explains our underlying nature must always command special attention. I think that almost every concept relevant to human sociality (such as rationality, conscience, guilt, consciousness, altruism, and egoism) has its meaning changed—or made more precise—by applying the new refinements of evolutionary theory. I also feel that the true realization of intellectual advances in biological theory comes from their eventual application to human conduct: from their effect on humanity's view of itself, and, in turn, the effect of changes in self-views on human conduct and, consequently, the future of all existence. In this case the changes in self-views involve principally two items: First, is a more precise awareness of the nature of the long-term history that has shaped our life interests, most especially the idea of fulfillment through relatives and their surrogates. Second, is the realization that ethics, morality, human conduct, and the human psyche are to be understood only if societies are seen as collections of individuals seeking their own self-interests (albeit through use of the the group or group cooperativeness, and given that, in historical terms, the individual's self-interests can only be realized through reproduction, by creating descendants and assisting other relatives). In some respects these ideas run contrary to what people have believed and been taught about morality and human values: I suspect that nearly all humans believe it is a normal part of the functioning of every human individual now and then to assist someone else in the realization of that person's own interests to the actual net expense of those of the altruist. What this "greatest intellectual revolution of the century" tells us is that, despite our intuitions, there is not a shred of evidence to support this view of beneficence, and a great deal of convincing theory suggests that any such view will eventually be judged false. This implies that we will have to start all over again to describe and understand ourselves, in terms alien to our intuitions, and in one way or another different from every discussion of this topic across the whole of human history. It is also a goal of this book to contribute to this redescription and new understanding, and especially to discuss why our intuitions should have misinformed us.

A major illustration of what this redescription means involves the resolution of the problem of duality (selfishness and altruism) in human nature, paradoxical to the earliest philosophers and not resolved in any writings that do not take modern biology into account. We have every reason to believe that our view of human nature can now be reunified, with David Hume's (1750) "elements of the serpent and the wolf" referring to the serving of our own interests by assisting ourselves at others' expense, and his "particle of the dove" representing the serving of our own interests through (1) relatives who carry our genetic materials and (2) friends and associates who may be expected to reciprocate our kindnesses with interest.

Only six authors (Alexander, 1979–1985; Campbell, 1972–1983; Singer, 1981; Mackie, 1978, 1982; Ruse, 1979–1986) have previously made extensive attempts to apply recent evolutionary theory to the study of ethical questions, although several (e.g., see Barash, 1977; Boehm, 1979; Caplan, 1978; Dawkins, 1976, 1982; Stent, 1978; E. O. Wilson, 1975, 1978; Richards, 1982–1986) have discussed the topic briefly. One author, Kitcher (1985), criticizes extensively what he sees as E. O. Wilson's (1975, 1978) and Lumsden and Wilson's (1981) views on evolution and ethics (and their and my more general views of how evolution has affected human behavior). Flew (1967) and Richards (1986a,b) review a good part of the literature on evolution and ethics that preceded the recent refinements of evolutionary theory (see also Ebling, 1969). I see the outstanding efforts by older authors to relate evolution and ethics as those of Darwin (1871), Thomas H. Huxley (1896), and Sir Arthur Keith (1947) (see pp. 168–177).

## SOCIOBIOLOGY AND IDEOLOGY

A caution is necessary, especially for the nonbiologist audience. As I see it, the greatest distortions of the recent advances in evolutionary biology are discussed under the label "sociobiology," whether by its most enthusiastic supporters or (more especially) its most severe critics. These include implications that behavioral causation can sometimes be reduced to genetic factors alone; undue emphasis on the sterile dichotomy of innate versus acquired (or genetic versus learned, social, or cultural); suggestions of identifiable but unchangeable limits on human learning in the conduct of social and ethical activities; implications that one or another brand of social Darwinism deserves reviving; casual, careless, or otherwise flawed imputations of function; and arguments for some version of the naturalistic fallacy (see pp. 165–168). Opponents of sociobiology argue that most or all evolutionary biologists support these errors and fallacies.

Some people asked why I did not use the label of sociobiology in my 1979 book; the main reason is that distortions by both proponents and opponents, which are involved in most so-called sociobiological writings about human behavior, detract from the real issues. The other reasons are: (1) outside biology the label is more closely associated with certain views of behavioral ontogeny and ethics (which I often do not share—see Alexander, 1979a), than with advances in evolutionary theory per se; (2) those efforts to apply evolution specifically to analyses of human behavior, which parade the adjective "sociobiological," have sometimes been the least scholarly (especially in the sense of distinguishing hypotheses from conclusions or "explanations"); and (3) even if sociobiology were to be accepted as simply "the study of the evolution of social behavior" (rather than someone's view of the developmental or genetic background of behavior), the label does not suggest any clear or logical boundaries for a discipline. Thus, it is not easily seen to include applications of evolutionary theory to apparently "nonsocial" topics like senescence, sex ratios, and life histories. I believe it is confusing to suggest that refinements of evolutionary theory create new disciplines, that they can be restricted to something like social behavior, or that they are properly part of one particular approach. This confusion has contributed to the term sociobiology becoming a target of derogation and ridicule by nonbiologists, and this has almost certainly delayed the acceptance and use of evolutionary principles by human-oriented scholars (Alexander, 1987). The attachment of labels like sociobiology to advances in evolutionary thinking that explicitly concern human behavior tends to create ideologies and to divide the intellectual world into proponents and opponents. Too many of those involved in the ensuing "debates" do not trouble themselves to understand the underlying issues, drawing their conclusions instead from the popular literature and what they (or popular writers) see as the political or social implications. This is characteristic of ideological as opposed to scientific arguments.

The label "sociobiology" also seems to have suggested to some social and political scientists, and philosophers, that there is an easy shortcut into a deep understanding of biology. If that is true, one only needs to examine the rash of publications by nonbiologists under the label of sociobiology to see that very few have discovered the shortcut. I believe, instead, that the route to appropriate understanding of organic evolution is through a broad understanding of basic biological principles, and that significant curricular revisions will be required, introducing biology where it is now often completely absent, in the training of human-oriented scientists, lawyers, philosophers, and others. It is this general absence of deep understanding of biology that has caused most of the controversies about "genetic" determinism, and about the relationship of evolution by natural selection to behavioral development, learning, and culture (cf. Flinn and Alexander, 1982; Irons, 1979). Nonbiologist readers may view the first section of this book as something that can be skipped over, in order to get directly to the topic of moral systems. On the contrary, I believe that unless the arguments in this chapter, and those in the first chapter of *Darwinism and Human Affairs*, are understood thoroughly, what I say in the latter parts of this book is virtually certain to be misinterpreted.

Paradoxically, within biology, terms like sociobiology are not particularly controversial. This is partly because most biologists understand genetics, development, and physiology well enough not to make the naive mistakes of both critics and enthusiasts from outside biology. And it is partly because no one is very upset if someone is wrong about the developmental basis of behavior in a frog, a bird, or an insect. To be similarly wrong about humans, however, can have decidedly pernicious effects.

Three decades ago Konrad Lorenz also tried to name a "new field" which he also said consisted of the evolutionary study of behavior. The label he used, "ethology," also came to be associated with his particular views concerning the physiology, development, and inheritance of behavior and as a result eventually became obscure and less frequently used. The label "sociobiology" appears to be suffering a similar fate; and I suspect that the causes of evolution, biology, and especially humanity's understanding of itself, will thereby be served. The reason is that whatever arguments from biology are useful in understanding human behavior will then melt more easily into the human-oriented disciplines and not be held outside in an artificial subdiscipline, thus perpetuating hostilities and impeding the flow of understanding.

## MEANINGS AND MISINTERPRETATIONS

It is necessary that I comment further on definitions, because even the words in the title of this book have some likelihood of being misinterpreted.

### Biology and Biological

The word "biology" has diverse meanings, especially for people from different disciplines. For many (especially in the social sciences, philosophy, and medicine) biology translates as "genetic" or "physiological," and is contrasted with "psychological," "social," or "cultural." I do not so mean it, and, indeed, I reject these usages. People who have fallen into this erroneous and, I believe, harmful dichotomy are often those who search for ways to alter human behavior. In their professions they are required to ask more or less continually: can I alter this behavior by changing only the psychological, social, or cultural environment, or must I (by some other means) alter the internal physiological, chemical, or hormonal environment, or even use a genetically different individual to get a different behavior? It is understandable that this kind of problem leads them to ask whether or not a behavior is "biologically" determined. But the dichotomy is misleading. Biologists also study what social scientists call "psychological" and "cultural" aspects of behavior, even in nonhuman organisms, and not merely physiological and genetic aspects: examples may be found in nearly every paper published in journals like *Behaviour, Animal Behaviour, Zeitschrift für Tierpsychologie,* and *Behavioral Ecology and Sociobiology.* Biologists, moreover, have no justification for being more deterministic than others in their view of behavior, or for neglecting ontogenies, plasticity, or psychological, social, and cultural stimuli and causes. Learning, after all, is essentially universal among animals, and prominent behavioral variations in even simple organisms—such as those of the different castes of social insects, and indeed the morphological and physiological uniqueness of the castes—are determined by environmental not genetic variations.

My dictionary defines biology first as the *science of life,* and the central question of this science is the evolutionary background or adaptive function of traits and tendencies. I mean to ask: How can biology, the science of life, contribute to our understanding of moral systems? What procedures, information, concepts, and theories from the science of biology may be useful to human-oriented scholars? In what ways are moral and ethical questions related to our background in organic evolution? What has been the *natural history* of moral systems? One aspect of this usage that distinguishes it from the use of "biology" by many nonbiologists is that it explicitly includes environmental as well as genetic effects, and, indeed, it always includes the *interaction* of genes and environment. When the Harvard paleontologist Steven J. Gould said on the television news program "60 Minutes" (broadcast on April 22, 1984) that the human mind is so flexible and the potential scope of human behavior so broad that "it scarcely behooves us to consider biology at all," he was obviously using "biology" as many nonbiologists use it—to refer to genetic variations. If he interpreted biology, as I do, to mean evolutionary background (i.e., to refer to the more or less common heritage of genes and culture given to us across all of history), he would surely have been hesitant to make the same comment. Similarly, Lewontin *et al.* (1984) state (p. 7) that "Biological determinism (*biologism*) has been a powerful mode of explaining the observed inequalities of status, wealth, and power in contemporary industrial capitalist societies, and of defining human 'universals' of behavior as natural characteristics of these societies." Deterministic views have undoubtedly so been used, but biologists, whether they are dealing with humans or nonhumans, are in no way restricted to universals or to variations that correlate with genetic variations: natural selection also fixes genes that lead to environmentally alterable traits. Whether or not they are deliberate efforts to do so, I believe that such narrow references to biology tend to denigrate and illegitimize a scientific discipline by synonymizing it with particular approaches or with ideologies.

"Biological" is often used in the popular press to refer to the relationship between parent and offspring, siblings, or other genetic relatives (e.g., "the biological father . . . "). By itself this usage is not as misleading as that implying "physiologically or genetically determined"; but the two usages are allied and that indicating relationship undoubtedly abets the restriction of "biological" to genetic or physiological backgrounds of traits. In either case "genetic" or "physiological" rather than "biological" is the correct adjective that does not mislead.

As a consequence of the general ignorance of biology, many discussants of human behavior fail to realize that nearly all traits of organisms are variable or plastic. Those traits that in usual environments are not so plastic, and that still reflect genetic variation within the human species (like eye color, nose shape, ear lobe attachment, and hair patterns on the back of the hand), are actually rare and probably will require special explanations. Many such traits in humans are involved in individual and kin recognition (Alexander, 1979a). As such they are valuable only when unequivocal and not too common, and so (1) they will tend to be rigid in their expressions and (2) the relative frequencies of the alleles (alternative genes) giving rise to their alternative expressions will fluctuate and tend not to go to fixation (i.e., no allele is likely to eliminate all others: each time any becomes common its value in recognition will diminish; see Lacy and Sherman, 1983). But alleles that behave this way—and traits determined in this fashion—appear to be less the rule than the exception.

Modern authors who consider how biology might contribute to human social enterprises seem to divide into two camps. The first group supposes that biology will be principally useful in locating a core of "basic" or essentially unalterable behaviors that will tell us how far we realistically can go in adjusting human social behavior. Such people see specific physiological and genetic mechanisms as the link between the biological and social sciences. A second group, of which I am a part, sees biological information as, rather, a means of altering human social behavior—of rerouting it so as to avoid such things as devastating wars or pathological conditions that develop because of faulty self-images. This second group uses as its chief inspiration the elaboration of predictive and explanatory subtheories from general evolutionary theory, not the elucidation of particular physiological or hereditary mechanisms (as important as they may be in many cases), and not patterns of social behavior shown by nonhuman species. This enterprise depends on evolution being a more or less singular process with long-term cumulative effects (which it is, evidently in large part as a correlate of the universality of DNA as genetic materials). It also depends upon a thorough understanding of adaptive trends as relative success in reproduction, and of flexibility in social strategies as an adaptive trend. As knowledge of the physicochemical underpinnings of human social behavior becomes extensive and detailed, the value of evolutionary theory in guiding our understanding of ourselves will necessarily diminish. But, currently, we are far from being able to discard such guidance without severe loss.

I am not optimistic about the usefulness of searches for unalterable or "basic" human social behaviors, as a method for solving our problems, because I see human social life evolving as flexible strategizing. The relevant environment of human social success is the collection of flexible strategies employed by other human individuals or groups. Inflexibility or preprogramming would be the worst possible strategy in the face of conflicts of interest, competition, the importance of cooperation, and other aspects of sociality. Understanding the relationship between human sociality and the environment is not like understanding how organisms survive, for example, winters or earthquakes, for in social behavior the winter and earthquake equivalents are not passive but have their own interests (i.e., are chiefly other humans) and may be expected to seek them. I will argue that human social behavior is even more unusual, in that the environment of its evolution is a within-species phenomenon to a greater degree than perhaps for any other form of life. Social behavior evolves as a succession of ploys and counterploys, and for humans these ploys are used, not only among individuals within social groups, but between and among small and large groups of up to hundreds of millions of individuals.

The value of an evolutionary approach to human sociality is thus not to determine the limits of our actions so that we can abide by them.

Rather, it is to examine our life strategies so that we can change them when we wish, as a result of understanding them.

The difficulty I have in dealing with the "biological constraints" approach to human behavior could not be illustrated more starkly than by the subtitle to Mel Konner's (1982) book, *The Tangled Wing: Biological Constraints on the Human Spirit*. Taking Konner's usage of "biological" as "physiological" or "genetic," the phrase making up the subtitle seems to me internally contradictory, in an intriguing and perhaps enlightening way. If one translates "spirit" roughly as "imagination," he sees immediately that only a nonhuman (presumably extraterrestrial) being could identify constraints on the human spirit that existed because of biology, for only a nonhuman could imagine things that humans are incapable of imagining. Whatever flights of fancy any or all human spirits, or the collective human spirit, may be capable of, are realities *because* of our evolutionary heritage, and included are all flights of fancy having to do with what it is imagined the human spirit cannot imagine.

I made a similar argument in the epilogue of *Darwinism and Human Affairs* (pp. 279–280). Kitcher (1985, p. 283) dismissed it as "specious" because "Not only can we identify limits on our cognitive abilities without specifying the content of things that we cannot come to know (as, for example, when we find out that the answers to certain questions will forever be unobtainable or that our brains are too small to carry out certain kinds of computations), but we are perfectly able to recognize things that we cannot learn to do." Kitcher's view is narrower than mine, in that I would include computations conducted with devices constructed deliberately and explicitly to enable us to carry out computations we found we wanted to do but could not, and others that would enable blind people to do the equivalent of seeing or deaf people to hear. Many questions that have seemed forever unanswerable, moreover, were not. Kitcher's quote of my statement also stopped at the point where the statement began to make his criticism less reasonable. [This comment is not restricted to this particular argument of Kitcher's; the tendency is also evident in his criticism of my argument (pp. 59–60) that Darwin provided useful falsifying operations for his theory and his implication (p. 188) that I present "the idea that rape violates the sexual rights of a male with a proprietary interest" as if it were ethically appropriate rather than by way of suggesting reasons why rape laws seem to have been constructed as if their goal were something other than justice for women.]

The question of "biological constraints" is not trivial. Therefore, I have repeated the central paragraph in the epilogue of *Darwinism and Human Affairs* so that the reader can judge the argument himself. Some of the qualifying phrases that may otherwise not be given sufficient attention are italicized:

> As it concerns *social* behavior, human nature would seem to be represented by our learning capabilities and tendencies in different situations. The limits of human nature, then, could be identified by discovering those things that we cannot learn. But there is a paradox in this, for to understand human nature would then be to know how to change it—how to create situations that would enable or cause learning *that could not previously occur. To whatever extent that is so*, the limits of human nature become will-o'-the-wisps that inevitably retreat ahead of our discoveries about them. *Even if this is not true in all respects*, I believe that it must be true in *some of the most important and practical ones*. I regard it as illusory to identify social behavior far outside present human capabilities (or interests) and then suggest that one has somehow said something significant about the limits of human nature, and similarly illusory to note any current human failure in social matters and regard it as unchangeable.

The question is not one of whether or not humans can learn any and all things with equal ease; they cannot. It is not a question of whether or not they can learn new things; they can. Moreover, one finds out how to teach or learn new things by playing around with "old" behaviors that come closest to the desired or perceived new possibilities. One thus finds out how to surpass the "border" of learning, or learning ability, as previously perceived. If there are any truly unalterable limits to human social learning (and I am not willing to admit that there are), then I would still contend that (1) they have not been identified, and to do so would be extremely difficult, and (2) they are of little significance to anyone. In this sense, the questions of *identifying* and *using* any such limits cannot be divorced from the question of their existence.

Just as biological scientists cannot ignore environmentally induced plasticity, social scientists are not justified in viewing any activities or attributes of humans as independent of this influence of the genetic materials. Such independence is a logical impossibility. Evidence from every quarter indicates that learning is not "writing-on-a-blank-slate," and if it were in some organisms at some times, it would only be appropriate to hypothesize that this too is either directly or indirectly a result of natural selection.

It follows that my use of the word biology in no way implies that moral systems have some kind of explicit genetic background, are genetically determined, or cannot be altered by adjusting the social environment. Nor am I about to espouse a Social Darwinist view of morality or claim that organic evolution offers a means of identifying proper modes of behavior. I mean simply to suggest that if we wish to understand those aspects of our behavior commonly regarded as involving morality or ethics, it will help to reconsider our behavior as a product of evolution by natural selection. The principal reason for this suggestion is that natural selection operates according to general principles which make its effects highly predictive, even with respect to traits and circumstances that have not yet been analyzed, or perhaps even encountered by scientists.

In summary, the widespread hostility toward efforts of biologists to analyze human behavior appears related to the manner in which the adjective "biological" is used outside of biology. Because the problems of human behavior are of such immense proportions, and because I believe that biology has definite and unique contributions to make, I cannot dismiss this misuse as trivial (see also Alexander, 1985a, 1986a).

## Moral Systems and Morality

By the phrase "moral systems" in my title, I mean to refer to what philosophers imply by this term: systems of ethics or normative conduct—the question of how agreements or contracts about right and wrong are generated and maintained within human societies, and why they differ. As the philosopher, Ralph B. Perry (1954) stated, " . . . a morality or moral value system is some kind of action guide, some kind of standard for conduct, character formation, and life . . . ."

If the concept of "moral systems" is an easy one, the same is not true of "morality." On the meaning of this term even Perry (p. 86) is less confident: " . . . there is something . . . in the world to which it is appropriate to give the name 'morality'. Nothing is more familiar; nothing is more obscure in its meaning . . . ."

Aside from its reference to values, the concept of morality implies altruism or self-sacrifice. Not all moral acts call for self-sacrifice, however, and not all self-serving acts, by any means, would be termed immoral. On the other hand, I suspect most would agree that a moral life will inevitably call for *some* acts with net cost to the actor. Similarly, many acts with a net value to the actor would be judged immoral because alternative courses of action of value to others are available at the time but are not taken. Generally speaking, then, *immoral* is a label we apply to certain kinds of acts by which we help ourselves or hurt others, while acts that hurt ourselves or help others are more likely to be judged moral than immoral. As virtually endless arguments in the philosophical literature attest, it is not easy to be more precise in defining morality.

But this is our central problem: to find out what people mean when they speak of moral and immoral actions, how they make the distinction, and then to relate all of this to our history of evolution by natural selection. My approach is initially descriptive or analytical rather than normative. I am interested, first, not in determining what is moral and immoral, in the sense of what people ought to be doing, but in elucidating the natural history of ethics and morality—in discovering how and why humans initiated and developed the ideas we have about right and wrong. I am interested in unravelling and understanding the fabric of human sociality right down to the smallest threads of interaction. I trust that appropriateness in norms, however defined, will be enhanced as knowledge about moral issues becomes detailed and is widely dispensed. My reasons for this assumption are partly that I expect collective interests to be better served when decisions are made with more information and by a larger proportion of the people involved, and partly that I expect deception to be more difficult as knowledge about morality is enhanced. By this, of course, a normative view is suggested—namely, that we ought to study evolution and we ought to dispense as widely as possible whatever we learn about human actions as a result. This is a point to which I will later return.

## PROXIMATE CAUSES AND THE REDUCTIONISM OF EVOLUTIONARY BIOLOGY

To social scientists, humanists, medical people, lawyers, and philosophers—all of the investigators most closely concerned with humans—biology inevitably implies reductionism of some kind. I will argue, however, that there is more than one form of biological "reduction" (or explanatory simplification), and the one employed here does not (extensively) involve the common meaning of reduction to *proximate mechanisms* (or proximate causes or physically identifiable components). Seeking proximate-mechanism reduction is what Mayr (1961) called answering the "How?" question. It is partly a concentration on this "How?" meaning of reduction that causes human-oriented scholars to contrast "biological" and "social." As suggested above, the implication of "biological" in this case is that it refers to structural or physiological components or mechanisms—nerves, muscles, or hormones—or to variations in such attributes. The extreme version of this kind of reductionism asks: "Is that trait (variant) genetically determined?" At the very least students of human behavior who deal in this form of biological reductionism, which might be called the search for partial or proximate causes, must continually keep on their guard against unnecessary or unjustified assumptions of determinism or preprogramming.

The second kind of biological reductionism, which forms the theme of this book, is not typically employed by human-oriented scholars in the form that biologists use it. It is most easily understood as the development of general evolutionary principles, and is usually referred to as the search for *ultimate causes*. Mayr termed it the "How come?" or "Why?" question (see Tinbergen, 1951; Daly and Wilson, 1983; Alcock, 1984; Wittenberger, 1981. Evidently Baker, 1938, originated the terms *proximate* and *ultimate* as I am using them—see Lack, 1954, and Hailman, 1982). Physicists tend to use the term "unification" for the process of principle generation, and biologists frequently use "synthesis." My use of reduction for this process may be novel, but I believe it is useful, for the reasons given below.

To establish principles is indeed reduction (or simplification), but not the kind of reduction that primarily seeks partial or proximate causes. Rather, the "Why?" approach seeks generalizations explaining phenomena that, in the absence of such generalizations, appear more complex as well as (sometimes) more mysterious. Rather than seeking to identify individual physiological, structural, or genetic contributions, each partly explaining some complex phenomenon, the "Why?" approach seeks broad generalizations about, for example, the goals of humans, or, in the most general sense, human motivations. These principles are necessarily sought in the evolutionary process that has given rise to all of our traits and tendencies, or at least to the potentials for them. One seeks general formulations that explain how natural selection has shaped, for example, sex ratios, senescence, differences between the sexes, parental behavior, or the length and nature of juvenile life. (Evolutionists tend to assume that there are multiple possible proximate routes by which similar evolutionary adaptations may occur. Because of this assumption they often postpone the study of physiological, ontogenetic, or other proximate mechanisms.) The perhaps unique applicability of this kind of reduction to living forms causes it appropriately to be termed *evolutionary reductionism*. The reason for this appropriateness is that formulating simplifying principles that apply to life is an effort to analyze the cumulative effects of the long-term operation of natural selection. This is done so as to predict or understand the effects in different environments of the collections of genetic materials now present in living things. The histories of nonliving phenomena are not as complex as those of living things, and the simplifying principles of physics and chemistry are as a result almost nonhistorical. In contrast, the principle of natural selection is dramatically simplifying primarily because of its relationship to the cumulative history of life. Because this aspect of reductionism in the evolutionary approach has not been generally recognized or accepted outside evolutionary biology, previous discussions of proximate and ultimate mechanisms have not fully elucidated the reductionism of evolutionary biology. One consequence is that the kind of reduction practiced by evolutionary biologists is erroneously regarded as simply the invoking of genetic mechanisms as proximate causes. This is another way in which the approaches of biologists to human behavior are seriously misrepresented and under-estimated.

Consider, as an example, a hungry human male. He has an immediate goal of eating. To achieve this goal he may leave an office and walk or drive his automobile some distance to his home, or to a favorite restaurant or a grocery store, and proceed appropriately. Or he may pick up his spear, say farewell to his family, and vanish into the bush. Carrying out either of these procedures involves an uncountable combination of con-tributing proximate causes or operations—the actions of nerves, muscles, hormones, sense organs, and thought processes. Each of these contrib-uting proximate mechanisms may also function in many contexts other than hunger. Quite different sets of such proximate mechanisms may lead to what appears to be the same goal in different individuals, or to different goals in the same individual at different times and in different circumstances. With no understanding of the concept of hunger, and of the modes of its satisfaction, we might have great difficulty inducing the singularity of function (assuaging of hunger) from the multiple proximate parts or aspects of the activities relating to hunger.

Because confusion about the two kinds of reductionism lies at the heart of so many controversies about human behavior, the contrasts between them deserve further attention. The "How?" or partial causes approach is most likely to evoke criticism (1) because understanding is sometimes better achieved by dealing with the original whole (e.g., the effort to assuage hunger rather than the underlying morphological and physiological components of the effort), (2) because it is noticeable that similar ends may be achieved by many different kinds of subordinate or contributing mechanisms (causing the individual mechanisms to be less important), and (3) because of the likelihood that something important may be missing when reconstitution of the dissected phenomenon is attempted. All three realizations cause us to regard even essential contributing proximate phenomena as usually more trivial than the functional results of their collective and cooperative interactions.

*In contrast*, the "How come?" or ultimate cause approach seeks to simplify, explain, or "reduce" complex phenomena such as human activities by hypothesizing directly that they are parts of even grander sets or combinations of actions. Thus, merely to identify a complex set of activities by a hungry human as an effort to eat is a step in this kind of reduction; another step is to see that effort as part of a lifelong effort to build (as a juvenile) and maintain (as an adult) a soma (phenotype, self) in the further interest of using it in the reproduction of one's genetic materials. This reduction by generalizing, because it seeks the adaptive significance of acts, also tends to identify the larger contexts within which specific acts or functions are carried out, and as a result identifies likelihoods of compromise or adjustment in the act that would not be obvious from any other approach. Without knowledge of food or ingestion, for example, we might be puzzled about failures to optimize other observed uses of lips and teeth like kissing, biting, or speaking. Similarly, without generalization from evolutionary reductions (principles), we could not easily predict that a hungry adult human might give all of its food to a mate or an offspring; nor could we develop a reasonable hypothesis about such behavior if we observed it. Discussions of proximate and ultimate mechanisms usually do not explain that reduction by generalization can profitably be carried much further. Thus, biologists proceed as if the lives of *all organisms* can be understood better by seeing them first as predictable patterns of somatic and reproductive effort (see pp. 40ff. ). In the hierarchy of explanatory principles governing the traits of living organisms, evolutionary reductionism—the development of principles from the evolutionary process—tends to subsume all other kinds.

Proximate-cause reductionism (or reduction by dissection) sometimes advances our understanding of the whole phenomena. This happens when the mechanism discovered or elucidated is unique or new, has a special kind of practical application, or itself represents a simplification through generalization. Discovering that diseases are caused by microorganisms, that cancer results from mutated genes, or that the genetic materials of all life are likely to be deoxyribonucleic acid are obvious examples.

When evolutionary reduction becomes trivial in the study of life it is for a reason different from incompleteness; rather, it is because the breadth of the generalization distances it too significantly from a particular problem that may be at hand. For example, if a group of political scientists or physicists meeting to avert an imminent nuclear disaster were presented with a discussion of the general principles of conflict strategies and confrontations throughout the history of life (nonhuman as well as human), they might think that someone had changed the subject. Even if they realized that this was background material they should have had available to them to make the best decisions, there might be no time to review or absorb it.

*As a second contrast,* reduction by dissection, or the seeking of partial causes or mechanisms, involves the discovery and examination of smaller and smaller units. In biology, this is the kind of reduction that leads to Nobel Prizes in physiology and medicine. It depends to some extent on new techniques and equipment, and does not frequently yield new information bearing directly on the analysis of complex human social behaviors (although when it does there is likely to be great excitement—as, for example, when someone discovers how to eliminate a problem that correlates with a specific genetic background, such as diabetes or Down's syndrome).

Reduction by generalization, on the other hand, depends more upon new ideas, and quite commonly influences our interpretations and understanding of even the most complex human behavior. Indeed, as critics have frequently pointed out, the greatest weakness of reduction by generalization is not that it is likely to be trivial but that errors are probable through unjustified leaps from hypothesis to conclusion, by either those who generate hypotheses or those who hear about them.

Critics such as Gould and Lewontin (1979) and Lewontin et al. (1984) seem to condemn all evolutionary approaches to human behavior by arguing as though students of the evolutionary background of human behavior always talk in terms of unverified conclusions rather than going through the process of generating and testing hypotheses. These critics imply that evolutionists who write about human behavior are, like Kipling, constructing "just-so" stories. Either consciously or unconsciously they have tended to publicize the worst cases, almost invariably already criticized and dismissed within evolutionary biology. They ignore or condemn by implication those they cannot as easily criticize.

They also typically ignore the best work in the areas they are criticizing. For example, Levins and Lewontin (1985), in a long diatribe against the "adaptationist program," direct their criticism at the notion of adaptation as perfection or optimization of traits, cite only two modern authors they say use this criterion, and fail to cite any modern evolutionist discussing or defending the concept of adaptation. Thus, they do not mention Williams (1966a), although his argument that adaptation means only better versus worse in the immediate situation is widely accepted, and Williams is almost certainly the most widely cited author on the concept. The omission may be considered all the more surprising because Lewontin (1966), in a review of Williams' book on adaptation, wrote " . . . I believe that Williams' book is excellent in its totality and that it is 95 percent correct. Most of the characteristics of organisms, including social behavior, must be the result of differential fitness at the level of individual genotypes."

Critics such as Gould and Lewontin (1979) and Lewontin et al. (1984)

also do not acknowledge that the method of science—of progress in understanding in this as in other fields of endeavor in which knowledge is cumulative—is to identify the core of accuracy and correctness in the works of all writers in a field, excise the flawed portions, and then build from the best that is left. Rather, they give the impression that their mission is to locate and emphasize the weakest parts of the arguments of individuals they are criticizing, then use those weakest parts to declare that the entire enterprise with which those parts are connected must be discarded—i.e., that the weakest components in an intellectual edifice can be used to prove that there is no core of accuracy and correctness, no possibility of a cumulative growth of knowledge. This approach is reminiscent of the humanities, where rhetoric is the methodology (Raymond, 1982), there is no cumulative growth of knowledge only a cumulative change of attitude or sophistication in regard to meaning, and criticism is to a greater degree partitioned around the efforts (or "projects") of individuals (Alexander, 1988). Sahlins (1976) and Kitcher (1985) argue similarly, but unlike Gould and Lewontin they do not have backgrounds that suggest to the reader that they are arguing in the manner of scientists.

Critics such as Gould and Lewontin also fail to acknowledge that they are capitalizing on difficulties in analyzing humans that are universal whatever the approach—namely, that we are analyzing ourselves and therefore must (1) use the attributes to be analyzed to do the analyzing, (2) avoid letting our own personal biases or interests influence the results, and (3) collect data from subjects whose best interests may be served by giving inaccurate or false information (and who, unlike most other organisms, are expert at deceiving other humans). They imply wrongly that all evolutionary biologists necessarily make the same mistakes. They do not discuss the facts that (a) *all* students of human behavior (not just those who take evolution into account) run the risk of leaping unwarrantedly from hypothesis to conclusion and (b) just-so stories were no less prevalent and hypothesis-testing no more prevalent in studies of human behavior before evolutionary biologists began to participate. Indeed, many of their examples predate the last two or three decades of modern evolutionary biology. It is one thing to criticize studies of human behavior because they do not meet current (or past) standards in the field, and quite another to reject them unless they meet some kind of Popperian ideal of procedure that has never previously been achieved. One wonders if such critics believe that merely to pursue knowledge about human evolution may yield undesirable directions of change in human society; I expect that this belief is held by many, including some whose views of "undesirable" would conflict dramatically with, say, those of Gould and Lewontin (see Maynard Smith, 1982, and Thornhill and Alcock, 1983, for other and somewhat different critical analyses of Gould and Lewontin's arguments. Also, compare the review of Lewontin *et al.*, 1984, by Gould, 1984, with those of Konner, 1984, Bateson, 1985, and Dawkins, 1985).

*As a third contrast*, investigations of proximate causes are typified by controlled laboratory experiments, and their practitioners are likely to criticize investigations of ultimate causes as being oversimplified, imprecise, or incomplete. Students of ultimate causes, on the other hand, are more likely to be theoretical and philosophical in their approach, and to use a broadly comparative method to secure answers. As already noted, they are also likely to see an identified proximate cause as one of several or many possible routes to realization of an ultimate function, therefore (in philosophical if not practical terms) as less vital as a first step to understanding.

Evolutionary reduction, when it is successful and accurate, tends to deepen our understanding of all of our immediate and primary behaviors, motivations, and emotions because their evolutionary significance and the involved compromises are almost never a part of our conscious knowledge before we pursue them deliberately. It changes our perceptions of nearly all that is dear to us. Unfortunately, it does not lead to dramatic "quick fixes" of serious human problems, although, and even more unfortunately, those who embrace it with inadequate understanding all too often act as though it does. The value of evolutionary generalization is difficult to grasp because it consists primarily in suggesting hypotheses. We forget that without considerable guidance in hypothesis construction our research efforts—indeed, our efforts at satisfactory day-to-day living—would nearly always be impotent.

Feinberg (1970, p. 5) followed a long line of philosophers in unknowingly connecting the general problems of moral philosophy directly to evolutionary reduction when he said that " . . . 'pleasure' and 'happiness' [are] the leading candidates, historically speaking, for the status of supreme goods or ultimate goals," and (p. 7) "It is plain that finding one large genus for the analysis of all our enjoyment-idioms as they apply to the multifarious things we are said to enjoy will be no easy task." Finding this "one large genus," however—namely, discovering that our history of evolution by natural selection has been one of tuning "enjoyment idioms" (or proximate mechanisms) in the service of survival of our own genetic materials, via reproductive success in all its guises—is precisely what evolutionary reductionism has accomplished.

Humans are not accustomed to dealing with their own strategies of life as if they had been tuned by natural selection. As Maynard Smith

(1982) points out, one consequence is that game theory, designed for economics, has been applied with more difficulty to humans than to nonhuman organisms. But I do not share Maynard Smith's reluctance to accept that "financial rewards, the risks of death and the pleasures of a clear conscience" (the economists' "utility") can be turned into a supposition that humans too can be understood as products of the maximizing of "Darwinian fitness." Maynard Smith sees Darwinian fitness, as applied to nonhuman organisms, as providing "a natural and genuinely one-dimensional scale" for the employment of game theory, arguing (1974) that:

> A major difficulty in applying game theory to human conflicts lies in the need to place a numerical value, or "utility," on the preferences the players place on the possible outcomes. How for example does one put the utilities of financial reward and of injury or death on the same numerical scale? This difficulty does not arise, at least in principle, in applying game theory to animal behaviour. In human conflicts, strategies are chosen by reason, to maximize the satisfaction of human desires—or at least it is in those terms that they are analyzed by game theorists. Strategies in animal contests are naturally selected to maximize the fitness of the contestants. Thus apparently incommensurable outcomes can be placed on a single scale of utility according to the contribution they make to reproductive success. This equivalence between utility and contribution to fitness is the main justification for applying game theory to animal contests. (p. 212)

It seems to me that Maynard Smith is not describing a special difficulty, in principle, of applying game theory to humans but simply an inadequacy so far of efforts to do so. To compare fitness, investigations of nonhuman strategies must also calculate the costs of deaths and risks and the value of resources gained or lost. The fact that such investigations ignore motivations or "desire" equivalents in nonhuman organisms does not mean that these do not exist but that they can (at least, for the moment) be safely ignored. Some might argue that they cannot be ignored in humans because we have introduced so much evolutionary novelty so swiftly into our environments. But novelty also exists in the environments of nonhumans. The difference is at least one of degree only, and to understand ourselves we simply have to deal with the problems of novelty anyway; even the particular nature of our responses to novelties is only likely to be understood as a result of evolutionary knowledge.

I believe that failure by biologists and others to distinguish proximate- or partial-cause and evolutionary- or ultimate-cause reductionism (and to use the latter) is in some part responsible for the current chasm between the social and the biological sciences and for the resistance to so-called biological approaches to understanding humans. Anyone who sees science as solely a matter of seeking partial causes by laboratory experimentation is very likely to regard the hypothesis-seeking and comparative and cross-cultural studies of evolutionary biologists as nonscientific, or even as useless speculation. If those with this bias were to have their way, however, a good deal of the direction would be eliminated from the investigation of both proximate and ultimate causes in biology. This direction is provided by the predictive value of principles derived from knowledge of the process of organic evolution, i.e., by evolutionary or ultimate-cause analysis, or reduction. Both approaches are essential to progress in biology and the social sciences, and it would be helpful if their relationship, and that of their respective practitioners, were not seen as adversarial.

## THE PROBLEM OF CULTURE

Any claim that biology holds important keys to understanding ourselves will be viewed skeptically by those who believe that culture has somehow liberated us from our history of natural selection. Such skeptics would note that the human arms races and resource competition proceed through cultural and not genetic change, and therefore are, as I have indicated, merely parallels to changes that proceed as a result of natural selection (see Alexander, 1979a, p. 66 ff., for a fuller exposition of the views discussed here). But such skeptics often view the process of natural selection too narrowly. Natural selection has two effects (Flinn and Alexander, 1982). First, it sorts among existing genetic variations that produce different phenotypic effects or traits, saving some and eliminating others. Cultural change can occur without such genetic change, and may do so massively and for many generations. Cultural change, however, is never independent of the second effect of natural selection, which is to accumulate and maintain genetic units that in particular environments lead to particular effects (or traits or phenotypes), and in other environments lead to other such effects—in other words, to accumulate and maintain genetic units that yield functional plasticity. Every organism, including ourselves, is a bundle of effects from such accumulated and maintained genetic units having realized one or another potential in one or another environment, and in some sense no organism can be understood otherwise. The very concept of "phenotype" or "individual" connotes plasticity because the evolutionary *raison d'etre* of the phenotype is that it gives genes flexibility in dealing with the environment. As suggested earlier, variations in the phenotype that correlate (within species) only with genetic variations require more special explanation than do those which vary according to environmental cues.

That plasticity of the phenotype is an inevitable consequence of the most basic facts about organic evolution is too often forgotten or ignored. To accept it is to realize that biologists are in no way restricted to studying species-wide traits, and that phenotypic variations need not be demonstrably correlated with genetic variations before traits can be assumed to be relatable to a history of natural selection. It is a main effect of natural selection to eliminate genetic variation associated with phenotypic variations that correlate with environmental variations. Stated differently, when trait differences correlate directly with genetic differences the reproductively inferior trait is maximally vulnerable to elimination by selection. Genetic backgrounds producing traits that can be varied to match the circumstances, on the other hand, are expected whenever circumstances vary unpredictably among predictable alternatives, as they do continually in the environments of living forms. It is not reasonable to use the demonstrated existence of a predicted effect of natural selection—plasticity associated with phenotypic variations in the absence of genetic variations—to deny the potency or relevance of natural selection. Some people, unfortunately, still try to do that.

There are some further points of great importance, I believe, in understanding the widespread failure of even educated and open-minded people to recognize the significance of an organic evolution guided principally by natural selection. First, an absence of heritable variations in phenotypic traits that track environmental changes virtually precludes identifying any part of the genetic underpinnings of the trait: genetic backgrounds of traits are identified only by studying heritable variations in the trait. So both strong directional selection (leading to homozygosity) and selection favoring plasticity (concealing heritable variations) lead to the impression of much phenotypic variation without any genetic correlates. At the same time, electrophoresis and other modern methods have revealed heretofore unsuspected amounts of genetic variation within populations. These genetic variations are uncovered by methods that do not relate them to particular traits. Moreover, genetic variations that persist are expected to relate either to persisting environmental variations (also not revealed by the methods used to locate the genetic variations) or to have neutral or relatively trivial effects on the phenotype. On the one hand, we are presented with great amounts of phenotypic variability that cannot be related to genetic variability, and indeed for which the genetic underpinnings are presently inscrutable. On the other hand, we observe large amounts of genetic variation that are not only unrelated to the observed phenotypic variations but are believed to be trivial in their effects. The two seem unconnected. Anyone willing to give natural selection its due, however, must realize that all of these conditions would be predicted in complex, changing environments in which cues to the changes are potentially available to the evolving organisms. Because of the prevalence (or universality) of such environments, conditions they are expected to produce cannot be used to deny the significance of natural selection as the principal guiding force of evolution.

Even if culture changes massively and continually across multiple generations, even if our problems and promises arise out of the cultural process of change, even if there are no genetic variations among humans that significantly affect their behavior, *it is always true that the cumulative history of natural selection continues to influence our actions by the set of genes it has provided humanity*. Our learning biases and emotional responses, for example, are not random or manufactured from thin air; they are the products of the unbroken process of evolution by natural selection that extends across the whole of history, into our prehuman past, and millions of years before that. This is why even a seemingly "purely cultural" phenomenon, such as an arms race, may be most effectively dealt with from a perspective that includes a thorough understanding of our history of natural selection. This is true even in the case of rapid introduction of environmental novelties (such as excess amounts of sugar or drugs, birth control devices, and almost any other result of technology) because the particular nature of our response to the novelty, whether reproductively adaptive or maladaptive, will be most predictable to those with knowledge of our selective (adaptive) history. Moths fly to their deaths around electric lights; this maladaptive response to an environmental novelty is understandable, and likely would have been predictable, only by knowing the nocturnal behavior of moths prior to the introduction of electric lights. Given the seriousness of current world problems deriving from human social behavior, and the impasses in our confrontations that are paraded daily in the news media, are there really reasons for believing that we can understand ourselves well enough without finding out about novelties in our own environment and their significance; without examining our long-term as well as our short-term history; without analyzing our cumulative genetic history as a part of the reason for our cumulative cultural history?

People are sometimes comfortable with the notion that certain activities can be labeled appropriately as "purely cultural" because they also believe that there are behaviors that can be labeled "purely genetic." Neither is true: the environment contributes to the expression of all behaviors, and culture is best described as a part of the environment. The often-used axis of genetic *versus* cultural, in respect to human behavior, is inappropriate because it omits all noncultural aspects of environment and suggests wrongly that there are behaviors at the two ends of the spectrum which lack, respectively, environmental and genetic input (Lumsden and Wilson, 1981; Flinn and Alexander, 1982).

Harris (1979) provides an excellent example of this confusion about culture, and about evolutionary analyses of human behavior, partly because he makes some assumptions that even many biologists make. He discusses Dickemann's (1979) evolutionary analysis of female infanticide as an example of " . . . the lack of parsimony and the redundancy involved in the behavior scaling version of sociobiological theory." Involved is female-biased infanticide among elite castes in stratified societies. Harris cites the evolutionary prediction (Alexander, 1974; Trivers and Willard, 1973) that female preferential infanticide is more likely among women married to high-ranking men and less likely among women married to low-ranking men, and notes that when male infants can be reared with confidence, their fitness (i.e., number of offspring) will tend to exceed that of females, since men in polygynous societies can have more "reproductive episodes" than women.

> Hence in elite castes and classes, where males have an excellent chance of surviving because living conditions are good, the maximization of reproductive success of both male and female parents will be achieved by investing in sons rather than daughters. On the other hand, in the low-ranking castes and classes, where male survival is very risky, reproductive success will be maximized by investing in daughters, who are likely to have at least some reproductive episodes rather than none at all. To complete the model, elite men can be expected to marry beneath their station, while lowly women can be expected to marry up if their parents can provide them with a dowry to compensate the groom's family . . . .

Harris says that the "cultural materialist" explanation for this phenomenon does not require that the pattern has been selected for "genetically," or that it is part of a "genetic program" that is activated as a result of either poverty or wealth, respectively. He suggests that men are more valuable because they dominate the "political, military, commercial, and agricultural sources of wealth and power"; he argues that this domination is a result of cultural rather than genetic selection.

> Sons have the opportunity to protect and enhance the elite family's patrimony and political-economic status. But daughters, who have access to significant sources of wealth and power only through men, are an absolute or relative liability. They can only be married off by paying dowry. Therefore, preferential female infanticide is practiced by the elite groups to avoid the expense of dowry and to consolidate the family's wealth and

power. Among the subordinate ranks, female infanticide is not practiced as frequently as among the elites because peasant and artisan girls can readily pay their own way by working in the fields or in cottage industry.

Harris argues that all of this has to do with efforts to maintain and enhance power and wealth, and *not* "the struggle to achieve reproductive success." He says the proof lies in the fact that high-status males marry beneath their station, such marriages taking the form of concubinage and not bestowing the right of inheritance upon the offspring. He says elites thus "systematically decrease their inclusive fitness by failing to provide for their own children." He thinks the whole system is a way of preventing elites from having too much reproductive success, so as to "maintain the privileged position of a small number of wealthy and powerful families at the top of the social pyramid."

Harris believes that the reason models based on reproductive success have "a degree of empirical validity" is that the factors which promote reproductive success

> . . . do so through the intermediation of biopsychological benefits that enhance the economic, political, and sexual power and well-being of individuals and groups of individuals. The exploitation of lower-ranking women by higher-ranking men, for example, is the kind of stuff out of which theories of reproductive success can easily be spun. But exploitation confers much more immediate and tangible benefits than genetic immortality on those who can get away with it. Because of the bias toward reproductive success, the principle of behavior scaling [ = evolved phenotypic plasticity] leads away from the most certain and powerful interests served by infrastructure toward the most remote and hypothetical interests served by having genetic survivors.

First, evolutionary models for female-based infanticide among elites do not call for the *survival* of males necessarily to be in doubt in lower class families (Alexander, 1974; Dickemann, 1979). Rather, because males in polygynous societies have more difficulty than do females in securing mates (and high-quality mates or multiple mates *a fortiori*) the question is the likelihood of one's son reproducing successfully or not rather than surviving or not. Because status correlates with desirability as a mate in stratified human societies, high-status males are more valuable reproductively if polygyny is permitted.

As Harris states, sons are also more valuable in protecting and enhancing the elite family's patrimony and political-economic status—in consolidating its wealth and power. On this point Harris, Dickemann, and the evolutionary biologists are, I think, in perfect agreement.

The second difficulty arises when Harris says that this means that "The genesis of the system lies in the struggle to maintain and enhance differential politico-economic power and wealth, *not* in the struggle to achieve reproductive success" (emphasis added). To clarify the difficulty let us suppose that someone argued that humans are interested in sex because of the pleasure associated with it and *not* because of procreation. Sexual intercourse in humans may (unlike nearly all or all other organisms) have acquired significance beyond fertilization of eggs per se (e.g., in long-term pair bonding) but this cannot detract from the facts that (1) historically it has been the only way babies were created, (2) the creation of babies is the only reason for our continued existence, and (3) those of us alive today carry in preponderance the genes of those who produced and raised the most babies.

Happiness and its anticipation are thus proximate mechanisms that lead us to perform and repeat acts that in the environments of history, at least, would have led to greater reproductive success. This is a central hypothesis in evolutionary biology. Paralleling it in importance is the hypothesis that control of resources is the most appropriate route to reproductive success (the juvenile lives of all organisms represent a process of increasing control of resources up to the point—through growth and development—that reproduction becomes possible). Similarly, I presume that status is typically a vehicle toward resource control and an outcome of it. If these ideas are correct, then humans should always experience pleasure when they gain in status or increase their control of resources (unless they do so at large expense to close relatives or spouses), and they should experience some converse feeling when they lose status or resource control (except, sometimes, when they transfer it to relatives or spouses).

Harris' analysis takes economic or "productive" ends as ultimate rather than as means to the end of reproductive success. Such analyses are like those which take pleasure and happiness as ultimate ends. They cannot explain why the proximate mechanisms of pleasure and happiness (Harris' "bio-psychological benefits") operate as they do, or even why they exist. Evolutionary theory from the science of biology does have the possibility of such explanations, whether or not in particular cases its individual practitioners err in their testing or interpretations, and whether or not contemporary humans actually use their striving for resource control to enhance their reproductive success (Vining, 1986, summarizes evidence that they often do not; but see Betzig, 1986, Hill, 1984, Alexander, 1988; reviews of Vining following his article). Harris implies that reproductive success, representing "remote and hypothetical interests," is somehow an *alternative* explanation to more proximate "bio-psychological benefits" as "the most certain and powerful interests served by infrastructure." He sees the "struggle to maintain and enhance differential politico-economic power and wealth" as *opposed* to "the struggle to achieve reproductive success." In the sense of comprehensive explanation, however, the relationship between such proximate and ultimate factors is not adversarial. Rather, neither can be explained without the other. The real problem that this aspect of Harris' discussion may be used to emphasize is that of determining the degree to which the exercise of proximate mechanisms may produce consequences different from those that led to their establishment and their present forms. Regardless of the answer to this question, I cannot imagine how cultural materialist explanations of human behavior and institutions can ever make real or complete sense except in light of a continuous history of natural selection of genetic alternatives.

Harris says that the proof of the accuracy of his opposing reproductive and economic success lies in the fact that elites "systematically decrease their inclusive fitness by failing to provide life-support systems for their own children." He is referring specifically to children of hypogynous marriages or via concubines. He ignores the essential certainty, however, that polygyny by elite males is a way of increasing inclusive fitness by adding children; that additional children, even poorly provided for, can be more reproductive than no additional children; and that it is more reproductive to concentrate parental investment on children of higher-ranking spouses because of their greater opportunities to join or remain in the elite than to distribute it evenly among offspring whose likelihoods of success vary greatly for reasons more or less beyond the elite polygynous father's control (Dickemann, 1979).

Even if males in elite castes and classes are sometimes more likely to survive, it is the rank they inherit socially that will make them likely to outcompete others in sexual and parental matters and thus likely to produce more offspring as well as to maintain and consolidate resources (Alexander, 1974; Betzig, 1986). This outcome explicitly requires the male dominance and polygynous tendencies that Harris implies associate only with a cultural materialist model. When Harris argues that male dominance is a matter of cultural *rather* than genetic selection we have to suppose that he means not only that males are not dominant over females because of male–female genetic differences but that, as well, *variations among societies* are not owing to genetic *variations*. (Males are not more politicoeconomically dominant in hierarchical polygynous societies because they are genetically different from the less dominant males of other societies.) No biologist I know would disagree with the second point; but probably none would say, either, that *male–female* genetic differences *within* societies are uninvolved in tendencies for males to dominate females, or that "genetic selection" has had nothing to do with male–female power asymmetries or their variations. There is no reason to doubt that the genetic selection that led to the physical ability of males to dominate females, thus to the whole system under consideration here, had its genesis in differential reproductive success among males of differing strength, power, and status (Alexander *et al.*, 1979). In no way am I implying that such ability justifies its use, any more than any unusually powerful individual necessarily has a "right" to use his strength to deny others access to resources.

Dowry is paid, at least partly, to secure a higher-ranking mate for one's daughter than would otherwise be the case, this, in turn, having probable beneficial effects on the status of the daughter's family (Dickemann, 1979). All of this is of questionable value for elites, who already have high status, so avoidance of dowry payment seems a doubtful reason for female infanticide by elites (who are also likely to be wealthy). Rather, females are not as valuable to elites, so investing in males what would have been invested in females is reproductively more profitable; there are other possible factors, such as that the necessity of marrying a daughter hypogamously may cause her to detract from the family's status sufficiently (when hypergamy cannot be accomplished because of the high rank of her family) to offset the value of her reproduction. In Harris' argument status would not be a commodity of great reproductive value; the argument from biology is clearly the reverse.

Harris thus (1) unduly restricts the nature of the hypotheses from the science of biology; (2) mixes biologists' hypotheses with his own, often confusingly; (3) asserts (but does not demonstrate) that efforts normally enhancing reproductive success are not involved in social stratification and hypergamy; and (4) treats proximate and ultimate factors as alternatives rather than as complementary and mutually dependent. Harris also states:

> Sociobiologists propose that human beings are preprogrammed to switch from infanticide to mother love; from cannibalism to vegetarianism; from polyandry to polygyny; from matrilineality to patrilineality; and from war to peace whenever the appropriate environmental conditions are present. Cultural materialists also maintain that these changes take place whenever certain infrastructural conditions are present. Since both cultural materialists and sociobiologists take the position that the enormous diversity represented in the alleged genetic scaling of human responses is at least genetically possible—within the "envelope"—the need for the scaling concept itself seems gratuitous. The focus in both strategies has to be on the question of what kinds of environmental or infrastructural conditions are powerful enough to change human behavior from war to peace, polygyny

to polyandry, cannibalism to vegetarianism, and so forth. To the extent that sociobiologists sincerely pursue this issue, they will inevitably find themselves carrying out cost–benefit analyses that are subsumed by the infrastructural cost–benefit analyses of cultural materialism. (p. 139)

On the contrary, I would argue, the cost–benefit analyses of cultural materialism are necessarily subsumed under those which take into account the history of human strategies of reproductive success and analyze the effects of technological and other novelties in that light. The reason it is not gratuitous to consider the nature of phenotypic plasticity (or "behavior scaling") very carefully is that the evidence is overwhelming that it is not random in its expressions. The only theory with a possibility of understanding why comes from biology. Harris' analysis suggests that we will always end up doing those things that are beneficial to us, regardless of environmental change; evolutionary theory from biology does not, and it can be uncannily predictive about the kinds of errors we will make. It is a central problem in biology and the social sciences, and one of the most exciting prospects in these disciplines, to explore the question of the evolutionary-historical basis for the kinds of plasticity that are expressed in cost–benefit analyses such as those discussed above.

The argument is common that selection cannot be effective if the situation in which a particular trait is favored appears only infrequently, and this argument has been made to me with respect to female-biased infanticide in elites, menopause, and other human traits. Using menopause to illustrate, if, throughout most of history, women had on average died before the usual age of onset of menopause, then, the argument goes, menopause could not have been favored by selection. The first question that has to be asked is what proportion of reproduction is affected by the event in question? How much effect on reproductive success occurs after the event (in the case of menopause, how much is overall, long-term reproductive success affected by a postmenopausal woman turning all her attention to tending the offspring she has already produced, as opposed to starting additional offspring she has low probability of rearing)? Without this qualification we might be led to the conclusion that if, say, only one in a thousand individuals reached adulthood, selection on adults could not be effective. In the case of female-biased infanticide the question has been asked: How could such a tendency be favored if only a tiny fraction of individuals in a small proportion of the societies of the world ever become elites in a polygynous stratified society? The question implies that infanticidal elites are genetically different from noninfanticidal elites or nonelites and betrays precisely the simplistic view of the development of behavior in the individual and the evolution of sociality in humans that I am trying to dispel. Thus, it is only necessary to hypothesize the obvious—that humans have evolved keen abilities to learn how to observe and mimic success in others and to avoid or "anti-imitate" failure (Flinn and Alexander, 1982).

Like Harris, Kitcher (1985) uses Dickemann's (1979) analysis of infanticide as a principal vehicle for criticizing evolutionary analyses of human behavior. Most of Kitcher's argument is virtually the same as that of Harris, although he does not cite Harris; the remainder does not oppose proximate and ultimate factors or culture and "biology," hence is not appropriate to the question discussed here (see Alexander, 1987).

## THE PROBLEM OF RESISTANCE TO SELF-UNDERSTANDING

Consider the differences and similarities between two scientific searches. First, within the past decade theoretical physicists have begun to construct what they call the Grand Unifying Theory of the Universe (see Georgi, 1981; Ross, 1985). This activity entails the identification and characterization (sometimes in the reverse order) of ever more fundamental units in the physical structure of the universe, until those known and confidently predicted come to account for every event and effect relevant to the effort. This search is concerned almost entirely with items and events beyond our human senses, and even beyond the limits of the knowledge and imagination of most of us—a search conducted primarily by exotic and indirect means, guided by predictions sufficiently complex to allow complete characterization, in some cases, of phenomena still unencountered. It is a search necessarily involving language so arbitrary as to be whimsical: charmed quarks, colored gluons, etc. It is a search about which most of us can only marvel, without feeling competent to be skeptical, or even desiring to be skeptical, although the actual proof of its stepwise progress is essentially beyond our comprehension. It is also a search that has no significance for our social life proximate enough to generate interest in that context (even though it may affect one's religious views or self-understanding if these had previously called for particular conditions with respect to the physical universe and its origin). As a consequence the theoretical physicists are able to proceed in their awesome and all-encompassing task, involving the *physical* universe, without hostility or negative intervention from those who either fully or only partly understand.

Now contrast this search with that involving the sources and bases of human sociality—seemingly a simpler investigation, yet in some respects far more difficult. This search begins not with particles or forces beyond our senses but with the everyday and directly observable. More than that, it begins with phenomena that we are all expert in dealing with already, and about which we probably regard ourselves as more expert than we really are. The search proceeds from everyday phenomena, in not one direction but two; on the one hand, toward still unobservably small yet astonishingly intricate and somehow powerful genetic units, and the mysteries of their performance in different environments; and, on the other hand, toward the massively complex and in some sense also unobservable social phenomena that involve the combined minds, wills, and purposes of thousands, millions, and even hundreds of millions of human actors. This too is a search guided by predictions about the unknown, but one that simultaneously is seen as explaining the familiar; and one that, paradoxically, may provide directly and immediately the means for changing what it analyzes. Sometimes, even inadvertently, the search causes social alterations before the analysis is complete; and it is quite possible for erroneous hypotheses about human behavior, either seen as correct or desired to be so when they are not, to cause alterations in society that otherwise would not have occurred.

The search for the bases of human sociality, unlike those for the physical basis of the universe, affects nothing so much as it does our social lives and futures, individually and collectively. It is chapter one of the search for the foundations of ethics, the chapter missing, I believe, from the grand search as it has been conducted before this time in our history. It is a quest that, again unlike that of the theoretical physicists, leads not merely to skepticism but to hostility, fear, resistance, and even bitter and vituperative rejection. These emotions are aroused, I think, because the effort to understand the *social* universe involves ourselves, because it is seen as threatening to affect our everyday lives. Indeed, as I shall argue below, it threatens to affect our *individual* rights and opportunities to seek happiness and success in our own *individual* fashions. We do not hesitate to call the efforts of the physicists "science," but we are more apt to ridicule and dismiss the efforts of the behavioral scientists who study humans. In all the universe, the only topic we literally do not wish to be too well understood is human behavior (including, necessarily, our own) even, it would seem, if that kind of understanding represents the only clear way to diminish the threat of self-extinction. The reason for this resistance, and for the threat mentioned above, is that human behavior involves conflicts of interest. Anyone who understands some aspect of it very well will likely be able to use the knowledge to serve his own interests and thwart those of others. Social research, for example, does not flourish when its results threaten the policies of the government that furnishes its financial support. Nor are those people viewed with favor who speak of seeking to understand human behavior so as to "manipulate" or "control" the actions of the populace in respect to as yet unspecified goals. By resistance to self-understanding, then, I mean not resistance to knowing about ourselves personally, or to understanding others (both of which we seem to approach with relish), but rather resistance to the concomitant condition of *being* understood by *others*.

Despite these negative aspects, I believe that to respond effectively to the crisis into which our world of dwindling resources, changing sociality, and devastating weaponry is moving requires the kind of self-analysis that must begin with deep biological understanding. Only then can the findings from the two "ultimate" kinds of searches—those of the theoretical physicists and the social behaviorists—be combined to enable us to improve the lot of humanity. Only then, perhaps, will we be likely to restrict technology largely or solely to developing widely or universally shared ways of enhancing human life, and to resist its use in developing more efficient ways of destroying human life.

Obviously I have been assuming all along that the reader agrees that there has been a process of organic evolution, guided principally by natural selection, and that this process stands alone as responsible, in some sense, for the traits and tendencies of all organisms, including the behavior of humans. In *Darwinism and Human Affairs* I argued at length why this assumption seems presently to be the only reasonable one and, I believe, showed that the myth of evolution as a nonfalsifiable proposition can be destroyed—even by referring back to Darwin alone. (Kitcher, 1985, criticizes my 1979 argument. He does so, however, by citing only a single falsifying procedure discussed by me, and by stopping his discussion short of my description of several reasons for the value of that one proposition. Anyone interested in my examples can locate nearly all of them under "Evolution, falsifying propositions" in the index of *Darwinism and Human Affairs*.) I caution again that I do not mean that any traits of any organisms are owing alone to the genes and gene combinations that natural selection has saved. I do mean that none of the traits of life can be produced without genes, as well as, of course, environments. Learning does not occur without genes, nor without environments. Intelligence does not occur without genes, nor without environments. Moral judgments cannot be made without genes, nor without environments.

The concept of hunger, used above to explain evolutionary reductionism, is obvious to us because it is a conscious part of our everyday lives. It is a major thesis of this book, however, that there are concepts associated with morality that are neither obvious nor entirely conscious. To use such concepts to help understand and adjust our everyday behavior sometimes requires hard intellectual effort and is not always pleasant. But the consequence of ignorance about ourselves is no longer merely a vague uncertainty or uneasiness. I am by no means alone in believing that it is quite likely to lead us to self-extinction.

My concern in this first chapter has been to introduce the problems in understanding morality, and their importance, and to suggest the kind of approach I intend to take toward their solution. The next few chapters analyze in turn each of the items that I have indicated to be important, turning first to the crux of the matter, the nature of human interests and their conflicts.

## Human Interests and Their Conflicts: What Lifetimes Are About

Moral and ethical problems and questions exist solely because of conflicts of interest; moral systems exist because confluences of interest at lower levels of social organization are used to deal with conflicts of interest at higher levels.

To analyze conflicts and confluences of interest—therefore, morality and moral systems—a theory of interests is required.

A theory of interests is a theory of lifetimes—how they are patterned and what they are designed (by evolution) to accomplish.

> What we are seeking to do and must do in a civilized society is to adjust relations and order conduct in a world in which the goods of existence, the scope for free activity, and the objects on which to exert free activity are limited, and the demands upon those goods and those objects are infinite. To order the activities of men in their endeavor to satisfy their demands so as to enable satisfaction of as much of the whole scheme of demands with the least friction and waste has not merely been what lawmakers and tribunals and jurists have been striving for, it has also been put . . . by philosophers as what we ought to be doing.
>
> Today, in my judgment, the most important problem which confronts the jurist is the theory of interests. . . . I should define an interest . . . as a demand or desire which human beings either individually or in groups or in associations or in relations, seek to satisfy, of which, therefore, the ordering of human relations must take account. . . . It is not group demands or desires, but the strivings of men in (or perhaps one should say through) groups and associations and relations to satisfy certain demands or desires. . . . Conflicts or competition between interests arise because of the competition of individuals with each other, the competition of groups or societies of men with each other, and the competition of individuals with such groups or societies, in the endeavor to satisfy human wants.

. . . in determining scope and subject matter of the legal system we have to consider five things: (1) we must take an inventory of the interests which press for recognition and must generalize them and classify them; (2) we must select and determine the interests which the law should recognize and seek to secure; (3) we must fix the limits of securing the interest so selected . . . (4) we must consider the means by which the law may secure interests when recognized and delimited, that is, we must take account of the limitations upon effective legal action which may preclude complete recognition or complete securing of interests which otherwise we seek to secure, as, for example, in the case of the rights of husband and wife to consortium as against each other; (5) in order to do these things we must work out principles of valuation or interests.

Roscoe Pound, 1941, pp. 251, 259, 261.

## WHAT ARE HUMAN INTERESTS?

In some sense, conflicts and confluences of interests are the warp and woof of the fabric of society. Those who agree cooperate; those who disagree conflict or compete; and those who cooperate also use their enhanced abilities from cooperation to compete with those with whom they have conflicts of interest. Conflicts and confluences of interest are reflected at every level in society from the most closely related and intimately associated individuals to globally distant nations with populations of hundreds of millions.

What is implied is that the world is filled with people who are following their own interests. I suggest that this is true, and that they do it individually, and, when their interests overlap or coincide, they do it collectively in groups and coalitions of every imaginable size, shape, and description. They do it in families and clans and neighborhoods, and in unions, guilds, syndicates, cooperatives, corporations, tribes, municipalities, partnerships, nations, and even coalitions of nations. That people are in general following what they perceive to be their own interests is, I believe, the most general principle of human behavior. It is obviously not a new idea, but its current interpretations and consequences are different from those in previous developments of this idea, and not all of them are intuitively obvious.

Presumably, if all humans everywhere shared precisely the same interests there would be no ethical or moral problems. Our goals would all be the same, and our cooperation to achieve them would be complete. Society would be relatively simple in its structure, unless the complexity of its functioning as a unit were much greater than now is the case; and I believe that the human psyche, as well, would be a relatively simple phenomenon. Without conflicts of interest, it seems to me, the very concepts of ethical and unethical, moral and immoral, and right and wrong would not exist. My reading of the literature in moral philosophy and the social sciences indicates that these assertions represent general agreement among those who have pondered the issues; I am aware of no contrary arguments, even though the conclusion of moral relativism that seems to follow is by no means universally accepted.

If ethical and moral problems arise out of conflicts of interests, then, to some extent, humans must be striving for the same things, and things which not everyone can possess, or possess equally, or to a degree that satisfies. To discover how to describe or model conflicts of interest in a quantitative fashion we must seek to understand the general nature of the goals of humans and the patterns of their striving. What do humans actually strive to achieve? What, after all, are their interests? How can they be classified and understood in everyday terms? Ultimately, how can we develop an appropriate set of subtheories from general evolutionary theory that will predict and account for variations in ethical and moral behavior?

By "conflict of interest" I do not refer to either (1) difficulties by individuals in making decisions—for example, because of inadequate information about costs and benefits of alternatives—or (2) the common situation that an individual cannot serve in a particular capacity because he has two sets of interests in relation to the two sets of interactants involved whose interests conflict. In the latter case we say that the individual involved—say, a judge or a mediator—has a "conflict of interest." In fact there is no internal conflict within that individual. Rather, he has a *potential* conflict with one or both of the parties whose interests he is supposed to be serving, and one or both of them may legitimately fear that he will see his own interests as best served by settling the matter in favor of the other party.

If only the relatively mild point is acceptable that most of the time most people are doing things that could readily and justifiably be termed "pursuing their own interests," then enormous significance is attached to the question of what people's interests really are. To know this would be to know what is actually going on in the world. To the extent that, from generation to generation, people continue to pursue their own interests as individuals and groups, then those activities and their effects, taken collectively, must account for the institutions and concepts that we refer to as society, culture, laws, ethics, and morality, and for the changes in these institutions and concepts and their cumulative growth and development. As a result, we cannot even have a general behavioral theory until we have a reasonable answer to this question of *what are people's interests*.

There are problems in seeking an answer. First, people often keep to themselves the nature of their own personal interests as they see them. They conceal their interests from others—at least they conceal some interests all of the time, and other interests part of the time. This fact is part of the evidence, I believe, that people do indeed follow their own interests and that the interests of different people conflict. There are many questions we do not wish to answer publicly or that we would regard as an invasion of our privacy. It is difficult to draw any conclusion other than that such concealment is part of following one's own interests when they conflict with those of others.

Second, there are reasons for believing that even though people are usually pursuing their interests, they do not themselves know precisely, in the general sense, what those interests are. By this I mean that such information is not a part of their conscious knowledge, and that if you asked people what they *think* their interests are they would usually give wrong answers, even though in many specific situations they would indeed know precisely which alternatives are in their own best interests. People are not generally aware of what their lifetimes have been evolved to accomplish, and, even if they are roughly aware of this, they do not easily accept that their everyday activities are in any sense means to that end.

All of this seems paradoxical. How can we possibly hope to examine conflicts and confluences of interest in the social interactions of people if those people do not themselves know what their interests are, and how can they be acting in their own interests if they do not know what their interests are? How can we tell what their interests are, moreover, if they are concealing them? And why should they accept the analyses of others if they did not wish anyone else to know about their interests in the first place? Is it really possible that people do not always know exactly what it is that they are keeping to themselves—concealing from others? Or even that they are concealing anything?

To think on these questions, consider nonhuman organisms for a moment. It is not so incongruous to imagine that they may be acting in their own interests without "knowing" it in the human sense of conscious understanding that can be communicated by language. The question, then, is whether or not we, as human observers, could find out what the interests of the individuals of other species are if we tried, and how we could do it. Of course that is precisely what the science of biology is all about: finding out about the interests of nonhuman organisms and their manners and extents of realization. Surely we can also secure at least partial answers to the question of what human interests have evolved to be and the extents and manners of their realization.

## LIFE INTERESTS AS REPRODUCTIVE

Lifetimes have evolved so as to promote survival of the individual's genetic materials, through individuals producing and aiding offspring and, in some species, aiding other descendants and some nondescendant relatives as well.

To regard a theory of interests as a theory of lifetimes is not necessarily a new idea, but it is firmly grounded in the new evolutionary theory. The idea was developed by a succession of authors, including Fisher [(1930) 1958] and Williams (1957–1966). For recent reviews see Stearns (1976, 1977).

It is part of the recent revolution in evolutionary theory that we know that natural selection is generally more powerful at lower levels in the hierarchy of organization of life, such as genes, chromosomes, and genomes (e.g., Fisher, 1958; Williams, 1966b; Lewontin, 1970; Dawkins, 1976, 1982; Alexander and Borgia, 1978; Alexander, 1979a; Leigh, 1977). We know this, first, because effectiveness of selection depends on the amount of difference between the involved entities, the heritability of differences, and generation time (Fisher, 1958; Lewontin, 1970). All of these features are more conducive to selection being potent at levels approaching the gene and less potent at group and population levels (Alexander, 1979a).

Second, the proponents of group (or population-level) selection (e.g., David Sloan Wilson, 1975, 1980; Michael Wade, 1976, 1978) have been forced to postulate populations with attributes much like those of individuals. They invoke groups that are founded by one or a few individuals (thus as near as possible to being single broods of offspring), and last about one generation (hence, have the same generation time as individuals). In the laboratory they create populations with minimal within-population genetic variance and maximal between-population genetic variance, and so forth.

Finally, many easily made observations on organisms indicate that selection is most effective below group levels. These include such things as evidence of conflicts among individuals within social groups, failure of semelparous organisms (one-time breeders) to forego reproduction when resources are scarce, and strong resistance to adopting nonrelatives by individuals evidently long evolved in social groups. None of these observations is likely if the individual's interests are consistently the same as those of the group or if, to put it differently, allelic survival typically were most affected by selection at the group level (see also Alexander, 1979a).

If organisms are not evolved to use their lives explicitly to benefit their group as a whole, then what does all of their effort during life, their risk-taking, and their competing stand for? What is the evolutionary *raison d'etre* of lifetimes and effort? In particular, why do individuals so often *seem* to be altruistic—to be striving to assist others?

One might at first assume that the goal of an organism's life is survival. Humans think and talk a great deal about survival, and obviously we all do things that increase our likelihood of survival. But we also do a very large number and variety of things that jeopardize survival. Most of this risk-taking has to do with status-seeking, resource control, and mate competition. If selection had always favored survival, risks should never be taken except in connection with acquiring basic resources, such as food, to enable continued survival.

Another powerful argument against survival as the function of lifetimes is that most lifetimes of organisms are extremely short; the vast majority are normally under one year. In a frequency distribution of the lifetimes of a wide variety of organisms (Figure 1.1), the skew is the opposite of what we should expect if natural selection had been maximizing the lengths of lifetimes. If natural selection had been maximizing life spans, we should all be more like bristlecone pines and redwoods, and there should be many species with life cycles longer than a few thousand years. After all, if natural selection can produce such wonderful things as giant squid, crickets, honey bees, naked mole rats, and people, it should have no trouble producing a few species with million-year life cycles.

The theory of lifetimes most widely accepted among biologists is that individuals have evolved to maximize the likelihood of survival of not themselves, but their genes, and that they do this by reproducing and tending in various ways offspring and other carriers of their own genes—descendant and nondescendant relatives. In this theory, survival of the individual—and its growth, development, and learning—are proximate mechanisms of reproductive success, which is a proximate mechanism of genic survival. Only the genes have evolved to survive. This theory is necessarily fairly new, since the gene concept is less than 100 years old. This means that if the theory is correct humans could not have *evolved* to know it, and to act directly and consciously in respect to it. We could have evolved to do a great many things that would make it *look* as though we know, and we might think that we know. But genes

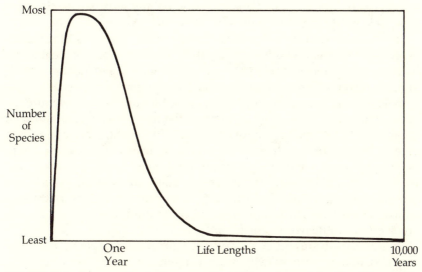

FIGURE 1.1. A generalized diagram of numbers of species with different life
            lengths. This general shape of curve derives whether one consid-
            ers only a single group, such as mammals, insects, or plants, or all
            organisms, and whether one uses maximum or average life spans
            (e.g., see Altman and Dittmer, 1964; Spector, 1956; Altman, 1962).

remained outside of the range of our senses in all respects until the
twentieth century—and they are still outside the knowledge of most
people—so any effects of our conscious understanding of genes upon
our conduct and our views of ourselves must be viewed as an evolutionary novelty.

Because of the novelty of knowledge of the genes, it is reasonable that
individual humans might not be able to describe their life interests
accurately in evolutionary terms. Nor is it surprising that it is difficult for
us to accept that we could have evolved to enable the survival of our
genes, and that our lifetimes may have been molded to serve that
function, rather than what we might nowadays regard as our own,
personal, selfish interests as individuals. Indeed, when we are told
about genes, we tend to see them as alien manipulators, the very
phenomena we are likely to be evolved to resist most intensively in our
social behavior. It is perhaps understandable that we have a kind of
xenophobia not only toward the genes, and ideas that such unchanging
objects could somehow underlie our behavior, but also toward anyone
who may argue that he has some special insight into our interests
(implying, also, ability to manipulate or control them). There is also the
possibility that pursuit of one's own interests may be viewed so

negatively by others as to cause us to avoid any such suggestion and even to keep the possibility outside consciousness.

It will seem strange to many to use the term "interests" to refer to evolved tendencies whether or not these are conscious or deliberate. Nevertheless, there seems to be no reason (not even dictionary definitions of "interest") to demand that interests refer only to what people consciously believe are their interests or intentions. As I have already noted, biologists continually investigate the life interests of nonhuman organisms, while lacking knowledge on this point, and nonhuman organisms live out their lives serving their interests without knowing, in the human sense, what those interests are. Moreover, it is axiomatic that we are not consciously aware of all that motivates us, and that consciousness (including which parts of our knowledge and attitudes are conscious and which parts are not) could not have evolved if it did not serve reproductive interests.

To say that we are *evolved* to serve the interests of our genes in no way suggests that we are *obliged* to serve them. In today's novelty-filled environments, human activities may often be directed in ways that do not in fact lead to increased success in reproduction or the perpetuation of one's own genes. Moreover, people aware of their background in evolution may be able to use conscious reflection and deliberate decisions to live their lives contrary to, or irrespective of, whatever their evolutionary background has prepared them to do. Recognizing that interests are reproductive provides us with the means for understanding and quantifying their conflicts. This can only be true because of the particular manner in which we have evolved to acquire most of our knowledge (through learning, principally via social interactions or from others). Evolution is surely most deterministic for those still unaware of it. If this argument is correct, it may be the first to carry us from *is* to *ought*, i.e., if we desire to be the conscious masters of our own fates, and if conscious effort in that direction is the most likely vehicle of survival and happiness, then we *ought* to study evolution.

## LIFETIMES AS EFFORT

Lifetimes can be regarded as composed of effort, and they can be divided into somatic and reproductive effort. Somatic effort increases residual reproductive value, reproductive effort reduces it.

A theory of interests is also a theory of effort (meaning expenditure of calories and taking of risks) in lifetimes. Organisms are commonly

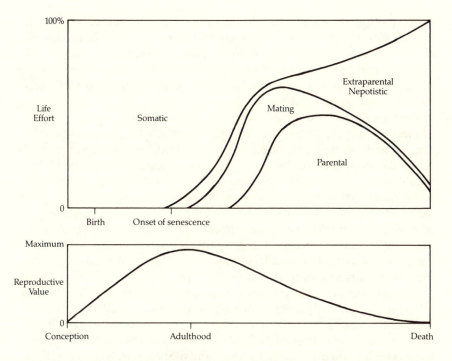

FIGURE 1.2.  A hypothetical human lifetime, showing a plausible distribution of different kinds of effort and changes in reproductive value. All early effort is somatic, which continues until death. Reproductive effort onsets before adulthood, here postulated in the form of extraparental nepotistic effort (e.g., help, or yielding of resources, to siblings). Senescence onsets shortly afterward, when the expense of reproductive effort becomes sufficient to reduce residual reproductive value. Mating and parental effort onset later, and each of the three forms of reproductive effort is postulated to maximize at a different time during adult life.

regarded by biologists as engaging in two general kinds of effort during their lifetimes; somatic and reproductive (Fig. 1.2). Somatic effort is, in general, that exerted in the prereproductive or juvenile stage and may be regarded as building the soma (phenotype, body, self) that will later be used in reproduction. It also maintains the soma of adults, when that soma still has some reproductive likelihood. In a sense somatic effort is personally or phenotypically selfish, while reproductive effort is self-sacrificing or phenotypically altruistic but genetically selfish. Somatic effort amasses resources, while reproductive effort redistributes them.

Somatic effort evolves to increase residual reproductive value by rendering subsequent reproductive effort more effective. Reproductive effort evolves to increase actual reproduction, thereby incidentally (via mortality and the fostering of the evolution of senescence—see below) reducing the residual reproductive value of the individual (Williams, 1966a; cf. Alexander and Borgia, 1978).

Perhaps the best examples to illustrate the existence of different kinds of effort across lifetimes are such extreme cases as certain butterflies. The juvenile is first a caterpillar, then a pupa. In most species the caterpillar does nothing but feed and protect itself from enemies. It is wholly involved with growth. It cannot produce offspring (although in some forms siblings move together in clusters and may show special forms of beneficence toward one another that would be regarded as reproductive effort). The pupa appears to be nothing more than a necessarily complex means of making the dramatic transformation from the caterpillar, highly specialized for somatic effort in one environment, into the remarkably different adult butterfly, just as highly specialized for the production of offspring in a different environment. The pupa, in other words, is wholly a developmental stage. Some adult butterflies are apparently wholly reproductive, not even giving much evidence that they protect themselves from predators. They do not feed at all, and have even lost their mouthparts and alimentary tracts; they do nothing but locate appropriate mates, copulate, and lay eggs in places where they are likely to hatch and grow up successfully. In most organisms somatic and reproductive effort are not so dramatically separated; but they exist, nevertheless, and together make up the *raison d'etre* of the phenotype.

## Reproduction and Senescence: Why Lifetimes Are Finite

Except when accidents intervene, senescence is the proximate reason for the finiteness of lifetimes, and for their general trajectories. Senescence evidently occurs throughout the entire adult human lifetime. Its effects are responsible for much of the trauma of human existence. In understanding lifetimes, therefore, senescence is a process and a concept just as important as those of somatic and reproductive effort, and ontogeny or development. It is curious that Williams' (1957) evolutionary theory of senescence, involving one of our most inexorable and disturbing characteristics, has not been adequately tested and has occupied very little research time and effort, despite its obvious explanatory potential and the expenditure of millions each year on gerontology.

Rose and Charlesworth (1980, p. 141) define senescence as "the post-maturation decline in survivorship and fecundity that accompanies advancing age" (see also Charlesworth, 1980). In a sense this decline is more properly an effect of senescence. The changes that cause the decline are what actually represent senescence. Williams (1957, p. 402) hypothesizes that these changes result from "adaptively unfavorable morphogenetic changes that were brought in as side effects of otherwise favorable genes, and which have only been partly expurgated by further selection." One could also describe senescence as an increasing susceptibility to environmental insults, which seems to begin at about the usual age of first reproduction. It is a change that occurs across all of our adult lives. As the effect that ultimately causes lifetimes to be finite, it is a phenomenon that must be understood if we are to develop a general comprehension of human interests. Indeed, I believe that the existence and nature of senescence is the proof that the reproductive view of human interests is correct. One of the reasons I am going to treat senescence in detail is that my experience tells me that most people are still skeptical of this view of human interests.

Senescence is an odd concept, a bit intangible and difficult to grasp. This is partly because it is apparently not something that has evolved directly but rather something that natural selection has been unable to prevent; and, as William D. Hamilton has pointed out to me, partly because senescence evidently has not a single or a few causes, but a large number of contributing causes. The questions are: Why are we, and other organisms, mortal? Why do we and they deteriorate, become increasingly fragile, susceptible to disease, incapacitated, and eventually senile? Why, in the absence of accidents, do they and we fail to live forever? Why do life lengths of the individuals of different species vary from a few minutes, hours, or weeks to a few thousand years? Why are lifetimes in most species so brief compared to those in the longest-lived ones? Why has selection not favored the longest possible lifetimes? What general principles may be involved? These are the kinds of questions a theory of senescence—really, a theory of life lengths and life patterns—may be expected to resolve. The evolutionary theory of senescence discussed here seems to resolve such questions in such a way as to substantiate the view that lifetimes are vehicles of genic survival, and to justify utilizing this proposition to understand morality.

## THE OLDER THEORIES OF SENESCENCE

Williams (1957), in what might be called the introduction to modern evolutionary theories of senescence, reviewed earlier theories. Unfortunately, outside evolutionary biology, his careful discrediting of these early theories has had little effect; they persist and predominate in the medical and social literature, and in research on human senescence. I believe that, as with cancer research which largely ignores the evolutionary background of life, the short-sightedness of theoretically deficient senescence research imposes an unjustifiable burden upon taxpayers, and stirs unreasonable hopes in the minds of people. To illustrate the distance between the arguments presented here and those currently considered in gerontological research, one can read almost any semipopular treatment of senescence such as the article, "Are we programmed to die?" in the *Saturday Review* of 2 October 1976 (see also, Fries, 1980).

The outmoded arguments, largely based on a proximate causes approach without the guidance of evolutionary reductionism through generalization, are given below.

## Wearing-Out

Machines wear out; so do some parts of organisms, such as teeth. Some people have supposed that living organisms also simply wear out. But machines are composed of static parts; organisms regenerate themselves continually. The wearing out of parts such as teeth, then, is not in itself senescence. What we are concerned with is loss of the ability to replace wornout teeth, loss of the ability to rebuild or regenerate the body's parts at least as rapidly as they deteriorate. As Williams (1957, p. 398) notes: "It is indeed remarkable that after a seemingly miraculous feat of morphogenesis [development from a single cell] a complex metazoan should be unable to perform the much simpler task of merely maintaining what is already formed." The wearing-out hypothesis thus explains nothing.

## Accumulation of Toxins

Products of metabolism accumulate in some tissues, giving them the appearance of old or aging structures (Curtis, 1963). The theory that this explains senescence is also a proximate one: it gives us no explanation for the *tendency* of tissues to allow accumulations of deleterious products of metabolism, for differences between species, or for changes in such tendencies with age. Hence, it gives us no way to explain why senescence is generally restricted to individuals past the usual age of first reproduction, regardless of the length of juvenile life, or (especially) why some organisms, such as fruit flies, mayflies, and annual plants, senesce rapidly while others, like turtles, elephants, parrots, and people, live thousands of times as long. Other theories of senescence share this shortcoming and are eliminated (as general theories or explanations) by the same reasoning; one such explanation is that somatic cells accumulate deleterious mutations (Curtis, 1963).

## Death Mechanisms

Many theories of senescence implicitly or explicitly incorporate the idea of a death mechanism, supposing that organisms commonly senesce and die to make room for other younger ones. August Weismann (1891) included such a mechanism in his "wear-and-tear" theory, and Curtis (1963, p. 694) included one in his theory of accumulated mutations in the slowly dividing or nondividing somatic cells. "It is suggested that the mutation rates of somatic cells are very much higher than the rates for gametic cells, and that this circumstance insures the death of the individual and the survival of the species."

The essential flaw in postulating general death mechanisms is that they call for a kind of altruism contrary to evolutionary principles except when relatives are assisted. No gene leading to death could spread on account of that effect unless other individuals carrying that gene were helped disproportionately as compared to individuals not carrying the gene. In a highly social organism, such as humans, tendencies to suicide in individuals who were causing an uncompensated drain upon the resources of their relatives could spread by natural (genic) selection (de Catanzaro, 1980, 1981; Chanley, ms.). But no general explanation of senescence appears derivable from this special case. For example, this theory has no way of explaining why rapid mortality occurs in semelparous organisms following reproduction, even when the eggs giving rise to the next generation will not hatch for weeks or months.

## Selective Irrelevance

Comfort (1956) argued that senescence is not affected by selection because few wild organisms survive long enough to become senile. Thus, long life would be so infrequent that gene effects occurring late in life would always be trivial or irrelevant. But the processes leading eventually to senility begin early: mortality rates increase with advancing age, beginning remarkably early in the adult life of the organism.

This is what we are required to explain. Senescence and senility are not the same thing. Comfort's argument does not account for any relationship between mortality rates at different ages in the same species, and it does not explain the grossly different life patterns of different species, or of different forms within species, such as males and females or queens and workers in honeybees, ants, and termites (see pp. 60, 67). Moreover, the question of whether or not selection can be effective always involves not just how frequently it can act but how significant are its effects on reproduction when it does. If this were not true, for example, we might suppose that any genes acting only in adult codfish would be trivially significant because only one in a million or so codfish eggs survives to produce an adult.

## WILLIAMS' PLEIOTROPIC THEORY OF SENESCENCE

As Williams (1957, p. 399) noted, " . . . other things being equal, a long-lived individual will leave more offspring than a short-lived one. If there is no specified death-mechanism, it is just as obvious that an individual that deteriorates slowly would be favored over one that deteriorates rapidly. Natural selection should ordinarily proceed toward lengthening life, not shortening it."

From this, Williams concluded that senescence is an unfavorable character, opposed by selection. To account for senescence, then, one is forced to postulate an opposing force of selection, with the existence and rate of senescence a compromise between the costs and benefits of the selective force incidentally resulting in senescenece, and the costs and benefits of selection against senescence. This idea is immediately attractive, as it conforms to the general supposition that all attributes of all organisms represent compromises among opposing selective forces.

Williams' (1957) paper on senescence was the initial contribution to the refinements of evolutionary theory that created the current revolution in humanity's understanding of itself. It is therefore ironic that the principal criticism leveled at this revolution is that its practitioners are "adaptationists" in the sense that they insist on finding an adaptive function for every trait of every organism. Williams' argument, however, was that senescence is a maladaptive consequence of other adaptive traits. Moreover, he also argued, in his pivotal 1966 book, that adaptation is an onerous concept to be invoked only with great care and after considerable investigation. The primacy and prominence of these two arguments alone put the lie to the attack on evolutionary biologists as glib "adaptationists" who see evolved function in all effects of all traits. The only way this attack can be justified is by assuming that it is

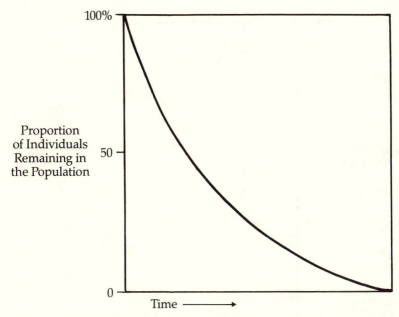

FIGURE 1.3. Effects of mortality on proportions of individuals remaining in a population. After Williams, 1957.

reasonable to attack the worst arguments in a field as showing that everyone in the field is careless or misguided rather than to strip those worst arguments away from the good ones and use the latter to build a better argument. As I have suggested earlier, publicizing the worst arguments rather than building from the best does not seem to be the typical approach of scientists.

Williams (1957) noted that many previous workers had been aware of the decline in selective pressures with increasing age, and had suggested that senescence might result from processes or effects that were favorable early in life but deleterious later. Williams continued the development of this general proposition by noting that if genes have effects both early and late in life (multiple effects of genes, whether occurring at different times or not, are referred to as pleiotropy), those acting early are likely to be more important. This is so because genes acting earlier during the period of reproduction affect a greater proportion of the reproduction of their bearer (Figs. 1.3 and 1.4). Other things being equal, early-acting beneficial genes will thus spread more rapidly than late-acting beneficial genes (that is, early effects of genes will have greater consequence for the genes' spread and persistence than later

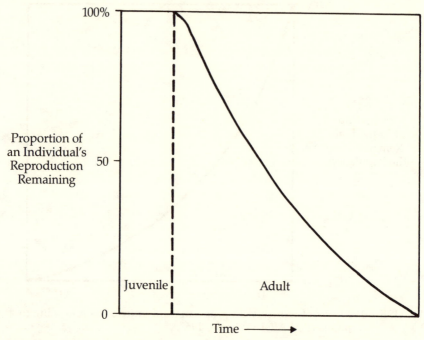

FIGURE 1.4. Effects of reproductive effort and mortality on the proportion of an individual's reproduction remaining. After Williams, 1957.

effects). Moreover, if early and late effects of genes should happen to be opposed, deleterious late effects will accumulate, because alleles will be saved as a result of their early effects and in spite of their later ones. This will lead to deteriorative effects that can be identified as the process of senescence.

Williams' pleiotropic theory (i.e., his theory of multiple effects of individual genes, here early beneficial ones and later deleterious ones), whether correct or not, unlike all others so far discussed, is an appropriate kind of biological theory. Medawar (1955, 1957) came closest to developing the same theory, but he did not take the step of distinguishing between linkage and pleiotropy to explain perpetuation of both beneficial and deleterious effects. In developing the theory, Williams pointed out that linkages can be broken, while pleiotropy would require substitution of alternative alleles. Simultaneously, Williams' theory provides a possible "ultimate" explanation, and a focus for identifying or analyzing genetic, physiological, or other proximate mechanisms. Williams' theory is a genetic theory in the sense that it argues that organisms are programmed to senesce in particular fashions in the successions of environments in which they have evolved. It is a useful theory because it is both testable and provides a focus for all investigators of senescence, whatever the approaches, goals, or organisms. Until demonstrated to be erroneous, or replaced by a more convincing theory of similarly broad applicability and usefulness, it will be ignored by investigators only at the peril of having their results declared trivial and their efforts wasteful.

Now let us analyze the bases and the consequences of the theory and evaluate its apparent validity 30 years after its formulation.

## THE NATURE AND EXTENT OF PLEIOTROPY

> *Heredity is particulate, but development is unitary. Everything in the organism is the result of the interactions of all genes, subject to the environment to which they are exposed.*
>
> Dobzhansky, 1961, p. 111

The above quote clearly implies that all genes are simultaneously pleiotropic (have multiple effects) and epistatic (affect one another's effects). The more one reflects on this suggestion the more significant and the more convincing it seems. We usually think of individual genes in terms of obvious or dramatic single effects; but, as Dobzhansky points out, the unity of development makes multiple effects essentially certain. Different effects are also highly likely to be manifested at different times in the life of the organism.

It does not follow that such differently timed effects are likely to be known. Typically, biologists have examined gene effects individually without either the means or the curiosity to determine all of the effects of single allelic substitutions. As Williams remarked (1957, p. 400) " . . . we seldom know the total survival value of a gene in a wild population, let alone its values in different parts of the life cycle." This is almost certainly the reason that the weakest part of the pleiotropic theory of senescence is the paucity of examples of appropriately acting genes.

Williams regarded it as being relatively unimportant to document the existence of appropriately pleiotropic genes, and one can scarcely disagree. To discredit the existence of the kind of selection relevant to his theory one would have to suppose (1) that most genes have single effects or (2) that the different effects of pleiotropic genes either (a) usually occur at the same time in the life cycle or (b) are equally beneficial or harmful. I suspect that geneticists would be in general agreement that the evidence indicates that none of these things is true.

Different effects of the same gene, such as at different times of life, would be owing to differences in the soma, not in the gene itself. The soma may be viewed as an ever-changing environment of the genes. Different effects of single genes could occur at different places in the soma, at different times, or both. The greater the complexity of the life cycle or the greater the changes in the organism's makeup, activities, or circumstances during its lifetime the greater the likelihood that there will be changes with time in a gene's effects on the organism. Different effects of a single gene may have obvious connections to one another or be seemingly autonomous, although it is difficult to see how they could be completely independent. The same effect of a gene can be beneficial in one circumstance, or in one stage of life, and deleterious in another.

Hamilton (1966, p. 35) argued that "Williams may have been unnecessarily restricting the scope of his theory by making it depend upon genes which are pleiotropic in the ordinary sense of the word." He pointed out that in a sense all age-specific genes are pleiotropic, simply because they yield effects at some ages and none at others; such genes are abundant (e.g., see Schneider, 1978, Charlesworth, 1980, and any of the journals of genetics). He explained this by describing the events resulting from appearance of age-specific genes with net positive or beneficial effects:

> the mutant will spread, the spread will be accompanied by a rise in population, and this rise will in time be checked by density-dependent adverse factors of the environment which bear on the life schedules, raising mortalities or reducing fertilities in a pattern that has nothing to do with the particular pattern of the positive effect which initiated the sequence. When population has been made stationary again, the overall result will tend to be that fertility has been down-graded and mortality up-graded all along their length, so that the beneficial effect is itself slightly down-graded and all the null effects [absence of effects at other times in life] now appear as slight disadvantages. (pp. 35–36)

I believe that the idea, expressed earlier, that even the same effect of a gene is unlikely to be equally beneficial throughout a lifetime—especially a long-lived organism with its life patterned around complex sociality—represents a third reason (in addition to pleiotropy, *sensu strictu*, and age specificity) why Williams' theory is reasonable.

Hamilton then developed a "picture of the evolution of the curve of force of mortality." He saw it as

> continually being "nibbled" from above, the nibbles representing the spreading of more or less age-specific advantageous mutations through the

population. They may be closely age specific or they may involve a lowering of the curve along a strip of considerable length. Following each nibble the whole curve, after more or less delay, makes a small ascent. The delay corresponds to the period of increasing population; the ascent to the coming into operation of the Malthusian [density-dependent] checks to increase. The nibbling takes place fastest at the left-hand end of the curve and towards the right-hand finally with infinite slowness at the age where reproduction ends. The greater the speed with which nibbles occur [with which mutations with advantageous effects spread] the sooner they can be succeeded by others. Thus the irregular downward movement is occurring fastest at the left-hand end, and the compensatory general upward movement results in a kind of dynamic equilibrium in which the curve trails upward indefinitely at the right. In the absence of complications due to parental care or other altruistic contributions due to post-reproductives, the curve should be roughly asymptotic to the age of the ending of reproduction. (p. 36)

Elsewhere in his paper, to test the probability of failure to senesce, Hamilton (1966) developed a model of a volvox-like organism with its cells undergoing synchronous division, every two divisions producing an independent daughter cell from each tetrad of cells. Even if (1) there is no mortality, (2) population expansion continues indefinitely, and (3) each individual expands its fecundity exponentially, he still found that "any mutation causing an improvement in early fecundity at the expense of an equal detriment later will . . . gradually come to numerical preponderance in the population; and if we allow any incipient incidence of mortality we likewise see that selection will favour resistance to it at early ages to a certain extent at the expense of greater vulnerability at later ages." (p. 25)

Hamilton then conceded that despite his argument that Williams had unnecessarily weakened his theory by restricting it to genes with beneficial early effects and detrimental late ones, his effort to model failure to senesce makes it "evident that Williams' [kind of] pleiotropic effects certainly do exist. . . . " Hamilton's findings with his immortal volvox-like model contradict Williams' arguments that asexual clones and protozoans should not show senescence (pp. 403–404) and, together with the above argument about pleiotropy, eliminate one of the four assumptions Williams regarded as essential to his theory (p. 400) and alter a second. The three remaining necessary assumptions are, then: (1) a soma essential to reproductive success but not passed on during reproduction, (2) natural selection of alternative alleles in a population, and (3) genes which either have opposite effects on fitness at different ages or are at least age-restricted in regard to beneficial effects. As Hamilton (1966, p. 26) concluded: ". . . for organisms that reproduce repeatedly, senescence is to be expected as an inevitable consequence of

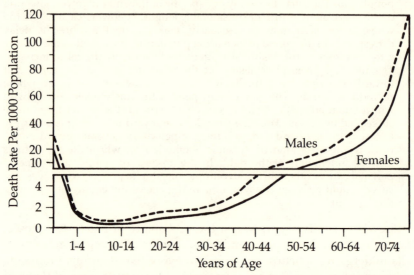

FIGURE 1.5. Mortality rates in modern America in 1950 (from Alexander, 1979a).

the working of natural selection." Thus, either a gene with early beneficial effects and late deleterious effects, or one with beneficial effects
early in life and none at any other time, would lead to senescence unless
it could be replaced by an allele with equally beneficial effects at all times
in life—which is highly unlikely because selection is not equally effective, and does not always operate similarly, across the whole life span.

## THE GENERAL SHAPES OF MORTALITY CURVES

Figures 1.5 and 1.6 depict rates of mortality throughout the lifetimes
of people in modern America (Alexander, 1979a) and Taiwanese
in the late 19th century (Hamilton, 1966). The curves are similar (as
are those from widely different societies all over the world; cf.
Alexander, 1979a) raising interesting questions about the effects of
technological and other environmental changes. One difference is
noticeable: in 19th century Taiwan, juvenile females had a higher
mortality rate than juvenile males, while in modern America, juvenile
males, as with males at all ages, die more frequently than juvenile
females. We can only speculate about this difference. It could represent a change in the activities of juvenile females, or it could reflect
the fact that in some Asian societies male offspring tended to receive
more parental attention, including better nutrition, causing female

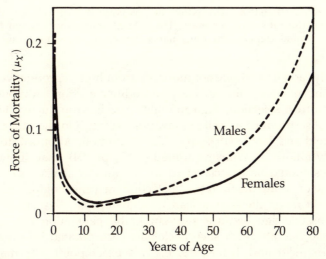

FIGURE 1.6. Mortality rates for Taiwanese in the late 19th century (from Hamilton, 1966).

offspring to succumb to disease more frequently, especially during famines and epidemics. It is unlikely to reflect infanticide except at around the time of birth.

## THE EFFECT OF MORTALITY RATES ON SENESCENCE

Williams (1957, p. 402) noted that:

> Any previously established genes that cause senescence will increase the rate of decline in $p$ [reproductive probability] and make it easier for other such genes to become established. In this way senescence becomes a self-aggravating process. (p. 402)

He then added that senescence is nevertheless unfavorable and that:

> The direct action of selection will always be opposed to it. The establishment of an important "senescence gene" in a population would cause the favorable selection of other genes that would reduce or delay the unfavorable effects. . . . As the suppression approached completion, however, the selection pressure for further suppression would diminish. Complete suppression would probably never be realized. Senescence might be regarded as a group of adaptively unfavorable morphogenetic changes that were brought in as side effects of otherwise favorable genes, and which have only been partly expurgated by further selection. There are, therefore, two opposing selective forces with respect to the evolution of senescence. One is an indirect selective force that acts to increase the rate of senescence by favoring vigor in youth at the price of vigor later on. The other is the

direct selection that acts to reduce or postpone the "price" and thereby decrease the rate of senescence. The rate of senescence shown by any species would depend on the balance between these opposing forces. (p. 402)

Similarly, accelerated rates of mortality from high reproductive effort increase the relative value of early reproductive effort. Although retarded by direct selection, high mortality late in reproductive life will evidently also produce a "self-aggravating" effect. On the other hand, as Hirshfield and Tinkle (1975, pp. 2228–2229) pointed out, it does not necessarily follow, as Williams argued (1957, p. 404), that "Low adult death rates should be associated with low rates of senescence. . . . " Regardless of adult death rates "Selection in (unchanging) environments could favor alleles that lead to high reproductive effort at the earliest possible age because shortening the generation time would increase the rate at which such alleles are incorporated into the gene pool" (Hirshfield and Tinkle, 1975). This exact point was made by Hamilton (1966) with his volvox-like model.

## MALE AND FEMALE MORTALITY

Why is male mortality generally higher than female mortality at all ages? For various reasons the net benefits of additional matings are usually greater for males than for females (see Trivers, 1972; Williams, 1966b, 1975; Alexander, 1979a). When this is true males tend to invest more in mating effort (partly because sex ratio selection is not altered by differences in intensity of sexual selection, owing to the sex ratio, if sexual selection occurs after termination of parental care; Fisher, 1958), and only in species with such males should male mortality exceed female mortality.

Not only do direct contests for mates involve high risks of injury that may lead to death, but the phenotypic attributes that evolve in males as a result of sexual selection often reduce viability even though increasing mating success. As Williams (1975, pp. 138–139) stated:

In many species a typical adult female will enjoy something like the mean reproductive success. A male, especially in polygynous species, may not reproduce at all. Perhaps only the fittest 25% of the males will reproduce, and the top 1% may enjoy many times the mean reproductive success. At every moment in its game of life the masculine sex is playing for higher stakes. Its possible winnings, either in immediate reproduction or in an ultimate empire of wives and kin, are greater. So are its possibilities for immediate bankruptcy (death) or permanent insolvency from involuntary but unavoidable celibacy.

Greater variance in male fitness not only affects optimization of reproductive behavior, but all tributary aspects of adaptive organization. A male's developmental program must gamble against odds in an effort to attain the upper tail of the fitness distribution. A female's need merely canalize against malfunctions. Female mortality will be found to exceed male, not in species with female heterogamety, but those with female masculinity.

In other words, because males typically gain more by increasing numbers of offspring via multiple matings, while females typically gain more by giving more parental care to fewer offspring, even the human male competes sexually a little more intensively. On average, he takes more risks than the female, and is more likely either to fail completely in reproduction or to outreproduce the average female. As a result, he has a higher rate of mortality and, correspondingly, has evolved to senesce sooner, a fact reflected in the relatively large number of widows around the world. The difference in senescence rate is not likely to be erased by an evolutionarily novel shift in women's activities, such as an increase in women taking over what have traditionally been men's jobs, or an increase in women's smoking, drinking, or assuming other risky activities formerly restricted to men. Equally risky activities by the two sexes may be expected to bring the mortality curves closer together, but they will only make the two curves coincident if there is no evolved difference between the sexes in senescence patterns. It is difficult to believe that there is not such an evolved male–female difference.

We can add that a female's reproductive success, especially in species with extended parental care, depends upon her ability to tend the offspring she has produced. A male's success, in species in which males invest more of their reproductive effort in mating, depends more upon activities that in many cases can be completed in a short period. A male highly successful during his first breeding season may lose little if he dies immediately afterward; a female in a parental species who dies shortly after mating may lose everything. Likewise, an old male may produce offspring that will be successful because of parental care from the mother; but an old female's youngest offspring may be unlikely to survive. One is tempted to speculate that this accounts for the evolution of menopause in human females and for sperm production and sexual potency in males that are much older than menopausing females (Williams, 1957; Alexander, 1974, 1979a; Dawkins, 1976).

Not all changes with age need be regarded as senescence. As an example, suppose that females sometimes favor older males largely because their greater age indicates a phenotypic success which may reflect a genotype superior in coping with the fluctuations in the species' environment (e.g., in maintaining resistance to rapidly evolving parasites and diseases). In the case of older males which are also obviously successful breeders, the relevant environment includes competing conspecific males. In such cases, attributes in males suggesting greater than actual age may be favored because they imply either resource control or power (as through ability to marshal assistance or assemble coalitions). Also, perhaps for all these reasons, they may enhance a male's attractiveness to females, as attributes in females suggesting youthfulness (hence, ability to bear and tend offspring well) may enhance their attractiveness to males. It would be inaccurate to regard such male attributes as simply evidence of maladaptive senescence, even if they started out as such. We may wonder, until someone figures out a way to test these ideas, if some tendencies toward gray hair or balding patterns in human males, or the "silver backs" of adult gorillas, might not represent effects of such selection.

Whenever different "morphs" within species maximize reproduction according to different routes, such as (1) male and female, (2) different kinds of males (e.g., large, flashy aggressive morphs versus small, drab, sometimes female-mimicking morphs in some birds, fish, beetles, and others), or (3) reproductives, workers, and soldiers (social insects), they may prove useful in analyzing the significance of different mortality schedules in relation to life functions and the history of selection upon factors leading to senescence. Unfortunately, not much advantage has yet been taken of the opportunity to compare such similar forms in these regards (although it is well known that queens in eusocial insects, living in the safe parts of nests and undertaking only relatively safe tasks, outlive by many times workers and soldiers who take on the riskiest tasks; for additional comparisons, see below, and Alexander and Noonan, in prep.).

## SEMELPARITY, ITEROPARITY, AND SENESCENCE

Semelparous organisms, such as salmon and soybeans, reproduce but once in their lifetimes; iteroparous organisms, such as trees, fruit flies, humans, and most others, reproduce repeatedly. Semelparous organisms differ from iteroparous organisms in regard to effects of selection on senescence in at least two important ways:

1. Selection on the iteroparous organism will tend to result in a gradual senescence, beginning in each individual after it has achieved the usual reproductive age, whether or not actual reproduction is occurring (i.e., once the sum effect of its life activities is to reduce rather than increase the probability of future reproduction); contrarily, that of

the semelparous organism will tend to a greater degree to maintain its vigor, or prevent any senescence, until reproduction actually occurs. This is so because the iteroparous organism undergoes a gradual reduction in the proportion of its reproduction that still remains (residual reproductive value—Williams, 1966a), while the semelparous organism tends to retain more nearly its full reproductive probability (leaving aside the inevitable probability of mortality) until the act of reproduction, except when there is a history of gradual deterioration in the environment, and this deterioration sometimes begins before the organism is able to reproduce. In effect, if timing of its single act of reproduction is essential to the semelparous organism, the period before reproduction actually occurs, during which timing is possible, is more a part of juvenile life than is the case with an iteroparous organism; by timing its one act of reproduction carefully through delaying it, the semelparous organism is to a greater extent still increasing its reproductive probability. This argument predicts the common observation that both iteroparous and semelparous organisms prevented from reproduction will tend to live longer; but it also predicts that the effect will be less dramatic in iteroparous organisms, in which senescence is likely to be more significant after the usual age of onset of reproduction.

2. The last act of reproduction may be indefinite in the iteroparous organism, but will always be definite in the semelparous organism because it is also the first. Hence, iteroparous organisms will tend to deteriorate suddenly only in response to environmental insults that in the past have consistently terminated all further reproduction (such as, for insects, freezing temperatures in autumn).

On the other hand, the act of reproduction itself may in the semelparous organism lead to fatal chemical or other events which cannot be selected against. Unlike genes in the iteroparous organism, any one or all of the thousands of genes that may participate in the success of a semelparous organism's reproduction may, without prejudice to the survival of its copies, incidentally produce effects leading to instant death, just after reproduction.

One therefore does not have to regard the semelparous organism as literally depleting all its phenotype in reproduction and dying afterward for that reason. Instead it can be thought of as converting all of the phenotype it can into offspring without prejudicing the phenotype's ability to complete the act of producing the offspring and putting them into optimal circumstances and physical condition. The quick postreproductive death of the semelparous organism, then, is a consequence of the failure of selection after the point at which the act of reproduction is completed. In a relevant experiment, Sokal (1970) found that when adult *Tribolium castaneum* (flour beetles) were killed just after first reproduction for 40 generations, they evolved a significantly shorter adult life; unfortunately, he did not verify if there had also been an increase in early fecundity. Rose and Charlesworth (1980), in a breeding experiment with *Drosophila,* claimed results that "provide evidence for (Williams') pleiotropy theory. . . . " They are correct, but their support of Williams' theory is weak because they did not perform the most useful test. Rather than breeding *Drosophila* for an early high rate of reproduction, and testing to see if senescence appeared early and more intensively as an *incidental side effect,* they bred for later high rates of reproduction and found that senescence was delayed. Several authors have recently obtained the same result but also failed to produce early rapid senescence (Rose, 1984; Luckinbill *et al.,* 1984; Clare and Luckinbill, 1985; Luckinbill and Clare, 1985). It is strange that in the 30 years following its publication no one has been able to perform the most appropriate test of Williams' theory (see Bell, 1984, for an additional effort in this direction, comparing organisms that reproduce by budding with those that produce young via gametes). Possibly, it has proved difficult to select for early high reproductive effort in laboratory animals because they have already been selected in this direction for long periods. It is also possible that most species with rapid generation times (such as *Drosophila*) will have been similarly selected, so that to test the theory adequately will require results from species with long generation times, such as some domesticated mammals. If so, the time required for experimentation will be prohibitive, and the most convincing data may ultimately come from comparative study of unplanned long-term changes in directions of selection (e.g., in Holstein-Friesian dairy cattle, Alexander, ms.).

The remarkable difference between the patterns of senescence in semelparous (one-time breeding) and iteroparous (repeat-breeding) organisms is probably one of the best simple demonstrations of the central significance of reproduction in the individual's lifetime. How, otherwise, could we explain the fact that those who reproduce but once, like salmon and soybeans, tend to die suddenly right afterward, while those like ourselves who have residual reproductive possibilities after the initial reproductive act decline or senesce gradually? Both kinds of organisms, in other words, continue somatic effort until their possibilities of further reproduction have disappeared, even though they accomplish this in strikingly different fashions. Stated another way, once an organism has completed all possibilities of reproducing (through both offspring production and assistance, and helping other relatives), then selection can no longer affect its survival: any physio-logical or other breakdown that destroys it may persist and even spread if it is genetically linked to a trait that is expressed earlier and is reproductively beneficial.

It is conceivable that within the same species one sex may be iteroparous, while the other is semelparous and their senescence patterns differ accordingly. For example, this may be the case in octopuses in which females lay only one clutch of eggs and tend it until the young more or less abruptly disperse, while males of the same species presumably mate with one female, and then seek others. We expect the females to die suddenly, normally at the time when their young disperse, and the males to senesce gradually (speaking compar-atively). Wodinsky's (1977) results with females, and his mention of failure to obtain the same results with males, imply that this is the case, although further testing is obviously required.

## PARENTAL CARE AND OFFSPRING REPLACEMENT

To demonstrate the changing effects of selection on alternative genetic units across a human lifetime, Hamilton (1966) compared four hypothetical genes (we can regard them as alternatives, thus competing alleles), each of which gives complete immunity against a lethal disease for 1 year of life in human females. The affected years are the 1st, 15th, 30th, and 45th. He assumed no parental care, and menopause before the 45th year (and, obviously, no ability afterward to help relatives), and then considered the relative selective advantages of the genes. The gene acting in the 45th year thus gives no advantage, and that acting in the 30th year gives less than the two acting earlier because women at 30 years have completed some reproductive years. It is less obvious that if reproduction never occurs by the 15th year, the genes acting at ages 1 and 15 will have equal likelihood of spreading. The reason is that, although the earlier-acting gene affects more individuals, the reproduc-tive probabilities of those individuals are lower than those of individuals affected at age 15, and the amount by which their value is lower necessarily varies with the mortality rate between 1 and 15 precisely as to compensate the raised value of 15 year olds. Unless the immunity given by the gene is different at different ages or the disease affects different proportions of individuals at different ages, then, age-specific effects before the onset of reproduction are not more valuable if they occur earlier. This is the reason for Williams' statement that the usual time of reproductive maturation should mark the onset of senescence. Once the age of reproduction is achieved, the inevitable lowering of residual reproductive value from that time on precludes compensatory increases in the value of individuals saved at later ages and causes earlier effects of genes to be more valuable.

One complication in applying this argument involves reproduction by juveniles via nepotism to nondescendant relatives. Diversion of calories or the taking of risks in such activities should cause senescence to begin during juvenile life, and consistent, large, successful expenditures of reproductive effort before adulthood may have caused a ballooning of such effects in special cases, like the termites, until individuals were eventually produced (termite workers) which have (by investigators unaware of this theory) been termed "permanent juveniles." These individuals live out their lives without producing offspring, without becoming sexually mature, and continuing to resemble juveniles rather than adults (see p. 67).

Trivers (1974) argued that juveniles evolve to take from their parents, as individuals, more than it is advantageous for the parent to give, but not enough to reduce the juvenile's inclusive fitness because of the consequent deprivation of its siblings. If this view of parent–offspring conflict is reasonably accurate—that is, if offspring really do refrain from taking resources from siblings—then senescence must begin as soon as the juvenile typically engages in such behavior to an extent that its likelihood of future reproduction is reduced. It would be interesting to look for evidence of senescence among juveniles in all of those species in which nepotistic acts occur regularly before adulthood. It is not idle to ask whether or not child labor—especially explicitly nepotistic forms like care of younger siblings—has occurred sufficiently long and intensively in any human societies to induce an earlier onset of senescence and a measurable modification of the life pattern. As suggested later, however (p. 82), it will be necessary to distinguish nepotism (as reproductive effort) from indirect somatic effort as social investment in reciprocity to determine this effect.

Hamilton's (1966) description of the mortality curve has it reduced most powerfully early in life. Nevertheless, most organisms probably suffer greatest mortality early in life, whether or not there is parental care, because they are intrinsically more vulnerable. Parental care evolves because it is more valuable reproductively to reduce early mortality than to produce a larger number of offspring, each with less parental investment and, accordingly, a higher probability of mortality. Parental care is probably the most important "nibbler" at the left side of the mortality curve. High juvenile mortality relative to that later on does not mean that lowered early mortality is not valuable but that juvenile mortality is more difficult to reduce.

Extensive parental care may not merely lower the mortality of juveniles but may also change the shape of the juvenile mortality curve in iteroparous species because of the possibility of offspring replacement. Thus, if inferior offspring, or offspring produced during times when they cannot be satisfactorily reared, are terminated early, the parent will benefit from having invested less. This effect should lead to a steepening of the early part of the curve of juvenile mortality in relation to the later parts, even if parental care is simultaneously lowering juvenile mortality at all points.

Abandonment or cannibalism of offspring, infanticide, abortion, and miscarriage may all be mechanisms in some mammals by which offspring replacement or "culling" is effected at minimal expense. The evidence for widespread superovulation in mammals (ovulation of more eggs than can survive) appears also to be evidence of offspring replacement, although if selection of superior offspring is involved it is not clear whether in many cases the selection is occurring before or after fertilization.

Humans are unique in that parental care may sometimes continue until offspring have themselves terminated their reproductive lives, at least in terms of actual production of offspring. Nevertheless, more or less dramatic alteration of the kinds and amounts of parental care often occur at about the time of reproductive maturity. This effect is especially evident in societies in which female offspring are sold or preferentially passed to men of other groups—or other village or clans. If such females are passed to a group containing none of their relatives they may be relatively vulnerable until they have produced dependent offspring by a man with power or prestige.

At about the same age young men may frequently suffer high mortality, not only because of high-risk activities obviously associated with within-group sexual competition and the establishment of a suitable resource base for their reproductive lives, but also from activities less obviously significant in these contexts, especially participation in organized aggression such as wars.

## THE WONDERFUL ONE-HOSS SHAY EFFECT

Finally, Williams pointed out that selection continually works against senescence, but is just never able to defeat it entirely. Perhaps the most important practical consequence of Williams' theory is that senescence leads to a generalized deterioration rather than one owing to a single effect or a few effects (Williams, 1957, pp. 406–407). In the course of working against senescence, selection will tend to remove, one by one, the most frequent sources of mortality as a result of senescence. Whenever a single cause of mortality, such as a particular malfunction of any vital organ, becomes the predominant cause of mortality, then selection will more effectively reduce the significance of that particular defect (meaning those who lack it will outreproduce) until some other achieves greater relative significance. As soon as a source of mortality has been rendered barely second in importance, selection will be more effective in counteracting the new most important source of mortality. The new defect will also be selected toward insignificance, and the result will be that all organs and systems will tend to deteriorate together. Fries (1980), evidently unaware of evolutionary theories of senescence, presents data supporting the notion that when "acute" and accidental sources of human death are removed the consequence is a sharp compression of senescence without any great increase in maximum life lengths.

The point is that as we age, and as senescence proceeds, large numbers of potential sources of mortality tend to lurk ever more malevolently just "below the surface," so that, unfortunately, the odds are very high against any dramatic lengthening of the maximum human lifetime through technology. This prediction is consistent with the finding of Fries (1980) that maximum life spans in the United States have increased little or none since 1900. This kind of selection also accounts for the fact that mortality curves for human populations in different times and places, and in different kinds of societies or cultures, are remarkably alike (compare Figs. 1.5 and 1.6 with Fig. 2, Alexander, 1979a). Similarly, the male and female curves tend to hold their relationships to one another cross-culturally.

Although this argument renders impractical research designed to locate the causes of senescence and thereby *dramatically* prolong human life, medical technology and bionics will undoubtedly continue to be directed at correcting deteriorations before they cause death (what Fries, 1980, called "progress in the elimination of premature death"). In consequence, *small* advances in average life length will continue to be achieved, and the significance of particular sources of mortality will be reduced. Others, in turn, will achieve new significance, and new crusades will be mounted against them. It is entirely possible, though, that gerontological research would lose a great deal of its support if it became quite apparent that no magic formula for dramatically length-ening life is likely to be discovered.

Supreme Court Justice Oliver Wendell Holmes may have presaged this part of Williams' argument over 100 years ago. In the nineteenth century, when transportation was principally via horse-drawn vehicles (wagons, buggies, shays), he wrote about the maddening tendency of all such vehicles to have one or another weak or short-lived component. According to his verse, "The Deacon's Masterpiece," one buggy was constructed so as to have no parts any weaker than all the others, with the consequence that it ran a hundred years then fell to pieces all at once.

## SUMMARY

The reason, then, that natural selection has not been able to prevent senescence is that natural selection maximizes the likelihood of genetic survival, which is incompatible with eliminating senescence. The reason for this, in turn, is that genetic survival occurs through success in reproduction (presumably because throughout the history of life environments have been sufficiently unpredictable as to preclude indefinite avoidance of mortality), and such success is always relative. Senescence, and the finiteness of lifetimes, have evolved as incidental effects of the evolution of lifetimes as efforts to maximize success in genetic reproduction. Organisms compete for genetic survival and the winners (in evolutionary terms) are those who sacrifice their phenotypes (selves) earlier when this results in greater reproduction. The proximate vehicles of senescence are evidently multiple or pleiotropic effects of genes, with the different effects occurring at different times of life. Early effects are reproductively more important than later ones, with the evolutionary consequences that early beneficial effects will be saved even if they are absent later in life or actually replaced by deleterious effects of the same genes.

Senescence theory, together with sexual selection and parental investment theory, therefore predicts (or explains) a large number of differences between human males and females, including their relative body sizes, mortality and senescence rates, relative frequencies in the population (i.e., sex ratios), relative amounts of parental care, relative times to maturity, relative rates of lawbreaking, etc. (Trivers, 1972; Alexander et al., 1979; Alexander, 1978, 1979a). Understanding these phenomena is a necessary part of understanding the nature of human lifetimes and which, in turn, is central to understanding conflicts of interest and thus the nature and roles of morality and ethics.

## Reproduction and Cooperation: Special Cases

Interests of different organisms tend to coincide in three major kinds of circumstances:

1. When relatedness in genes identical by immediate descent is high.

2. When two or more unrelated individuals reproduce via the same third parties (e.g., in lifetime monogamy or eusocial insects that live in huge nuclear families).

3. When external threats can only (or best) be dissipated by cooperation.

## GENETIC INDIVIDUALITY AND INDIVIDUALITY OF INTERESTS

If the life interests of organisms are in maximizing genetic reproduction (that is, if organisms have evolved by the repeated preservation of those genetic alternatives leading the individual to develop so as most effectively to promote the survival by reproduction of all its genetic materials), then it is out of this fact that a general theory about conflicts of interest must arise, namely: sexual reproduction causes individuals to be genetically unique. It creates genetic individuality because it consists primarily of random recombination in each generation of very large numbers of independently assorting genetic units (Williams, 1975; Maynard Smith, 1978; Parker, Baker, and Smith, 1972). A long history of genetic individuality means that individuals will evolve to behave as though their life interests are individually unique. Moreover, social organisms should be expected to be adept at judging partial overlaps of interest with other individuals through (1) proximate mechanisms that correlate with numbers and kinds of genealogical links and (2) opportunities to achieve goals or deflect threats by cooperative efforts with others. The longer the usual lives of individuals, and the longer individuals continue to interact significantly and repeatedly with one another, the greater will be their adeptness at assessing and acting appropriately with respect to partial confluences of interest, as well as conflicts of interest, and the more complex will be society. This, then, is the basic biological theory of conflicts of interest and therefore of moral systems. To understand our social and moral systems we have to unravel their fabric until we begin to see precisely how it has been created from the interlacing of the threads of individual reproductive striving.

Several facts support the hypothesis that conflicts of interests arise out of a history of genetic individuality. First there are evidently no reports of conflict among genetically identical individuals within clones among species that have for a long time reproduced asexually; and evidence of extraordinary cooperativeness in such cases abounds (cf. E. O. Wilson, 1975; Aoki *et al.*, 1981; Alexander and Noonan, in prep.). Second, altruism appears generally to diminish with decreasing degrees of relatedness in sexual species whenever it is studied—in humans as well as nonhuman species (for reviews, see Sherman and Holmes, 1985;

Holmes and Sherman, 1983). Third, in cases in which identity or near-identity of genetic interests is achieved in sexual species (without genetic identity per se), cooperation is also dramatic. Examples are the two partners in lifetime monogamy and the members of the large social insect colonies that are actually nuclear families of enormous size (e.g., honeybees, ants, termites). In each case the cooperating parties (spouses; workers and queens) reproduce via the same third parties (offspring; siblings and offspring), to which they are more or less equally related genetically, and which are usually the closest (needy) relatives available to each of them (Hamilton, 1964; West Eberhard, 1975; Wilson, 1971; Noonan, 1981; J. E. Strassmann, 1981; Alexander and Noonan, in prep.). These various cases represent tests of the idea that lifetimes have evolved to maximize the likelihood of genic survival through reproduction. This idea is likely to represent the greatest difficulty in acquiring support for the biological theory of morality developed in the following pages. Therefore it is important to review briefly some of these special cases.

## THE PINNACLES OF ULTRASOCIALITY: HOW THEY EVOLVED

One kind of evidence that genetic reproduction is the *raison d'etre* for the individual is the manner in which what E. O. Wilson (1971) calls the four "pinnacles" of complex sociality or "ultrasociality" (Campbell, 1975) have been achieved in clones, eusocial insects, nonhuman mammals, and humans. Here I will concentrate on the first two and the last— for nonhuman mammals, see Jarvis (1981) and Jarvis, Sherman, and Alexander (in prep.).

Complex sociality should be expected to arise only when confluences of interest produce benefits that override the costs of conflicting interests (see also Alexander, 1974, 1979a; Alexander and Noonan, in prep.), leading first to cooperative group living and later to complex sociality. It seems to me that there is one basic functional substrate for trends toward *cooperative* group living and that is active and cooperative defense against some common extrinsic threat or uncertainty (e.g., a predator or a powerful or elusive prey or food item). Three conditions promote cooperation as a means of overcoming such threats or hostile forces: (1) genetic similarity or identity (as in clones, e.g., of aphids; Aoki *et al.*, 1981), (2) tendencies for close relatives to remain in close proximity (Hamilton's 1964 "population viscosity"), and (3) reproduction via the same third party (as with unrelated parents cooperating to produce and protect mutual offspring to which they are equally related).

One indicator of the degree to which conflicts of interests among social individuals have been minimized is the size of the group: only when conflicts are minimal should very large group sizes be reached. The reason is that there are automatic costs to group living, mainly involving access to resources (Alexander, 1974, 1978; Hoogland and Sherman, 1976). These costs tend to increase as group sizes increase, so that net benefits tend to disappear above certain sizes (Alexander, 1979a).

Another indicator of minimal conflict is the level of cooperativeness, measurable partly by the complexity of tasks performed by individuals, especially considering groups like modern nations of hundreds of millions or even more than a billion (in China). Such human groups are necessarily highly cooperative, and this is especially true in wartime or when they are threatened externally. The tasks they have been able to accomplish by cooperative division of labor are without parallel among other sexually reproducing organisms.

## Clones

Conflicts of interest are not expected when all group members are genetically identical. This is the case in clones of aphids, rotifers, or any other organisms in which reproduction occurs through parthenogenesis or fission without sexual recombination of the genetic materials—and has so occurred for a very long time. To my knowledge, no one has ever reported evidence of conflict or competition between individuals in such groups under natural or normal conditions, and I believe that any such reports would require careful scrutiny for the possibility of alternative explanations; mistakes would be easy when observers are accustomed to studying nonclonal forms. Parthenogenetic organisms, such as aphids, often remain together in clones of enormous size, and in some cases (Aoki *et al.*, 1981) some individuals sacrifice their lives for the others, and are morphologically and physiologically specialized to do so. Of course, the cells of the bodies of metazoans such as ourselves are also clones of genetically identical units, and not only do they reach enormous numbers, but their cooperation is so complete that the result is unitary: a human being composed of hundred of millions of cells can think about a single goal and direct all of its attention to its realization. This astounding feat is so commonplace that we scarcely think about it.

In addition to the above examples, which are consistent with expectations from evolutionary theory, there are some unusual cases in which little is yet known of the interaction of the individuals involved but complete cooperation can be predicted. Thus, littermates of the North American nine-banded armadillo are monozygotic—products of a single egg and thus genetically identical. This has apparently been the case for thousands (perhaps millions) of generations. One predicts that if the argument being advanced here is correct, armadillo littermates should show signs of competitiveness or conflict only in circumstances when confusion with interlopers from other litters is likely (Alexander, 1974). So far no one has learned enough about armadillo social behavior to test this rather startling hypothesis. (Dawkins, 1982, seems to reject this line of reasoning because in parthenogenetic forms genotypes are "frozen"; but this only means that, depending on mutations for novelty, they would evolve more slowly.)

## Eusocial Insects

Aside from clones and humans, the largest cooperative groups are those of certain social insects, reaching colony sizes of thousands and millions, the largest (certain ants and termites) estimated at more than 20 million individuals (Wilson, 1971). These colonies also accomplish astonishing feats, as a great deal of literature, scientific and popular, attests. Humans and social insects, unlike clones, are composed of genetically different individuals: their cooperativeness does not arise out of genetic identity. They have reduced their competitiveness within colonies or groups, moreover, in two entirely different fashions. The term "eusocial," applied to ants, termites, and some wasps and bees by Wilson (1971), refers to forms in which the tendency has been to evolve colonies in which one or a few individuals produce all of the offspring, while the rest serve as helpers (workers, soldiers) in rearing them. In eusocial insects the reproductive individuals have become highly specialized during evolution to produce enormous numbers of eggs (e.g., one every few seconds for years, or possibly decades, in termites), and have sometimes become essentially helpless otherwise, being fed and cared for by their offspring. The millions of individuals in the largest social insect colonies are commonly the members of a single nuclear family comprising mother (and, in termites, father as well) and offspring. One interesting consequence of this arrangement is that the workers in a colony of modern eusocial insects, such as honeybees, have very little to disagree about, even though they are not genetically identical (Hamilton, 1964). The reason is that they all reproduce through the same individuals: those siblings, produced by their mother, who are destined to be males and queens in the next generation. This means, for example, that one should not expect to find conflicts or deception in the signals transmitted from worker to worker among social insects with respect to food, danger to the hive, or many other aspects of everyday life. This expectation, surprisingly, is unlike that for the vast majority of animal signals (Otte, 1974; Lloyd, 1977; Dawkins and Krebs, 1978; Dawkins, 1982; see also pp. 73 ff.). Further, when the members of a colony consistently have complex events about which they may profit from communicating, we should expect that their communication would become extraordinarily effective. Of course this is precisely the case. Biological and social scientists have long marveled at the incredible communicative abilities of honeybees, with respect to rich food sites that may be distant from the hive in different directions and temporally restricted in their availability: they are able to tell one another the directions, distances, and nature of pollen or nectar sources miles away from the hive (von Frisch, 1954; Lindauer, 1961; Gould, Henerey, and MacLeod, 1970; Gould, 1976). I suggest that the two basic reasons for honeybees having evolved such potency in their communication are (1) they have something complicated and important to communicate about and (2) conflicts of interest have been dropped to near zero among workers. The objects of communication for honeybees are bonanza food sources—nectar and pollen—that last long enough, and are sufficiently difficult to locate, to make it pay for individuals in a sedentary or nesting species to be able to tell their nestmates how and when to exploit such bonanzas. Probably later in evolution, honeybees began to use the same signals to guide emigrant swarms to high-quality nest sites (Lindauer, 1961).

The reduction of conflicts in eusocial insect colonies is accomplished, then, not just by a high degree of relatedness (Hamilton, 1964), but by the workers in modern forms depending for their genetic success on exactly the same third parties—siblings produced by their mother. This fact, of course, does not tell us why the ancestors of modern eusocial insects initially were more successful in groups than alone (Hamilton, 1964; Wilson, 1971; Alexander, 1974; Charnov, 1978); because their social life originated millions of years ago this specific question may never be answered. Whenever stay-at-home helpers (helpers at the nest) produced more copies of their own genes by assisting with the rearing of siblings (or other relatives) rather than by having their own offspring (either at home or elsewhere), the route toward eusociality was begun. Close relatedness and some kind of group effect (predator defense, better provisioning of food, etc.) would both have been involved (this topic is discussed further by Alexander and Noonan, in prep.).

## Humans: Ultrasociality Based on Reciprocity

Humans have taken a route to ultrasociality entirely different from that of the social insects. In the largest and evidently most unified or stable human groups (i.e., large, long-lasting nations) partial (rather than complete) restrictions on reproduction have the effect of leveling or equalizing opportunities to reproduce. Socially imposed monogamy and graduated-income taxes are examples of such *reproductive opportunity leveling*. The tendency in the development of the largest human groups, although not always consistent, seems to be toward equality of opportunity for every individual to reproduce via its own offspring, rather than toward specializing baby production in one or a few individuals and baby care in the others. However humans specialize and divide labor, they nearly always insist individually on the right to carry out all of the reproductive activities themselves. One consequence is that the human individual has evolved to be extraordinarily complex (and evidently to revere individuality), and another is that the complexity and variety of social interactions among human individuals is without parallel. Because human social groups are not enormous nuclear families, like social insect colonies, a third consequence is that competition and conflicts of interest are also diverse and complex to an unparalleled degree. Hence, I believe, derives our topic of moral systems. We can ask legitimately whether or not the trend toward greater leveling of reproductive opportunities in the largest, most stable human groups indicates that such groups (nations) are the most difficult to hold together *without* the promise or reality of equality of opportunity (see also Alexander, 1974, 1979a; Alexander and Noonan, 1979; Strate, 1982; Betzig, 1986).

## OTHER SPECIAL CASES OF COOPERATION

### Genes in Genomes

A corollary to reproductive opportunity leveling in humans may occur through mitosis and meiosis in sexual organisms. It has generally been overlooked that these very widely studied processes are so designed as usually to give each gene or other genetic subunit of the genome (= the genotype or set of genetic materials of the individual) the same opportunity as any other of appearing in the daughter cells. Alexander and Borgia (1978) and Williams (1979) have speculated that this equality of opportunity came about because only alleles with equal (or better) likelihoods of being present in daughter cells have survived; possibly, more generalized mechanisms have come to be involved in modern forms. It is not inappropriate to speculate that the leveling of reproductive opportunity for intragenomic components—regardless of its mechanism—is a prerequisite for the remarkable unity of genomes, some of them comprised of thousands or hundreds of thousands of recombining, potentially independent genes and other subunits (Leigh, 1983; Alexander and Borgia, 1978).

## Monogamous Pairs

To the extent that males and females (of any species) commit themselves to lifetime monogamy, the interests of two individuals in a pair approach being identical. This point is often confused by biologists and social scientists alike (e.g., Dawkins, 1976, and Sahlins, 1976, both thought that unrelated spouses necessarily disagree more than relatives). The reason is the same as that causing identity of interests in the different individual workers in a eusocial insect colony: the two different individuals realize their reproduction through identical third parties which each of them gain by helping a great deal. In the case of worker insects the third parties are the reproductive brothers and sisters produced by the queen, their mother. If the queen dies and is replaced by one of the workers' siblings, the situation may not be altered even though the workers are less closely related to a sister's offspring than to their sisters, and less closely related to a sister's offspring than is the sister herself. When a queen changeover occurs, unless workers retain some ability and likelihood of themselves becoming the queen (and in many modern species they have lost this ability), they can do no better than by cooperating fully with one another to produce reproductive nieces and nephews.

Given that the members of monogamous pairs are evolved to invest parentally, then, to the extent that (1) philandering is unlikely or too expensive to be profitable, and (2) the relatives of one or the other are not significantly more available for nepotistic diversions of resources, each member of the pair will profit from complete cooperation with the other to produce and rear their joint offspring. In humans this condition is most likely in (1) societies in which (a) families live and work separately and (b) husband and wife are in fairly close contact most of the time and (2) societies in which married couples are "neolocal," living in some new location apart from both sets of relatives but close enough to be affected by the interests of their kin networks in sustaining the marriage. In such societies (which historically have probably been most often agricultural), I predict that the devotion of husband and wife will be measurably most complete.

Aside from clones, social insects and humans have developed the largest known societies, measured by numbers of complexly interacting individuals. They are also the most complexly communicating organisms. They have both accomplished this by expanding confluences of interest and reducing conflicts of interests, and it is at least possible that monogamy was involved in both cases, early in the evolution of social insects and late in the evolution of the largest human societies. What we have to understand, for both social insects and humans, is how the situations develop in which workership and monogamy, respectively, come to be the rule or norm. I believe I am correct in saying that in neither case are the answers yet available.

## MONOGAMY AND REPRODUCTIVE OPPORTUNITY LEVELING

Our understanding of the manner in which monogamous pairs come to cooperate is not much better than our understanding of why social insect colonies sometimes become huge and sometimes do not. Because monogamy in large technological nations is imposed socially (meaning that the costs of its alternatives are imposed by the rest—or some part—of society), understanding its background becomes a part of the effort to understand moral systems. Alexander *et al.* (1979; see also Alexander, 1975) have argued that socially or legally imposed monogamy is a way of leveling the reproductive opportunities of men, thereby reducing their competitiveness and increasing their likelihood of cooperativeness. The imposition of monogamy by custom or law has the interesting effect of reducing both male–male and male–female conflicts to a minimum, especially when clans are discouraged (as in nation states: see Alexander, 1979a, pp. 256–259), and when married couples do not have differential access to their respective relatives (e.g., when they are "neolocal" or reside in a new locality rather than becoming a part of one or the other extended family of relatives). Moreover, the combination of socially or legally imposed monogamy, neolocality, and close association of the married couple in work not only leads to minimizing of philandering and conflict of interest between husband and wife, but also characterizes the largest (and perhaps the most unified—or durable—of all large) human societies. Young men at the age of maximal sexual competition are the most divisive and competitive class of individuals in human social groups; they are also the pool of warriors. It is not trivial that socially imposed monogamy (and the concomitant discouragement of clans as extended families that control members) correlates with (1) justice touted as equality of opportunity; (2) the concept of a single, impartial god for all people; and (3) large, cohesive, modern nations that wage wars and conduct defense with their pools of young men (Alexander, 1979a). To a large extent socially imposed monogamy has spread around the world by conquest. The social imposition of monogamy thus simultaneously (1) inhibits the generation of certain kinds of within-group power dynasties that might compete with government and lead to divisive within-group competition and (2) promotes those activities and attitudes that generate and maintain success in the wielding of reciprocity as the binding cement of social structure (honesty, sincerity, trust).

Humans almost certainly began to evolve their social tendencies and capabilities in small kin groups. If so, during that process they incidentally acquired the capability to maintain social organization in ever larger and more complex social groups through systems of reciprocity rather than nepotism per se. In such groups there is only one way to approach an equalization of reproductive opportunity, and that is by sets of rules or moral systems. In humans the laws and mores of larger and larger groups seem increasingly to (1) guarantee to every individual the right to produce and rear its own offspring and (2) restrict the amount and likelihood of variation in reproduction among families. China is currently an extreme in both size (over one billion) and regulation of reproduction (Keyfitz, 1984). Until 1981 or 1982, government assistance was given for a first child, but funds were withdrawn if a second was born. More recently it was reported (e.g., Ann Arbor, Michigan, News, 1982; Nova and 60 Minutes television programs, 1984) that enormous pressure for sterilization followed the birth of a single child. Not long ago, India briefly attempted to require sterilization after three children were born to any person; the government of India now pays individuals who submit to sterilization. More subtle, but also more widespread, are laws that reduce variance in access to resources, such as graduated income taxes, the vote, representative government, elected (not hereditarily succeeding) officials, and universal education.

MacDonald (1983) discusses the "leveling" effect of monogamy, although he seems to find it puzzling, in evolutionary terms, perhaps because he does not consider the significance of equality of opportunity as a basis for social unity in the face of extrinsic threats. Once this factor is weighed in, one sees that the real puzzle is not, as MacDonald supposes, to account for leveling processes, but to account for the maintenance of despotic societies, within which the greatest disparities in opportunities for individuals occur (e.g., Betzig, 1986); or, rather, to explain why some sizes and kinds of societies involved huge disparities in individual opportunity (those intermediate in size; Alexander, 1979a), while others (large and small) have leveled them to extreme degrees. I think the answer will come from comparing the histories of interaction between neighboring societies, effects of physical or physiographic barriers on their sizes, and separation of warriors (soldiers) from their families.

Despite their obvious and dramatic differences from one another, then, the most extremely ultrasocial systems of humans and other species are apparently all based on reproductive opportunity leveling. The essential difference is that in (some) clones and eusocial forms all individuals realize their reproduction through the same sets of babies and have specialized baby production and baby care in different individuals, and humans have done neither of these things.

## CONFLICTS OF INTEREST AND DECEPTION IN COMMUNICATION

A measure of the effects of the new precision in evolutionary theory on biology can be taken by considering that until a few years ago biologists had interpreted "communication" as little more than the honest, accurate transfer of information between and among individuals. Similarly, linguists have tended to regard the function of human language as to serve as a vehicle for transmitting accurate information. Now biologists realize that the conflicts of interests that exist because of histories of genetic difference imply instead that nearly all communicative signals, human or otherwise, should be expected to involve significant deceit (Otte, 1974; Lloyd, 1977, 1980; Dawkins and Krebs, 1978; Dawkins, 1982; Payne, 1983). Indeed, it is instructive to classify communicative signals according to the amounts of deception they may be expected, on evolutionary grounds, to involve, and the reasons for deception. I have already suggested that in rare circumstances, such as honeybee workers dancing about food sources or a pair of parents wholly committed to lifetime monogamy, signals may be *totally honest*. It is the rarity of this expectation from biological considerations that is most intriguing to us at this point. Conversely, signals involved in predator–prey relations, such as the mimicking of a poisonous prey species by a harmless one, may be expected to be *totally deceptive*. There is no overlap of interest between a predator and its prey, and no reason to expect any truth in their signals to one another. Neither will gain by doing anything at all that will help the other, and neither has any likelihood of evolving to tell the truth to the other. Anyone who has examined under a microscope a palatable butterfly that mimics in its color pattern or otherwise an unpalatable or poisonous one will recognize that this prediction is upheld: at a distance the resemblance is remarkable, but up close the similarities are often so superficial that one is astonished that he could have been deceived.

Most communicative signals, such as nearly all that pass among humans, lie between the extremes of *total deception* and *total honesty*. I suggest two categories, which might be called *restrained embellishment* and *unrestrained embellishment* (Fig. 1.7). These two categories differ both in the proportion of deception involved in the signals and in the reason for the extent of the core of truthfulness within each of them. *Restrained embellishment* involves signals such as those passed between relatives or

Totally Honest, No Deception

The overlap of
interests between
signaler and signalee
is complete

(e.g., honeybee worker's dance
indicating to sisters the direction
and distance of sources of food
to be fed to other sisters)

Totally Deceptive, No Truth

There is no overlap
of interests between
signaler and signalee,
no reason for truth

(e.g., Batesian mimicry)

Restrained Embellishment

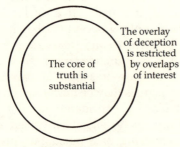

The core of
truth is
substantial

The overlay
of deception
is restricted
by overlaps
of interest

(e.g., signals between bonded mates
or close relatives, as in parent-
offspring or sibling-sibling interactions)

Unrestrained Embellishment

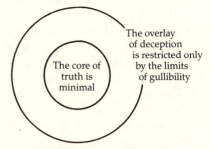

The core of
truth is
minimal

The overlay
of deception
is restricted only
by the limits
of gullibility

(e.g., signals between sexual
or other intense competitors,
especially when they are unrelated)

FIGURE 1.7. A classification of kinds of communicative signals, based on the
amount of deception expected, and the reasons.

cooperative mates, in which the signaler would lose by too much
deception because it shares so many of its interests with those of the
individual to which it is signaling. The core of truth is large and the
amount of embellishment rather small, because too much deceit is
contrary to the interests of the signaler. Included are most signals
between close relatives such as parents and offspring and siblings, and
most signals between male and female in bonded pairs if either or both
sexes invest parentally to any large degree (unless philandering or
channeling of assistance to one's own relatives, as opposed to those of
the spouse, is possible, thus interfering with a likelihood of complete
sharing of interests and honesty in signaling). Similarly, restrained
embellishment should typify communication between long-term or

lifetime friends who may reasonably expect repeated and reciprocal interactions.

*Unrestrained embellishment* characterizes signals passed between sharply competitive individuals, such as brief interactants and nonrelatives, in which the degree of embellishment is determined, not by shared interests between signaler and signalee, but by how much the signaler can get away with—what Otte (1974) called "the limits of gullibility" in the responder. I can appear taller by wearing shoes that are *slightly* built up, but if the heels are too high everyone will laugh; I can wear *small* shoulder pads in my jackets but not too large or, again, the deception will be too apparent; and so forth. Unrestrained embellishment involves most signals between unrelated or distantly related competitors, and those between even close relatives when resources are severely restricted. Included would be individuals competing for the same mate or territory. Two sibling honeybee queens fighting for sole control of a hive, even though three-quarters alike genetically, may be an example; as may two sisters in our own species trying to divide the family heirlooms when their parents die without a will; or two brothers fighting over a single female or a single indivisible farm or kingdom. Unrestrained embellishment differs from total deception mainly because gullibility may be reduced among conspecific competitors.

# 2

## A BIOLOGICAL VIEW OF MORALITY

### Conflicts and Confluences of Interest:
### A Theory of Moral Systems

> . . . although a society is a cooperative venture for mutual advantage, it is typically marked by a conflict as well as by an identity of interests. There is an identity of interests since social cooperation makes possible a better life for all than any would have if each were to live solely by his own efforts. There is a conflict of interests since persons are not indifferent as to how the greater benefits of their collaboration are distributed, for in order to pursue their ends they each prefer a larger to a lesser share."
>
> Rawls, 1971, p. 4

Moral systems are systems of indirect reciprocity. They exist because confluences of interest within groups are used to deal with conflicts of interest between groups.

Indirect reciprocity develops because interactions are repeated, or flow among a society's members, and because information about subsequent interactions can be gleaned from observing the reciprocal interactions of others.

To establish moral rules is to impose rewards and punishment (typically assistance and ostracism, respectively) to control social acts that, respectively, help or hurt others. To be regarded as moral, a rule typically must represent widespread opinion, reflecting the fact that it must apply with a certain degree of indiscriminateness. Moral rules are established and maintained primarily by application of the concepts of right and wrong.

## CONFLICTS OF INTERESTS

It is difficult to exaggerate the significance of conflicts of interest. One has only to read a newspaper or a news magazine, or listen to his associates discussing what they regard as the significant issues of the day, to realize that nearly all that is newsworthy involves conflicts of interest. However massive may be the areas of thought and action on which all people everywhere may truly agree, it is their areas of disagreement and contention which remain as the cutting edge of strife, risk, and danger to individuals and societies the world over. It is conflicts of interest that people write about, worry over, and ponder most intensely, that fill the literature and all forms of the condensed versions of life that in the broad sense can be called "theater." It is how we deal with *conflicts of interest* that will determine the fate of the world and the future of humanity.

Not all organisms with conflicts of interests possess moral systems or ethical rules; neither do conflicts of interest automatically give rise to ethical and moral considerations, or puzzlings over justice and what is right and good. There obviously are ways of resolving conflicts of interest that do not involve these human concepts. Two trees sprouting in a spot of gravel along a city sidewalk cannot carry on a discussion of the issue of which is going to possess eventually the small patch of living space that is obviously too small for both; neither does the outcome in any sense involve ethics or morality. Thus, while conflicts of interest are necessary for the appearance of ethical and moral questions, they are not sufficient. The question is thus raised: what must be added to the conflicts of interest that characterize all life to create the conditions sufficient to produce systems involving ethical and moral questions? I will argue that the reason the concepts of moral and ethical are peculiarly human is the same as that accounting for the evolution of self-awareness, consciousness, purpose, conscience, and many other human attributes that seem tied to our complex and almost indefinitely iterated social interactions (see pp. 81ff.). I see these special attributes of the human psyche as a system for prediction and manipulation of the future—especially the social future—when the main actors will be other humans. From a complex beginning in interactions between cooperating parents and between parents and offspring, then among kin of several sorts and other unrelated but repeated interactants, humans have evolved to recognize one another individually and to cooperate and compete in groups with respect to partial confluences and conflicts of interest. It is the general awareness of multiple confluences of interest, and the uniquely human ability to translate this awareness into rules, enforced and used by groups and subgroups—ultimately in their competition with other similar groups and subgroups—that created the systems of indirect reciprocity that we now call moral systems. I will argue (see pp. 79ff.) that this condition arose because for humans, unlike any other species, other humans became the principal hostile force of nature—the principal cause of failure to survive or reproduce. The primacy of this group-against-group competition *within the species* meant that the resulting evolutionary race would be an unending one. Competing groups would tend to be only one step ahead of or behind one another so long as they remained conspecific and mingled their genetic materials, thereby continually melding as well their ability to absorb one another's culture. Hence, the race that created the human psyche, and the unique and complex social capabilities of humans.

## WHY DO HUMANS LIVE IN GROUPS?

Elsewhere, I and others (e.g., Alexander and Tinkle, 1968; Bigelow, 1969; Alexander, 1971, 1979a; Strate, 1982) have developed the argument that human evolution has been guided to some large extent by intergroup competition and aggression. Because this argument is central to the theory of morality presented here, and because my view of it has developed somewhat since 1979, a short review seems appropriate.

I have already noted that group living entails automatic costs to individuals, which must be overcompensated by specific benefits if group living is to evolve; this view could not develop until the nature and relative potency of selection at individual and genic levels had been explained (Williams, 1966a; Lewontin, 1970; Alexander, 1974; Dawkins, 1976; Alexander and Borgia, 1978). Larger groups involve greater costs to individuals, and this fact causes us to realize that, even if cooperative group hunting was the original context of human grouping, it cannot explain much of the history of human sociality. As hunting weapons and skills improved, group sizes should have decreased. Cooperative group hunters among nonhumans tend to live in small groups (canines, felines, cetaceans, some fish, and pelicans), and large groups are typically what Hamilton called "selfish herds," whose evolutionary *raison d'etre* is security from predation. Even groups evidently evolved to cooperate against predators are typically small (chimpanzees, baboons, musk ox).

If an external threat is invoked to explain human social groupings— as appears necessary—the only one adequate to the task is other groups of humans (Alexander, 1971–1985). This proposition is immediately satisfying, for it can explain any size of group (as parts of balance-of-power races); it accords with all of recorded human history; it is consistent with the fact that humans alone play competitively group-against-group on a large and complex scale; and it accords with the ecological dominance of humans as a species. In effect, organized in competitive groups, humans have become their own principal "hostile force of nature." Most of the evolution of human social life, and I will argue the evolution of the human psyche, has occurred in the context of within- and between-group competition, the former resulting from the latter. Without the pressure of between-group competition, within-group competition would have been mild or nonexistent—or else dramatically different—because groups would have been smaller and would have required less unity and cooperativeness. Strate (1982) supported this view when he concluded from a cross-cultural study that defense against other human groups accounts for variations in social organization better than any alternative.

No other sexual organisms compete in groups as extensively, fluidly, and complexly as humans do. No other organisms at all play competitively group-against-group. Most importantly, so far as we know, in no other species do social groups have as their main jeopardy other social groups of the same species—therefore, the unending selective race toward greater social complexity, intelligence, and cleverness in dealing with one another (see Alexander, 1979a, and references therein).

To make the above argument requires some way of distinguishing primary causes of social grouping and secondary responses to it. On the other hand, one must also consider that *any* cooperative cause of group living cannot be expected to last and be elaborated unless it leads to increased reproductive success among all participants, which by definition means in relation to members of other groups, thereby establishing at least an indirect intergroup competition. No one, I think, imagines that humans—given their recorded history of interactions—have evolved to be a kind of organism that tends to allow such competition to be indirect and mild. We have consistently done the opposite.

Despite my earlier remarks that indirect reciprocity may be unique to humans, we cannot ignore the possibility that there may be a parallel to morality in many nonhuman social groups that cooperate—canines, for example. Is it not possible that in such cooperative social groups any individual who deviates too far from some behavioral pattern or repertoire may be punished, ostracized, or killed by essentially any individual or subgroup of individuals within the whole group? Baboon babies are said to play silently (Irven DeVore: Film on baboon ecology and social behavior, Univ. of Calif.), and we can suppose that the significance of this fact lies in the possibility that noises attract predators. It would be interesting to see who does what in the case of noisy juvenile baboons. If the arguments in this book are correct, rudimentary moral systems (indirect reciprocity) will appear where outside threats most powerfully dictate group cohesion, when such threats are combated best by complex social organization within the group, and when the actions of single individuals or small subgroups can threaten, from within, either the group as a whole or its most powerful elements.

The theory of moral systems that I am espousing is obviously *contractarian*, as opposed to *utilitarian* (cf. Grant, 1985; Rawls, 1971); it is also a particular form of contractarian theory in which (1) individuals seek their own interests; (2) their interests are ultimately reproductive—hence, include to varying and predictable degrees the interests of relatives and those with whom relatives are shared (such as spouses); (3) interests of individuals can be furthered by cooperating with others—both relatives and nonrelatives; (4) the mechanisms are direct and indirect reciprocity, the latter involving a very complex significance of reputation or status; and (5) the rules consist of *restraints* on particular methods of seeking self-interests, specifically on activities that affect deleteriously the efforts of others to seek their own interests. What is new in this theory is that (a) interests are seen as reproductive, not as individual survival, and, accordingly, pleasure and comfort are postulated to have evolved as vehicles of reproductive success, and (b) the mechanism of indirect reciprocity is made explicit as the central feature. These are not trivial refinements, since together they can account for aspects of beneficence that have perplexed philosophers, theologians, and all students of morality who have previously postulated either contractarian or utilitarian models.

## CLASSIFYING HUMAN EFFORT: THE "ATOMS" OF SOCIALITY

If ethical, moral, and legal systems are ultimately understandable in evolutionary terms, then we ought to be able to explain them eventually, at even the most complex and synthetic levels, by beginning with the "atoms" of sociality proposed out of the life history and effort theories of modern evolutionary biology (see Table 2.1). We can note, first, that lifetimes are divisible into somatic and reproductive effort, and, second, that reproductive effort can be subdivided, at least in humans, into mating effort (on behalf of gametes), parental effort (on behalf of offspring), and extraparental nepotistic effort (on behalf of collateral or nondescendant relatives and descendants other than offspring). Next it is useful to emphasize that humans are unusual among organisms in that all of their life effort that is *social* in nature is permeated with *reciprocity*. The possibility of mutually beneficial reciprocal interactions can cause both somatic and reproductive effort to be *socially mediated* (nepotism, for example, can involve reciprocity in which the return benefit goes to a relative of the originally beneficent individual). In turn, reciprocity itself can be direct (A helps B, B helps A) or indirect (A helps B, B helps C, C helps A. Or A helps B; C, observing, later helps A; A helps C). Reciprocity is probably never complete, or balanced. (For further explanation, see below and Fig. 1.2 and 2.1; Tables 2.1–2.5.) The effects of reciprocity and other forms of social mediation (competition, pseudoreciprocity) multiply the number of different "atoms" of sociality that must be elucidated if a biological approach to human social behavior is to be integrated with the approaches of philosophers and social and political scientists.

1. *Direct Somatic Effort.* In this category of phenotypically selfish behavior are included those aspects of somatic effort (i.e., directed toward growth, development, and maintenance of one's own phenotype or soma) that explicitly do not involve benefits routed through other individuals. Direct somatic effort is mediated by neither nepotism nor reciprocity. Examples are eating, drinking, seeking shelter, and avoiding danger, when these actions are carried out without the assistance or positive intervention of others. This category of behavior, which probably corresponds most closely to the moral philosophers' *egoism* (particularly when the latter specifically involves seeking to promote one's own welfare *rather* than someone else's), is not as common as might be thought in today's specialized social environment. We can actually do very little for ourselves without some kind of assistance, however indirect, by others.

2. *Indirect (Socially Mediated) Somatic Effort.* This kind of phenotypically selfish behavior is routed through other individuals. Thus it may involve social investments (initial costs, beneficent acts) in *direct and indirect reciprocity.* These investments are expected eventually to be repaid to one's self (as opposed to one's relatives, which would identify them as indirect nepotism). Examples are purchases of goods to be used by one's self (which may represent reciprocity in the form of mutually beneficial exchanges of resources between buyer and seller) and all social and other benefits given to others as investments in reciprocity when the returns are realized through assistance to one's self. There are two kinds of mediation of somatic effort: (a) direct assistance to Ego (*i*) by a relative (repayment to the relative's phenotype is likely not necessarily to be expected or required) and (*ii*) by a nonrelative (eventual repayment is likely to be expected, to either the benevolent individual or its relatives) and (b) assistance to Ego as a return on an investment made by Ego as a part of somatic effort (i.e., direct reciprocity, such as, Ego helps a nonrelative, expecting return assistance from the helped person at some later date). We can predict that infants and very young children, especially, are evolved to exhibit effort that elicits the (a) (*i*) kind of assistance above. What Trivers (1971) called "reciprocal altruism" would include both the nepotistic and somatic (egoistic) effects of investments in both direct and indirect reciprocity (thus, while *beneficent*, or initially costly, it would be only temporarily phenotypically altruistic and not *genetically* altruistic or costly at all).

Table 2.1. Kinds of Effort and Their Outcomes[a]

| "Atoms" of sociality | Kinds of effort | Phenotypically | Genotypically |
|---|---|---|---|
| | I. Somatic effort | Selfish | Selfish |
| | A. Direct | | |
| 1. | 1. Immediate payback | | |
| 2. | 2. Delayed payback | | |
| | B. Indirect | | |
| | 3. Via direct reciprocity | | |
| 3. | a. Immediate payback | | |
| 4. | b. Delayed payback | | |
| | 4. Via indirect reciprocity | | |
| 5. | a. Immediate payback | | |
| 6. | b. Delayed payback | | |
| | II. Reproductive effort | Altruistic | Selfish |
| | A. Mating effort | | |
| 7. | 1. Directly nepotistic (no social mediation) | | |
| | 2. Indirectly nepotistic (social mediation) | | |
| | a. Via direct reciprocity | | |
| 8. | (1) Immediate payback | | |
| 9. | (2) Delayed payback | | |
| | b. Via indirect reciprocity | | |
| 10. | (1) Immediate payback | | |
| 11. | (2) Delayed payback | | |
| | B. Parental effort | | |
| 12. | 1. Directly nepotistic (no social mediation) | | |
| | 2. Indirectly nepotistic (social mediation) | | |
| | a. Via direct reciprocity | | |
| 13. | (1) Immediate payback | | |
| 14. | (2) Delayed payback | | |
| | b. Via indirect reciprocity | | |
| 15. | (1) Immediate payback | | |
| 16. | (2) Delayed payback | | |
| | C. Extraparental effort | | |
| 17. | 1. Directly nepotistic (no social mediation) | | |
| | 2. Indirectly nepotistic (social mediation) | | |
| | a. Via direct reciprocity | | |
| 18. | (1) Immediate payback | | |
| 19. | (2) Delayed payback | | |
| | b. Via indirect reciprocity | | |
| 20. | (1) Immediate payback | | |
| 21. | (2) Delayed payback | | |

[a]Direct somatic effort refers to self-help that involves no other persons. Indirect somatic effort involves reciprocity, which may be direct or indirect. Returns from direct or indirect reciprocity may be immediate or delayed. Reciprocity can be indirect for two different reasons, or in two different ways. First, returns (payment) for a social investment (positive or negative) can come from someone other than the recipient of the investment, and second, returns can go either to the original investor or to a relative or friend of the original investor.

Although also egoistic in its consequences, socially mediated somatic effort that involves initial costly investments (beneficence) may often be misinterpreted as altruistic (that is, as *genetically* costly). Because of divisions of labor and social interdependency in the modern world, this kind of egoism is also more commonplace than direct somatic effort.

3. *Direct Nepotism*. Included here are all investments in relatives for which the return may be expected in genetic terms, through the reproduction of the assisted relatives.

Mating effort is the most problematic form of effort placed here: it may be viewed as selfish (hence, be confused with somatic effort), particularly in males, who usually, as in mammals, strive to place their sperm inside the body of the female, hence are in a better position to abandon the offspring to its mother's care than vice versa. A gamete, after all, is not an individual, and it possesses no genetic materials other than those of its producer. But gametes are also not merely parts of the phenotypes that produce them, and (except in species with haploid males) are not genetically identical to their producers. Mating effort, moreover, is reproductive effort that involves risks and expenditure of calories. Effort exerted on behalf of gametes lowers the reproductive value of the individual as surely as that exerted on behalf of offspring or other relatives. Perhaps the example is confusing primarily because mating effort involves interactions of two individuals, and there is a tendency to compare the *relative* "selfishness" of the two. Also, in mating effort, as compared to other reproductive effort, the *genetically selfish* aspects of acts may be relatively more apparent than their *phenotypically altruistic* aspects. We are more likely to regard a male mammal's effort to place his gametes in a warm, safe place where they can fertilize an egg as an act of reproductive selfishness that benefits him in relation to the female involved than we are to see it as an act of phenotypic altruism benefiting his gametes.

4. *Indirect (Socially Mediated) Nepotism*. This category of reproductive effort includes investments in reciprocity in which returns from one's beneficence may reasonably be expected to be realized by relatives rather than one's self (e.g., heroism or good will created by one's benevolent acts may cause benefits to accrue to one's family).

Although the last two categories of behavior are not easily understood as a part of the moral philosophers' category of "egoism," neither are they either indiscriminately or genetically altruistic or utilitarian; if carried out appropriately in evolutionary terms, all of the above four kinds of behavior are *genetically selfish*, even those which are *phenotypically self-sacrificing* or *(temporarily) altruistic* (or *beneficent*) (Alexander, 1974, 1979a).

*5. Reciprocity (Direct and Indirect).* It appears to me that all reciprocity so far documented in nonhuman organisms is appropriately termed *direct reciprocity*, in which the return from a social investment in another (i.e., an act of "temporary" altruism) is expected from the actual recipient of the beneficence, although not necessarily in the same currency (Trivers, 1971; Axelrod, 1984). In *indirect reciprocity* (Alexander, 1977a,b, 1979a, 1982, 1985b), the return is expected from someone other than the recipient of the beneficence (Tables 2.2–2.4). This return may come from essentially any individual or collection of individuals in the group. Indirect reciprocity involves reputation and status, and results in everyone in a social group continually being assessed and reassessed by interactants, past and potential, on the basis of their interactions with others. I do not exclude the possibility that indirect reciprocity, in this sense, will eventually be documented in some primates—especially, chimpanzees (e.g., de Waal, 1982, 1986) social canines, felines, cetaceans, and some others.

What I am calling "indirect reciprocity" Trivers (1971) referred to as "generalized reciprocity." I avoided the latter term because of the way Sahlins (1965) used it—cf. Alexander (1975, 1979a, 1985). Sahlins typified generalized reciprocity as involving one-way flows of benefits in which the expectation of return is vague or nonexistent. He included nepotism, citing the case of a mother nursing her child, and with respect to nonrelatives seemed to be referring to what we would now call genetic or reproductive altruism. Perhaps both terms will survive: indirect reciprocity for cases in which the return explicitly comes from someone other than the recipient or the original beneficence, and generalized reciprocity for social systems in which indirect reciprocity has become complex and general.

Reciprocity in nonhuman organisms (Trivers, 1971; Axelrod and Hamilton, 1981) may have arisen between bonded males and females in species with both maternal and paternal care. In such cases it may have developed out of mating effort (e.g., a male gives a gift to a female and is allowed to copulate), subsequently as indirect nepotism through effects on offspring produced jointly by the pair (e.g., a female copulates with a male and he gives her a gift which she uses to rear his offspring). Alternatively (and perhaps more likely), reciprocity may have arisen as a modification of direct nepotism in which flows of benefits began to pass in both directions successively rather than just one direction from one relative to another. Benefits can be returned to a social investor as a part of the egoistic behavior of the individual returning it—i.e., at no cost to that individual. In such instances, possibilities for cheating are essentially nonexistent and the overall complexity of the mental activi-

Table 2.2. Indirect Reciprocity

---

Rewards (why altruism spreads)
    1. A helps B
    2. B helps (or overhelps) A
    3. C, observing, helps B, expecting that
    4. B will also help (or overhelp) C
       (ETC.)
Or
    1. A helps B
    2. B does not help A
    3. C, observing, does not help B expecting that, if he does
    4. B will not return the help
       (ETC.)

---

Table 2.3. Indirect Reciprocity

---

Punishment (why rules spread)
    1. A hurts B
    2. C, observing, punishes A expecting that, if he does not,
    3. A will also hurt C
Or
    4. Someone else, also observing, will hurt C, expecting no
       cost
       (ETC.)

---

Table 2.4. Indirect Reciprocity

---

Deception (why cheating spreads)
    1. $A_1$ makes it *look* as though he helps B
    2. $C_1$ helps $A_1$, expecting that $A_1$ will also help him
    3. $C_2$ observes more keenly and detects $A_1$'s cheating and
       does not help him (avoids or punishes him)
    4. $A_2$, better at cheating, fools $C_2$
    5. $C_3$ detects $A_2$'s cheating (ETC.)

$C_1 \rightarrow C_2 \rightarrow C_3$ }    Either learning or evolution
$A_1 \rightarrow A_2 \rightarrow A_3$ }         (or both)

---

ties accompanying evolution of the act will be reduced in comparison to reciprocity per se. Connor (1986) calls such interactions "pseudoreciprocity." In terms of my examples, it would be pseudoreciprocity if the female receiving a gift from a courting male copulated with him strictly because it was to her immediate advantage. If the act was at least temporarily costly—e.g., if she was initiating a longer-term exchange of beneficence—then the step into direct reciprocity would have been taken. I agree with Connor that most discussions of "reciprocity" in nonhuman species probably involve pseudoreciprocity instead.

It will be seen that subdividing somatic effort into direct and indirect—and reproductive effort into mating effort, parental effort, and extraparental nepotistic effort—creates five major "atoms" of sociality. The overlays of reciprocity and pseudoreciprocity, with the possibility of immediate or delayed returns, brings the number of such "atoms" to 21 (Table 2.1). Further complicating the picture are additional overlays involving consciousness and deliberateness in different kinds of acts (Table 2.5).

Identifying atoms or units of sociality for the purpose of understanding the flow of human social interactions seems to be a matter of locating units or transactions that can substitute for one another in the functioning of nepotism or reciprocity. I mean to suggest units for which cost-benefit analyses can be accomplished more or less independently, units that can be regarded as alternatives or options for the purpose of compensating beneficence or cheating. I believe that without very large numbers of such units, and large numbers of alternative players, reciprocity could not become complex. Human sociality seems composed of countless such units, and I think we are constantly separating the flow of our social interactions into units (acts, interactions, transactions) that we can use for our own purposes (e.g., investments intended to test the readiness of another to repay social debts with interest).

In light of the biological separation of lifetimes into somatic and reproductive effort, it is curious that moral philosophers' views of moral behavior usually require either 100% selfishness or 100% altruism but scarcely ever combinations of the two; with a few exceptions (e.g., Whiteley, 1976; MacIntyre, 1981b), philosophers seem to find it impossible to combine the two. The reason seems to be the view that consistency is required in moral behavior (i.e., to be moral one must advocate for himself only those rights and privileges he will advocate equally strongly for all others), and a dual human nature (i.e., involving both egoistic and altruistic tendencies or acts) has inconsistency built into it. Whiteley (1976) and MacIntyre (1981b) believe it is possible to be consistently (morally) egoistic, but I find it difficult to imagine that a true egoist would be likely to advocate the right of others to resources that egoism would require him to seek for himself. One has to presuppose that resource seeking does not involve conflict and ignore the argument that success is relative. The only time that utilitarianism (promoting the greatest good to the greatest number) is predicted by evolutionary theory is when the interests of the group (the "greatest number") and the individual coincide, and in such cases utilitarianism is not really altruistic in either the biologists' or the philosophers' sense of the term. It seems more likely that restraints on individuals and subgroups serving their own interests occur solely because of the likelihood of prohibitive costs being imposed by some part of the rest of society; this is precisely the definition of moral systems I am developing here.

Moral philosophers have not treated the beneficence of humans as a part, somehow, of their selfishness; yet, as Trivers (1971) suggested, the biologist's view of lifetimes leads directly to this argument. In other words, the normally expressed beneficence, or altruism, of parenthood and nepotism and the temporary altruism (or social investment) of reciprocity are expected to result in greater (genetic) returns than their alternatives.

If biologists are correct, all that philosophers refer to as altruistic or utilitarian behavior by individuals will actually represent either the temporary altruism (phenotypic beneficence or social investment) of indirect somatic effort or direct and indirect nepotism. The exceptions are what might be called evolutionary mistakes or accidents that result in unreciprocated or "genetic" altruism, deleterious to both the phenotype and the genotype of the altruist; such mistakes can occur in all of the above categories (see also Alexander, 1979a, Table 1, for a discussion of genetic and phenotypic altruism). Part of our analysis (p. 100ff.) will involve the effects of certain kinds of indirect somatic effort and nepotistic altruism on the numbers and significance of such accidents by others. The question involved is whether or not we are evolved to promote such mistakes in others, and to resist them in ourselves, and the effects of any such tendencies on the nature of our moral and legal systems.

## PHILOSOPHY AND CONFLICTS OF INTEREST

Among social and political scientists, moral philosophers, ethicists, and others who study and think about moral questions, probably everyone would agree that conflicts of interest, and the human attitudes, tendencies, and actions that derive from histories of conflicts of interest, are alone responsible for ethical, moral, and legal questions. On the other hand, not everyone who writes in this arena headlines his discussions with the question of conflicts of interests. I think of such recent and influential volumes as John Rawls' (1971) *A Theory of Justice*, Richard Brandt's (1979) A *Theory of the Good and the Right*, William Frankena's (1973, 1980) *Ethics and Thinking About Morality*, and Lawrence Kohlberg's (1981) *The Philosophy of Moral Development*. One cannot find general discussions of the nature of interests or the quantification of their conflicts; or do phrases like "conflict of interest," "differences of opinion," or even "disagreements" and "interests" appear in either the tables of contents or the indexes. Similarly, if one keeps the question of conflicts of interest, at both individual and various group levels, in mind while reading the essays of Richards (1986b) and the responses to them. I believe some of the seemingly most difficult questions are simplified.

The general theory of interest, called for by Pound (quoted pp. 33–34; see also Pound, 1959) has not been developed, and is discussed by few other authors. Although everyone who writes in this arena may recognize that disagreements and conflicts about interests are what underlie moral systems, for some reason few have been compelled to generalize about them or dwell on their bases.

It is my impression that many moral philosophers do not approach the problem of morality and ethics as if it arose as an effort to resolve conflicts of interests. Their involvement in conflicts of interest seems to come about obliquely through discussions of individuals' views with respect to moral behavior, or their proximate feelings about morality— almost as if questions about conflicts of interest arise only because we operate under moral systems, rather than vice versa.

An excellent example of a philosophical discussion that does not directly confront the question of whether the whole flow of social interactions depends on conflicts and confluences of interest is that of Callahan (1985). Writing on "What Do Children Owe Elderly Parents?" Callahan alludes to interests driving the interaction only twice. On p. 32 he notes "As a piece of practical advice, however, it [honoring fathers and mothers] once made considerable sense. In most traditional and agricultural societies, parents had considerable power over the lives of their offspring. Children who did not honor their parents risked not only immediate privation, but also the loss of the one inheritance [land] that would enable them to raise and support their own families." On p. 36, speaking of "The poor," he comments ". . . adults with elderly parents ought not to be put in the position of trying to balance the moral claims of their own children against those of their parents, or jeopardizing their own old age in order to sustain their parents in their old age. Though such conflicts may at times be unescapable, society ought to be structured in a way that minimizes them." It is as if Callahan did not consciously consider whether or not conflicts of interest were the central issue in the topic he was discussing.

Most of Callahan's article attempts to resolve the problem of care for the elderly in contemporary society by wrestling from every possible direction with proximate mechanisms, such as the feelings of children toward their parents, of parents toward their children, and of "society" toward both. This exercise ends inconclusively, as if presaged by his statement (p. 35). "I am searching here with some difficulty for a way to characterize the ethical nature of the parent–child relationship, a relationship that appears almost but not quite self-evident in its reciprocal moral claims and yet oddly elusive also."

The trouble is, there is no one "parent–child relationship" and the whole problem of care for the aged has arisen, not so much because lives have been prolonged, but because familial bonds have been fractured, explicitly in ways that have made confluences of interest between aged parents and their children much less likely. Self-interested reasons for children to care for aged parents have all but disappeared, and I suggest that this is why their care is being thrust upon "society" and why it has become so expensive. This expense to society is, in turn, why "society" has become concerned to discuss the question of children's moral and ethical obligations to their parents. I see no likelihood that such questions can ever be elucidated by confining the arguments to proximate mechanisms. Callahan does conclude that "A minimal duty of any government should be to do nothing to hinder, and if possible do something to protect, the natural moral and filial ties that give families their power to nurture and sustain." He does not delve deeply into the basis for this (or any other) "should," however. Somehow he also realizes that "To exploit that bond by coercively taxing families is, I believe, to threaten them with great harm . . . It . . . presupposes a narrower form of moral obligation . . . than can naturally be defended . . . [and] promises to rupture those more delicate moral bonds . . . that sustain parents and children in their lives together." I think that what Callahan is describing here are the probable repercussions of forcing children to care for their parents, repercussions that will exacerbate the overall problem and cause even greater expense to "society." I am not suggesting that intensive analyses of the feelings (and other proximate mechanisms) that underlie moral dilemmas are not useful; I think it is obvious they are essential. I am, rather, saying that cases like the relationships between parents and children in different societal milieus show that the underlying conflicts of interest drive the proximate mechanisms at least as significantly as the reverse. To try to understand one without the other seems futile.

In contrast to Callahan's discussion, Strong (1984) develops an excellent and well-documented discussion of conflicts of interest among neonates, parents, and physicians, which I believe shows well how thinking directly in terms of conflicts and confluences of interest of the involved parties can lead to potentially satisfying ways of making decisions. At one point (p. 15) he describes three useful reasons for " . . . The general principle that the patient comes first":

> One is the utilitarian consideration that people will be more likely to seek health care if they trust doctors, and people are more likely to trust doctors if it is generally perceived that doctors put the interests of patients first. Another consideration is that a trusting relationship has therapeutic advantages in that it reduces anxiety and enhances compliance. In addition, because physicians in general are known to espouse the principle of putting patients first, patients assume that doctors will act accordingly. As Albert Jonsen and Andrew Jameton see it, patients have a right to make that assumption, and doctors are morally obligated not to disappoint them.

> When patients are incompetent, society itself prudently (and rightfully) requires physicians to put patients first, since any of us might some day become incompetent patients. In addition, there may be an implied agreement with the incompetent patient's family to do what is best for the patient.

> None of these considerations, however, seems to support the premise that the infant comes first even if that means great sacrifice by the family. The therapeutic advantage and the implicit agreement with the patient do not apply in the case of newborn patients. Neither does the prudential reason, since none of us will be neonates again. Besides, the utilitarian goal of encouraging parents to seek medical care for their children would seem to be served just as well, if not better, by the principle of putting the infant first, unless doing so creates a great burden for the family. Furthermore, concerning any implied agreement with an incompetent patient's family, it is doubtful that parents generally agree, either implicitly or explicitly, that the physician is to do what is best for the infant regardless of the burden to parents. I submit, then, that there is no basis for the view that the duty to the patient is absolute in the kind of case we are considering.

There is one curious omission in Strong's discussion: nowhere does he acknowledge that physicians might have interests of their own that could conflict with those of both parent and neonate, or most especially with those of parents in the matter of "aggressive treatment" to save neonates: "Thus, when doctors make unilateral judgments about newborns with the avowed or implicit purpose of protecting the infant's interests, they are not behaving paternalistically toward anyone." But separate interests on the part of the physician are an obvious probability, and I suggest that the forcing apart of physicians' and their patients' interests by the impersonality and nonrepetitiveness of physician–patient interactions in modern urban society is a principal reason for the rises in dissatisfaction, litigation, and the expenses of medical care. For example, excessive use of diagnostic procedures (that are often risky to the patient) are carried out to protect the interests of physicians and hospitals because, I believe, physicians and hospitals have lost the ability to convince patients that they have indeed assumed the medical interests of the patient as if they were their own. Family doctors in rural settings with stable populations of interrelated, interacting people suffered far less from such difficulties, partly because their reputations were constantly on the line. Patients had ways other than litigation to reciprocate inferior treatment, and more reasons to believe they were obtaining the best care the physician could give.

The closest Strong comes to acknowledging that physicians may have separate interests of their own is the following:

> . . . There are vested interests, in that an entire medical subspecialty has developed to care for impaired newborns. Just try to suggest to neonatologists and NICU nurses that their patients are not persons! (p. 14)

Contrary to most authors, a few who have dealt with moral issues have focused quite directly on conflicts of interest. Thus, Perry (1954, pp. 87, 165) noted that:

> It is an open secret . . . that morality takes conflict of interest as its point of departure and harmony of interests as its ideal goal. (p. 87)

> The ultimate data of moral science are not men's approbations and disapprobations, but conflicts of interest, and the organizations of interests by which they are made non-conflicting and cooperative. (p. 135)

The philosopher, Hans Kelsen (1957), is another example, and in his book *What is Justice?* he stated what is meant by conflicts of interests (pp. 2–4):

> Where there is no conflict of interests, there is no need for justice. A conflict of interest exists when one interest can be satisfied only at the expense of the other; or what amounts to the same, when there is a conflict between two values, and when it is not possible to realize both at the same time; when the one can be realized only if the other is neglected; when it is necessary to prefer the realization of the one to that of the other; to decide which one is more important, or in other terms, to decide which is the higher value, and finally; which is the highest value.

Despite this clear statement and the rather grand essay written 16 years earlier by Roscoe Pound (see pp. 33–34 ), neither Kelsen nor any other author I have discovered sets out to identify interests and quantify their conflicts and confluences (although Strong, 1984, comes close); most do not even acknowledge this as a matter of importance. Piecemeal efforts are as old as history, but there seems to have been no effort toward a general theory.

Why should it be true that the very disciplines preoccupied with conflicts of interest should deal with them as if they were something other than the central issue? Perhaps the authors involved would respond to this question by saying: "Rubbish! Of course we know that conflicts of interests are the heart of the problem. The reason we don't dwell on them is *because* we know their role and importance so well."

Perhaps. But precisely the same thing is sometimes said about altruism. At a recent meeting at the University of Michigan, a prominent moral philosopher said, in evident puzzlement, "We have been discussing altruism forever. What is all the recent excitement from biology about?" The excitement exists because theories of inclusive-fitness-maximizing (Hamilton, 1964) and reciprocity (Trivers, 1971) enable us to formulate testable hypotheses about aspects of altruism that previously could not be investigated scientifically. A new understanding of what human interests are all about might similarly justify a reexamination of the central question of conflicts of interest in connection with morality and ethics and the general conduct of people. I think we have such a new understanding and, as with our new understanding of altruism, it comes from biology. Grant (1985), for example, remarks that "When Rawls speaks of human beings as rational, he means that they are able to calculate their self-interest. . . . What men primarily calculate about are those good things which lead to comfortable self-preservation." It is a major argument of this book that this prevalent view simply will not allow us to analyze human sociality to the core. (A more extensive discussion of moral philosophy occurs later on pp. 145ff.)

## MORAL SYSTEMS AS SYSTEMS OF INDIRECT RECIPROCITY

The problem, in developing a theory of moral systems that is consistent with evolutionary theory from biology, is in accounting for the altruism of moral behavior in genetically selfish terms. I believe this can be done by interpreting moral systems as systems of indirect reciprocity.

I regard indirect reciprocity as a consequence of direct reciprocity occurring in the presence of interested audiences—groups of individuals who continually evaluate the members of their society as possible future interactants from whom they would like to gain more than they lose (this outcome, of course, can be mutual).

Returns from indirect reciprocity may take at least three major forms: (1) the beneficent individual may later be engaged in profitable reciprocal interactions by individuals who have observed his behavior in directly reciprocal interactions and judged him to be a potentially rewarding interactant (his "reputation" or "status" is enhanced, to his ultimate benefit); (2) the beneficent individual may be rewarded with direct compensation from all or part of the group (such as with money or a medal or social elevation as a hero) which, in turn, increases his likelihood of (and that of his relatives) receiving additional perquisites; or (3) the beneficent individual may be rewarded by simply having the success of the group within which he behaved beneficently contribute to the success of his own descendants and collateral relatives.

Obviously, various forms of punishment, including ostracism or social shunning, can also be applied to individuals repeatedly observed not to reciprocate adequately or follow whatever codes of conduct may exist.

Typically, then, in interactions solely involving direct reciprocity, individuals may be expected to seek a net gain, although (1) this does not necessarily come at the expense of the other interactant (i.e., both may profit) and (2) the net gain may only be realized after a long iterated series of interactions, any one or fraction of which may actually yield a net loss for the individual in question. Even in directly reciprocal interactions, however, net losses to self (and even explicitly greater losses than those of the partner) may be the actual aim of one or even both individuals, if they are being scrutinized by others who are likely to engage either individual subsequently in reciprocity of greater significance than that occurring in the scrutinized acts. In effect, what goes on in such cases could be termed "social hustling," in which a "player" more or less deliberately (though conscious purpose is not a requirement) loses in order to "set up" the observer for a later overcompensating gain. I am referring to all effects of such social scrutinizing as indirect reciprocity.

If current views of evolutionary processes are correct, reciprocity flourishes when the donated benefits are relatively inexpensive compared to the returns (Hamilton, 1964; Trivers, 1971; Alexander, 1974; West Eberhard, 1975). This kind of gain is possible under two circumstances: the first is when threats or promises extrinsic to the interactants cause joint similar efforts to be worth more than the sum of their separate contributions, leading to more or less symmetrical cooperation.

The second is when the contributions of partners in reciprocity are different, leading to division of labor. The second situation can arise out of different abilities or training in different contributors, or from differences in their accumulated resources.

Systems of indirect reciprocity as expressed in humans require memory, consistency across time, the application of precedents, and persistent and widely communicated concepts of right and wrong (Trivers, 1971, 1985; Alexander, 1977–1982; Axelrod and Hamilton, 1981). They become, automatically, what I am here calling moral systems. I believe that the feeling that human behavior is out of reach of biological analyses arises, not so much because we are confused by the existence of "culture" or socially heritable learning (the reason usually given), but because culture includes systems of indirect reciprocity (moral, ethical, and legal systems) by which the costs and benefits of acts deemed by others to be socially positive or negative can be manipulated. The "problem of culture," then, may not be so much one of ontogenetic disjunction (as most authors seem to imply—meaning that at some point learning or culture takes over and the human organism begins to operate independently of its evolutionary heritage), but rather a failure to appreciate the pervasiveness and the consequences of indirect reciprocity.

Systems of indirect reciprocity, and therefore moral systems, are social systems structured around the importance of status. The concept of status implies that an individual's privileges, or its access to resources, are controlled in part by how others collectively think of him (hence, treat him) as a result of past interactions (including observations of interactions with others). Status can be determined by physical prowess, as in those nonhuman (animal) dominance hierarchies in which coalitions are absent, or (as in humans) by mental or social prowess. Mental and social prowess, in this sense, includes (as in moral systems) effectiveness and reliability in reciprocity and cooperation.

Once social interactions become instrumental in establishing status, then testing and practice, as in the forms typically called "play," may become prominent. Play represents practice for later status-affecting interactions, but it also affects current and projected status. In humans, social-intellectual play in the form of humor has become uniquely elaborate. This kind of play, moreover, unlike most forms of play, is prominent across all of adult life. As with physical play in humans (Alexander, 1974), humor has also come to include unique group-against-group forms (i.e., "ostracizing" humor, such as ethnic and racial jokes) (Alexander, 1986b).

## WHERE DO RULES COME FROM

As soon as planning, anticipating, "expecting" organisms are interacting without complete overlap (confluence) of interests, then each of two interactants may be expected to include in (add to) its repertoire of social actions special efforts to thwart (intercept, alter) the expectations of the others—explicitly in ways designed to be costly to those others and beneficial to himself. Interruption of another's expectations will be costly to that other when the expectation involves some investment (cost), or when pursuing it has been done in a way that is less costly because it did not allow for the possibility of the kind of interruption that the first party caused. I suggest, then, that the expense of investing in expectations, and the possibility of doing so with less expense if certain kinds of interruptions are forestalled, are the essential reasons for the invention and maintenance of *rules*. Rules are aspects of indirect reciprocity beneficial to those who propose and perpetuate them, not only because they force others to behave in ways explicitly beneficial to the proposers and perpetuators but because they also make the future more predictable so that plans can be carried out. This proposition is subtly, but significantly, different from that implied by Rawls (1971, p. 6):

> In the absence of a certain measure of agreement on what is just and unjust, it is clearly more difficult for individuals to coordinate their plans efficiently in order to ensure that mutually beneficial arrangements are maintained. Distrust and resentment corrode the ties of civility, and suspicion and hostility tempt men to act in ways they would otherwise avoid. So while the distinctive role of conceptions of justice is to specify basic rights and duties and to determine the appropriate distributive shares, the way in which a conception does this is bound to affect the problems of efficiency, coordination, and stability.

The significance of indirect reciprocity has to do not only with rules, but with intent (Table 2.5), and the general levels of altruism prevailing in the society. Because systems of indirect reciprocity involve promises of punishment as well as reward they lead to avoidance of selfishness as well as positive acts of altruism. This is why, I believe, humans tend to decide that a person is either moral or not, as opposed to being moral in one time or context and immoral in another, and why intent is said to be "nine-tenths of the law." We use motivation and honesty in one circumstance to predict actions in others.

Seeing morality as self-serving because of indirect reciprocity enables us to visualize it in two stages or as involving two kinds of outcomes for acts widely regarded as immoral:

1. If I do that ("immoral thing") to someone I am apt to suffer costs greater than the benefits, imposed on me by the other members of my group as a result of indirect reciprocity (within-group indirect reciprocity).

2. If I do that ("immoral thing") to someone I will foster, or at least not restrain, the development of a pattern of within-group behavior that will *eventually* impose a cost on me greater than the benefits. These costs will be imposed on me either by a change of rules that I precipitate or promote against my long-term interests or by the ability of members of groups other than my own to injure or destroy my group because of its lack of unity (between-group indirect reciprocity). Awareness of this last possibility by my group members will cause them to be even more watchful of my behavior within the group, thus increasing the costs of "immoral" actions monitored by within-group reciprocity.

The consequences of indirect reciprocity, then, include the concomitant spread of altruism (as social investment genetically valuable to the altruist), rules, and efforts to cheat (Tables 2.2–2.4). I would not contend that we always carry out cost–benefit analyses on these issues deliberately or consciously. I do, however, contend that such analyses occur, sometimes consciously, sometimes not, and that we are evolved to be exceedingly accurate and quick at making them (Table 2.5).

## DISCRIMINATE AND INDISCRIMINATE BENEFICENCE

The beneficence involved in human nepotism and direct reciprocity is discriminative: different relatives, and relatives of different needs, are distinguished. Friends are treated individually. As yet, no organism outside clones has been shown to display population-wide indiscriminate beneficence, and I will argue that, with the exception of clones and certain kinds of eusociality (especially, in termites, ants, wasps, and bees), only in human systems of indirect reciprocity does a modicum of essentially indiscriminate beneficence or social investment exist in large groups.

Indirect reciprocity must have arisen out of the search for interactants and situations by which to maximize returns from asymmetrical, hence highly profitable direct social reciprocity. One consequence of large complex societies in which reciprocity is the principal social cement and indirect reciprocity is prevalent is that opportunities for such mutually profitable asymmetrical reciprocal interactions are vastly multiplied. This situation, in turn, fosters the appearance of tendencies to engage in *indiscriminate social investment* (or indiscriminate beneficence)—which I define as willingness to risk relatively small expenses in certain kinds of social donations to whomever may be needy—partly because of the

Table 2.5. Interactions of Motivations and Outcomes in Determining Morality and Immorality of Social Acts[a]

| Outcomes of social acts | Motivations | | | | | | | | |
|---|---|---|---|---|---|---|---|---|---|
| | Doesn't know or think about what he is doing | | Does these things deliberately | | | | | | |
| | Considered to be insane or incompetent (i.e., *cannot* know—includes non-humans) | Considered to be lazy or thoughtless—does these things without thinking about them (could know but doesn't) | Believes he is selfish and expects to win because of selfishness | | Believes he is altruistic and expects to win *because* of altruism | Believes he is altruistic but expects to win *despite* altruism | | | |
| | | | | | | Expects reward on Earth | | Expects reward in Heaven | |
| | | | Sees his way of life as satisfying; acts this way because he enjoys it | Sees his way of life as a burden (as compared to other lives possible) | Sees his way of life as either satisfying or as a burden | Satisfying | Burden | Satisfying | Burden |
| Helps only self | [1] Neutral (e.g., baby) | [2] Immoral | [3] Immoral | [4] Unlikely | [5] Immoral | [6] Immoral | [7] Unlikely | [8] Unlikely | [9] Unlikely |
| Helps only self and relatives | [10] Neutral | [11] Immoral | [12] Immoral | [13] Unlikely | [14] Prob[b] | [15] Prob[b] | [16] Prob[b] | [17] Prob[b] | [18] Prob[b] |
| Helps self, relatives, and friends who are likely to reciprocate with interest | [19] Neutral[a] | [20] Immoral? | [21] Immoral | [22] Unlikely | [23] Prob[c] | [24] Prob[c] | [25] Prob[c] | [26] Prob[c] | [27] Prob[c] |
| Helps self, relatives, reciprocating friends, and others in the presence of potential reciprocators | [28] Neutral[a] | [29] Moral? | [30] Immoral | [31] Unlikely | [32] Prob[c] | [33] Prob[c] | [34] Prob[c] | [35] Prob[c] | [36] Prob[c] |

98

| | 37 | 38 | 39 | 40 | 41 | 42 | 43 | 44 | 45 |
|---|---|---|---|---|---|---|---|---|---|
| Helps all of the above, and also helps strangers when it is not too costly, even when not in the presence of reciprocators | Neutral[a] | Moral | Unlikely? | Unlikely | Moral | Moral? | Moral? | Moral | Moral |
| | 46 | 47 | 48 | 49 | 50 | 51 | 52 | 53 | 54 |
| Helps anyone who needs it even if the immediate cost is great | Neutral[a] | Moral | Unlikely | Unlikely | Moral | Moral? | Moral? | Moral | Moral |
| | 55 | 56 | 57 | 58 | 59 | 60 | 61 | 62 | 63 |
| Helps others indiscriminately while maintaining self at approximately the lowest level consistent with doing this effectively | Neutral[a] | Moral | Unlikely | Unlikely | Moral | Moral? | Moral? | Moral (Saint) | Moral (Saint) |

[a]I have speculated as to how each category of act is likely to be judged. Problematic cases illustrate the difficulty of deciding questions of morality when self-interest is broadened to include reproductive (genetic) interests, and when motivation comes to include realizations of the nature of such interests. Squares 25–32 and 41–48 would probably be marked "moral" by those unaware of biological considerations because they seem to involve self-sacrifice. An evolutionary biologist might regard all squares as representing possible behaviors, and as all possibly representing self-interested behaviors, but he might also regard squares 55–63 as less likely than would nonbiologists. Biologists would also be more likely to search for ways in which squares 55–63 could represent behaviors that serve the actor's interests.

[b]Behaviors that will probably be seen by most as immoral because of outcomes and despite motivations. Prob, problematic.
[c]Behaviors that will probably be seen by most as moral because of outcome and motivation combined.
[d]Desirable behavior even if morally neutral.

prevalence of interested audiences and keenness of their observation, and the use of beneficent acts by others to identify individuals appropriate for later reciprocal interactions. In complex social systems with much reciprocity, being judged as attractive for reciprocal interactions may become an essential ingredient for success. Similarly, to be judged harshly because of failure to deliver small social benefits indiscriminately in appropriate situations may lead to formidable disadvantages because of either direct penalties or lost opportunities in subsequent reciprocal interactions.

I suggest that indirect reciprocity led to the evolution of ever keener abilities to observe and interpret situations with moral overtones. In such a milieu, I would argue, a modicum of indiscriminate beneficence would arise, as social investment, because of benefits to individuals who are viewed as altruists. Beneficence can approach being indiscriminate in two ways: (1) *some acts* can be indiscriminately beneficent and (2) *all acts*, or social behavior in general, can tend in the direction of being indiscriminately beneficent. These two different expressions of beneficence will not necessarily have the same consequences for the actor.

Population-wide indiscriminate beneficence might also evolve when small "populations" are regularly composed of relatives related to a similar degree, and if the individuals of other populations are never contacted and therefore not discriminated against. This may be an unlikely situation for mammals or even vertebrates in general. This kind of indiscriminate beneficence would require no special proximate mechanisms—no social learning; but there is yet no undisputed evidence for unlearned recognition of relatives in any species (see reviews by Sherman and Holmes, 1985; Alexander, 1985).

Figure 2.1 describes hypothetical social stages through which the evolving human species might have passed (many times), and seeming to lead (but, as argued here, probably not actually doing so) toward a utilitarian or idealized model of morality in which *all* social investment becomes indiscriminate beneficence.

As already noted, complete and indiscriminate beneficence, as in the utilitarian system of philosophers (i.e., systems promoting the greatest good to the greatest number), would not always be a losing strategy for individuals, even in evolutionary terms. Indiscriminate beneficence would not lose, for example, when the interests of the group and the interests of the individuals comprising it are the same. Such a confluence of interests would occur when all group members were equally and most closely related to the individuals destined to reproduce. It could also occur (temporarily) whenever the group was threatened externally in such fashion that complete cooperation by its members would be

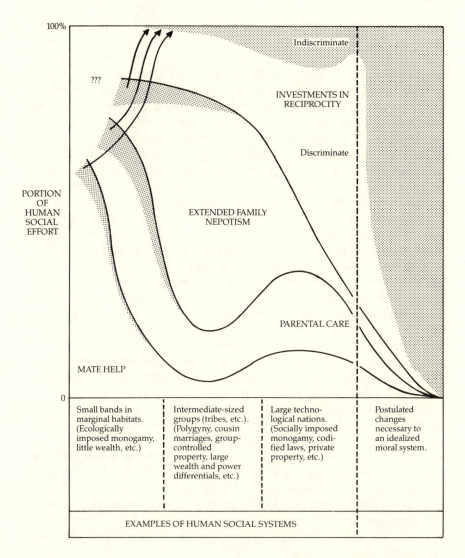

FIGURE 2.1. A speculation about the relative importance of different kinds of social interactions in some different kinds of societies. The principal purpose is to show the probable origins of indiscriminate altruism, its probable significance in different societies, and the changes from existing societies that would be necessary to realize an idealized model of morality in which everyone was indiscriminately altruistic.

necessary to dissipate the threat, and when failure of the group to dissipate the threat would more severely penalize any remaining individuals than would the group's survival after that individual had used all of its effort to support the group. In such cases it is not trivial to consider the different treatments likely to be accorded those individuals who contributed wholeheartedly and unselfishly to the well-being of the group when it was threatened, and those who did not, or who in fact selfishly betrayed their fellows or ignored their needs.

General encouragement of indiscriminate beneficence, and general acceptance of its beneficial effects, results in a society with high social unity. This encouragement and acceptance is expected to occur partly because of the likelihood, much of the time, that nearly everyone benefits from living in a unified society (as opposed to a socially divisive one), but also partly because individuals gain from portraying themselves as indiscriminate altruists, and from thereby inducing indiscriminate beneficence in others (and often from inducing degrees of it that are deleterious to those others). This means that whether or not we know it when we speak favorably to our children about Good Samaritanism, we are telling them about a behavior that has a strong likelihood of being reproductively profitable. In a small social group this can be true for the Good Samaritan even if he or she is never identified, but Good Samaritan acts seem likely to be most profitable to the actor if his responsibility for the act is discovered accidentally, and most importantly through no effort of his own.

I would postulate that self-serving indiscriminate social investment—because it was seen as net-cost (i.e., genetic as well as phenotypic) altruism and was interpreted wrongly as part of a real trend toward universal indiscriminate (net-cost) altruism—provided the impetus for the idealized modern model of morality portrayed in Fig. 2.1. The value of self-serving beneficence, it seems to me, is what sets the stage for the evolution of the ability and tendency to develop a conscience, which I have interpreted (Alexander, 1979a) as the "still small voice that tells us how far we can go in serving our own interests without incurring intolerable risks."

The implication is that approaches to morality are expressed consistently, and to the degree they are usually realized in society, because there is continual pressure to bring about a condition of more nearly ideal morality. If so, this pressure is likely to be applied by each individual so as to cause his neighbor, if possible, to be a little more moral than himself. Stated differently, it would be to the advantage of each individual in a society that other individuals, especially those not most closely related to him, actually achieve or approach the ideal of completely moral behavior. Ideally moral (indiscriminately beneficent) people would tend to "help" others in the society, however slightly, to achieve the goals that evolutionists believe have driven evolution by natural selection. They would contribute slightly to everyone else's interests by (1) helping their interactants directly, (2) hurting themselves in relation to others, and (3) setting an example that others may follow, thereby contributing to the interests of the group as a whole. Accordingly, one expects that the individuals in a society would gain from exerting at least a little effort toward encouraging other individuals to be more moral (altruistic, beneficent) than they otherwise might have been. Among the many ways of accomplishing this is included the setting up of an idealized morality as a model or goal, and the encouragement of everyone (else) to become like that. One way of promoting this situation is to designate as heroes those who approach the ideal moral condition. One expects that sainthood may be awarded to individuals who spend their lives on explicitly antireproductive behavior. The prevalence among saints of asceticism, self-denial, celibacy, isolation from relatives, devotion to the welfare of strangers, and otherwise indiscriminate tendencies to be altruistic supports this hypothesis. So does the fact that sainthood is generally awarded (long) after the death of the awardee (thus, the awardee cannot personally gain from this heroic designation).

The long-term existence of complex patterns of indirect reciprocity, then, seems to favor the evolution of keen abilities to (1) make one's self seem more beneficent than is the case; and (2) influence others to be beneficent in such fashions as to be deleterious to themselves and beneficial to the moralizer, e.g., to lead others to (a) invest too much, (b) invest wrongly in the moralizer or his relatives and friends, or (c) invest indiscriminately on a larger scale than would otherwise be the case. According to this view, individuals are expected to parade the idea of much beneficence, and even of indiscriminate altruism as beneficial, so as to encourage people in general to engage in increasing amounts of social investment whether or not it is beneficial to their interests. They may be expected to locate and exploit social interactions mimicking genetic relatedness leading to nepotistic flows of benefits (e.g., to insinuate themselves deceptively into the role of relative or reciprocator so as to receive the benefits therefrom). They may also be expected to depress the fitness of competitors by identifying them, deceptively or not, as reciprocity cheaters (in other words, to moralize and gossip); to internalize rules or evolve the ability to acquire a conscience, interpreted (Alexander, 1979a) as the ability to use our own judgment to serve our own interests; and to self-deceive and display false sincerity as defenses against detection of cheating and attributions of deliberateness in cheating (Trivers, 1971, 1985; Campbell, 1975; Alexander, 1974, 1977b, 1979a, 1982, 1985).

So we are provided with the general hypothesis that tendencies toward moral behavior, and the establishment of moral systems, are vehicles for promoting the goals of society as a whole: that they develop because all of the individuals of society often share the same goals, that, ultimately, these goals involve competition with and defense against other human groups; that, except in times of severe external threats recognized by everyone as requiring extreme cooperativeness, the ideal of universal indiscriminate beneficence is not met within groups; that the ideal morality has never even been approached between societies or nations; and that, because some degree of within-society competition probably occurs nearly all of the time, every individual may be expected to use the impetus toward realizing the goals of everyone to his own advantage by promoting a slightly greater degree of "morality" in his neighbor than in himself (i.e., a net-cost or genetic altruism).

The question may be raised, however, why anyone should be vulnerable to manipulation unduly far in the direction of beneficence, if we have been subjected to such manipulations a very long time? Why, in other words, should moralizing ever be effective? I think there are at least four contributing factors. First, the degrees of beneficence that are actually reproductively appropriate will vary dramatically as societies move between periods of extreme danger and relative security, making it difficult to know how to behave. When will a specified degree of failure to accede to exhortations to be beneficent cost more than it yields, because of (a) failure of the group on which one depends for success, or (b) responses within the group to one's failure to be beneficent? Second, individuals may be expected to take advantage of this dramatic shifting to deceive others about the degree of danger so as to induce unduly beneficent behavior in others. Sometimes aspiring leaders may use such deception to promote their own leadership as an antidote to the supposed threat, and as a promoter of unity. Third, we may expect that the individuals in a society such as we have been describing will evolve to deceive others about the degree of beneficence they themselves are exhibiting: Everyone will wish to appear more beneficent than he is. There are two reasons: (1) this appearance, if credible, is more likely to lead to direct social rewards than its alternatives; (2) it is also more likely to encourage others to be more beneficent. If one's associates are beneficent, then he can afford to be (or is forced to be) more beneficent than if they are not (we may note the additional feedback from these facts that would cause everyone to be concerned that everyone else appear beneficent so that people in general will feel comfortable with a higher degree of beneficence than would otherwise be the case). Fourth, if kin recognition is *learned* (Alexander, 1977a; 1979a; 1985a; Greenberg, 1979; Sherman and Holmes, 1985; Mintzer, 1982), mistakes are likely, and one may insinuate himself into the role of a relative so as to receive inappropriate nepotism, or even pretend to be nepotistic so as to receive the appropriate beneficent responses. Playing upon the tendency of everyone to strive to appear more beneficent than he is, and using the other ploys just described, may lead to much success in social manipulation.

The introduction of indirect reciprocity, whereby society as a whole or some large part of it provides the reward for beneficence and the punishment for selfishness (fines for running stop signs; tax rebates for donating to charity, etc.), simultaneously served both society and the individuals comprising it, and provided a vehicle for manipulating individuals socially to levels and kinds of beneficence detrimental to them (or to their reproductive success). It is somewhat paradoxical that the tendencies and pressures in the direction of idealized moral systems should serve everyone in the group up to a point, but then be transformed by the same forces that molded them, into manipulations of the behavior of individuals that are explicitly against the interests of those being manipulated and *in* the interests of those ostensibly contributing to *everyone's* interests by promoting trends toward morality in the system.

One consequence (and a saving grace) of the pressure within societies for everyone to be a little more moral than would pay, and of keen abilities by people in general to determine tendencies and willingness to behave beneficently or not, is that no one can afford to lag too far behind relative to everyone else. As beneficence continues to be promoted, *everyone* has to follow along, so that the most selfish individuals would be forced to be less selfish, and perhaps as well variance in readiness to be beneficent would narrow as the "front" of beneficence advances in the direction of the ideal of indiscriminate investment and true justice in the form of equal opportunity and equal treatment under the law. It is possible that the societies in which moral philosophers operate have actually changed so much in this direction during the past two or three centuries as to alter the preoccupations of moral philosophy toward a greater concern for utilitarian ideals and a less jaundiced view of humanity. If so, there is likely no greater irony than the fact that modern technological societies, whatever the degree of egalitarianism or approach to the philosophical ideal of morality within some of them, are teetering us on the brink of world disaster as a result or their interactions with one another. The problem has become one of inducing *between* and *among* societies the same processes of moralizing pressure and democratization that have developed so intricately within them.

It is also true that, in the absence of overriding power differentials, dramatic departures from usual levels of benfience in the direction of serving one's own interests are virtually certain to result in net losses as a result of shifts of reputation or status, or subsequently diminished beneficence from others. On the other hand, dramatic departures from usual levels of beneficence in the direction of *indiscriminateness* may raise status and multiply subsequent benefits so as to produce a net return to the actor. This asymmetry of effects would seem likely to cause acts of cheating and selfishness to depart minimally from norms while promoting dramatic or extreme acts of heroism, charity, and saintliness. Perhaps, to some extent, the asymmetry of these two effects is involved in the "creep" of certain kinds of closely knit, stable societies toward more highly cooperative, democratic opportunity-equalizing structures.

I believe that the various factors discussed here are the essential elements that produce and maintain what we commonly call moral systems, and moral behavior in individuals. Understanding them represents the means for resolving the existing paradoxes with respect to morality, eliminating the aura of mystery that has surrounded the concept, and understanding not only why moral systems have always fallen short of our ideals but why we nevertheless establish and maintain such ideals. If accurate, these arguments may also clarify the routes by which we can most closely approach what are seen as idealized moral systems, and perhaps most confidently avert moral disasters.

> Moral talk is often rather repugnant. Leveling moral accusations, expressing moral indignation, passing moral judgment, allotting the blame, administering moral reproof, justifying oneself, and above all, moralizing— who can enjoy such talk? And who can like or trust those addicted to it? The most outspoken critics of their neighbors' morals are usually men (or women) who wish to ensure that nobody should enjoy the good things in life which they themselves have missed and men who confuse the right and the good with their own advancement. (Baier, 1965, p. 3)
>
> Seeking to protect the autonomy that we have learned to prize, we aspire ourselves *not* to be manipulated by others; seeking to incarnate our own principles and stand-point in the world of practice, we find no way open to us to do so except by directing towards others those very manipulative modes of relationship which each of us aspires to resist in our own case. (MacIntyre, 1981b, p. 66)

## Morality and the Human Psyche

*Morality is like a cultivated field in the midst of the desert. It is a partial and precarious conquest. Ground that is conquered has to be protected against the resurgence of original divisive forces. The moralized life is never immune against demoralization. At the same time that morality gains ground in one direction it may lose ground in another. Changes in the natural and historical environment and the development of man himself are perpetually introducing new factors and requiring a moral reorganization to embrace them. In the last analysis all depends on the energy, perseverance, and perpetual vigilance of the human person.*

Ralph Perry, 1954, p. 100

*Why does man, knowing what is right, so often choose to do what is wrong? Is not this the critical question?*

Lack, 1965, p. 66

*The heart of man is made so as to reconcile contradictions.*

Hume, 1772, p. 203

*. . . the foundation of morality is to have done, once and for all, with lying.*

T. H. Huxley, 1896, p. 146

Humphrey (1976) and Alexander (1979a,b) hypothesized that consciousness is a vehicle for building and testing alternative scenarios in regard to future aspects of, particularly, social life. I speculated that self-awareness is a way of seeing ourselves as others see us so that we can cause them to see us as we would like them to rather than as they would like to, and as opposed to ways that will not serve our own interests. I proposed that free will does not really involve the question of physical causation but represents our ability to act upon whichever of the scenarios that we draw up seems to us most likely to serve our own interests. And I described conscience as the still, small voice that tells us how far we can go without incurring intolerable risks or costs to our own interests. At that time I had no clear way of combining these ideas with the Balance-of-Power hypothesis for human evolution. Now, however, I believe that a connection between the human psyche and intergroup competition can be hypothesized.

It is rather remarkable to contemplate that the structure of the human psyche could ultimately have been molded in some large part by the necessity and manner of societal defense. Yet, the argument continues to gain force that the evolution of humanity, and the rise of nations and of complexity in political structure, has been guided by balance-of-power races among societies (e.g., Pitt, 1978; Strate, 1982; Betzig, 1986). To draw the connection between such events and the nature of individual humans, let us review the assumptions about humans and human society developed so far, which I speculate have universal application:

1. Each person is programmed by the history of natural selection to maximize the likelihood of survival of his/her genetic materials through reproduction and nepotism, both of which depend on the acquisition and redistribution of resources. More precisely, we are programmed to develop and respond to the proximate stimuli of particular environments in ways that *at least in the general past* would have accomplished this end.

2. In general, anyone has at least the possibility of giving or receiving benefits from anyone else (ignoring for the moment the specific costs and benefits).

3. There are many inexpensive ways to give benefits that are nevertheless of great value to others.

4. There are many useful endeavors that cannot be carried out, or carried out as effectively, by one person alone, or even by small (as opposed to large) groups; *the outstanding and pivotal example has for a long time been defense against other competitive and aggressive human groups.* These endeavors call for cooperativeness, and social investment in others.

5. When social competition begins to take place through cooperation of individuals in social groups, and when reciprocity becomes a significant element in the social cement, then social capital can be acquired through investment even in others who themselves are unlikely to reciprocate, because of the value of being identified as a reliable and effective reciprocator.

6. Within groups there are formalized retributions, which can be effected when anyone secures "too much" ("too many" resources, too much power) and there are also formalized charities for those who become unusually "needy" (i.e., so needy that their plight, if not attended to, may directly or indirectly affect society, and each of us, in adverse fashions).

Given conditions (2–6), what strategies of beneficence will be best for the kind of human described in (1) above? In other words, what factors govern the nature of moral systems as devised by collective agreements and subgroups, and the nature of the human psyche evolved in such a social milieu? I propose that moral systems are constructed via the following "giving" behaviors or "rules"—that is, humans who have evolved in societies with the above six features will tend to develop (learn) their beneficent behavior as follows:

a. Give, when the benefit goes to a genetic relative (sometimes via a spouse or in-law) and its return to the giver via the improved reproduction of the relative is likely to be greater than the expense of the act multiplied by the fractional relationship of the recipient to the giver (in Hamilton's 1964 terms, $k>1/r$ when $k$ is effects from the environment and $r$ is degree of relatedness. This kind of giving represents investment in relatives or direct and indirect nepotism).

b. Give, when the recipient is likely to give back more than he or she receives (= investment in direct reciprocity).

c. Give, when failure to do so is likely to cause others to impose costs greater than the expense of the beneficence.

d. Give, when the act is likely to cause a sufficient number of appropriate people to regard the act as indicating a significant probability (in other interactions) of the actor giving back more than is received, hence indicating that the actor is himself a good object of social investment by the observers (= investment in indirect reciprocity).

e. In all other situations do not give.

There are four main conditions under (b) that may enhance the likelihood that a recipient of beneficence will give back more than it receives: (i) the recipient is a relative: (ii) the beneficent act is inexpensive for the beneficent individual but very valuable to the recipient: (iii) the recipient has previously acted like a benefit-giver (altruist): (iv) if it does not give back more than it receives, the recipient is placed in a position of being judged a nonaltruist or nonreciprocator by a sufficient number of appropriate people, so as to force either reciprocation or a net loss from social interactions.

Similarly, I hypothesize that failure to give, or "taking" (selfish, spiteful) behavior, has been programmed to develop (ontogenetically, by learning or whatever mechanisms) in the individual as follows: (i) Take from relatives whenever the benefit to one's own reproduction is greater than the effect of the same benefit on reproduction of relatives otherwise likely to receive it, devalued by the fractional relationship of the relative to the taker. (ii) Take from nonrelatives whenever the act is likely to be undetected, the cost of being detected is likely to be lower than the benefit of taking, or the taking is part of a reciprocal interaction that the benefit-giver anticipates being to his own ultimate benefit.

Finally, and in many ways most important of all in understanding ourselves, I expect any and all aspects of these strategies to be concealed—sometimes via self-deception as a means of deceiving others—

whenever revealing them is likely to have adverse effects on inclusive-fitness maximizing.

I speculate that these general conditions and responses characterize humans in all societies, and that—given the value to humans of grouping to defend against other human groups, and the consequent evolution of such traits as foresight, conscience, intelligence, and self-awareness—they are both necessary and sufficient to account for the general nature of moral systems and the behavior of individuals within moral systems. In discussions of moral behavior, (1), (c), and (d)—and the manner and the extent of concealment of strategies—have most often been misunderstood or left out.

## HYPOTHESES ABOUT THE EVOLUTION OF CONSCIOUSNESS

The following six hypotheses connect the central and unique aspects of the human psyche to (1) a history of evolution in which success corresponds to genic survival via reproduction and (2) a human history dominated by intergroup competition, i.e., a history in which the principal threat to reproductive success (or hostile force of nature) was other humans, both within one's own society or group (group living being a necessity because of intergroup aggression) and in other hostile groups.

These hypotheses represent for me the first plausible connection between the "Balance-of-Power" hypothesis for human evolution (cf. Alexander, 1979a) and the extraordinary and unique aspects of the human psyche. Development of this view of the human intellect was initiated by Alexander and Tinkle (1968), Bigelow (1969), and Alexander (1971, 1977b, 1979a); see also Campbell (1965), Fox (1971), Humphrey (1976), Dickstein (1979), and Hoffman (1981).

*Hypothesis 1.* Consciousness, foresight, self-awareness, conscience, and related aspects of the human psyche have evolved as a set of *"overrides"* of more widespread (and not necessarily solely human), generalized indicators of *immediate* costs and benefits. The most prominent and perhaps most general of such indicators of immediate costs and benefits are pain and pleasure. Pleasure is here thought of as having evolved because it causes organisms to seek events and repeat acts that tend to increase reproductive success, pain because it causes organisms to avoid events and not repeat acts that tend to decrease reproductive success.

Presumably, generalized indicators of immediate costs and benefits, such as pain and pleasure, evolve because there are consistencies between such costs and benefits and eventual reproductive success (that is, *later* costs and benefits). Presumably, also, overrides would only evolve when there are otherwise unpredictable reversals in the relationship between immediate costs and benefits and later ones. Even if what is (currently) seen as an immediate cost (for example, risking or giving one's life) comes to be related consistently to an ultimate benefit (for example, survival of one's offspring and their eventual reproduction), pain and pleasure can evolve to indicate appropriately with respect to reproductive deficits and benefits. That is, it could become an actual pleasure to give one's life for offspring if this relationship were consistent and could reliably be separated from other life-threatening situations that would not lead to reproductive success if engaged. The question is: What happens when such consistency is not the case?

The concept of overrides suggests that it is a common social situation for humans, more so than for any other organisms, that immediate costs or benefits may lead to *either* later costs or later benefits, depending on *longer-term* contingencies that can be identified and dealt with via consciousness and all of the other attributes typically associated with the human psyche, or at least better developed in humans than in any other species. The question raised by this hypothesis is: Why in human life should it be true, more than in the lives of other species, that short-term benefits may turn into *either* long-term costs or long-term benefits, and that contingencies available to us may assist us in determining which of these is going to be the case?

*Hypothesis 2*. The above situation arose as reciprocity became the binding cement of human social life. The changes in cost–benefit relations that caused the rise of consciousness and related phenomena were human manipulations, and as such represent a part of the manner by which competing humans became the principal hostile force influencing the evolution of humans.

Reciprocity involves social investment, which represents a short-term cost that may (but never certainly does) yield a long-term benefit. Something similar occurs with nepotism, but in its simpler forms nepotism does not require (is not improved by) consciousness, since the long-term genetic return can be made reliable simply by differential behavior toward individuals with whom one has had certain specific and different social experiences. This mechanism will work when the number and diversity of relatives do not vary greatly and the reproductive likelihood of relatives does not fluctuate widely in different circumstances. It will not work (well enough, or be the best mechanism) when relatives are very numerous, vary widely in their relatedness to an actor, and also vary widely or fluctuate in their reproductive probability. This last situation, which has evidently been typical for humans for a very long time, places a high premium on nepotistic investment strategizing that is essentially the same as in reciprocity. It is probably the situation that caused reciprocity to become involved in human nepotism, and to become so central in human society. It is probably also the situation that resulted in selection for consciousness and its related attributes.

*Hypothesis 3.* Reciprocity arises out of nepotism (becomes prominent) when large numbers of long-lived individuals related in differing degrees live together in social groups within which there is more or less constant directional selection favoring facilitators of (a) complex cooperation and (b) ability to move back and forth between complete cooperation (in the presence of threats to the whole group) and advantage-taking (in the absence of such threats). Coalitions and competitions may come and go at any level.

*Hypothesis 4.* Intergroup competition and aggression—that is, social situations in which other human groups are the principal extrinsic threats—represent the only circumstance that can maintain the situation in Hypothesis 3 and account for the large groups whose social behavior is guided principally by reciprocity in which indefinitely numerous and complex manipulations of costs and benefits can create selection leading to the human kind and degree of consciousness and its related overrides of other proximate indicators.

*Hypothesis 5.* Group hunters of mammals (themselves evidently always mammals)—whether canines, felines, or primates—tend to become so fearsome (such ecological dominants, such powerful manipulators of their own environments) that they approach becoming, incidentally, their own main competitors. Thus, cooperativeness, of whatever origin, sets the stage for "ganging up" two on one (and upward) in within-species competitions. Chimpanzees evidently gang up to murder (de Waal, 1986; Goodall, 1986). I suspect that one-on-one murders in humans are principally postculture (i.e., followed the availability of weapons that upset the "balance-of-power" at that and other levels), and that elaboration of culture derives from changes postulated above. Cooperatively hunting species can themselves be dominated by other group hunters (or group cooperators). Humans did this to all other such species, and in the process became not only their own principal hostile force (group-against-group), but the enslavers of canines and felines, and the jailers of their closest remaining relatives, the great apes. Finally, and incidentally, they have also become the one species capable of annihilating itself by within-species aggression.

Consciousness and related aspects of the human psyche (self-awareness, self-reflection, foresight, planning, purpose, conscience, free will, etc.) are here hypothesized to represent a system for competing with other humans for status, resources, and eventually reproductive success. More specifically, the collection of these attributes is viewed as a means of seeing ourselves and our life situations as others see us and our life situations, so as to outguess, outmaneuver, outdo those others—most particularly in ways that will cause (the most and the most important of) them to continue to interact with us in fashions that will benefit us and seem to benefit them.

Consciousness, then, is a game of life in which the participants are trying to comprehend what is in one another's minds before, and more effectively than, it can be done in reverse. This is the reason for the great significance of time, foresight, and planning in human activities, and for the bringing of time-related and -sequenced activities into consciousness. Wilson and Herrnstein (1985, *Crime and Human Nature*) present a formula that they believe illustrates how humans project and evaluate the costs and benefits of criminal behavior. They argue that the decision whether or not to engage in criminal behavior depends on the likelihood and extent of success and immediate benefits weighed against the likelihood and extent of later costs, all of this tempered by an "impulse factor." The impulse factor is a combination of (1) previous learning about both costs and benefits and (2) restraints on capabilities affected by evolutionary history (which can be translated as individual differences in ease of acquiring abilities to carry out specific acts, at least in comparison with others—hence, in ease of likelihood of realizing proximate rewards or punishments such as, respectively, pleasure and pain). I think that Wilson and Herrstein's arguments can be made compatible with an evolutionary approach, perhaps largely because they are willing to assume a kind of egoism or selfishness in criminal behavior that is not typically assumed in discussions of morality or ordinary social behavior, and that their arguments are much more general than is suggested by their consideration of only tendencies to behave criminally or not.

The above assumptions and hypotheses may be regarded as part of the development of a new theory of the nature of the human individual from a modern view of evolution. It seems to me that we are in an enviable position, significantly altered from that of Darwin, Freud, and other great thinkers who pioneered such theorizing, from biology, in the past. We can start with clear and complete assumptions about overall design and motivations—the life interest—of our subject, the human individual. This can be done because of the refinements of theories about natural selection that began with Fisher (1930, 1958) and included Hamilton (1964), Williams (1966a), and Trivers (1971).

Life would surely be easier, and our intellects and emotions more relaxed, if all of the above things could suddenly be rendered untrue. Then, if I should decide to truly devote my life to the benefit of others I could simply tell them so, and because history might give them reason to believe me, we could both relax. Similarly, if all those around me were devoted to serving my interests in preference to their own, then if serving my own interests were also my goal, my own life would be much more relaxed.

On the other hand, if everyone knew that everyone else was continually serving only his own interests in all circumstances, and the only defense is to keep all others from hurting one's self when possible, it does not seem that human society and human nature would be nearly as complex as they are now. But things are more complex than either of these cases, because we have become so astoundingly clever at deception and manipulation.

## CONSCIOUSNESS AND DECEPTION

Let us go now to the assumption that sometimes people make (evolutionary) mistakes and serve the interests of others rather than their own.

We, therefore, would expect the evolution of abilities and tendencies to deceive potential altruists into serving inadvertently the interests of others. Obviously, we expect as well the evolution of abilities and tendencies to resist such manipulations (Trivers, 1971). Thus, the race toward social, mental, and emotional complexity is on.

If efforts by others to manipulate our social actions to their own ends are sometimes successful, then we are given a new way to deceive: by giving the impression that we are indeed serving their interests when in fact we are not—by behaving like altruists while actually serving our own interests. This possibility becomes a virtual certainty once reciprocity among social interactants reaches the level of involving delayed rewards. Then it can pay to give the impression of being an altruist even if you are not.

But now a new set of responses may be expected to evolve in those vulnerable to being cheated by others pretending altruism—keener and keener abilities to detect such falseness, including particularly finely honed abilities to detect *deliberate* deception or lying.

We are just beginning. The next level of deception involves convincing others by word, gesture, expression, and other ways—outside our *costly* interactions with them—that we are *truthful* people and that *honesty* is our general nature. Now we can also cash in on "good will" built up by displaying beneficence when it is inexpensive for us and valuable to its recipients. We can build up "debts" of this sort and expect benefits even from mere observers of our beneficence if we have occasion to interact with them later.

Provided with a means of relegating our deceptions to the subconscious—indeed, provided perhaps only at this point in the evolutionary process with a subconscious (cf. Daniels, 1983)—false sincerity becomes easier and detection more difficult. There are reasons for believing that one does not need to know his own personal interests consciously in order to serve them as much as he needs to know the interests of others to thwart them. A child learns first to serve his own interests, but initially in a situation in which all of his contacts—his caretakers—also wish to serve them. But what are the first things he does with his consciousness? I have suggested that consciousness is a way of making our social behavior so unpredictable as to allow us to outmaneuver others; and that we press into the subconscious (as opposed to forgetting) those things that remain useful to us but would be detrimental to us if others knew about them, and on which we are continually tested and would have to lie deliberately if they remained in our conscious mind (I am here using "subconscious" as psychiatrists and others sometimes use the term "preconscious," to mean that part of nonconscious knowledge that can be made conscious, and as well everything that has passed from the conscious into the nonconscious).

The subconscious category of motivation or drive could be used as a general storage area for sets of rules, mores, or cultural do's and don'ts, that (in some fashion or for some reason) seem to be rules that, if we follow them, will in the end serve our own interests. Perhaps the punishment for transgressions is very severe, or the chances of detection great—or erratic and outside our control or ability to perceive them. Perhaps following those rules automatically yields such extraordinary social rewards that we can only gain by giving the impression that we accept them absolutely without question. So we internalize our society's most important rights and wrongs. We develop a conscience, and we have in this discussion passed already from some version of Freud's id (primitive self, bald egoism, direct somatic effort) to the ego (direct and indirect somatic effort) and the superego which, in approximation, adds nepotistic beneficence (reproductive effort) to direct and especially indirect somatic effort [note the relationship to the discussion, in evolutionary terms (pp. 129ff.) of Kohlberg's studies of moral development in the individual]. Included in the function of the superego would be not only the discriminative altruism of nepotism and directly reciprocal contracts but the deceptions and manipulations of indirect reciprocity—causing us to appear more beneficent than we are, and leading others sometimes to be more beneficent than is to their benefit.

Is it possible that the conflicts Freud thought he identified among the id, ego, and superego are in part the consequences of a "reality check" designed into humans (Dierdre Block, pers. comm.)? Such a reality check could involve grave mental-emotional hurdles if the rules accepted or forced upon us, especially at early ages, turn out not to be serving our interests in the real world in which we have later come to live. Some marvelously special methods of such truth-seeking must have become an activity of the subconscious almost coincidentally with its ability and tendency to internalize preferred or taught rules.

Similarly, I would suggest that much of the confusion about the significance of dreams dissipates if one sees them as instances of scenario building, or repetition, in the interests of (1) cementing prior events of great significance for retention and (2) testing series of alternative possibilities with respect to social events yet to transpire. This is not a new idea. Ira Progoff, quoted in *Psychology Today* (Kaiser, 1981) asserts that:

> Dreams reach back into the past and call our attention to those experiences that can give us a clue with which to solve our present problems and move into the future. Our dreams can give us these clues, however, in the only mode of functioning that is available to them—that is, on the conscious level, by indirection, allusion, imagery, and symbolism. In all of these considerations we ought to keep in mind that the complexities just described are all involved in the psychological, mental, and moral development of every human individual.

Is it the special attribute of humans that they compete socially by having evolved the capability of assuming the other person's position as well as their own in the process of best serving their own interests (Symons, 1979)? That they serve their own interests partly by recognizing so well what others' interests are? They could do this first in the context of helping kin of all ages and then use the ability to identify the interests of others to best or cheat them while simultaneously evolving to conceal their own individual interests. Concealment of interests would acquire importance as (1) interests became individualized and (2) sociality became more prevalent or intense.

With respect to their effects on the evolution of the human psyche I would hypothesize that overlaps of human interests are appropriately classified as follows:

1. Always universally shared
   a. No ethical or moral problems are involved
   b. Best characterized as (or most likely to be) *nonconscious*

2. Shared within subgroups; different between subgroups; overlapping but different among individuals

   a. The realm in which the word *ethics* is most employed

   b. Best characterized (or most likely to be) *conscious*

3. Individually distinctive; personally unique

   a. The realm in which the word *moral* most applies

   b. Most likely to include *subconscious*

## SELF-DECEPTION

> *Were a portrait of man to be drawn, one in which there would be highlighted whatever is most human, be it noble or ignoble, we should surely place well in the foreground man's enormous capacity for self-deception.*
>
> Fingarette, 1969, p. 1

In the world of sociality, behavior can be divided into categories with respect to acceptability or desirability. Thus, some forms of seeking one's own interests are either universally unacceptable or nearly so—like raping small children, murdering competitors, or stealing a neighbor's resources. Other behaviors that are just as clearly efforts to serve one's own interests are generally acceptable—like shooting a burglar, assaulting someone who physically attacks a family member, or seeking one's own child in a school fire.

Similarly, some forms of beneficence are generally expected—like helping old ladies across busy streets or holding the door for someone on crutches. Still other beneficent acts are "desirable" (or highly appreciated) and sometimes happen, but are not really expected—like the donation of a new park by a wealthy person or the repeated passing of the lifeline to the next person in a flood.

I would describe this scale going from deplorable to desirable acts as including four categories: (1) unacceptable egoism, (2) acceptable egoism, (3) expected beneficence, and (4) desired (but not expected) beneficence. This raises the question of how we decide how much egoism is acceptable? What effect does the acceptance of some egoism have on the individual's development and behavior? Ruse (1982), in denying moral relativism, says (p. 275):

> Because of our common evolutionary heritage we share an ultimate moral code, and can indeed make judgments of right and wrong, distinguishing them from personal preference.
>
> The man who says that it is morally acceptable to rape little children, is just as mistaken as the man who says that $2+2=5$.

Maybe the two hypothetical men in Ruse's example would be equally mistaken, but not for the same reasons. One might find it easier to retain for a longer time universal agreement about the mistake along the route, $2+2=4.9$, $2+2=4.8$; $2+2=4.7$ than about that along the route leading to sexual intercourse forced to lesser and lesser degrees with females closer and closer to maturity. It seems to me that Ruse's example, by specifying an extreme along a gradient, sidesteps the issue raised in his first statement above. I can find no evidence for even a core of absoluteness in morality. Rather it appears that our judgments about it are always cost–benefit decisions (including unconscious and subconscious acts as a result of conscience) made in relation to our own personal history of lessons and the structure of our society. Universality of some moral rules about selected extremes does not seem to be a criterion for denying this assertion.

Ruse also stated (p. 324) that

> Children must be taught not to lie, cheat, steal, bully, and a host of other behaviors associated with proper interpersonal conduct. Moreover, children should be taught to behave properly, not simply because it is expedient, but because it is right. If you avoid cheating, only because you fear being caught, then the educational system has failed you.

Ruse thus touches upon the question of why internalizing rules, or using one's conscience well, is so valuable. In this connection we may consider four possible kinds of people in respect to sociality (see also Table 2.5):

1. The brazen cheater or open egoist who does not internalize ( = pass to the subconscious?) concepts of right and wrong and does not seek to hide that he operates egoistically and nepotistically. Such people do not gain much good will.

2. The sneaky cheater (insincere altruist) who, like the brazen cheater, operates consciously to serve his own ends but attempts to conceal this fact. Sneaky cheaters may succeed sometimes, but if discovered they lose big, and their reputations spread quickly, partly because anyone who exposes such exploiters gains so much good will by the act.

3. The honorable egoist who accepts and internalizes rules taught or given to him and yet, excluding those rules per se, knowingly operates to serve his own ends (i.e., he accepts that acknowledging those rules also serves his own ends).

4. The self-professed altruist who accepts and internalizes the rules and believes, partly from them (and either rightly or wrongly), that he is indeed an altruist whose life is largely or wholly concerned with serving others, as opposed to himself. Such persons can be subdivided

into self-deceiving, self-serving moralists and true self-sacrificers or altruists. The latter,in turn, may either gain or lose, in evolutionary terms, because of the particular system of indirect reciprocity in which they practice their indiscriminate altruism.

Of course all people do not behave consistently according to one or another of these patterns. I suspect that most people, for example, know someone who appears to be a "true altruist" with respect to family, and who may parade this tendency and seek to be judged by it, yet is a brazen or sneaky cheater in business dealings; or vice versa. If they can detect these different ways of operating, I think people prefer to interact over long periods with honorable egoists over all the others (except, perhaps, true altruists, at least under some conditions). Certainly, honorable egoists are likely to be preferred over cheaters, and probably brazen over sneaky cheaters if the latter's strategy is detected. Is not this, and the value of the effort to detect cheaters, the evolutionary basis for the subconscious?

There are differences between teaching people to "help others or else" (you will be punished) and to "help others and (in the long run) you'll be helping yourself." For example, consider these two different possible strategies in educational efforts to develop the professional self-images of, say, physicians and lawyers. The former produces a cynic who tests each immediate situation to see if he can avoid the negative effects of failing to help. The second may produce a naive altruist who seems to bumble away whatever he accumulates. The trouble is, though, that in most social circumstances the chance to pay someone back (for either helping or not helping), and to avoid him or seek him out for establishing a reciprocal relationship if it were not actually you he was helping, are multiple and extend across long periods. If he were careful enough to assess his costs in the *immediate situation* (hence, seemed to be acting like a cynical cost–benefit assessor who contemplates the effects of each act upon his own interests), then astute observers would avoid him in future interactions in favor of others more likely to be more beneficent or less careful about their own or immediate self-interests, and he could lose mightily on that account. Also, he could err and fail to help when he should have on other grounds. In either case his tendency to be a conscious, deliberate, cynical, cost-benefit tester in each circumstance would cause him to lose. On the other hand, if he occasionally erred in the specific situation on the side of beneficence this would label him as a good interactant to seek out, and one to whom help could be given with little fear of being short-changed.

In any society in which coalitions and harmonious reciprocal interactions often lead to large gains for all participants (as compared to loners or those who must participate in less satisfactory or harmonious interactions or coalitions), he who errs on the side of beneficence has some likelihood of gaining in the long run. In this sense, the "rule utilitarian" (as opposed to the act utilitarian) would be best off. (A rule utilitarian is said to be one who supposedly always asks himself about each act, "What if *everyone* did this?" "What if there were a *rule* that this act is permissible?"; an act utilitarian asks, "What if *I* do this?") Indeed, it would be beneficial to parade one's self as an adherent to rule utilitarianism because of the implication of altruism (doing what is best for the group as a whole) and the effect of that implication on potential interactants. In this sense the very worst thing one could reveal to associates and potential interactants is that he is, first and foremost, a self-interested individual. One way of avoiding the impression that this might be so is to deny that hedonism or self-interest could possibly be a reasonable creed. Another is to believe sincerely that one is not self-interested. We see in these arguments a reason for promoting an ideally moral model of society that carries benefits for the promoter: it is a way of assisting others to believe that we ourselves are more moral than we are.

Lyons (1965) begins a discussion of the two kinds of utilitarianism with a story about a man and woman driving past an orchard. The woman says, "Oh, look, the apples are ripe, let's pick a few!" The man replies (*driving slower*), "No . . . what if everyone did the same." In his discussion of this conversation Lyons does not mention the possibility that the man may gain from convincing his companion (whether it is true or not) that he does not really believe in individuals opportunistically acting according to their own interests in individual situations. Since the story is about the interaction of a him and a her, the implication is that it is concerned with the ultimate situation with respect to the virtues of showing that one is not a cynical cost-benefit tester with one's own interests at heart.

Perhaps the most difficult question is how, if people have always been self-interested cost-benefit testers, any other impression could ever occur. The answer may lie partly in the differences in the way one treats relatives and nonrelatives. The testing of an associate may be a continual probing to see if weaknesses in his information or strategy can be exploited, including whether or not he can be induced to treat you like a relative.

Conscious concealment of interests, or disavowal, is deliberate deception, considered more reprehensible than anything not conscious. Indeed, if one does not know consciously what his interests are, he cannot, in *some* sense, be accused of deception even though he may be using an evolved ability of self-deception to deceive others. So it is not always—maybe not usually—in our evolutionary or surrogate-evolutionary interests to make them conscious (i.e., it does not always satisfy evolved proximate mechanisms even if interests are no longer reproductive). Maybe we resist finding out about the genes and their mission not only because bringing genes into our consciousness makes them seem like alien manipulators (which we are evolved to resist), but also because talking directly about our evolutionary background and the mission of our genes and our phenotypes is like making public our most importantly secret secret. Accepting the arguments of evolutionary biologists is like admitting that one is, after all, an egoist; I have just argued that this is a poor social strategy, at least for those whose actions do not speak louder than their words. It may also seem to be an acceptance that humans are immoral and can never be otherwise.

Each individual has a sphere of secrecy about him, small or large, that includes, I suggest, all those items he believes it would be detrimental to him (and sometimes to his relatives and friends) for others to know about; I further suggest that all through history we have tended to transfer this acceptance of secrecy, and desire for secrecy, upward as we have sought our goals through collective action in groups. In other words, we also seek to fulfill our personal interests by permitting and promoting secrecy in the interactions of different kinds of groups, including (especially) nations, for it is at "national" boundaries that our interests seem to change most sharply—national boundaries most dramatically define the alien, the strange, the enemy.

But we do not always draw boundaries so sharply, as is witnessed by the fact that we sometimes extend the concept of "rights" to include nonhuman organisms such as domesticated animals. The philosopher, Peter Singer (1981), in his book, *The Expanding Circle*, alludes to his arguments (expanded elsewhere) that rights must be extended even beyond sentient beings, to include rocks, trees, and other inanimate objects. (As a point of interest, until he makes that extension, his argument is unknowingly—apparently—extremely similar, using even similar words, to one made by Darwin, 1871.)

One's sphere of secrecy—of personally unique interests—can expand or contract according to certain specific aspects of behavior. Thus, if one marries, so long as he or she holds an absolute commitment to the partner, there is no necessity to hold any secrets about time, money, commitment, thoughts, or anything else in respect to one's partner (except information that might threaten the bond). If the partner is equally committed, the pair becomes a unit of interests against the world, without secrets from one another. Either lopsided family associations or opportunities to philander change this. Long-term monogamous fidelity is encouraged by others, and by governmental apparatuses as the extension of others' interests, perhaps because there is a stabilizing effect on the group as a whole. This may be owing both to the symmetry of interests within monogamous nuclear families and to the restriction of sexual competition monogamy imposes on men. Men are a divisively competitive subgroup in any human society and, historically, the subgroup upon which, in terms of defense, the survival of the group depends. So the particular route toward realization of one's interests that correlates with monogamy and devotion to the nuclear family has been encouraged in apparently every nation, and has tended to characterize those that have achieved and long maintained great sizes and unity (Alexander, 1978, 1979a; Alexander *et al.*, 1979; p. 71).

In effect, the realms in which secretiveness in behavior are required, or of considerable self-interest, expand as one tends to operate contrarily in respect to rules generally accepted by others. Since it is in everyone's interests to identify anyone not committed to the rules that are generally accepted and followed, it becomes increasingly difficult, risky, and self-consuming to add to the list of generally accepted rules one is going to avoid following. More and more of conscious time is used up in the effort to deceive successfully, and discovery becomes an increasingly expensive threat because of the significance of deliberateness in the effort, if it is discovered. Hence, also, at least part of the virtues of moralizing.

If people can be fooled—some all the time and all some of the time—then there will be continual selection for becoming better at fooling others (Trivers, 1971). This may include causing them to think that it will be best for them to help you when it is not. This ploy works because of the thin line everyone must continually tread with respect to not *showing* selfishness. If some people are self-destructively beneficent (i.e., make altruistic mistakes), and if people often cannot tell if one is such a mistake-maker, it might be profitable even to try to convince others that one is such a mistake-maker so as to be accepted as a cooperator or so that the other will be beneficent in expectation of large returns (through "mistakes") later. Of course, one may also be deceiving about his *ability* (as well as tendency) to give so that the other will think he has lots to expect later or that he and the deceiver can really help one another by *cooperation*. Reciprocity may work this way because it is grounded evolutionarily in nepotism, appropriate dispensing of nepotism (as well as reciprocity) depends upon learning, and the wrong things can be learned.

Self-deception, then, may not be a pathological or detrimental trait, at least in most people most of the time. Rather, it may have evolved as a way to deceive *others*. Self-deception is unlike at least *some* deception of others in that it need have no conscious aspect: the self-deceiver does not (necessarily) know he is deceiving himself. The *direct* other-deceiver usually (at least) does (see also Trivers, 1985).

Some aspects of religion and law and ethics contribute to deception of others by self-deception; Donald T. Campbell (1975) calls it "sincere hypocrisy" (see also Alexander, 1974, 1979a; Trivers, 1971, 1985). Righteousness is a source of motivation. We gain by thinking we are right, and by convincing both our allies and our enemies, because of the motivation it gives us. People often seem to *like* this aspect of self-deception: it provides an excuse or a rationale for sinking deeper into self-deception about motives and for justifying acts that could not otherwise be justified. This argument implies some control over self-deception, and I believe there may be a great deal of such control.

Fingarette (1969) illustrates what is probably the general view of self-deception: First, he sees self-deception as disadvantageous, speaking of the " . . . self-deceiver, the one who is both the doer and the sufferer" (p. 1). Second, he subscribes to the notion, quoting Bulwer-Lytton (p. 2), that "the easiest person to deceive is one's self." Third, he notes that various authors have agreed that self-deception occurs in regard to egoistic acts or impulses, quoting Camus (p. 2) "Then I realized, as a result of delving in my memory, that modesty helped me to shine, humility to conquer, and virtue to oppress . . . " He speaks (p. 9) of " . . . the retrogressive movement into self-deception" and " . . . the movement out of self-deception and into personal integrity and responsibility." Later (p. 32) Fingarette says: "The swindler's failure (to see the outcome of his swindle) does not involve loss of moral integrity; the self-deceiver's success does." Fourth, he notes (p. 4) that " . . . an analysis of self-deception will have an intimate bearing upon such concepts as 'conscious,' 'unconscious,' and 'defense,' and upon the elucidation of psychoanalytic and psychiatric theory more generally." Fifth, he discusses (p. 14 ff.) the "inner conflict" (quoting Demos) "supposedly involved in self-deception," noting that Demos says " . . . that there probably exists contradiction in self-deception, and that certainly there is a paradox inherent in the very notion of lying to one's self." He speaks (p. 19) of a mother who denies that her son is a scoundrel when everyone knows he is. He does not remark that if a person who *is expected to know*, or is in a position to know, declares, fervently and sincerely on an issue, we are quite likely to believe: " . . . the self-deceiver must, with a certain sincerity, not only deny believing but also deny seeing that the conclusion is established by the evidence" (p. 27).

Fingarette says (p. 28): "If our subject *persuades* himself to believe contrary to the evidence *in order to evade*, somehow, the unpleasant truth to which he has already seen that the evidence points, then and only then is he clearly a self-deceiver." He does not indicate that the manner of evasion of the "unpleasant truth" involves anyone else, or indeed goes beyond deceiving one's self about the unpleasant truth. Hence, his statement supports the notion that self-deception is maladaptive. If, on the other hand, the self-deception ("easy" to effect; effected through "persuading" one's self; etc.) has as its function the deception of others, much of the paradox disappears. In effect, we expect all of Fingarette's other characterizations of self-deception if it is in fact adaptive or advantageous for the self-deceiver. That would explain why it tends to involve egoistic behaviors, why it is easy to effect, and why it involves "defense" and the subconscious; it also resolves the central paradox in the concept, the "inner conflict," and the question of how it could ever come about, let alone be an apparently universal and central feature of the human psyche. None of Fingarette's various hypothetical (yet reasonable) examples of self-deception seems intractable to the notion that its function is to deceive others: a mother denying that her son is a scoundrel; a man denying that he has terminal cancer. This is not to argue that self-deception is *always* adaptive. The mother who at first denies that her child has been killed, later continuing the charade, may become obviously pathological. I think it is confusing to link this kind of denial of reality, or self-delusion, with the sincerity of everyday self-deception. The former may become more likely because the latter has evolved via a reproductive function or value, but this in no way negates the general adaptive hypothesis.

Later (p. 4), Fingarette comes close to an adaptive view of self-deception when he argues that:

> In general, a person in self-deception is a person of whom it is a patent characteristic that even when normally appropriate he *persistently* avoids spelling-out some feature of his engagement in the world . . . There is a trend of genuineness to his "ignoring"; it is not simple hypocrisy, or lying, or duping of others . . . The adoption of the *policy* of not spelling-out an engagement is a "self-covering" policy. To adopt it is, perforce, never to make it explicit, to "hide" it."

And (p. 62):

> . . . the self-deceiver is one whose life-situation is such that, on the bases of his tacit assessment of his situation, he finds there is overriding reason for adopting a policy or not spelling-out some engagement of his in the world

. . . it continues to be the case that the fabrications he tells us he also tells himself.

But Fingarette never does take the next step of arguing that self-deception is a *complex* "hypocrisy, or lying, or duping of others. . . . " In effect, if the hypothesis about self-deception proposed earlier (Alexander, 1979a) and discussed here is correct, it amounts to a proof that morality as seen by philosophers is a pursuit only and that humans are basically selfish (in reproductive terms).

One possible aspect of self-deception involves finding explanations for phenomena important to us that we cannot for some reason understand directly—such as our evolved *raison d'etre* before we knew about evolution, reproduction, and genes. Another may involve a value in not remembering or remembering wrongly. Still another involves justifying actions or attitudes that are selfish when it is not in our interests that they be so interpreted, and doing it so as to avoid the difficulties of conscious lying—in other words, a value in believing in one's own truthfulness, altruism, or sincerity while engaged in (or as a part of) deceiving someone else.

Prior to knowledge of evolution and genetics we could not know about genes, so if conscious thought has reproductive consequences we should have found the closest substitute for this concept, which, in practical terms, I think, is *family* (and we count genealogical links to determine relatedness and how to treat relatives). We should be expected sometimes to make up substitute or wrong reasons. For example, the real reasons for outbreeding have also been inaccessible, since even biologists cannot yet explain it fully (because their under-standing of the function of sexuality itself is still incomplete). Accord-ingly we *use* whatever deleterious effects arise, and we also use the social machinery, to make incest a horror: we revile those who engage in it. Consider, for example, the fear that a relative might marry a person whose relatives—because of their social access to that person and a failure to abhor incest—might cuckold one's own relative. Such a fear could lead to a severe and general ostracizing of incestuous families—especially of their young females as potential mates.

Given that ethical, moral behavior is learned, and that we somehow know this, it would seem that mere repetitions of assertions about what constitutes morality might teach in the direction desired. Is it, then, surprising that people cling to and repeat phrases such as "Justice will prevail," "People are really basically fair," and "We all know what is right and what is wrong"? And, as well, is it surprising that people should recoil, automatically and violently, from analyses (by biologists or whomever) that publish conclusions such as "People are basically selfish," "Justice is necessarily incomplete and imperfect," and "Right and wrong are not absolutes but depend on the circumstances, and opinions may vary"?

> . . . by the cultivation of large and generous desires . . . men can be brought to act more than they do at present in a manner that is consistent with the general happiness of mankind. (Bertrand Russell, 1935, p. 255)

## MYTHS AND SELF-IMAGES

CYNIC:

> . . . a misanthrope, specif., one who believes that human conduct is motivated wholly by self-interest
>> Webster's Dictionary (5th ed., 1974,
>> Springfield, MA: G. and C. Merriam Co.)

> A blackguard whose faulty vision sees things as they are, not as they ought to be.
>> The Devil's Dictionary (Ambrose Bierce, 1911,
>> NY: Crowell)

If ability and tendency to form a self-image is evolved, then we expect a self-image to consist in large part of a view of the kinds of actions or attitudes one supposes will best serve his own interests. Once evolved, the tendency to form a self-image must have become a target of the reproductive striving of competitors. It should be a common ploy to attempt to manipulate the self-images of others to serve not their interests but one's own. Probably the most significant area of manipulation of self-image is the parent–offspring interaction. There can be no doubt that parents strive to create and adjust the self-images of their offspring, and humans may have evolved to accept many such efforts, especially while young and naive.

A presumed value of self-image seems to me to underlie many of what I would call the prevalent myths about sociality. I have just argued that resistance to evolutionary analyses of human behavior partly involves a myth of self-image—the notion that if we have been cruel or racist or selfish during history and if we uncover and publicize biological reasons for such behavior *in the past*, then by acknowledging that history and accepting that those reasons may be accurate, we are producing a self-image of humanity, and ourselves as parts of it, that will increase our tendencies to carry out and accept cruelty, racism, and selfishness in the future.

Let us consider some of these myths. First is the myth of creation, and all myths bound up in biblical narratives about supposedly subsequent events. There is no pretense in this myth that humans are basically good—at least not following the "fall from grace." The central point is that no matter how bad humanity may be, there is a just and all-powerful God who is the source of the moral rules or notions about right and wrong, and of moral laws, and it is God's laws that must be followed. So long as what are interpreted as God's laws seem designed to produce the self-image in everyone of being an altruistic contributor to society, such laws are unlikely to encounter much opposition even from those who do not accept them as God's word. In a world of egoists, the only one who suffers from exhortations that "Everyone should try to be like Jesus" is the one who succeeds (or, more accurately, succeeds *too soon*, before society has developed the machinery to reward a rush of indiscriminate altruism).

The second myth of this sort that intrigues me I will call the central myth of modern anthropology. It says that humans lived 99% of their existence as small, peaceful, nomadic, separated family groups of hunter-gatherers whose life was almost solely made up of cooperation with scarcely any competitiveness, aggression, or nastiness of any kind. Symons (1979) says that "The hunting and gathering way of life is the only stable, persistent adaptation humans have ever achieved." He describes this as " . . . a way of life characterized by small groups, low population densities, division of labor by sex, infanticide, and nomadism." Alexander and Tinkle (1968), Alexander (1971, 1979a), Bigelow (1969), Dawkins (1976), and others have argued that this description, which is the standard description of modern hunter-gatherers, could not be true of anywhere near 99% of human history, and that it describes humans that today exist in low population densities and are nomadic because they have been pushed by the rest of humanity to the ecological outposts of the world—the harshest deserts and the Arctic: it is a way of life that is stable because it has so far been *forced* on those who follow it. I have argued (Alexander, 1979a) that modern hunter-gatherers more than likely came from richer habitats and regions of higher population densities rather than vice versa. Ember's (1978) demonstration that such isolated peoples are capable of considerable aggressiveness seems to me to support this hypothesis, as does the present general richness of human habitat across the world and the densities of human populations. It is part of my argument that hunter-gatherers in rich habitats do not behave like hunter-gatherers in the sparsely populated ecological outposts of the planet.

Later in his book (1979, pp. 146–158), Symons argues for precisely the same view of human history that I (and others, e.g., Bigelow, 1969; Strate,

1982; Betzig, 1986) do. This argument is not consistent with the central myth of separated, low-density, nomadic hunter-gatherer groups struggling against climatic extremes. Symons also discusses chimpanzees as "model human ancestors" doing many of the things we humans have done continually throughout recorded history: stealing women, killing strangers, and ganging up to fight, test neighbors, and capture prey.

Modern society is filled with myths perpetuated because of their presumed value in regard to self-images: that scientists are humble and devoted truth-seekers; that doctors dedicate their lives to alleviation of suffering; that teachers dedicate their lives to their students; that we are all basically law-abiding, kind, altruistic souls who place everyone's interests before our own; that our country (church, family) is always right and benevolent and has never done anything with malice or malevolence as a part of the motivation; that our nation is on the side of right (and we alone sit down to arms negotiations because of our "good will"); that God is on our side; etc.

Recently, a branch of anthropology calling itself "symbolic anthropology" has argued that human history is largely to be understood by analyzing the meanings of myths—as some say, the meaning of meaning. If so, one has to believe as well that much of the future depends upon our responses to our own myths. I have little doubt that this is true. I would argue, first, that there is no better reason for understanding our mythologies—both in terms of how particular myths have generated and why they have taken their particular forms. Second, I would argue that the only reasonable way to progress toward such an understanding is through scientific analysis, by which I mean simply analyses that have built into them the criterion of repeatability so that their assumptions, speculations, and hypotheses can be falsified if they are indeed false, and their results can be verified by careful repetition to test their accuracy. No other procedure allows us to generate a cumulative growth of true understanding of any topic, particularly human behavior where our different interests conflict so directly.

An especially good example of how myths and self-images can lead us in unwanted directions lies before us at the moment. Anyone can inform himself of its nature and its danger by reading the book *Countdown to Armageddon* by Hal Lindsey (1980). This book puts into a compelling narrative a particular version of the biblical prophesy that has been developing across the past decades, mainly by fundamentalist Protestants. This account seems so constructed as to interrelate closely with current events, particularly the arms race and U.S.–Soviet relations. It contends that the biblical prophesies include a set of events beginning with the restoration to the Jews of their homeland, which, as subsequent events fall into place, leads inevitably to Armageddon, apparently seen as nuclear holocaust. Russia is suggested as a dark force from the north that will attack Israel, initiating the step that makes Armageddon inevitable. This last step occurs after Russia becomes the most powerful nation in the world. Because, as Lindsey and others see it, the United States is not alluded to in any fashion in the Bible, Armageddon will presumably be prevented so long as the U.S. is more powerful than Russia. The conclusion seems to be that if one is indeed a true believer he will welcome Armageddon and the opportunity to meet his maker and see God's will be done. If he is not quite this dedicated then the interpretation could be that postponing Armageddon depends upon our ability to support the U.S. in some kind of all-out nuclear arms race in which we absolutely reject the possibility of being the second most powerful nation.

Hal Lindsey's books are read by millions; the jacket of this particular book describes him as one of the few authors to have three books on the bestseller list simultaneously, and this book has sold 15 million copies. The New York Times designated him as the writer of the decade of the 1970's. It is disturbing that circumstances could prevail in which the end of civilization, or of life on earth, could be brought about by enough people, and the right people, accepting his scenario. Who would not be frightened to find, say, the President of the United States, or his Secretary of State or Defense, or any other high official, quoting this scenario? As Martin (1982) has pointed out, it is not beyond credibility that a high official, faced with a critical decision, might be more likely to push a button if he believed he was thereby carrying out the will of God (*Newsweek*, 5 November 1984, reported that some religious leaders are concerned that the president may be "unduly influenced in foreign affairs by a 'theology of nuclear armageddon'").

To reduce the banal possibility of Lindsey's kinds of prophecies becoming self-fulfilling we must understand ourselves and our mythologies much better than we do now. Science is the only means, unless we are prepared to accept divine revelation as a source of information. Only science, among human activities, comes close to being a self-correcting method of pursuing the truth. Ironically, we must be no less constrained, in "scientific" pursuits of self-understanding, to recognize self-fulfilling myths.

## Life History Theory and the Ontogeny of Moral Behavior

Studies of the development of attitudes toward moral questions in individuals can be correlated with theories about sequences of different kinds of effort in biological theories of lifetimes.

## INTRODUCTION

The transfer of the individual's interests from itself alone (direct somatic effort) to include others (indirect somatic effort and reproductive effort) not only involves some of what we ordinarily term altruism (here discussed as social beneficence), it also involves a shift from more immediate to less immediate consequences. I am going to use the extensive studies of the psychologist, Lawrence Kohlberg (see Kohlberg, 1981, 1984), to show how the findings of social and biological scientists may be joined to make more sense from each. If one looks at Kohlberg's proposed stages in the development of morality one sees shifts that seem to reflect (1) the appearance of reciprocity in systems of rewards and punishment between parents and child, (2) the use of indirect reciprocity as a way of gaining long-term benefits, (3) the onset of tendencies (a) to take less than possible for one's self and (b) to help others, (4) the onset of tendencies to use one's own judgment rather than that of others to make the decision to be beneficent (or invest socially), and (5) a general shift from being a relatively powerless acceptor of imposed costs and benefits (a rule-follower) to being first a rule-enforcer and finally a rule-maker. These are my interpretations, not those of Kohlberg, but they clarify for me why it might be expected that some individuals in all cultures and most individuals in some cultures do not achieve one or both of Kohlberg's final "stages" of "moral development." If one sees himself as principally a victim of the rules of others, and as never having (enough of) a hand in devising the rules, he is scarcely as likely to become a defender of the rules.

In Kohlberg's Level A the child depends on immediate rewards and punishments: nothing is given up for later or long-term rewards. In Level B immediate rewards are foregone in the interests of longer-term rewards, and the decisions or actions are based on an expectation of reciprocity (reward) from the individuals in the child's immediate group or actual presence. In Level C the individual has so effectively absorbed knowledge of the systems of rewards and punishments within society at large that (I suggest) it profits from using its own judgment, or following its conscience, and sometimes reaps rewards not solely from persons and groups involved at the time or in its immediate group.

I have repeated here Kohlberg's (1981) description of his six stages of moral development (pp. 409–412), adding, for each stage, an evolutionary-biological hypothesis. I am aware of the extensive literature critical of Kohlberg's conclusions (well reviewed by Kohlberg, 1984), and I do not regard certain of the dogmas, such as that these "stages" are absolutely developmental, hence never reversible, as satisfactorily demonstrated. Nevertheless, it seems to me that if one begins with the concepts of somatic and reproductive effort, acknowledges their sequencing in the organism's lifetime, and then goes on to subdivide them, as I have done above, he is drawn to the hypothesis that some sort of predictable sequence of stages will emerge eventually from increasingly astute analyses of life patterns. [The criticism that Kolberg's approach does not provide explanations for individual differences (cf. Wilson and Herrnstein, 1985) bears on the usefulness of the conclusions in certain contexts, not on their general validity or overall significance.] It is possible that examining Kohlberg's results in light of a biological view of human sociality and the structure of lifetimes may resolve some of the controversies.

## KOLBERG'S STAGES, WITH AN EVOLUTIONARY HYPOTHESIS FOR EACH

Level A. Preconventional Level

Stage 1. The Stage of Punishment and Obedience

*Content*

Right is literal obedience to rules and authority, avoiding punishment, and not doing physical harm.

1. What is right is to avoid breaking rules, to obey for obedience' sake, and to avoid doing physical damage to people and property.
2. The reasons for doing right are avoidance of punishment and the superior power of authorities.

*Social Perspective*

This stage takes an egocentric point of view. A person at this stage doesn't consider the interests of others or recognize they differ from actor's, and doesn't relate the two points of view. Actions are judged in terms of physical consequences rather than in terms of psychological interests of others. Authority's perspective is confused with one's own.

*Evolutionary Hypothesis.* Kohlberg is close to describing a stage of juvenile life in which all activities represent direct somatic effort. If there is at first truly an absence of concern with others' viewpoints, even with those of parents and other caretakers, what is implied is that human children have been so altricial (helpless) for so long that adults have evolved to accept (tolerate) their total attention to their own interests. If Kohlberg's "physical consequences" include punishment by other humans, however, and if "confusion" of authority's perspective with one's own involves tendencies to adopt the views of those with power, then the implication (which I think is Kohlberg's) is, rather, that indirect somatic effort is mixed with direct somatic effort more or less from the start. Either possibility is compatible with an evolutionary approach, although I would favor the suggestion that very young children at first exhibit only direct somatic effort in their interactions with others. The question of interest comes to involve degree of altricialness and its effects on social interactions between children and (principally) parents.

Stage 2. The Stage of Individual Instrumental Purpose and Exchange

*Content*

Right is serving one's own or other's needs and making fair deals in terms of concrete exchange.

1. What is right is following rules when it is to someone's immediate interest. Right is acting to meet one's own interests and needs and letting others do the same. Right is also what is fair; that is, what is an equal exchange, a deal, an agreement.
2. The reason for doing right is to serve one's own needs or interests in a world where one must recognize that other people have their interests, too.

*Social Perspective*

This stage takes a concrete individualistic perspective. A person at this stage separates own interests and points of view from those of authorities and others. He or she is aware everybody has individual interests to pursue and these conflict, so that right is relative (in the concrete individualistic sense). The person integrates or relates conflicting individual interests to one another through instrumental exchange of services, through instrumental need for the other and the other's goodwill, or through fairness giving each person the same amount.

*Evolutionary Hypothesis.* Kohlberg seems to give an almost perfect description of purely somatic effort in a social situation in which a mix of direct and indirect (socially mediated) somatic effort is the only way best to serve one's own interests. The only departure is his suggestion of "through fairness giving each person the same amount." One is inclined to take more seriously the preceding phrase implying instead whatever contributions are required to secure "the other's goodwill." But there are obviously circumstances in which the participants' keenness of observation requires "giving each person the same amount" if "the other's [others'] goodwill" is to be secured. Powerful awareness of direct reciprocity is implied, with indirect reciprocity obviously becoming involved. It is possible that a more satisfactory classification could be developed by trying to identify the manner and timing of introduction of awareness of indirect reciprocity. Birth order and spacing might be important variables.

Level B. Conventional Level

Stage 3. The Stage of Mutual Interpersonal Expectations, Relationships, and Conformity

*Content*

The right is playing a good (nice) role, being concerned about the other people and their feelings, keeping loyalty and trust with partners, and being motivated to follow rules and expectations.

1. What is right is living up to what is expected by people close to one or what people generally expect of people in one's role as son, sister, friend, and so on. "Being good" is important and means having good motives, showing concern about others. It also means keeping mutual relationships, maintaining trust, loyalty, respect, and gratitude.
2. Reasons for doing right are needing to be good in one's own eyes and those of others, caring for others, and because if one puts oneself in the other person's place one would want good behavior from the self (Golden Rule).

*Social Perspective*

This stage takes the perspective of the individual in relationship to other individuals. A person at this stage is aware of shared feelings, agreements, and expectations, which take primacy over individual interests. The person relates points of view through the "concrete Golden Rule," putting oneself in the other person's shoes. He or she does not consider generalized "system" perspective.

*Evolutionary Hypothesis.* Here Kohlberg's description has clearly brought indirect reciprocity to the fore. Although Kohlberg says that "shared feelings, agreements, and expectations . . . take primacy over individual matters," consistency with the arguments presented here would mean that shared feelings, agreements, and expectations represent the avenues by which individual interests are most likely to be realized. Similarly, putting oneself in the other person's shoes (including concern with the "concrete Golden Rule"), "having good motives, showing concern about others," and "keeping mutual relationships, maintaining trust, loyalty, respect, and gratitude" are all part of participating in systems of indirect reciprocity. Kohlberg carefully distinguishes between such participation and the awareness of a "generalized 'system' perspective" in order to make clear how the next stage differs.

There is no easy way to decide when and how reproductive effort begins to be involved in moral development as Kohlberg describes it. Indirect reciprocity is involved in both somatic and reproductive effort. It seems to me, though, that the particular kind of concern for the rules that begins to be powerfully in evidence in the next stage is more consistent with concern that one's social contributions result in benefits to relatives.

Stage 4. The Stage of Social System and Conscience Maintenance
*Content*

The right is doing one's duty in society, upholding the social order, and maintaining the welfare of society or the group.
1. What is right is fulfilling the actual duties to which one has agreed. Laws are to be upheld except in extreme cases where they conflict with other fixed social duties and rights. Right is also contributing to society, the group, or institution.
2. The reasons for doing right are to keep the institution going as a whole, self-respect or conscience as meeting one's defined obligations, or the consequences: "What if everyone did it?"

*Social Perspective*

This stage differentiates societal point of view from interpersonal agreement or motives. A person at this stage takes the viewpoint of the system, which defines roles and rules. He or she considers individual relations in terms of place in the system.

## Level B/C. Transitional Level

This level is postconventional but not yet principled.

*Content of Transition*

At Stage 4½, choice is personal and subjective. It is based on emotions, conscience is seen as arbitrary and relative, as are ideas such as "duty" and "morally right."

*Transitional Social Perspective*

At this stage, the perspective is that of an individual standing outside of his own society and considering himself as an individual making decisions without a generalized commitment or contract with society. One can pick and choose obligations, which are defined by particular societies, but one has no principles for such choice.

## Level C. Postconventional and Principled Level

Moral decisions are generated from rights, values, or principles that are (or could be) agreeable to all individuals composing or creating a society designed to have fair and beneficial practices.

*Evolutionary Hypothesis.* Kohlberg here describes a stage at which the rules of society begin to be important to the individual. If we continue to interpret moral development in terms of somatic and reproductive effort, then I would interpret this stage as the beginnings of serious concern that *others* behave in ways beneficial to one's self and one's relatives. In other words, I am (perhaps more importantly) hypothesizing that Kohlberg has now begun to talk specifically about individuals concerned with reproductive effort. I see Kohlberg's Stage 4 as representing a transition from being primarily a rule-follower to being also concerned with rule enforcement. This interpretation is consistent with the idea that after having learned and followed the rules one's self, having invested in the system, and having produced and instructed relatives with whose welfare one is ultimately concerned, there is reproductive value in ensuring that one's investment is safe, i.e., that the rules do not change.

Here my interpretation begins to take an increasingly serious divergence from that of Kohlberg and, indeed, from those of most contemporary interpreters of morality. I see these final "stages" of moral "development" as being just as self-serving (in reproductive terms) as the first three stages. They represent the transitions to (1) reproductive effort being paramount (somatic effort having been reduced toward maintenance per se), (2) seeking positions of power, and (3) concern with enforcement of the rules under which one has learned to operate and according to which one has made his investments in society. The difference between this reproductively self-serving interpretation and the increasingly altruistic interpretations of others is very great indeed. Its implications for the understanding of society, and for the question of why some individuals do not enter into the last three stages of moral "development" are enormously important. If one has been prevented from investing significantly, if one has been thwarted in the gaining of power (or the *feeling* of having invested successfully or having gained power), then it will likely serve one's interests to resist becoming a rule-enforcer.

Stage 5. The Stage of Prior Rights and Social Contract or Utility
*Content*
The right is upholding the basic rights, values, and legal contracts of a society, even when they conflict with the concrete rules and laws of the group.
1. What is right is being aware of the fact that people hold a variety of values and opinions, that most values and rules are relative to one's group. These "relative" rules should usually be upheld, however, in the interest of impartiality and because they are the social contract. Some nonrelative values and rights such as life and liberty, however, must be upheld in any society and regardless of majority opinion.
2. Reasons for doing right are, in general, feeling obligated to obey the law because one has made a social contract to make and abide by laws for the good of all and to protect their own rights and the rights of others. Family, friendship, trust, and work obligations are also commitments or contracts freely entered into and entail respect for the rights of others. One is concerned that laws and duties be based on rational calculation of overall utility: "the greatest good for the greatest number."

*Social Perspective*
This stage takes a prior-to-society-perspective—that of a rational individual aware of values and rights prior to social attachments and contracts. The person integrates perspectives by formal mechanisms of agreement, contract, objective impartiality, and due process. He or she considers the moral point of view and the legal point of view, recognizes they conflict, and finds it difficult to integrate them.

*Evolutionary Hypothesis.* Here much of Kohlberg's description suggests more or less complete commitment to the notion of rule enforcement. This is consistent with the discussion of Stage 4, except for Kohlberg's final statement (of content). If Kohlberg means to imply that a significant proportion of the populace of the world either implicitly or explicitly favors a system in which everyone (including himself) behaves so as to bring the greatest good to the greatest number, then I simply believe that he is wrong. If he supposes that only a relatively few— particularly moral philosophers and some others like them—have achieved this "stage," then I also doubt the hypothesis. I accept that many people are aware of this concept of utility, that a small minority may advocate it, and that an even smaller minority may actually believe that they behave according to it. I speculate, however, that with a few inadvertent or accidental exceptions, no one actually follows this precept. I see the concept as having its main utility as a goal toward which one may exhort others to aspire, and toward which one may behave as if (or talk as if) aspiring while actually practicing complex forms of self-interest. In other words, I see this form of utilitarianism as a concept useful to those with *more* power and influence in getting those with *less* power and influence to behave in fashions more useful to the former than to the latter. It represents a transition from rule-*enforcer* to rule-*maker*, and is consistent with the acquisition of power by those engaged in reproductive effort (note, however, that general preoccupation with this idea or goal, and shifts induced in its direction whatever their basis or motivation, will—as discussed elsewhere in this book—expose those who lag or deviate too far and thus provide a self-reinforcing propulsion in the direction of utilitarianism). I have not seen this hypothesis advanced before. It is a radical departure from current interpretations, and at the least it seems to deserve inclusion in the mix of ideas and propositions currently being developed in the efforts to unravel human sociality.

Stage 6. The Stage of Universal Ethical Principles

*Content*

This stage assumes guidance by universal ethical principles that all humanity should follow.

1. Regarding what is right, Stage 6 is guided by universal ethical principles. Particular laws or social agreements are usually valid because they rest on such principles. When laws violate these principles, one acts in accordance with the principle. Principles are universal principles of justice: the equality of human rights and respect for the dignity of human beings as individuals. These are not merely values that are recognized, but are also principles used to generate particular decisions.

2. The reason for doing right is that, as a rational person, one has seen the validity of principles and has become committed to them.

*Social Perspective*

This stage takes the perspective of a moral point of view from which social arrangements derive or on which they are grounded. The perspective is that of any rational individual recognizing the nature of morality or the basic moral premise of respect for other persons as ends, not means.

*Evolutionary Hypothesis.* I see Kohlberg's Stage 6 as a logical outgrowth of his interpretation of earlier stages. From his viewpoint it is a culmination of step-by-step progress toward an ideal of morality as universal indiscriminate altruism. For me it is rather a culmination of the tendency to become preoccupied with rule-following, rule-enforcement, and rule-making by those increasingly concerned with reproductive effort, use of power, and confidence that one's investments in reciprocity were not in vain and will continue to serve one's relatives after one's own demise. There is, however, much more to it than this. Discussions of indiscriminate altruism recur throughout this book.

In a sense, even indirect reciprocity in the human child may ordinarily precede nepotism developmentally, since the child may, in effect, be coerced by its parents to be more beneficent or to be beneficent earlier, than would otherwise be in its own interests. In such cases, the child is actually behaving more like an adult involved in a system of reciprocity (with its parent), or submitting to an imposed moral system, than like an adult in a nepotistic system, since it behaves "altruistically" to avoid punishment or to secure approval, the latter leading to later benefits. The development of a satisfactory or effective view of reciprocity in a child may depend on the consistency of reward and punishment that we are told by psychologists is so important in child training. It is interesting to contemplate the steps by which a child might be led into the one-way beneficence of nepotism, in which the only expected return is the pleasure of witnessing or knowing about the success (or pleasure) of the recipient of one's beneficence. It would appear that because of the nature of this return, the relationship between nepotism and reciprocity is much more complex than has been suspected. I would speculate that the evolution of reciprocal beneficence has occurred in the following sequence:

1. Simple reinforcement, without consciousness involved (at first)
2. Nepotistic beneficence (at first only parent to child, without consciousness or deliberateness)
3. Discrimination of different relatives with respect to degree of relatedness and need (again, not involving conscious awareness)
4. Reciprocity (social investment) involving relatives
5. Discrimination of nonreciprocating relatives
6. Reciprocity to nonrelatives

In contrast, it seems likely that in the moral development of the individual child the sequence may be something like (1) (4) (5) (6) (3) (2), with conscious awareness involved in the last two or three. I also speculate that the reasons for this shift are (a) the extraordinarily complex and central role of reciprocity in human social life, causing attention to its skills to be more important to the developing individual than any other effort and (b) shifts in the use and prominence of what I have been calling conscious awareness in social interactions. The addition of conscious awareness I would see, both phylogenetically and ontogenetically, as principally a way of refining responses and increasing their reproductive appropriateness. This would seem especially relevant in assessing the significance of indirect reciprocity in some instances.

It is apparent that to leave the beneficence of nepotism out of the picture in experimental, developmental, or social psychology as well as moral and legal philosophy is to handicap severely the probability of progress toward explication. To connect child development as well as adult attributes and tendencies to the social actions and systems by which individual interests are realized in biological terms thus seems to me a potentially valuable enterprise. Martin (1954), for example, writes as follows:

> The child values food, rest, activity, and freedom from pain. In this sense, he is not a creature without values. But his values are rooted in his biology. The exact nature of that which satisfies his searching is only grossly defined. He must yet develop the specific goals, but the general direction and orientation is there. (p. 211)

In other words, the child is at first selfish, because he is still wholly a bundle of somatic effort. Martin continues:

> The man also values food, warmth, rest, activity, and freedom from pain. But he has come to value other things more. He will do without adequate rest in order to get a work assignment finished. He will endure pain in order to gain social approval. He will accept all kinds of biological deprivations in order that the members of his family may enjoy certain comforts and advantages.
>
> What is the nature of the process by which man takes on a different set of values, values derived from the society in which he lives, values which are often in conflict with his biological needs, values which give him a new orientation and direction? (p. 211)

Martin's descriptions of child and adult are entirely consistent with evolutionary theory, and the questions he poses are those posed by life history or "effort" theorists in biology. It seems to me that there is no source other than biology for an answer.

Dawkins also (1976) raises issues in child development when he states:

> Be warned that if you wish, as I do, to build a society in which individuals cooperate generously and unselfishly towards a common good, you can expect little help from biological nature. Let us try to *teach* generosity and altruism, because we are born selfish. (p. 3)

This statement obfuscates things because it implies that if we are "born selfish" that is somehow our nature, or it is immutable during development unless combated directly. It implies that to "try to *teach* generosity and altruism" is difficult because it goes against human nature. But generosity and altruism are older than Dawkins implies, and far more complex. I hypothesize that they are as integral a part of human nature as being "born selfish." They are, however, a part of reproductive effort, and being "born selfish" speaks only of somatic effort. If generosity and unselfishness are *reproductively* selfish because they are typically directed at relatives or at others who will reciprocate with interest, this has little to do with the kind of selfishness shown by newborns. It is even more removed to deal with the question of "common good." The important points are that we do not remain as we are when born, and because generosity and unselfishness as usually expressed and identified are evidently complex forms of reproductive selfishness, it might sometimes be more difficult to prevent their appearance in the developing human than to cause it. Moreover, generosity and unselfishness are probably not taught because otherwise we would grow up to be selfish, but because otherwise we would grow up to be bumblers rather than experts at self-interested activities. Up to now, I would argue, social learning has been all about becoming better at self-interest—indeed, about becoming so good at it that we will be regarded as honest, kind, fair, impartial, reliable, and altruistic not only by our social interactants but also by our own conscious selves.

## General Conclusions

I have now completed what might be called the preliminary arguments. They lead to the following conclusions:

1. All of the great and worrisome problems of the world involve moral and ethical questions.

2. Moral and ethical questions derive from conflicts of interest, and from the social responses of humans as organisms whose genetic materials have accumulated as a result of evolution by natural selection.

3. To understand conflicts of interest we must first develop a theory of interests. In terms of evolutionary history the ultimate interests of organisms, including humans, are in maximizing the likelihood of survival of their genetic materials through reproduction; we expect organisms to find pleasure in, seek out, or be satisfied by activities that in the environments of history would accomplish this end.

4. Human "interests," then, may be said to be reproductive, whether or not and to whatever extent (a) such knowledge is conscious and (b) evolutionary novelties in the environment thwart realization of reproductive interests.

5. In sexually reproducing organisms like ourselves conflicts of interest arise and exist because of histories of genetic individuality; they are evidently absent within clones in species with a long history of asexuality.

6. In sexually reproducing social organisms degrees of genetic difference, and therefore degrees of difference in reproductive interests, are expected to correlate in nonnovel social environments with degrees of conflict and cooperation (as Hamilton, 1964, and others have noted, this correlation must be considered in light of other variables, such as differences among relatives of equal degree in ability to use resources to reproduce). Quantification of conflict and cooperation thus begins with knowledge of degrees of genetic relatedness and how these correlate with proximate mechanisms of kin recognition to pattern the structure of social behavior (differences in information and perception may lead to apparent conflicts of interest; we would expect these to be minimal or absent without a history of conflicts of interest resulting from a history of genetic differences).

7. A theory of interests is a theory of lifetimes. Lifetimes are evolved to be composed of (a) somatic effort and (b) reproductive effort. Somatic effort increases reproductive value (if, in evolutionary terms, appropriately directed); reproductive effort leads to reproduction and lowers residual reproductive value. Reproductive effort is divisible into mating, parental, and extraparental nepotistic effort.

8. Effort in humans may be more easily understood by regarding somatic effort as direct and indirect, the latter involving both direct and indirect reciprocity. Similarly, reproductive effort (gametic, parental, and extraparental nepotistic) may be divided into direct and indirect nepotism, the latter involving indirect reciprocity.

9. In direct reciprocity the return is from the recipient of the beneficence; in indirect reciprocity the return comes from someone other than the originally beneficent individual. Returns from indirect reciprocity may take any of three (or more) forms: (a) The beneficent individual may be engaged in profitable reciprocal interactions by others who have observed his behavior in reciprocal interactions and judge him to be a potentially rewarding interactant, (b) the beneficent individual may be rewarded with compensation from all or part of the group (such as with money or a medal or social elevation as a hero) which, in turn, increases his likelihood of receiving additional perquisites, or (c) the beneficent individual's relatives may be compensated ( = indirect nepotism).

10. The "egoism" discussed by philosophers and other nonbiologists can be understood in biological terms as direct somatic effort which is both personally and reproductively selfish. The "altruism" discussed by

philosophers and other nonbiologists, which (except for evolutionary "mistakes") is reproductively (genotypically) selfish and sometimes phenotypically selfish, can be understood in biological terms as indirect somatic effort and direct and indirect nepotism.

11. We are thus evolved to be nepotists, even though, because of the role of social learning and the nature of consciousness, purpose, and deliberation, we are not *obliged* to be nepotists.

12. In the development of the individual, reciprocity evidently appears before nepotism: acceptance of temporary one-way flows of benefits tied to promises of rewards precedes acceptance of long-term one-way flows of benefits. This situation may have appeared, in evolution, as a consequence of the way in which humans were evolving the ability to absorb through learning how to exploit most effectively the complexities of human social organization.

13. Senescence, defined as increasing susceptibility to environmental insults, is a central aspect of the patterning of lifetimes. It has evolved as an incidental, pleiotropic effect of the evolution of lifetimes as efforts to maximize success in genetic reproduction. It is expected to onset approximately when reproductive effort onsets (because residual reproductive effort diminishes from that point on and the effectiveness of selection is correspondingly reduced) and to occur gradually in iteroparous organisms and suddenly in semelparous organisms.

14. Within sexual species extreme cooperativeness correlates with similarity of genetic interests, whether in parents committed to lifetime monogamy, in the extraordinary nuclear families of the eusocial insects, or in humans or other groups temporarily subjected to extreme outside threats.

15. Clones became large and cooperative because the members are genetically identical (hence, have identical genetic interests), and are able somehow to enhance their collective interest by so doing.

16. Eusocial insects and monogamous pairs cooperate because they reproduce via the same third parties, which are their closest relatives, hence the cooperating individuals share genetic interests.

17. Communicative signals typically involve deception. Those between monogamous spouses or eusocial insect workers may be honest because their interests are (often, at least) identical. Signals passed between close relatives and some others have a large core of honesty and a "restrained" embellishment because of broad overlap of interests. Those passing between sharp competitors within species are restricted in their embellishment only by the limits of gullibility, and still others, as with some of those between predators and prey (e.g., mimicry), are expected to be totally deceptive.

18. Conflicts of interest become most intense and important in social groups of partial relatives or nonrelatives, because of (a) the proximity of competitors and (b) the power that results from cooperation. Group living—its causes and effects—thus becomes a focus of our interests.

19. Larger and larger social groups, human and otherwise, have evidently formed and maintained themselves by somehow moving toward leveling of reproductive opportunities among those with conflicts of interest. Generally speaking, the bigger the group, the more complex the social organization, and the greater the group's unity of purpose the more limited is individual entrepreneurship. (The relationship between size and reproductive opportunity leveling is not simple: in intermediate-sized groups despotism increases with increasing group size; Betzig, 1986; Alexander, 1979a.)

20. In humans reproductive opportunity leveling occurs via the establishment and enforcement of the rules, compromises, and contracts of moral, ethical, and legal systems. Unlike the only other sexually reproducing, nonclonal groups to achieve group sizes in the millions (eusocial insects), in humans the tendency has been for all individuals to be directly reproductive, with the opportunities of doing so in the largest groups leveled by socially imposed monogamy, suffrage, welfare, and other trends toward justice as impartiality.

21. Moral systems are systems of indirect reciprocity. They exist because of conflicts of interest, and arise as an outcome of the complexity of social interactions in groups of long-lived individuals with (a) varying conflicts and confluences of interest, (b) indefinitely iterated social interactions, and (c) multiple alternate interactants.

22. The function or *raison d'etre* of moral systems is evidently to provide the unity required to enable the group to compete successfully with other human groups. Only in humans is the major hostile force of life composed of other groups in the same species.

23. Although morality may now be seen as involving justice for all people, or consistency in the social treatment of all other humans, the concept may have arisen for what would now be seen generally as immoral reasons, as a force leading to internal cohesiveness within human groups, specifically excluding and directed against other human groups with different interests.

24. Consciousness and related aspects of the human psyche have evolved as a system for developing and utilizing social scenarios to one's own advantage in competing with others for status, resources, and eventually reproductive success.

The arguments of moral and legal philosophers have so far been independent of some of the considerations discussed in this chapter, which arise out of recent biological theory. To explain the significance of this fact, and the effect of adding biological considerations to philosophical arguments about morality, I will now go directly to an analysis of the arguments of philosophers and other human-oriented students of social life.

> I do not think that we have adequately determined the nature and number of the appetites, and until this is accomplished the inquiry will always be confused.
>
> Socrates
> [Cornford, 1941]

# 3

## MORALITY AS SEEN BY PHILOSOPHERS AND BIOLOGISTS

*. . . there is some benevolence, however small, . . . some particle of the dove kneaded into our frame, along with the elements of the wolf and serpent.*

David Hume, 1750

*It is almost as immoral to make exceptions in favor of one's wife, son, or nephew as in favor of oneself.*

Kurt Baier, 1958

*The main idea [of the principle of justice or fairness] is that when a number of persons engage in a mutually advantageous cooper- ative venture according to rules, and thus restrict their liberty in ways necessary to yield advantages for all, those who have submitted to these restrictions have a right to similar acquiescence on the part of those who have benefited from their submission.*

John Rawls, 1971

*The tribesman who works to exalt the name and fame of his tribe is rewarded by an advance of his own name and fame.*

Sir Arthur Keith, 1949

## INTRODUCTION

Anyone who studies moral systems will find that information and opinions regarding them come from several different sources, essen- tially independent of one another. First, there are ordinary people, who invariably have thought a great deal about right and wrong, and the rules they live under, and usually have definite opinions. Second, there are the formal constructors, enforcers, and interpreters of the rules: police, judges, lawyers, political and religious leaders, and teachers. Third, there are moral philosophers and ethicists, who have built an enormous and complex literature discussing what is, has been, will be, and might have been, with respect to moral systems. Fourth, there are groups of knowledgeable and educated people whose areas of expertise border on this realm but who are usually not directly concerned with it: sociologists, psychologists, anthropologists, historians, economists, po-

145

litical scientists, biologists, and others. Here I shall discuss mainly the writings of one or a few recent representatives in each of three major categories: (1) moral philosophers, (2) biologist-philosophers, and (3) philosophers of biology. I am not concerned to review the history of moral philosophy or even to trace the origins and priorities of ideas in that discipline (see Kupperman, 1983, MacPherson, 1979, and Grant, 1985, for useful reviews), but rather to relate some recent arguments from philosophy to those I am making, and to show how thinkers from different backgrounds have approached the problems discussed in this book.

## The Moral Philosophers

Egoism and altruism represent the main poles of argument with respect to morality. Yet no nonbiologist writer on this topic that I have found has been specific about what is meant by either one. In describing altruism or helping others at one's own expense, the nature of the expense is never described, no attempt is made to analyze all aspects of the probable rewards, and the significance of different individuals as objects of the altruism is usually not considered. In talking about eogism, Kalin (1957) uses the phrase "coming out on top"; Frankena (1980) uses getting "the best score." Neither one takes up the question of precisely what such phrases mean—nor does any other philosopher I have read. Let us see, then, how some philosophical arguments have developed on the topic of morality. In the analyses that follow I have tried always to use examples of the *best* rather than the worst or most vulnerable arguments of moral philosophers: Although I will discuss the writings of only a few individuals, to my knowledge there are no publications in the philosophical literature that escape the criticisms leveled here.

### RATIONALITY AND SELF-INTEREST

Good examples of the difficulty in understanding human interests without careful consideration of biological issues are the protracted discussions and arguments by philosophers on the question of rationality and self-interest. After defining morality so as to require self-sacrifice, philosophers often ask "Would a rational person ever act morally contrary to self-interest?" They then define acting contrary to self-interest as doing anything that risks one's "own welfare" or involves the possibility of getting killed or injured. Brandt (1979, p. 331 ff.), for example, divides the cases he examines into three categories.

First, he notes that a person may "act out of benevolence or other moral motivation before his self-interested desires . . . can become fully engaged. We might say that he acts morally before he thinks. . . . " His example is a soldier who falls on a grenade, saving his comrades, when a little rational thought (according to Brandt) would likely have caused him to fall in another direction and save himself but get his comrades killed. Brandt says that "Impulsive actions of this sort may, of course, be irrational; they might not have occurred if the person had had all the relevant facts vividly represented at the time of action." He says that "Such actions throw no light on the problem of concern to us." He does not deal with the questions of (1) whether or not such impulsive actions ever are rational, and if so, in what way, or (2) why it should be true that otherwise rational persons should (rather frequently, one may say) carry out the kind of impulsive actions that have a significant probability of making them dead heroes. It seems to me that both questions are likely to throw much light on the problem of what constitutes rational action in one's own self-interest, and, indeed, on the general topic of Brandt's treatise, the "good and the right." Surely it is not inconsequential to consider the difference between being a member of the family of a dead hero and being a member of the family of a living (or dead) coward. Everyone knows, and many cite excessively, the heroes among their ancestors; and the gains from being so fortunate as to have heroic ancestors may be large. Conversely, the "sins of the fathers" may be visited "upon the children unto the third and fourth generations." Cowards in one's lineage are usually unmentioned, and there are numerous cases in which even remote descendants have spent large amounts of time and money trying to clear an ancestor's name (such as the descendants of the man whose name was Mudd—Dr. Mudd who was alleged to have aided Lincoln's assassin). Unless one recognizes that we are here because of an evolutionary process in which success has always been measured by how much one helps genetic relatives, it is unlikely that considerations of these sorts can be placed into an appropriate perspective (Fisher, 1930, p. 265).

Brandt (1979, p. 332) describes his second kind of case: "Sometimes the morally right triumphs over long-range self-interest because a person happens to have non-self-interested desires which motivate him to do what is morally right." He means by this, "For instance, if someone involved is a friend or lover or one's pet dog; or if the issue arouses one's interest in some movement in art or literature or music; or if it touches on one's political loyalties. In such cases morality has powerful allies." He regards such situations as "rather special," but notes that "it does seem that if these non-self-interested desires are rational,

then a fully rational person would do what is contrary to self-interest."
He does not explore the possibility that the desires he mentions are, in
fact, self-interested in the terms that really count; yet anyone who has
considered self-interest as a reproductive phenomenon will understand
immediately that this is not only possible but likely to be the case.
Friends and lovers as objects of one's beneficences obviously may
enhance one's reproductive success. Pet dogs may also do so, although,
in today's world, it is likely that in many cases they become surrogates
for offspring and friends, and the kindness and money lavished on them
represent reproductively deleterious acts. This is not really different
from Brandt's first case.

What Brandt (1979, p. 332) calls the "third and most interesting type
of case" is that of "straight conflict between moral motivations and
self-interested desires, when the agent does not fail to represent the
relevant outcomes, and has no other type of relevant desire." He argues
that moral motivations are not like desires, such as for alcohol, that
conflict with ambition because "normally a life of concern for others,
and of strong moral commitments, is a richer and more enjoyable life
than one that is merely self-interested." He says "It seems unlikely that
it will be seriously urged that life would be better in the absence of
benevolence and moral motivations in the way it would be better
without addiction to alcohol." But he does not explore the question of
*why* this is so. Evolutionary considerations suggest that the life of the
benevolent person is richer because benevolence is commonly rewarded
richly, and also because a long history of such rewarding of benevolence
has caused us to evolve powerful feelings of well-being when we
perform benevolent acts that tend to indebt our friends and associates to
us. This will often be our feeling even if most of the rewards are actually
likely to accrue only to our relatives and descendants. Obviously, as
(sometimes) with pets, alcohol, tobacco, drugs, fast cars, and other
evolutionarily novel situations we may experience the proximate pleasures of reproductively appropriate behavior when we are actually
behaving contrarily to our reproductive interests. If we are to understand ourselves, deeply, however, we must somehow discover the
actual correlates of "richer and more enjoyable" lives and see when they
are consistent with our evolutionary background and when they are not
and why.

Brandt (1979, p. 333) then argues that it is unlikely that moral or
beneficence-giving behavior could be extinguished by conditioning
"Partly because the age of the development of benevolence is so early;
partly because it normally receives continuous support later in life, of
the kind that established it in the first place. Moreover, a rational person

would not have these thoughts, since it is just not true that the happiness of others usually stands in one's way." The latter statement would surely be challenged unless Brandt is exceedingly restrictive about his definitions of "others" or "happiness." Competition for mates, jobs, and other resources that one may have but two cannot would often be judged unequivocally to involve one person's happiness affecting that of another. The argument can be carried further, however, since biology suggests that our motivations are guided in social matters by the fact that success in reproductive matters is always a relative matter. This being the case, the happiness of *some* others nearly always "stands in one's way."

Brandt (1979, p. 333) pays lip service to the notion of reciprocity in his argument here, by remarking that "It is true that going to the aid of another may be costly in some cases, but it would not be hard to show, by many examples, that benevolence-expressing behaviour normally pays in terms of self-interest, as does having moral attitudes in general, provided the degree of benevolence does not go beyond a certain point." He then notes that "It would seem, then, that sympathy and benevolence pass the test of rationality." But he accomplishes this conclusion by making sympathy and benevolence into self-interested acts.

Brandt (1979) then refers to his earlier claim that some motivations are irrational—he so regards "Kant's and Rashdell's aversions to homosexuality." With respect to aversions to acts like homosexuality and suicide, Brandt does not explore the question whether or not there are reasons from biology to expect such aversions—such as the fear that their approval might lead to one's children or other relatives becoming homosexual or suicidal. He supposes that the notion that such activities are "not natural" is irrational because they must be owing to natural causes, therefore natural; and he argues that homosexuality, at least, does not hurt anyone else. Again, a background in biological training would scarcely allow one to draw such conclusions. There are obvious possible reasons why failures to censure homosexuality and suicide might adversely affect one's reproductive success; and it is easy to argue that some actions—even possibly both of these actions—are "unnatural" in the sense that they might derive from developmental experiences that are historically or evolutionarily novel. I caution that I am not arguing that such novelty is in fact the cause of homosexuality or suicide; that if so it makes such behaviors right or wrong; or that either is in fact "unnatural" in any sense bearing on morality. Nor am I arguing that the above *possible* reasons for aversion to homosexuality or suicide are the *actual* reasons for such aversion; only that it is rational to believe that they are.

Brandt (1979, p. 335) eventually concludes that "when the moral motivations in conflict with self-interested desires do control conduct, in the absence of a specific indication that there was mistake in factual belief or reasoning, or that the motivation would have been weaker in a person who had undergone cognitive psychotherapy, it is not irrational that they do so." He arrives at this conclusion without coming to grips with the nature of self-interest, without ever deciding whether or not the acts he calls self-interested and self-sacrificing really are, in any terms that count. He accomplishes it by the questionable assumption that if behavior enhances the *general welfare*, it is rational. No reason is given for making this assumption, which in evolutionary terms does not always make sense.

The philosopher Kurt Baier (1958, p. vii) says:

> . . . [The] reason why any and every agent *should be* a moral and not an immoral agent, . . . is that a general acceptance of a system of merely [sic] self-interested reasons would lead to conditions of life well described by Hobbes as "poor, nasty, brutish, and short." These unattractive living conditions can be improved by the general adoption of a system of reasoning in which reasons of self-interest are over-ruled, roughly speaking, when following them would tend to harm others. Such reasons are what we call "moral reasons," and we rightly regard them as overruling reasons of self-interest [sic], because the acceptance of self-interested reasons as over-ruling moral ones would lead to the undesirable state of affairs described by Hobbes. This is the reason why everyone has an excellent reason for so regarding them.

There is an obvious element of inconsistency here, since basically Baier is saying that to be moral will at least contribute to preventing one's life from being poor, nasty, brutish, and short—hence, it is in some sense in one's self-interest to be moral. He also suggests that we should be moral so that other people will too, " . . . to their best interests." But he does not add that inducing others to be altruistic may be in our own self-interests. His argument does not deal with the question of "free riders" who may escape being moral without seriously reducing the climate of morality insofar as it benefits them. Nor does he explain that it is also self-interested to be *regarded* as of *high moral worth*, although he goes on to say that " . . . doing right is not in one's interest and thus entitles one to *compensation* (positive retribution); and . . . doing wrong *is* in one's interest and therefore makes one liable to negative retribution." If these "retributions" reach certain levels, however, they obviously could make "doing right" self-interested behavior. This, I believe, is what systems of indirect reciprocity (moral systems) are all about. That is why I regard them as more closely related to legal systems than most philosophers seem to allow. It also explains why motivation is so important in both moral and legal questions. As Frankena (1980) states

> From the point of view of morality, the well-motivated person is better than the right-doing, because having such people around is likely to result in more right-doing than having people around who only happen to do what is right because it fits in with their ends. (pp. 48–49)

There is always the *internal* conflict in a person, at least one who is acting as a moral agent, whether what is "right" is (1) what is beneficial to him and his or (2) what is beneficial to others at the expense of him and his. Who would think a man moral for saving a stranger's child while letting his own drown, or immoral for saving his own while letting the other drown? Frankena (1980, p. 49) seems to be ignoring such problems when he says " . . . a moral agent who is sincerely asking what he should do will never in any particular situation have to choose between doing what is right or even what he believes to be right and acting from the best or right motive; the right thing to do is always the right thing to do."

The failure of moral philosophers to specify what egoism means, in the sense of what is meant by doing what is good for one's self, is part of the failure to come to grips with the problem of what human *interests* are. Frankena (1980, p. 67) argues that " . . . the belief in ego or me first as the source of all unethical behavior, both immoral and unmoral . . . is certainly largely correct." Even if this is true, however, it does not follow that behavior generally accepted as moral is not egoistic or must be self-sacrificing, and this is certainly true if egoism includes contributing to the survival of one's genes. Assuming that morality has to be self-sacrificing is what has led moral philosophers into their worst intellectual quagmires. Consider these quotes from Frankena (1980):

> I believe . . . that morality requires genuine sacrifice, and may even require self-sacrifice. (p. 87)

> It would, after all, be paradoxical if the only way to justify a nonegoistic enterprise like morality were by use of an egoistic argument. (p. 87)

> To give me my best score, a life must include my being around to collect the results, but a life involving self-sacrifice may not allow me to do this (pp. 89–90).

> When morality requires . . . the supreme sacrifice . . . it is in no way possible to maintain that one will always come out with the best score, if one ever does. (p. 88)

... it seems clear to me ... that a universal coincidence of being moral and achieving the best score can be shown to be false—unless it is posited that there is a hereafter in which God will readjust the balance (p. 91).

This kind of argument mires Frankena (and other philosophers) hopelessly in the effort to understand phenomena related to indirect reciprocity. Consider this analysis of self-respect by Frankena (1980):

... self-respect ... is a conviction that one's character and life will be approved by any rational being who contemplates it from the moral point of view .... The importance of self-respect is not so much that it improves one's score as that it may lead one to prefer a life in which it is present to one from which it would be absent but which would yield a better score.... Our need for self-respect and its dependence on our being moral are important evidence that we may prefer being moral to having the highest score. (pp. 92–93)

Baier (1965) carries the argument that morality requires self-sacrifice to an extreme, distinguishing between moral and immoral egoism as follows:

... [immoral] egoism differs from ... morality in that it fails to consider the interests of others even when the long-range benefits to oneself are likely to be greater than the short-range sacrifices. (p. 93)

For some philosophers the fact that egoism (even in the biologists' sense of serving one's genetic interests) means that justice can never be complete, because conflicts of interests are then not resolvable, is a reason for denying that egoism can be moral or can be part of a moral system. In their view moral systems are ways of reducing conflicts of interest, and some would contend that morality is achieved only with the complete disappearance of conflicts of interest.

If egoism, as self-interest in the biologists' sense, is the reason for the promotion of ethical behavior, then, paradoxically, it is expected that everyone will constantly promote the notion that egoism is *not* a suitable theory of action, and, *a fortiori*, that he himself is not an egoist. Most of all he must present this appearance to his closest associates because it is in his best interests to do so—except, perhaps, to his closest relatives, to whom his egoism may often be displayed in cooperative ventures from which some distant- or non-relative suffers. Indeed, it may be arguable that it will be in the egoist's best interest not to know (consciously) or to admit to himself that he is an egoist because of the value to himself of being able to convince others he is not. One context in which this is likely to be evident is the male–female interaction in species showing long-term parental care. Thus, in humans, intriguing questions surround the concealment of ovulation by females, evidently from themselves as well as their mates (cf. Alexander and Noonan, 1979; Alexander, 1979a; Benshoof and Thornhill, 1979; B. I. Strassmann, 1981; Symons, 1979; Hrdy, 1981). Alexander and Noonan argue, for example, that such concealment is not conscious because this would entail essentially long-term awareness of deception being practiced against one's lifemate—a practice in conflict with the most useful self-image, vulnerable to detection because of the deceiver's awareness of her deception, and contrary to the interests of a long-term bond of intimacy and otherwise shared interests.

## MISUNDERSTANDINGS OF RECIPROCITY

It is a common error to suppose that something additional to nepotism and reciprocity is required to account for the structure of society. I call this an error not because we know precisely how nepotism and reciprocity can account for society, but because the authors to whom I refer draw their conclusion as a result of an inadequate understanding of reciprocity, especially indirect reciprocity: "Rewards from society at large, or from other than the actual recipient of beneficence, may be termed indirect reciprocity" (Alexander, 1977b, p. 296). As examples I suggested rewards for "heroism, military and civil service, philanthropy, lawful behavior, inventiveness, leadership, etc." (Table 2.2; see also pp. 77, 89 and Alexander, 1979a, pp. 48–58, Fig. 5). Punishments for behaviors contrary to the rules or mores may also be considered part of the system. The function of such punishments and rewards, I have suggested, is to manipulate the behavior of participating individuals, restricting individual efforts to serve their own interests at others' expense so as to promote harmony and unity within the group. The function of harmony and unity, I have further argued, is to allow the group to compete against hostile forces, especially other human groups. It is apparent that success of the group may serve the interests of all individuals in the group; but it is also apparent that group success can be achieved with different patterns of individual success differentials within the group. So, among other things, it is in the interests of those who are differentially successful to promote both unity and the rules so that group success will occur without necessitating changes deleterious to them. Similarly, it may be in the interests of those individuals who are relatively unsuccessful to promote dissatisfaction with existing rules and the notion that group success would be more likely if the rules were altered to favor them.

A blatant misinterpretation of reciprocity was that of the anthropologist, Marshall Sahlins (1976), who suggested that for one to be suitably rewarded for saving someone from drowning he himself would have to be saved from drowning by the person saved. Perhaps Sahlins was trying to make a joke of the biological arguments about reciprocity by noting that since the second individual was the one originally saved he is probably a poor swimmer and an unlikely source of help for the person who saved him, should the tables ever be turned. It is difficult to believe that Sahlins really thought his discussion was germane, but he gives us no reason to think otherwise.

A less obvious and more typical misinterpretation is that of the philosopher, Peter Singer (1981), who writes:

> In Britain, blood needed for medical purposes comes exclusively from people who voluntarily give their blood to the National Blood Transfusion Service. These donors are not paid. They do not get preferential treatment when they themselves need blood, for the National Health Service provides blood free of charge for all those in Britain who need it. Nor can donors be rewarded—or even given a grateful smile—by the patients whose lives are saved by their gifts. Donors never know who receives their blood, and patients never know who gave the blood they receive. Common sense tells us that people who give blood do it to help others, not for any disguised benefit to themselves. (p. 133)

Singer (1981, p. 134) goes on to note that fewer than 2% of thousands of donors asked by Titmuss (1971) why they gave blood indicated that it was for self-interested reasons. He says that this system and the others like it in other countries "are working refutations of the contention that altruism can only exist among kin, within small groups, or *where it pays off by encouraging reciprocal altruism*" (p. 134, emphasis added). He concludes that "Genuine non-reciprocal altruism directed toward strangers does occur," and that "Any theory which entails that nonreciprocal altruism toward strangers cannot occur must be wrong." Singer (1981) then asks:

> Does this mean that the evolutionary theories of the origin of altruism discussed in the first chapter of this book must be wrong? It may seem that it does . . . . But recall the argument of the preceding chapter in which I suggested that altruistic impulses once limited to one's kin and one's own group might be extended to a wider circle by reasoning creatures who can see that they and their kin are one group among others, and from an impartial point of view no more important than others. (p. 134)

Singer's (1981, pp. 117–119) "argument of the preceding chapter" went like this:

> To reason ethically I have to see my own interests as one among the many interests of those that make up the group, an interest no more important than others. Justifying my actions to the group therefore leads me to take up

a perspective from which the fact that I am I and you are you is not important. Within the group other distinctions are similarly not ethically relevant. That someone is related to *me* rather than to you, or lives in *my* village among the dozen villages that make up our community, is not an ethical justification for special favoritism; it does not allow me to do for my kin or fellow villagers any more than you may do for your kin or fellow villagers. Though ethical systems everywhere recognize special obligations to kin and neighbors, they do so within a framework of impartiality which makes me see my obligations to my kin and neighbors as no more important, from the ethical point of view, than other people's obligations to their own kin and neighbors . . . , the next step is to ask why the interests of my society shall be more important than the interests of other societies. If the only answer . . . is that it is *my* society, then the ethical mode of reasoning will reject it. Otherwise we would simultaneously be holding: (1) if I claim that what I do is right, while what you do is wrong, I must give some reason other than the fact that my action benefits me (or my kin, or my village) while your action benefits you (or your kin, or your village); and yet (2) I can claim that what I do is right, while what you do is wrong, merely on the grounds that my act benefits my society whereas your act benefits your society.

If . . . from an ethical point of view I am just one person among the many in my society, and my interests are no more important, from the point of view of the whole, than the similar interests of others within my society . . . , from a still larger point of view, my society is just one among other societies, and the interests of members of my society are no more important, from that larger perspective, than the similar interests of members of other societies. Ethical reasoning, once begun, pushes against our initially limited ethical horizons, leading us always toward a more universal point of view.

Where does this process end? Taking the impartial elements in ethical reasoning to its logical conclusion means, first, accepting that we ought to have equal concern for all human beings . . . extending to all mankind the concern that we ordinarily feel only for our kin. The ideal of the brotherhood of human beings has now passed into official rhetoric; turning that ideal into reality, however, is another matter.

Singer asserts (1981, p. 120) that "The circle of altruism has broadened from the family and tribe to the nation and race [see Darwin, 1871, T. H. Huxley, 1896; Keith, 1947, for the same argument], and we are beginning to recognize that our obligations extend to all human beings." He goes further and says that, "The process should not stop there," that " . . . all beings with the capacity to feel pleasure or pain should be included; we can improve their welfare by increasing their pleasures and diminishing their pains." "The expansion of the moral circle should therefore be pushed out until it includes most animals." He speaks of a "momentous new stage in our moral thinking" in which "the moral status of animals has become a lively topic of debate" and asks whether we will "eventually go beyond animals too, and embrace plants, or perhaps even mountains, rocks, and streams?" he believes, however (p. 123), that "the boundary of sentience—by which I mean the ability to feel, to suffer from anything or to enjoy anything—is not a morally arbitrary boundary in the way that boundaries of race or species are arbitrary."

Singer's reference to "the point of view of the whole," and his arguments for "broadening" "the circle of altruism" to "members of other societies," "all human beings," and even beyond is not really a "momentous new stage in our moral thinking." As I have noted, Darwin (1871), T. H. Huxley (1896), and Keith (1949) all discussed the same possibility, and Darwin's discussion was actually similar to Singer's. There is also a parallel in the rise of the idea of God as representing the views of all the people (*Vox populi, vox Dei*); eventually all people everywhere, and not just the members of one's own society; and even the rest of the universe, in which God may be regarded as having interest because he created it (his eye, after all, is "on the sparrow").

The problem of why the boundary of the "moral circle" is so difficult to identify unequivocally can be understood by considering the nature of indirect reciprocity. If people are judged socially by their treatment of others—or by what they advocate as treatment of others—then they may be judged by their treatment of any organisms (or anything—perhaps even rocks and streams in some cases) that the observers feel have rights. Moreover, the maintenance of moral systems, and their nature, may be affected by how the members view themselves and their treatment of nonhuman organisms and amoral humans (such as severely retarded persons, fetuses, certain kinds of criminals, and the moribund; see also p. 100). I recently heard a philosopher lecture on the topic "Why animals have no rights," He argued that only humans construct and operate moral systems, and only organisms that do this have rights. He was concerned to advance the notion that it is not immoral to use nonhuman organisms in medical research to save human lives. He was immediately asked: Why not use severely retarded persons in medical research, as they are also certainly not moral beings and therefore by his reasoning should have no rights. His response was difficult to decipher, but it seemed to include some elements of the above explanation from indirect reciprocity for the fuzziness of the boundary of moral obligations and rights. This speaker did not seem to grasp that rights are given and denied by humans, in some kind of collective fashion (not as individuals—at least not in most societies today), and that if all humans were to decide that dogs, or rhesus monkeys, or laboratory rats have rights equally with humans they would indeed then have such rights, and this would surely be true using his own definition. So the question of how human moral systems would be affected by using retarded persons, fetuses, and prison populations in medical research could potentially become virtually the same question as how they would be affected by using dogs. It is all a matter of how people view dogs, how they view people who threaten dogs in particular ways, and how this in turn affects how people treat both dogs and people. It is my impression that issues of this sort become clearer when morality is seen as beneficial to the morally acting individual through the operation of indirect reciprocity. We are apt to judge others not only as a result of their treatment of other humans, but as a result of their treatment of even nonhuman organisms, and this, I believe, is why the limits of "rights" are indefinite, as the arguments of this philosopher, and Singer, would imply.

Singer's argument is probably the only one by a philosopher, on these points, that tries to take modern evolutionary theory from biology into account, yet also utilizes the kinds of arguments that philosophers generate about reason and altruism. Unfortunately, he does not even raise the possibility that reciprocity with respect to blood donations can involve something other than (1) direct payment by either the blood service or the person who ultimately uses the blood, or (2) later preferential treatment in relation to blood use. In other words, he does not indicate that he is aware that giving blood may be sufficiently important as a social criterion as to yield benefits, for those who are known to be blood donors, that are independent in all other regards from the blood service itself. That he is aware of this general feature of reciprocity is shown by his earlier analysis of reciprocity (pp. 43 ff.) in which he reiterates Trivers' (1971) note that "People who are altruistically motivated will make more reliable partners than those motivated by self-interests." For this very reason, a known blood donor may receive his "payment" from the members of society who accept him in social interactions or treat him deferentially compared to others known not to be blood donors or not known to be blood donors. After all, giving blood is a fine way of suggesting that one is so altruistic that he is willing to give up a most dear possession for a perfect stranger. On that basis it might be viewed as, rather than unreciprocatable altruism, a social investment with a very special and high likelihood of paying off handsomely. Who among us is not a little humble in the presence of someone who has casually noted that he just came back from "giving blood"? Questions that Richard Titmuss (1971) could have asked that bear on the social motivations of blood donors, and the benefits of giving blood, are: how many of them kept their blood giving a complete secret? Where and to whom did those who told others about it do that? What kinds of thoughts did they have about giving blood, about telling others, and about the personal qualities of those who give blood? Did they regard these things differently afterward, or see themselves differently?

The questionnaires Titmuss used asked none of these questions, nor does he discuss them. The closest he came to comments relevant to such questions was in the following statement:

> No donor type can, of course, be said to be characterized by complete, disinterested, spontaneous altruism. There must be some sense of obligation, approval and interest; some awareness of need and of the purposes of the blood gift; perhaps some organized group rivalry in generosity; some knowledge that fellow-members of the community who are young or old or sick cannot donate, and some expectation and assurance that a return gift may be needed and received at some future time (as with Mauss's examples of gift-exchange in other societies). Nevertheless, in terms of the free gift of blood to unnamed strangers there is no formal contract, no legal bond, no situation of power, domination, constraint or compulsion, no sense of shame or guilt, no gratitude imperative, no need for penitence, no money and no explicit guarantee of or wish for a reward or a return gift. They are acts of free will; of the exercise of choice; of conscience without shame. (p. 89)

This statement in fact includes the aspects of indirect reciprocity involved in the "social contract" ("sense of obligation, approval, and interest . . . ", "organized group rivalry in generosity"). Yet it also denies the existence of a "formal contract," influences of "power, domination, constraint or compulsion . . . sense of shame or guilt . . . explicit guarantee of or wish for a reward or return gift." The statement also mixes in irrelevant considerations like "free will" and some arguments that are on a different plane from the question of expectations of status shifts or other indirect rewards (as with knowledge that "young or old or sick cannot donate"). One can quibble about the significance of words like "formal" and "explicit." Titmuss was seeking to show that tendencies to give or not depend on the structure of the society and the "market system." Thus, he concludes:

> In certain undesired circumstances in the future—situations in which death or disability might be postponable—then the performance by a stranger of a similar action would constitute for them or their families a desired good. But they had no assurance of such action nor any guarantee of the continued existence of the National Health Service. Unlike gift-exchange in the traditional societies, there is in the free gift of blood to unnamed strangers no contract of custom, no legal bond, no functional determinism, no situation of discriminatory power, domination, constraint or compul-

sion, no sense of shame or guilt, no gratitude imperative, no need for the penitence of a Chrysostom. (p. 238, 239)

In not asking for or expecting any payment of money these donors signified their belief in the willingness of other men to act altruistically in the future, and to combine together to make a gift freely available should they have a need for it. By expressing confidence in the behaviour of future unknown strangers they were thus denying the Hobbesian thesis that men are devoid of any distinctively moral sense. (p. 239)

As individuals they were, it may be said, taking part in the creation of a greater good transcending the good of self-love. To "love" themselves they recognized the need to "love" strangers. By contrast, one of the functions of atomistic private market systems is to "free" men from any sense of obligation to or for other men regardless of the consequences to others who cannot reciprocate, and to release some men (who are eligible to give) from a sense of inclusion in society at the cost of excluding other men (who are not eligible to give).

These donors to the National Service we have described in much detail were free not to give. They could have behaved differently; that is to say, they need not have acted as they did. Their decisions were not determined by structure or by function or controlled by ineluctable historical forces. They were not compelled, coerced, bribed or paid to give. (p. 239)

Again, Titmuss' statement does not adequately take into account the power of indirect reciprocity, in the form of ethical and moral systems, to manipulate the costs and benefits of the acts of individuals.

Unfortunately, early in his book, Singer (1981, p. 43) requires, for a definition of altruism, not only that it "benefits others at some cost to oneself" but that, in addition, it "is motivated by the desire to benefit others." His reason for adopting this definition is that it is "the common meaning of the term." In the context of modern biological theory, however, that is scarcely a valid reason for failing to deal explicitly with the probability that our professed and even sincerely believed motivations may not at all reflect the evolutionary significance of our acts. For the same reason we are not compelled to accept his assertion that "common sense" is the right basis for deciding what is behind blood giving, especially when that common sense simultaneously denies the probability that what one thinks is the reason behind one's act may not convey its real significance, and does not take into account well established biological facts and theories.

Singer's "argument of the preceding chapter" is a way of explaining how nonreciprocated altruism can occur and how blood donors can give blood even though there is no possibility of their being repaid in any way, shape, or form. Since he has not demonstrated that this happens, or even, in my opinion, that it is likely, his argument is not needed to explain blood giving. Nor does he describe any other actual human behavior that requires an explanation from the ethical "disinterested," equal-concern-for-all point of view. We are still, then, in the position of asking whether such a point of view is really behind any human behavior, or if there is an alternative explanation; and we are not yet shown any beneficent behavior that cannot easily and logically be linked to nepotism and reciprocity. The kinds of behavior needed are such acts as privately giving blood or organ transplants to nonrelatives or strangers, as readily as giving them to relatives or friends or giving them publicly. Robert Smuts has suggested to me that even these acts require further examination because of the possibility that by convincing themselves that they are selfless, private donors may become better able to convey an appearance of selflessness to others. If such conditions seem to render the propositions virtually untestable, that is simply a problem that we must solve if we are to deal in a better way with the unparalleled difficulty of understanding ourselves.

Singer's assertions about expansion of the circle of morality entirely omit discussion of the only issue that stands in the way—and the issue that appears to lie behind all moral and ethical considerations: conflicts of interest. Were there no conflicts of interest, the question of extending morality or beneficent behavior outward to even rocks, mountains, and streams, as he mentions, would not be a problem. If there are conflicts of interest, then to fail to discuss them while asking the question of where the outer limits of moral considerations shall lie is to miss the point entirely. How can one argue that a reasoning person will not discriminate among associates if his own self-interest—however defined—will thereby be enhanced? Contrary to Singer, I would argue that carrying out such discrimination in one's own interests may be the very basis for the evolution of the ability to reason. I am not assuming that all (or even most) apparently selfless acts are in fact reciprocated, but that such acts would not be performed unless, during evolutionary history, the rewards were on average greater than the costs. This hypothesis directly contradicts Singer's assertion (quoted earlier) that "Any theory which entails that non-reciprocal altruism toward strangers cannot occur must be wrong" unless Singer means to restrict such altruism to direct altruism or evolutionarily novel situations (see also Thompson, 1980).

The question that Singer seems to beg is that of how and why an ethical point of view, or approach, ever came to be instituted, let alone discussed as a central issue, in societies that historically were composed of nepotistically, reciprocally selfish individuals. As he describes it, the ethical point of view seems to require an abandonment of all that, in evolutionary terms, is expected to be near and dear to the individual. Therefore, in a sense, the ultimate question about ethics and reason is:

Why should any rational person accept ethical reasoning, as Singer and philosophers in general define it? In other words, where did ethical reasoning come from? How did it benefit those who initially took it up? If morality and ethical reasoning require justice or fairness or impartiality or disinterestedness in the sense that Singer requires—and I am inclined to believe that they do—then what is the reason for their originating and becoming important in human social life?

## PROXIMATE AND ULTIMATE MECHANISMS AND SELF-SACRIFICE

Two major assumptions, made universally or most of the time by philosophers, are counter to the arguments presented here from biological considerations, and I believe they are responsible for the confusion that prevents philosophers from making sense out of morality or even being able to resolve the paradoxes. These assumptions are the following:

1. That proximate and ultimate mechanisms or causes have the same kind of significance and can be considered together as if they were members of the same class of causes: this is a failure to understand that proximate causes are evolved because of ultimate causes, and therefore may be expected to serve them, while the reverse is not true. Thus, pleasure is a proximate mechanism that in the usual environments of history is expected to impel us toward behavior that will contribute to our reproductive success. Contrarily, acts leading to reproductive success are not proximate mechanisms that evolved because they served the ultimate function of bringing us pleasure.

2. That morality inevitably involves some self-sacrifice. This assumption involves at least three elements:

a. Failure to consider altruism to relatives as benefits to the actor. Two consequences are that (i) self-interest is sometimes defined as survival of the individual (which is instantly recognizable as insufficient) and (ii) when self-interest is defined so as to include pleasure, and all similar proximate sensations or rewards, no procedure can be given to account for the differences between pleasurable and nonpleasurable social actions.

b. Failure to comprehend all avenues of indirect reciprocity within groups.

c. Failure to take into account both within-group and between-group benefits.

These several problems are especially well-illustrated in Nielsen's

(1978) paper on a question commonly asked by moral philosophers: *Why Should I be Moral?* After going through an array of different kinds of answers commonly posed to this question, Nielsen concludes, unlike most philosophers, that it is sometimes in one's rational self-interest to do what is wrong. Sartorius (1975, p. 218) evidently agrees: "Penal laws exist . . . because even an unanimous opinion that a certain line of conduct is for the general interest, does not always make it people's individual interest to adhere to that line of conduct." It is worthwhile to review the arguments by which Nielsen reaches his conclusion. In his opening paragraphs he mentions most of the assumptions listed above:

> Bradley seems perfectly right in saying: "A man is moral because he likes being moral; and he likes it, partly because he has been brought up to the habit of liking it, and partly because he finds it gives him what he wants, while its opposite does not do so." In other words, people are moral primarily because they have been conditioned to be moral. The human animal is a social animal and (as Butler and Hume observed) people normally tend to consider the welfare of others as well as their own welfare. People indeed act selfishly but they also take out life insurance, feel anxiety over the troubles of others, and even have moments of mild discomfort at the thought that life on this planet may someday be impossible. But . . . I am asking "What good reasons do people have for being moral?" . . . There is a short, snappy answer . . . "People ought to be moral because it is wicked . . . not to be moral" . . . . This short answer will not do . . . . (pp. 539–540)

> There is a more defensible answer . . . one of the very strongest and most persistent . . . desires is . . . to be free from the "tooth and claw" of a life in which each man exclusively seeks his own interest and totally neglects to consider the interests of others. In such a situation life would indeed be "nasty, brutish and short." We could not sleep at night without fear of violent death; we could not leave what we possessed without well-warranted anxiety over its being stolen or destroyed. . . . Where people's interests conflict, each man would (without the institution of morality) resort to subterfuge or violence to gain his own ends. A pervasive Dobuan-like suspicion would be normal and natural . . . even rational in such a situation. Every individual would be struggling for the good things of life and no rule except that of his own self-interest would govern the struggle. The universal reign of the rule of exclusive self-interest would lead to the harsh world that Hobbes called "the state of nature". (p. 541)

> When we ask: Why should we have a morality—any morality, even a completely conventional morality—we answer that if everyone acts morally, or generally acts morally, people will be able to attain more of what they want. It is obvious that in a moral community more good will be realized than in a nonmoral collection of people. Yet in the interest of realizing a commodious life for all, voluntary self-sacrifice is sometimes necessary; but the best possible life for everyone is attainable only if people act morally; the greatest possible good is realizable only when everyone puts aside his own self-interest when it conflicts with the common good. (p. 542)

> Yet an answer to the question "Why should people be moral?" does not meet the one basic question that the thorough-going skeptic may feel about the claims of morality. The "existing individual" may want to know why *he*, as an individual, ought to accept the standards of morality when it is not in *his* personal interest to do so. He may have no doubt at all about the general utility of the moral enterprise. But *his* not recognizing the claims of morality will not greatly diminish the total good. Reflecting on this, he asks himself: "Why should *I* be moral when I will not be caught or punished for not acting morally?" (p. 542)

In this short passage all of the problems mentioned earlier are present. Thus, Nielsen begins by discussing on a par with one another whether or not one "likes" being moral and whether or not morality "gives him what he wants." He shows no realization that there are historical reasons for one liking those activities that tend to "give him what he wants." Moreover, he considers that we are "conditioned" to be moral as if there is no historical background for our abilities and tendencies to accept certain kinds of learning or to learn certain kinds of things.

Second, he assumes, with nearly all modern philosophers, that morality involves people considering "the welfare of others as well as their own," and it is clear from what he says later that this means self-sacrifice. He regards acting selfishly as opposite to taking out life insurance. Since life insurance is almost invariably secured for the benefit of relatives, and since he does not elsewhere take up this question, we may assume that he has not considered that the reason for life itself—therefore, presumably, in some fashion, for morality too—is to produce and assist relatives.

Like Baier (above) and others, Nielsen also discusses what would happen if there were no morality. He notes that humans can accomplish more as a group if they cooperate (including being moral) than if they try to go it alone, but he speaks of this accomplishment as if it involved only the activities of the group being considered and does not mention the possibility that group cooperation has as its *raison d'etre* competition against other groups. This possibility—which I regard as a virtual certainty (Keith, 1947, 1949; Bigelow, 1969; Alexander and Tinkle, 1968; Alexander, 1971, 1974, 1977b, 1979a,c; Carneiro, 1970; Wilson, 1972; Strate, 1982)—means that any kind of cooperative effort within a group, including morality, may carry as one of its principal significances its general effect on the tendency and ability of the group to cooperate well when circumstances are dire. Thus, to cooperate and develop good will by strictly within-group activities when threats from other groups are minimal or nonexistent may have remarkably salutary effects on ability to cooperate as a group when threatened or attacked, and thereby benefit every individual to a degree that far more than compensates any temporary altruism during peaceful times. To fail to consider this all-important aspect of group-living, cooperativeness, and morality is to miss one way of answering the question that Nielsen cannot answer: How there can be a self-interested answer to the question; "Why should I be moral?" The remainder of Nielsen's article is well worth reading, for he goes through a number of philosophical arguments on this question and shows how none of them answers the question appropriately. That his own effort also fails is particularly instructive.

Another question is raised, however, by Nielsen's discussion. He asks what society would be like if everyone pursued his own self-interest, and then he describes it as Hobbes and others have also done. His description does not fit what most of us think about our own society, even if we do not regard society as wholly moral and without risk, and even if we recognize that some people do pursue their own self-interests at the expense of others. Yet I argue throughout this book that, whether they know it or not, people are indeed pursuing their own self-( = genetic) interests, at least insofar as current environments mimic those of the past. Why, then, is society not like what Nielsen and others suppose would be the case if everyone pursued his own self-interests? Why does it *seem* as though we are in general being moral in the sense that Nielsen and others imply when they say that morality means self-sacrifice, and that a society of self-interested people pursuing their own interests would be a harsh, nasty, brutish, suspicion-ridden society? Why, if we are not actually doing it, do we *believe* that we are continually self-sacrificing to help others, and that morality does indeed exist and does indeed involve self-sacrifice? These are serious questions. The answers, I believe, will come from a careful analysis of the nature of the human mind or psyche, developed out of the hypotheses that humans do seek their own self-interests, that self-interests are genetic, and have long involved complex nepotistic and reciprocal relationships with large and diverse sets of near and distant relatives (or effectively nonrelatives), that self-interests have only been realizable through cooperation in social groups that compete with one another, and that the full implications of these facts have not been accessible to human knowledge (see pp. 107ff.)

## The Biologist-Philosophers

The biologist-philosophers, who have considered ethics and morality as something to be understood in light of organic evolution or in conjunction with it, have consistently been ignored by moral philosophers and others trying to understand the human condition, even though, in terms of modern biology, the writings of some of them have not been far off target.

## THE NATURALISTIC FALLACY

Biologist-philosophers can be divided into three main groups: First are those like Wolfgang Wickler and Julian Huxley, and some others, who believe that by looking into the evolutionary process one can determine how we ought to proceed *because* what is "good" in evolution, they think, must be ethically good. Wickler (1972) asserts that

> . . . criticism of social norms . . . is a job that specifically belongs to the ethologist" (p. 21) [and] "The ethologist is therefore justified in criticizing many of the existing ethical norms and the ancient and more recent moral commandments, both positive and negative. He is also, I believe, fully entitled to suggest, on the basis of his scientific knowledge, where and how norms should be changed. (pp. 141, 142)

Julian Huxley (see Huxley & Huxley, 1947) leaves no doubt where he stands.

> . . . the evolutionist is able to provide new general standards or criteria for ethics . . . contributions from . . . [other] fields have been either incomplete—(as in theology) or limited in extent. It is only in relation to the evolutionary process as a whole that our ethical standards can be fully generalized, and the system be rounded out to completion. (p. 132)

> . . . evolutionary ethics must be based on a combination of a few main principles: that it is right to realize ever new possibilities in evolution, notably those which are valued for their own sake; that it is right both to respect human individuality and to encourage its fullest development; that it is right to construct a mechanism for further social evolution which shall satisfy these prior conditions as fully, efficiently, and as rapidly as possible. (p. 142)

He speaks of "progress" in evolution and calls (p. 128) for a "maximum of variety-in-unity." Huxley simply asserts what is right; and he calls on evolution:

> . . . it is clear on evolutionary grounds that the individual is in a real sense higher than the State or the social organism. . . . All claims that the State has an intrinsically higher value than the individual are false. (p. 126)

> The human individual is not merely inherently higher than the State, but the rightly-developed individual [sic!] is, and will continue to be, the highest product of evolution. . . . (p. 128)

Huxley's assertions presage those of Edward O. Wilson (1978), who gives as the first three principles the "new ethicists" must follow:

survival of the human gene pool, preservation of genetic diversity, and universal human rights. Whether or not these goals would all be judged admirable by humanity, Wilson does not connect his selection of them to biological principles. The first two seem to call for a group-selectionist view of things, but, after arguing that our biological background places limits (or "restraints") on human nature, Wilson does not comment on this leap. He speaks of diversity in the gene pool but of "an" enduring moral code (in the singular), seemingly calling simultaneously for genetic diversity and behavioral uniformity.

There are several different versions of the so-called "naturalistic" fallacy [e.g., Grant (1985) believes that " . . . the contractarian teaching of Hobbes and Locke is an example . . . because what they both say about justice is founded upon what they claim to know about the way things are"], and it creates very strange bedfellows indeed. For example, it places together those who may assert that one or another kind of nastiness—such as killing—is ethical because it occurs "naturally" with those who would plead that some activity that they see as peaceful, nonviolent, or positive—such as homosexuality—should be accepted ethically because it too occurs "naturally" or in nonhuman organisms.

As the archeologist-anthropologist, Sir Arthur Keith (1947, p. 11), pointed out, this "is-to-ought" fallacy also places together all of those who see evolution as God's mode of creation, if it is regarded as following from this that God's handiwork is not to be tampered with. Keith quotes Hitler: "It is not for men to discuss the question of why Providence created different races, but rather to recognize that it punishes those who disregard its work of creation." "God having created races," Keith goes on quoting to illustrate, "it is therefore the noblest and most sacred duty for each racial species of mankind to preserve the purity of the blood which God has given it." Keith remarks that for proponents of this view, " . . . even as an ethical doctrine it [efforts to maintain "genetic purity" or what Keith called "evolutionary isolation"] should not be condemned." He notes that not only was Hitler invoking "Providence" to support his racist doctrine, he was "also a eugenicist" (see also, discussions by Richards, 1986a,b).

Keith (1947), writing in the middle of the World War II, frequently used the war as an illustration of his points. For example, he used Hitler as a case of how someone employing the naturalistic fallacy could also use evolution to his own advantage:

> Hitler has sought on every occasion and in every way to heighten the national consciousness of the German people—or, what is the same thing, to make them racially conscious; to give them unity of spirit and unity of purpose. Neighborly approaches of adjacent nations are and were repelled;

the German people were deliberately isolated. Cosmopolitanism, liberality of opinion, affectation of foreign manners and dress were unsparingly condemned. The old tribal bonds (love of the Fatherland, feeling of mutual kinship), the bonds of "soil and blood" became "the main plank in the National social program." (p. 12)

"Germany is for the Germans" was another plank. Foreign policy was "good or bad according to its beneficial or harmful effects on the German *Volk*—now or hereafter." "Charity and humility are only for consumption"—a statement in which Hitler gives an exact expression of the law which limits sympathy to its tribe. "Humanitarianism is an evil . . . a creeping poison." "The most cruel methods are humane if they give a speedy victory" [shades of Nagasaki and Hiroshima!] is Hitler's echo of a maxim attributed to Moltke. Such are the ways of evolution when applied to human affairs. (p. 12)

Proponents of the is-ought fallacy, or the believers in "natural law," are not always as easy to identify as Wickler and Julian Huxley. Thus, the contemporary sociobiologist, Edward O. Wilson (1981), writes as follows:

The naturalistic fallacy has not been erased by improved biological knowledge, which still describes the "is" of life but cannot prescribe the "ought" or moral action. (pp. 430–431)

But Wilson follows this remark immediately with a statement that seems to suggest something else:

I believe that this criticism has lost a great deal of its force in the last few years. An understanding of the roots of human nature now seems essential to ethical philosophy. Any judgment concerning whether an act is natural or abnormal depends on such information, through behavioral categories as diverse as cousin marriage, homosexuality, territorial prerogatives, and cannibalism. All attempts to define "natural law" by unaided intuition are dangerously incompetent. This is equally true whether applied to such personal matters as the wisdom of birth control or to the supposedly inevitable trajectory of economic history. (pp. 430–431)

Wilson (1980) also writes as follows:

. . . homosexuality may have a genetic component. Its high frequency of occurrence in all societies could easily have arisen by kin selection and hence be as fully "natural" as heterosexual behavior. Suppression of homosexuals on the grounds that they violate natural law in any modern sense cannot be justified. And still another inference: incest is evil (this word can be used without embarrassment) by almost any conceivable standard, since it leads to a demonstrably high level of developmental abnormality due to the increased incidence of homozygosity of lethal and subvital genes. (p. 69)

The questions one feels are necessary in the wake of these remarks are: (1) are acceptances of "natural laws" of human behavior justifiable if one uses scientific knowledge rather than "unaided intuition," and (2) if homosexuality cannot be shown to have evolved by natural selection then would suppression of homosexuals be justified? Moreover, the assertion that the reason incest is evil is that it results in a higher level of (i.e., *sometimes* causes) developmental abnormalities in offspring leaves us with several questions. "Incest" usually refers to sexual relations not the production of offspring. Means are available for preventing absolutely the production of offspring as a result of sexual relations. Would such prevention render incest moral? Alternatively, if two persons marry who happen to carry genes that would cause their offspring to have abnormalities comparable to those Wilson believes (without references) to result from incest in humans, is the marriage then evil? And, one must add, whether or not the couple has or plans to have children? If an incestuous union results in normal children is it then no longer evil? It is not the case that all incestuous marriages result in abnormal offspring, nor is there a magic line with respect to degree of relatedness of marriage partners that makes a marriage "incestuous." Wilson's argument would identify as "evil" all marriages involving likelihoods of abnormal offspring similar to those in which the spouses are (unspecifiedly) close relatives.

In another instance, Wilson (1980) provides a puzzling discussion relevant to "natural laws" of behavior and the naturalistic fallacy. He says that "The primary functions of sexual behavior are pair bonding and the creation of genetic diversity, rather than reproduction per se. Thus the sexual revolution, but not promiscuity, is in concert with the innate learning rules." One is led to believe that he is implying by this that promiscuity somehow violates a "natural law." When asked following his oral presentation of this material (University of Michigan, Tanner Lectures, 1980) if he meant that promiscuous people cannot be happy, he hesitated, but responded affirmatively, stating that in regard to questions of monogamy and fidelity he was conservative. Again, after denying the validity of the naturalistic fallacy, Wilson is suggesting that there are natural laws determining or governing what is right and wrong about human behavior, and that only biologists or those with extensive biological knowledge are able to discover them.

## DARWIN'S GROUP SELECTION THEORY AND FISHER'S ALTERNATIVE

Darwin (1871) developed the first complete theory of morality and ethics, in the following words (p. 500):

Ultimately our moral sense or conscience becomes a highly complex

sentiment—originating in the social instincts, largely guided by the approbation of our fellow-men, ruled by self-reason, and confirmed by instruction
and habit.

It must not be forgotten that although a high standard of morality gives but
a slight or no advantage to each individual man and his children over the
other men of the same tribe, yet that an increase in the number of
well-endowed men and advancement in the standard of morality will
certainly give an immense advantage to one tribe over another. A tribe
including many members who, from possessing in a high degree the spirit
of patriotism, fidelity, obedience, courage, and sympathy, were always
ready to aid one another, and to sacrifice themselves for the common good,
would be victorious over most other tribes; and this would be natural
selection. At all times throughout the world tribes have supplanted other
tribes; and as morality is one important element in their success, the
standard of morality and the number of well-endowed men will thus
everywhere tend to rise and increase.

This is a group selection model, but one that depends on confluences
of interests within groups and does not deny the existence of countering
conflicts of interest within groups. Thus, it is an appropriate model
because, despite Darwin's ignorance of the genetic materials, it would
operate through the survival of alleles as a result of selection at the
group level.

Since Williams' argument that which alleles survive depends primarily on reproductive successes and failures of individual organisms
rather than of groups, several investigators (e.g., Wade, 1976, 1978; D.
S. Wilson, 1975; 1980) have worked to devise schemes whereby,
theoretically or in the laboratory, allelic survival depends primarily on
selection at the group level. As noted earlier (p. 37), it is fairly easy to
accomplish this. The more important question, however, is: How
important is group selection in nature? The answer seems to be that
biologists almost never have to invoke it to explain many if not most
findings with respect to social behavior (e.g., see Alexander, 1979a,
p. 22ff.). Nevertheless, as I suggested in 1974, humans are an excellent
model for the kind of group selection Darwin envisioned.

Darwin (1871) is not entirely clear in the above arguments, however,
as is suggested by his phrases (above) "slight or *no* advantage" and
"*largely* guided by the approbation of our fellow-men [and] . . .
self-reason . . . " (emphases added). He notes that:

It is obvious that the members of the same tribe would approve of conduct
which appeared to them to be for the general good, and would reprobate
that which appeared evil. To do good unto others—to do unto others as ye
would that they should do unto you—is the foundation-stone of morality.
It is, therefore, hardly possible to exaggerate the importance during rude
times of the love of praise and the dread of blame. A man who was not

impelled by any deep, instinctive feeling, to sacrifice his life for the good of others, yet was roused to such actions by a sense of glory, would by his example excite the same wish for glory in other men, and would strengthen by exercise the noble feeling of admiration. He might thus do far more good to his tribe than by begetting offspring with a tendency to inherit his own high character. (p. 500)

Darwin sometimes gives the impression that he sees the "approbation and disapprobation" of "fellow-men" as a manipulative device which turns what would otherwise be selfish acts into expensive ones or what would otherwise be altruistic acts into self-interested ones. I would see this as completely compatible with a modern biological view of moral systems. But Darwin does not ever clarify this point, and he frequently says something that suggests the opposite (e.g., p. 493): "Finally the social instincts, which no doubt were acquired by man as by the lower animals for the good of the community, will from the first have given to him some wish to aid his fellows, some feeling of sympathy, and have compelled him to regard their approbation and disapprobation." Accordingly, I think we must give authorship of the idea that "heroism" is reproductive to Fisher (1958, 1930): "The mere fact that the prosperity of the group is at stake makes the sacrifice of individual lives occasionally advantageous, though this, I believe, is a minor consideration compared with the enormous advantage conferred by the prestige of the hero upon all his kinsmen" (p. 265). Fisher at once shows that the group and individual level selection arguments are not entirely incompatible (both may be operative), while supporting the latter as of greater importance. His theory is, in general, the same as that I am presenting here. Considerable elaboration is needed, however, before a simple statement that heroic tendencies evolved because they help kin can be translated into a general theory of moral systems.

## T. H. HUXLEY, AND MORALITY AS CONTRARY TO EVOLUTION

Now let us turn to the second group of biologist–philosophers, of which Thomas Huxley was probably the most effective proponent. Huxley believed, along with some other evolutionary biologists such as David Lack, that ethics and morality operate against evolution, and that there is a breach between the two which makes it impossible even to understand moral and ethical behavior in evolutionary terms. But his reasons were different from those of Lack, whose Christian ideology apparently made him stop short, without adequate explanation, of considering the moral sense a product of evolution and the issue of morality as other than divinely inspired (Lack, 1957).

Thus, T. H. Huxley (Huxley and Huxley, 1947) argues that the imitation of "the cosmic process [the evolutionary process] by man is inconsistent with the first principle of ethics." He says (Huxley, 1896):

> Let us understand, once for all, that the future depends, not on imitating the cosmic process, still less in running away from it, but in combating it . . . the practice of that which is ethically best—what we call goodness or virtue—involves a course of conduct which, in all respects, is opposed to that which leads to success in the cosmic struggle for existence. "Ethical nature may count upon having to reckon with a tenacious and powerful enemy as long as the world lasts." (p. 83)

Huxley's understanding, however, was more complete than is implied in the above quote. Thus, he footnotes the middle sentence in the above quote:

> Of course, strictly speaking, social life, and the ethical process in virtue of which it advances toward perfection, are part and parcel of the general process of evolution, just as the gregarious habit of innumerable plants and animals which has been of immense advantage to them, is so. A hive of bees is an organic polity, a society in which the part played by each member is determined by organic necessities. . . . Even in these rudimentary forms of society, love and fear come into play, and enforce a greater or less renunciation of self-will. To this extent the general cosmic process begins to be checked by a rudimentary ethical process, which is, strictly speaking, part of the former, just as the "governor" in a steam-engine is part of the mechanism of the engine. (p. 83)

In this statement Huxley too seems to see moral systems as an *outcome* of the "general cosmic process" as well as something that combats or opposes it.

## DARWIN, KEITH, AND HUMAN EVOLUTION IN GROUPS

Sir Arthur Keith (1947) was an effective member of the third group of biologist-philosophers. Keith disagreed with Waddington (1941) and other proponents of the naturalistic fallacy "in supposing that evolutionary knowledge can provide a basis for modern ethics" (p. 6), and also with T. H. Huxley in supposing that the "cosmic process" and the "ethical process" (p. 7) are in opposition. Keith saw the two processes as working in harmony because he believed that Huxley's view of the evolution of humans did not include Darwin's theory that human evolution " . . . was carried out mainly as a struggle between communities—team against team, tribe against tribe. Inside each team or tribe the 'ethical cosmos' was at work, forging and strengthening the social bonds which made the members of such a team a cooperative whole. These mental bonds, Darwin supposed, had been evolved from those inborn ties that link members of a family together—the love of parents for their children, of children for parents, and of children for each other." (p. 7)

However, Keith's (1947) view approached that of T. H. Huxley when he described "The law of Christ" as "incompatible with the law of evolution . . . the two laws are at war with each other; the law of Christ can never prevail until the law of evolution is destroyed" (p. 15). Here I should note, incidentally, that Keith failed to distinguish genetic or organic evolution from cultural change; he simply lumped the two processes under evolution. This does not invalidate as much of what he said as one might expect, because many of his statements about culture can be taken as reflecting the effects of the history of genetic change on our current tendencies and abilities.

Evidently Keith also saw the difficulty of expanding ethical structures to a universal brotherhood of all peoples on earth (which he called "Universalism"). "Universalism is possible only if nations and tribes are deprived of their independence or sovereign rights; war is a means of asserting, maintaining, or extending national or tribal independence" (p. 50). He says of Universalism (p. 51) that " . . . our desired Utopia demands not only a new order of government, but a new human mentality. . . ." Keith then points out (p. 52) that "Universalism as an ideal is probably much more ancient than . . . the Christian ideal. . . . Universalism has no drive, no momentum . . . is not contagious . . . has behind it no missionary enthusiasm." But:

> Universalism, not as an ideal but as a political practice, has been and is at work in all parts of the earth. Nowhere is Universalism welcomed and encouraged by a people; everywhere governments have forced and are forcing Universalism upon unwilling and resistant subjects. There is something in the Universalist ideal which runs against the grain of human nature. Force and fear are the driving power behind this regional kind of Universalism. Love and brotherhood have no part in its spread. (p. 52)

Next Keith explains how this "regional Universalism" has advanced:

> No tribe unites with another of its own free will. It will surrender its independence only if first conquered by force; or in the face of a powerful and aggressive opponent it may be driven to unite with other tribes to resist a common enemy. Every tribe seeks to ensure its safety and its continuance by increasing its power above that of its competitive neighbors by an increase of its numbers or of its territory, or by both of these ways. Fear and force are the chief means by which civilization welds tribes into nations. The

same means are employed to weld small competitive businesses into large combines. (p. 87)

Tribes are being swollen by conquest, weaker tribes are driven by fear to unite and so withstand their conquering neighbor. By war, force, terror, and diplomacy, local "universalisms" have been accomplished in Europe; in place of a thousand independent tribes we have some twenty-six nations— some weak, some very strong. (p. 53)

Then, evidently with tongue in cheek, he says "Having accomplished so much, why not let the beneficent process go on and reduce Europe to one unit? That would be a big step toward the final goal of the Universalist—a world state." Why not, he asks, allow Germany (he was writing during World War II) to accomplish her goal of unifying Europe "under her domination"?

Keith notes that "the fight for the Universalist ideal is being waged under two different flags—one is the flag of naked force, the other is the flag of freedom. The one offers Europe a tyranny; the other an agreed federation. Yet neither the aim of the Allies, and much less that of Germany, is of the kind which moved the minds of early [and, one may add, late] Universalist philosophers. They hoped that sweet reasonableness and a feeling of brotherliness would conquer the world for their ideal. How are we to reconcile our sense of right and of justice to these ever-recurring frustrations of our hopes? I know of only one way—a better understanding of the laws of evolution and of the workings of man's inborn mentality." Perhaps my words would be different, but I at least share Keith's feelings on these topics.

In his chapter on "Universalism in theory and in pratice" Keith cites authors such as Condorcet, William Godwin, and Edward Carpenter as "a few of the great minds who have entertained the idea through the ages . . . " And he quoted Darwin from *The Descent of Man:*

As man advances in civilization and small tribes are united into larger communities, the simplest reason would tell each individual that he ought to extend his social instincts and sympathies to all the members of the same nation . . . ; this point being once reached, there is only an artificial barrier to prevent his sympathies extending to the men of all nations and races . . . unfortunately experience shows us how long it is before we look on them as fellow creatures . . . sympathy beyond the confines of man—that is, *humanity* to the lower animals—seems to be one of the latest moral acquisitions. This virtue [humanity] seems to rise incidentally from our sympathies becoming more tender and more widely diffused until they extend to all sentient beings. (p. 54)

Later

Darwin's Universalism is closely akin to the sentiment which Adam Smith names "universal benevolence" (*Moral Sentiments*, sect. ii, chapter ii). "Though our effectual good offices can very seldom be extended to any wider society than that of our own country, our goodwill is circumscribed by no boundary, but may embrace the immensity of the universe." (p. 55)

As I have argued earlier (Alexander, 1977, 1979a; above, p. 79), the rules of morality and law alike seem not to be designed explicitly to allow people to live in harmony within societies but to enable societies to be sufficiently united to deter their enemies. Within-society harmony is the means not the end. My arguments agree with Keith (1947):

> The benefits which have accrued to the peoples of Europe by the spread of a limited "Universalist" ideal, although still confined by national boundaries, are manifest. Nations have secured internal peace; tribal wars and raids have vanished; internal trade has prospered. New cooperations have replaced old antagonisms and rivalries; civilization has become an integral part of the mind and of the home. These are real and solid benefits. But then consider the liabilities which our heightened nationalism has hung around our necks. To preserve our national integrity has involved us in wars infinitely more deadly and cruel than ever afflicted any people in tribal times (p. 57–58)

Keith argues that Universalism is not a feasible scheme and would not lead to Utopia. He quotes T. H. Huxley (1898):

> Even should the whole human race be absorbed in one vast polity, within which "absolute political justice" reigns, the struggle for existence with the state of nature outside it and the tendency to the return of the struggle within, in consequence of over-multiplication will remain . . . every child . . . will . . . bring into the world the instinct of unlimited self-assertion . . . the prospect of attaining untroubled happiness or of a State which can, even remotely, deserve the title of perfection appears to me to be as misleading an illusion as ever was dangled before the eyes of poor humanity. (p. 59)

> The most recent gifts of civilization—broadcasting, speedy intercommunication between all parts of the world by air, by sea, by land, international postal and telegraphic services, the cinema, literature, the daily dissemination of news—were hailed by almost every writer as heralding the dawn of internationalization and Universalism. What these inventions really have done is to quicken national life. Aristotle regarded a community numbering a hundred thousand as an impossibility; by means of the inventions just mentioned a nation numbering a hundred millions and more can be given the unity of a small tribe. (p. 62)

Keith notes that scientists tend to favor Universalism as a solution to the world's problems, "statesmen" being "usually reticent." It is still true.

Keith next asks whether, if mankind is unlikely to become Universalist under a *secular* government, it might do so under a religious one. He doubts it, noting that:

> . . . the area of the world over which the Prince of peace is alleged to preside is the most nationally minded part of the world—the part where fierce war is endemic. Christianity has not conquered nationalism; the opposite has been the case—nationalism has made Christianity its footstool. (p. 65)

Keith argues that with the "Love thine enemies" "amendment of the tribal law" [the latter "law" being to love one's neighbors and hate one's enemies] "Christ annihilates the law of evolution, he throws a bomb right into the very heart of the machinery by which and through which nature has sought to build up races or breeds of mankind." Perhaps. But I think that Keith does not here give sufficient attention to the question of a proper strategy by a people out of power, surrounded by enemies and at their mercy. "Bless them that curse you, do good to them that hate you, and pray for them which spitefully use you and persecute you" is counsel for a subordinate people, and, I would suspect, the way to survival and reproductive success for the vanquished since time began. "Love thine enemies" is also a call for evangelism, increasing the size and strength of your group. It can be so used regardless of Christ's or anyone else's meaning or motivation in exhorting people to do it. Grant (1977, pp. 120–123) refers repeatedly to a tendency by Jesus to restrict his ministry and that of his disciples to Jews " . . . no mission to the Gentiles was set on foot until after the Crucifixion" (p. 120). "No doubt Jesus shared the general Jewish hope that the Gentiles would in due course be called to share the Kingdom of God. But, for all his emphasis on loving one's neighbours, he did not call them himself" (p. 122).

Keith refers to the evangelism of Christianity, throwing open the creed of Christianity to all mankind, as against Nature—"anti-evolutionary in its aim"—while Judaism, teaching an absence of evangelism, within-group marriage, and a fierce exclusiveness, remained separate: "The Jew preferred to shoulder his racial burden and save his evolutionary soul." He argues that the Jews managed "to survive [their] . . . ordeal and come down, still nationally minded, to this day . . . because their religion, their law, and their mentality are conformable to the law of evolution: isolation and inbreeding are the chief factors in the production of special people or races." Statements of this sort may have been responsible for Keith being labeled a racist in anthropological circles, and for the subsequent neglect of his arguments.

Keith notes that Christianity spread through "compulsion, force, and war . . . outlawry, ostracism, excommunication . . . persecution and . . . naked force to secure unanimity of tribal faith among the members of its congregation." (p. 75). He argues that by thus becoming linked to nationalism Christianity betrayed its original creed; and he sees this as evidence that "Christianity has failed because its methods are discordant with human nature, and are therefore anti-evolutionary. Nationalism, on the other hand, is a growing force because it is in harmony with human nature, and therefore pro-evolutionary." Again, I think that the teachings of, say, Christianity or Judaism as "universal benevolence" are adaptive only among a conquered or vulnerable people, tending to lose their force and become perverted when the proponents of Christianity or Judaism are transformed into powerful peoples.

Keith also believes that "Civilization . . . like Universalism and Christianity, is anti-evolutionary in its effects . . . " I wonder if we are not misled by our belief, expressed by Ruse (1982), that people do not follow the rules out of fear of detection and retribution but out of some inner knowledge of what is right. That is, we are led to believe that there is a basic difference between international deterrence and national law. Perhaps there is a difference, in that international (intertribal) dispute is always a matter of open scheming, conniving, plotting, and deliberate planning (within tribes or nations), while anyone detected to be so operating within his group or tribe would be ostracized or worse for this motivation. Each nation pretends it is using the same virtues in its dealings with the other that are used among its people in dealing with one another, but perhaps none really does.

But, contrary to Keith, civilization is no more anti-evolutionary than within-group or -family kinship bonds. He seems to be saying this later (p. 90) when he argues that civilization has not really changed "man's mentality" and that the feelings once reserved for neighboring tribes are now directed against other nations: "England, in building up her civilization, replaced tribalism by nationalism . . . the behavior of one European nation to another is . . . 'uncivilized.' "

Keith notes that "All thought of Nature's ancient evolutionary purpose has been dismissed from the civilized mind" and " . . . so largely do the affairs of civilization occupy the modern mind that many have come to regard the advance of civilization and the development of a perfectly civilized society as the true and sole object of human existence." Nevertheless, he argues,

> Civilization has not increased the mental capacity of its subjects; what it has done is to supply men with the opportunities, the leisure, and the means to develop the mental gifts already attained by man while living in a state of nature. We altogether underestimate the mental and emotional outfit required by people living in a state of nature. (p. 88)
>
> . . . like millions more, I followed the rise and fall of famous football teams.

All such irrational proclivities I attribute in my own case and in that of millions of others, to our comparatively recent origin from tribal ancestors. To "take sides" is a sure sign of tribal mentality. Even we rationalists . . . are not infrequently guilty. . . . But, of course, we take the "right" side. (p. 92)

If morality means true sacrifice of one's own interests, and those of his family, then it seems to me that we could not have *evolved* to be moral. If morality requires ethical consistency, whereby one does not do socially what he would not advocate and assist all others also to do, then, again, it seems to me that we could not have *evolved* to be moral.

David Lack, and other biological-philosophers who both try to take account of evolution and reject the "naturalistic" fallacy, seemed to be inclined to the view that these things are true. Rather than reject the idea that humans are moral in the senses of sacrifice and ethical consistency, however, Lack supposed that the moral nature of humans comes from somewhere other than evolution. Lack apparently was a devout Christian, and there are indications that he believed that morality is a God-given attribute or admonition. Moral philosophers, as I have said, have never concerned themselves with the problem of making the concept of morality consistent with knowledge of the evolutionary process.

The alternative to Lack's apparent position is to suppose that humans are not really moral at all, in the sense of "true sacrifice" given above, but that the concept of morality is useful to them. We have to ask now how this could be so. If it is so, then we might imagine that, in the sense and to the extent that they are anthropomorphized, the concepts of saints and angels, as well as that of God, were also created because of their usefulness to us. I have already argued that the usefulness of morality, which restricts it to one's own group members, or allies, lies in intergroup competition.

Some saints, at least, really do appear to act contrarily to their own interests, at least in the short run, and that is why they are singled out. It would seem that they are the models we embrace in our moralizing efforts to get others to carry their temporarily self-sacrificing behavior in the continuous game of social reciprocity a shade farther than we do. To coerce someone into helping all group members indiscriminately rather than his own relatives preferentially is to cause him to help all of the rest of us, even if ever so slightly; and one reason this is so is that reproductive success is always relative.

## The Philosophers of Biology

Michael Ruse (1981; 1982, p. 266; 1984), a philosopher of biology, has recently tried to link evolutionary knowledge and moral issues. Perhaps inadvertently, he uses only examples implying that morality means either giving the greatest good to the greatest number or else serving the needs of everyone. Thus (p. 269), he regards it as moral (actually he refers to it as "the very opposite" of "immoral") to have rid the world of smallpox. He uses this as an example contradicting the notion that whatever is, ought to be. But this is a case in which the interests of all humans coincided: No one, I presume, stood up for protecting the smallpox virus from extinction. Any moral issue would involve, not the extinction of smallpox as such, but the question of how much each person should be expected to invest—or how much public money should be used—in the effort to extinguish smallpox.

That Ruse (1982, p. 270) indeed fails to distinguish moral questions and phenomena involving universal agreement is also indicated by his statement that " . . . if something makes *everyone* unhappy, its moral value is certainly in question" (emphasis added). In fact, when anything makes *everyone* either happy or unhappy—no matter how important it may be—it is presumably not a moral issue at all. Because everyone would wish to change that which makes everyone unhappy, presumably no one acted willfully to bring it about, and no one would defend it: there would be no conflict of interest.

We try to move moral issues in the direction of involving no conflict of interest, always, I suggest, by seeking universal agreement with our own point of view. But Ruse (p. 272) argues that if morality involves conflicting interests then " . . . really . . . there is no morality at all! I want the cake; you want the cake. Whosoever is stronger, or trickier, or less of a fool, gets it. That is the end of the matter. There is no morality here. No real right and wrong, whatever anyone says." Later he resolves the issue, for himself, by saying (p. 273) that " . . . even when people have different desires, they can share a moral code. I want the cake; you want the cake. We may both agree that we ought to give the cake to a third person, who is far hungrier than both of us."

But Ruse stops too soon. He implies that giving the cake to a third person represents real sacrifice by the other two. He does not even consider the possibility that some larger, less direct gain—as in good will from observers or from the third, hungrier person, and all of the possible tangible benefits larger than a piece of cake that may accrue from good will—is what is really at stake. He does not ask if we would give the cake to a third party in any other circumstance. As a result, it seems to me, his version of morality vanishes again.

In still another instance Ruse tries (p. 273) to resurrect morality as true altruism by noting that even if "two people (say a man and a woman) have different genetic interests" they may "work in loving unison (say, in raising their children)." He overlooks the fact that a man and a woman raising *their* (jointly produced) children have identical genetic interests in the project. Daly and Wilson (1981) present evidence that when this is not the case "loving unison" is in greater jeopardy, and so is the child.

Ruse is arguing against what he calls "moral relativity," by which he means the notion that morality is "subjective" as a consequence of everyone having different interests. He believes that societies allowing different marriage systems, such as polygamy and monogamy, "at a higher level of abstraction . . . subscribe to some such rule as: 'Everyone who so wishes ought to have a reasonable opportunity to get married, compatible with environmental factors and so forth.'" Once again he seems to be supporting the notions that morality means true sacrifice and that humans do it (i.e., that some individuals take mates to allow them a chance of marriage and forego additional mates to allow others to have mates). He seems not to be considering the possibilities that, for example, males are allowed to have as many mates as they do in some polygynous societies because the costs of preventing it are too high; that polygyny occurs because the most powerful men are powerful enough to enforce their intent to have multiple wives; or that monogamy is enforced because power is so distributed and the sex ratio such that the majority gains from such a rule, and that the same majority represents the power structure in such societies. The question then becomes: Why do shifts in power differentials occur (Betzig, 1986)?

Ruse mistakes the effect of evolution by natural selection (p. 270) when he denies the validity of "evolutionary ethics" by arguing that "From an evolutionary perspective . . . what we humans ought to do is to have just about as many offspring as the world can possibly hold." What evolution effects, however, is differential survival of alternative genetic materials. That it does not always do this by maximizing numbers is indicated by the general reduction of brood sizes in favor of more parental care for each offspring. Ruse also confuses the issue by implying that the point of evolution has been to preserve species:

> As yet another move to save Darwinian evolutionary ethics, one might be tempted to argue that what really counts, what is really of ultimate moral value, is that in some loose sense the human species be preserved and encouraged on its course. (p. 270)

He then says that this "overall position collapses" because "If Darwinian evolution teaches us anything, it is that the key to success lies in reproducing as many of one's kind as one possibly can."

But this "key to success" is in a within-species competition, not as a means of saving the species per se. Once again, unless someone disagrees with the notion that we ought not all to be extinguished, whether or not the human species ought to survive, even if it is regarded as the only crucial issue, is not a moral issue: there is no conflict of interest. What is a moral issue is whether or not we ought to be allowed to carry out, in our own individual or subgroup interests, behavior that to this or that degree *threatens* everyone's (or, for that matter, anyone else's) survival.

Ruse remarks that:

> I cannot believe that it would be morally a good thing for some people to have many children, and for the rest of us to have none, even though this seems to be the consequence of unfettered biology. (p. 290)

This is a peculiar remark. First, one may ask if there are reasons for supposing that it would be a "morally good thing" for all people to have equal numbers of children. Second, it is obviously *not* the necessary consequence of "unfettered biology" that some people have many children and others none, unless essentially every aspect of human behavior in groups amounts to a "fettering" of "biology."

## Morality and Law

Moral and legal systems are commonly distinguished by those, like moral philosophers, who study them formally. I believe, however, that the distinction between them is usually poorly drawn, and based on a failure to realize that moral as well as legal behavior occurs as a result of probable and possible punishments and reward. There seems to be a general feeling that moral behavior does not require rewards and punishments such as are provided by laws. Thus Baier (1958) asserts that

> . . . moral rules differ from laws and regulations in that they are not administered by special administrative organs such as policemen and magistrates. Everyone "administers" them himself . . . unlike laws and regulations, moral rules have not been laid down by anyone. (pp. 98–99)

I think Baier is mistaken in this supposition, and that moral systems are also systems of "laws" in which the rules are "laid down" much as formal laws are, and in which rewards and punishment are administered by others, but are usually far more subtle and sophisticated—and often far more devastating—than those typical of legal systems. When Baier says that everyone administers moral rules himself he could mean (1) that everyone is watching to see that others follow the rules, (2) that everyone oversees his own personal morality (by the use of a conscience, for example), or (3) both. I believe that (3) is the case. Only (2) really implies that moral rules differ from laws, but it seems clear to me that we often internalize the rules of law as well as the rules of morality—and perhaps by the same process: some peoples' consciences bother them as surely if they pass through a stop sign as if they pass by a beggar without contributing to his cause.

It would seem that laws are simply a specialized, derived aspect of what in earlier societies would have been a part of moral rules. On the other hand, law covers only a fraction of the situations in which morality is involved, and it is probably concentrated in those realms in which (1) either majority opinion, or the attitude of a minority power structure, is more consistent and definite and (2) the issues involved are more public. This opinion is not unique. Gross (1979), for example, says that:

> The right to be free of . . . harm does not have its origin in law but in a general consensus of the rights enjoyed by any member of society . . . this consensus is a more fundamental element of society than even the law . . . (pp. 13–14)

Law also tends to characterize those societies that are more formally and complexly organized, because of (1) their size or the level of their technology, (2) the prominence of reciprocity in social interactions (as opposed to nepotism, in which the currency is more difficult to evaluate because of the genetically reproductive component, i.e., our rewards come partly from the reproductive success of the helped relatives), and especially (3) the importance of written records. Printing enhances the consistency of rules across generations and provides records (precedents) to which everyone can return for guidance, in effect facilitating the transformation of customs into laws and creating a milieu in which very complex systems of reciprocity can flourish. The printed word provides a source of precedents which is reliable and essentially unchanging. No longer is it necessary to rely upon the oral opinions or assertions of those in power. This takes away considerable ability to manipulate, and creates a trap for those who would argue for justice as equal treatment only when it is to their advantage to do so. When their words have been recorded they can be reviewed for confirmation and accuracy. William D. Hamilton has also suggested to me in conversation that the printed word tended to place the recording of opinions in the hands of people with attitudes and abilities different from those who wield authority in the absence of printed words. In a sense, the printed word broke up the monopoly or authority of those who previously held the power to wield it orally, and to whom it was always necessary to return for the rules.

These points can be illustrated by considering the remarks of moral philosopher, Kurt Baier (1958), quoted above (p. 180). I will argue that the sentence "Everyone administers them himself . . . " would be more nearly accurate if the word, "himself," were omitted; and that moral rules are "administered" by the whole or most of society—by the approval and disapproval of the group. If Baier means to refer to the internalizing of rules and regulations by each individual, through conscience, memorization, self-conditioning, or whatever (in the sense of Kohlberg's, 1981, final stage of "moral development"), then I would argue that we do essentially the same thing with respect to formal law.

When Baier says (p. 99) that "unlike law and regulations, moral rules have not been laid down by anyone," I am not sure whether the emphasis is on "laid down" or "anyone," but I think I would disagree in either case. A rule is just as surely "laid down" if it is orally or tacitly agreed to and universally understood as when it is a matter of written record; and, after all, many rules regarded as moral and not a part of the legal code are written down and discussed formally in diverse fashions. As for the notion that moral rules have not originated with *anyone*, the only alternative that I can fathom is a divine source, and this kind of "explanation" or rationalization has little analytical value unless divinity arises out of human thought, which returns us to the proposition that Baier rejects.

Some philosophers argue that legal systems differ from moral systems in that their methods of enforcement may involve "fear of penalties imposed by a minority of powerful persons" (Whiteley, 1976, p. 90). Thus, Whiteley (1976, p.90) says in writing about "Morality and Egoism" that he does not "count a rule as belonging to the morality of a society" if it is so enforced. "Moral rules and ideals are those which have the general support of the members . . . morality depends on common consent. . . . " But the actual sources and reasons for so-called moral rules are often obscure, and I can find no reason for believing that they are unlike formal laws in never involving compromises, subterfuges, and manipulations by minority power structures. It is not sufficient that some, most, or even all of us may regard some moral rules as highly palatable because of our personal backgrounds, beliefs, or statuses in society. The close relationship between moral and legal systems is suggested by so-called "Good Samaritan" laws in which bystanders or passersby who do not aid a person in distress can be fined (Gross, 1979).

The distinction I would suggest between moral and legal systems is that legal systems arise out of long-continued agreement, by either the majority or the power structure, on matters of right and wrong: such agreement leads to establishment of more or less permanent regulations, and this works because such a high proportion of the powerful people in the society agree. Moral systems, on the other hand, comprise belief systems of subgroups and proportions of the people that are small enough, or else belief systems that change often enough, to reduce the desires and tendencies of society as a whole to make them into definite, permanent, or irreversible regulations. Everyone knows that issues of morality and ethics present paradoxes; and many know that not merely ordinary people in their everyday activities but the intellectuals and formal students of moral systems across the ages have made little progress toward resolving the moral paradoxes since the first records of their consideration by the ancients.

All too often moral philosophers—who perhaps more than any other group of individuals might have been expected to resolve the moral paradoxes—have either become preoccupied with the meaning of words and phrases in one another's special arguments or else fallen into the trap of making pronouncements, of which the following are examples:

> An act is right when it conduces to the moral good, that is, to harmonious happiness; and it is wrong when it conduces to disharmony. (Perry, 1954, p. 107)

> . . . the belief in ego or me-first as the source of all unethical behavior, both immoral and unmoral . . . is certainly largely correct. (Frankena, 1980, p. 67)

> If the point of view of morality were that of self-interest, then there could *never* be moral solutions of conflicts of interest. . . . (Baier, 1958, p. 99)

Each of these statements is an unsupported assertion. Each also involves one or more areas of vagueness or ambiguity. Thus, how is one to identify "harmonious happiness" or "disharmony"? Who decides? If we were all agreed on what is conducive to harmonious happiness, morality as a topic of interest—perhaps as a topic at all—would fade. Baier also remarks (pp. 161–162) that " . . . the essential function of law is regulation. . . . not for the sake of regularity, but for the sake of adjusting human interests, and thereby achieving the good life of harmonious happiness." Was it wrong, then, for blacks in the South to create "disharmony" refusing to step to the back of the bus, or by trying to eat at the Woolworth counter? Many thought so. Was it wrong for the Supreme Court to rule against segregation in 1954, so as to disrupt the *apparent* harmony of the segregated South? Baier would surely say no, citing his phrase "adjusting human interests," but very large numbers of people regarded all three acts just described as conducing to disharmony, and therefore wrong. It is at least fair to ask whose opinions should be considered—just those in the South? Northerners too? Canadians? Ghanians? South Africans? Anyone interested? What kind of distribution of answers, or what size of majority, will we use to establish the rightness or wrongness of these acts? And what about asking the same questions in 1853, or any time other than 1953?

The same kinds of questions can be raised about Baier's and Frankena's assertions. It is worthwhile to take the ambiguity and arbitrariness out of such statements, and I think this can now be done, to a much greater degree than previously, by considering new theory and information from biology. Baier's statement, for example, is clearly inadequate: all that would be necessary to create what he says could *never* be created is for society, or its majority or power structure, to develop a system of rewards and punishments whereby it is in everyone's self-interest to follow the rules. This can be accomplished wherever group cooperativeness is in the self-interests of a sufficient number of individuals. I would argue that this is precisely what both moral and legal systems are all about, and that the easiest way to understand is by assessing costs and benefits in terms of evolutionary biological theory.

Law, then, seems to be little more than ethics written down. Both law and ethics are much more concerned with punishment than with rewards, because, I believe, they are systems of restraints against too-extreme acts of self-interest. Both law and ethics are most often a defense of the many against the few: the many who recognize the value (to themselves and theirs) of the unity, strength, and persistence of the group against the few with shorter (or longer) vision or alternative connections. The moralizer is one who is making a special effort to turn it all to his own personal gain within the group. He is damned only with faint resistance, for what he advocates is that ideal behavior which if universal would further the interests of the group. He has the possibility of gaining (1) because his advocacy not only is aimed to correspond to the group's interests but simultaneously portrays him as more a promoter of the ideal than his actions may reveal (i.e., his moralizing, if cleverly done, may draw attention away from his own transgressions), and (2) because he may induce self-deleterious behavior in others.

But the focus here is on the internal trend across history in human social structure. Does it tend to reduce conflicts of interest? I believe so; I think the general trend of law is toward equalizing access to the usual resources of reproduction, including mates. This trend may be opposed successfully only temporarily, in association with unusual imbalances of power between subgroups; the opposite is eventually divisive in its effects—thus tending to reduce group sizes and cohesiveness. Thus, despotism may be more characteristic of small- or intermediate-sized human groups such as tribes and "chiefdoms" (Alexander, 1979a; Betzig, 1986). Trends toward increased despotism in the rise of larger groups among the *smallest* human social groups (bands to chiefdoms) seem opposite to those that have occurred in the much larger groups (modern states or nations). Socially imposed monogamy, women's suffrage, affirmative action toward minorities, special assistance to the physically and mentally handicapped—all of these are very recent trends toward equalization of opportunity with respect to within-group interests that appear to operate in the greater interest of maintaining social unity in very large human groups. It is as if the smaller groups are able to unify in larger and larger coalitions in the balance-of-power race primarily by allowing or designating single leaders; these leaders accept their positions because of special perquisites, which become more lavish as despotism continues to be the means of organizing further for defense. Then (in humans as in social insects—the only real parallel in group sizes among sexual organisms; see Alexander and Noonan, in prep.), it seems that a dramatic reversal allows sudden and extraordinary expansion of group sizes: despotism is replaced by opportunity leveling; leaders of huge nations at least appear to accept far fewer perquisites. As young men become more and more crucial for defense, older men become less and less able to control the women and prevent access to them by young men. Thus, perhaps, polygyny begins to disappear, and monogamy becomes the rule. Men are able to marry younger. The extended family (in the anthropological sense of a cohesive, controlling influence on the lives of individuals) weakens or disappears as vengeance is forbidden to clans and enforcement of the rules passes to government. To a greater degree, then, young people begin to choose their own mates. Socially imposed monogamy may have been a pivotal issue, because of its involvement with the crucial resource of mates, its great effects on the young men of military age, its role in reducing conflicts of interest at the family level (by inducing symmetries of genetic relatedness among the central core of social interactants), and its close relationship to the general concept of justice as equality of opportunity in all matters (see also Alexander, 1979a).

Public interests arise because of the comprehension that there are broad bases or spreads of equality or identical interests that often oppose the interests of individuals. Recognition of "public" as opposed to "private" interests is a significant indicator of the social nature of things and of the problems in understanding reciprocity in a complex society.

Anyone who reads the literature on dispute settlement within different societies (e.g., Nader and Todd, 1978; Miller, 1976) will quickly understand that genetic relatedness counts: it allows for one-way flows of benefits and alliances. Long-term association also counts; it allows for reliability and also correlates with genetic relatedness. In long-term associations there is plenty of time and multiple and subtle opportunity for retribution. In small, stable groups use of disinterested third parties, an integral part of formal law, is often resisted, and its necessity is viewed as a loss of freedom, an invasion of privacy, and, at best, a necessary evil. The reason is obvious: instead of being required to avenge relatives, for example, one is forbidden to do so. Once formal law is instituted, its effective use tends to break up within-group sanctions, such as status shifts and other ways of denying access to resources, especially in societies in which individuals are highly mobile and can move away from their social debts and disputes. Use of disinterested third parties sets formal, generalized limits on the punishment or penance that can be exacted for a social transgression. Formal law reduces the power of local bullies and moralizers, and it is resented by them. The larger the social group, the more fluid its membership; and the more attenuated the social interactions of its membership, the more they are forced to rely on formal law (cf. Schwartz and Miller, 1964).

Formal law, partly because it is written down and represents a stable set of precedents, may require what I think of as the "creep" toward social systems that approach the idealized models of indiscriminate beneficence described earlier (p. 100). Two factors seem to me to be crucial in the continuation of this creep; roughly equal influence of different individuals, as in one vote per person; and relative openness in society so that individuals can understand the issues. How and why these institutions arise is more difficult, as is the question of why, in a society like that in the United States, changes that give rights to minorities or otherwise disadvantaged groups do not proceed at an even rate. Some fluctuations are caused by outside threats such as war, while others are caused by changes in economic conditions. Nevertheless, freeing of slaves, women's suffrage, social welfare, desegregation, affirmative-action programs, equal rights efforts, and provision in public places to accommodate the physically disadvantaged are all evidence of increased interest in indiscriminateness in social beneficence.

## Morality and Democracy

Part of the aura of mystery or paradox that seems to lie at the core of human nature and sociality can be clarified by considering what have been seen as the "contradictions" of democratic forms of government. Lipson (1985), for example, notes that the two concepts of liberty and equality are the "twin ideals" of democratic theorists:

It is these values preeminently which infuse into the democratic form of government its animating spirit. You cannot theorize about the goals of a democratic polity or evaluate the success or failure of any actual democracy without couching your thought in the context of these symbols. If one tries to compress the ethos of democracy into the briefest summary, it will run something like this: Democracy is the form of government which combines for its citizens *as much freedom and as much equality as possible* [emphasis added]. (p. 152)

As Lipson notes, his final phrase embodies the paradox: "When we say that our governing ideals are liberty and equality, and that the aim of democratic governments is to combine them in practice, what we have done is to propound a riddle with more double meanings than the Delphic oracle ever contrived." The reason, as we can now see, is ultimately biological (although, interestingly enough in view of earlier arguments in this book, Lipson compares the theorizing of political scientists only with that of physicists): individuals have separate interests. They join forces (live in groups; become social) when they share *certain* interests that can be better realized for all by close proximity or some forms of cooperation. Typically, however, the overlaps of interests rarely are completely congruent with those of either other individuals or the rest of the group. This means that, even during those times when individual interests within a group are most broadly overlapping, we may expect individuals to temper their cooperation with efforts to realize their own interests, and we may also expect them to have evolved to be adept at using others, or at thwarting the interests of others, to serve themselves (and their relatives). This is precisely why the "liberties" of individuals and subgroups must be limited and why "inequalities" must continually be curbed. The question is how these "twin ideals" interact in different situations. Lipson says that contradictions arise " . . . indeed, in logic, they are insurmountable— when liberty and equality, however defined, are held as absolutes. Pushed to its logical extreme, neither yields to the other. . . . The aim of public policy is to discover the appropriate distribution of specific freedoms and equalities *in contexts which continually change*" [emphasis added]. (p. 159)

Lipson goes on to remark that "Sometimes it is necessary to restrict certain liberties of certain persons in order, correspondingly, to enlarge the correlative freedoms of others. This is also . . . a process of equalization." He notes that in the U.S., "The Left, representing or leading the underprivileged, . . . hopes to reduce the inequalities of wealth and social status . . . . Contrariwise, the Right reflects the attitudes of those at the top of the heap, conservatives who are well satisfied with unequal privileges which they wish to retain. Their

emphasis is on the liberty of the individual, meaning primarily themselves, which they consider threatened by the programs of the welfare
state and the graduated taxes needed to finance them."

So Lipson identifies the problem as a conflict between those better off
who wish to retain their status and those worse off who wish to better
theirs. Each hopes to accomplish his purpose at the expense of the
other. Along with many writing on such topics, however, he implies
that the motivation of one of these parties is somewhat nobler than that
of the other: striving for "equality" somehow seems more moral by
definition than does striving for the freedom to practice entrepreneurship to one's own advantage. Perhaps striving by the "downtrodden
masses" to better their lot does have outcomes that come closer to
widespread ideals of justice, since, regardless of actual motivation, it
does tend to reduce the variance in status, wealth, or privilege, while
similarly motivated striving by those already having such perquisites
increases the variance. It must be true that the pattern of variation in
such perquisites determines where power lies, and ultimately influences
strongly the directions and kinds of change within societies.

There is another element, however, which I was puzzled not to find
in Lipson's analysis. To me it represents the knottiest problem of
government if not of morality. It is the problem of determining when
(and which) liberties (opportunities) for individuals and subgroups will
eventually *enhance* the liberties (opportunities) of others—even the
evidently most downtrodden or lowest in status and resource availability. Everyone knows that entrepreneurship can benefit everyone else as
well as the entrepreneur. It is much easier, I think, to see how
restrictions of the liberty of some give additional opportunities to others
than to predict accurately when efforts toward equality will restrict the
opportunities of all.

In this connection I find it particularly interesting to consider Rawls'
(1971) view of justice in relation to an "original [hypothetical] position"
in which those who formulate the rules do not know their places in
society, their "class position or social status," or their "fortune in the
distribution of natural assets and abilities, . . . intelligence, strength, and
the like." What Rawls wishes to create, by having the rules be formulated from behind such a "veil of ignorance," is a circumstance in which
each rule formulator imagines himself as potentially one of the most
vulnerable members of the society in which the rules will apply. The
reason he has to invoke such a veil of ignorance is that otherwise those
with status, goods, intelligence, strength, or whatever resources, may be
expected to promote rules that will cause the advantages to be even
more useful than otherwise would be the case. The reason I am

particularly interested in the approach is, first, that societal changes like universal suffrage give more say to those who will see themselves as most likely to be disadvantaged in the future. Second, the interest of people in the fates of the collection of their relatives now and in the future—emphasized in discussions of individual interests throughout this book—may often cause Rawls' "veil of ignorance" to approach reality. That is, the rule-makers and -maintainers of any generation cannot tell what particular statuses and resources their descendants and other relatives in future generations will possess. This will be most especially true in those societies, such as many democracies, in which social and financial mobility are greatest. This fact may contribute significantly to the "creep" toward equality of opportunity, or "justice as fairness," in such societies (see also, p. 106).

When the interests of all are most nearly congruent, it is essentially always due to a threat shared equally. Such threats almost always have to be external (or else they are less likely to affect everyone equally; exceptions are interracially or otherwise divided populations, as in South Africa—where unity is also restricted to *within* the adversarial subgroups—or, less clearly, internal threats such as famine from over-population, at least in societies already rigidly totalitarian, as in modern China). External threats to societies are typically other societies. Maintenance of such threats can yield situations in which everyone benefits from rigid, hierarchical, quasi-military, despotic government. Liberties afforded leaders—even elaborate perquisites of dictators—may be tolerated because such threats are ever-present (Betzig, 1986). Extrinsic threats, and the governments they produce, can yield inflexibilities of political structure that can persist across even lengthy intervals during which the threats are absent.

Some societies have been able to structure their defenses against external threats as separate units (armies) within society, and to keep them separate. These rigidly hierarchical, totalitarian, and dictatorial subunits rise and fall in size and influence according to the importance of the external threat. They represent everyone's vehicle for serving common interests when these become acute. When, for one reason or another, such defensive subunits take over or characterize the government, we typically regard the society as "less free" (Gastil, 1985).

It seems to me that western democracies are characterized by particular kinds of flexibility in allowing or promoting individual liberties, in which entrepreneurship is used relatively effectively by the society as a whole for the good of its membership. The entrepreneur gains, but in the process others gain too. The same societies manage to keep their military as a separated branch of government service. These societies respond to changing circumstances by changing the sizes and strengths of their armies and the freedom of entrepreneurs. Such flexibilities may be strengths or weaknesses in the presence of competing or aggresive neighbor societies. For example, they are strengths when they lead to useful technological breakthroughs or promote unity through pride of social structure or desire to maintain "freedom." They are weaknesses when the debates that characterize decision-making delay or cause equivocation in responses to aggressors. They are also strengths when they involve flexibilities in responding to novel situations (e.g. international disputes) that cannot occur in more rigid competing societies.

Discussion of liberty and equality in democracies closely parallels discussions of morality and moral systems. In either case, adding a perspective from evolutionary biology seems to me to have potential for clarification.

## The Goal of Universal Beneficence

To think of humans existing without conflicts of interest is to assume situations involving or mimicking what biologists have come to call group selection, in a way explicitly opposing the notion of individuals striving to maximize their separate reproductive successes. It seems to me that this thought returns us to the ideal state of morality postulated by philosophers, theologians, and social scientists, and to Darwin's "universalism" and Adam Smith's "universal benevolence." If so, biology supports the view of Perry (1954) and numerous other philosophers that morality (at least as expressed in the behavior of individuals) is in fact only an ideal or a pursuit, and never actually realized. If morality is defined in the philosophers' terms as self-sacrifice, and if this means (with knowledge of the significance of nepotism) genotypic as well as phenotypic sacrifice, then the idea of morality as an unrealized ideal is consistent with the approach from evolutionary biology that I have been describing. It is indeed common, if not universal, to regard moral behavior as a kind of altruism that necessarily yields the altruist less than he gives, and to see egoism as either the opposite of morality or the source of immorality; but, as we have already seen, this view is usually based on an incomplete understanding of nepotism, reciprocity, and the significance of within-group unity for between-group competition.

Returning to Singer's thesis, discussed earlier, it would seem that he expects or hopes, as does a large class of people who seek world peace and a new level of morality, that we can achieve these ends (only?) by expanding the kind of morality we now express within groups, and seen as group loyalty. Because Singer basically sees morality as altruism that

(1) costs the actor and (2) is motivated by the desire to benefit others, it follows that all one has to do is somehow widen the circle of persons we rationally (and morally) treat in fashions expensive to ourselves. Schell (1982), in his efforts to see how to save the planet from nuclear holocaust, seems to employ a similar kind of reasoning. As earlier quotes show, Darwin (1871) outlined the same thesis, in words surprisingly like those of modern writers.

My view of moral systems in the real world, however, is that they are systems in which costs and benefits of specific actions are manipulated so as to produce reasonably harmonious associations in which everyone nevertheless pursues his own (in evolutionary terms) self-interest. I do not expect that moral and ethical arguments can ever be finally resolved because conflicts of interest cannot be finally or ultimately resolved. Compromises and contracts, then, are (at least currently) the only real solutions to actual conflicts of interest. This is why moral and ethical decisions must arise out of decisions of the collective of affected individuals; there is no single source of right and wrong.

I would also argue against the notion that rationality can be easily employed to produce a world of humans that self-sacrifice in favor of other humans, not to say nonhuman animals, plants, and inanimate objects. Declarations of such intentions may themselves often be the acts of self-interested persons developing, consciously or not, a socially self-benefiting view of themselves as extreme altruists. In this connection it is not irrelevant that the more dissimilar a species or object is to one's self the less likely it is to provide a competitive threat by seeking the same resources. Accordingly, we should not be surprised to find humans who are highly benevolent toward other species or inanimate objects (some of which may serve them uncomplainingly), yet relatively hostile and noncooperative with fellow humans. As Darwin (1871) noted with respect to dogs, we have selected our domestic animals to return our altruism with interest.

Because of the value of models of extreme altruism and the prevalence of manipulative behavior I do not doubt that occasional individuals lead lives that are truly altruistic and self-sacrificing. However admirable and desirable such behavior may be from others' points of view, it represents an evolutionary mistake for the individual showing it. This only means that I do not suppose it likely that such behavior can easily be induced generally. I think there have been far fewer such truly self-sacrificing individuals than might be supposed, and most cases that might be brought forward are likely instead to be illustrations of the complexity and indirectness of reciprocity, especially the social value of appearing more altruistic than one is. I also appreciate the fact that these speculations will be viewed with distress by those who have great faith (or hope) in the value of what I see as the myth of ideal morality as a possible or likely universal. But I also believe that to understand the natural history of morality to its core is one of the ways to change this situation.

That I regard true altruism, in the sense of genetic self-sacrifice, as rare means that I also regard order and justice, as they now exist, as outcomes of self-interested behavior (in the sense of genetic interests). I also regard it as crucial that we test this hypothesis thoroughly, and, if it is correct, that we take it directly and plainly into account in our efforts to preserve or restructure society.

If moral systems are efforts to convince (other) people to behave as though they are products of group selection, one wonders how such "mimicry" began? Did it arise out of (1) a residuum of group-selective effects and efforts to magnify them or (2) manipulation of indiscriminate altruism expressed *within* groups (but not between them) as a result of either (a) groups being composed of close kin or (b) groups often passing through circumstances in which the interests of the individuals comprising them converge because of extrinsic hostile forces? To be able to answer such questions is not trivial because of the potential for contributing to our efforts to understand the proximate correlates of morality.

If morality tends to mimic the effects of group selection, if moralizing seeks to promote this mimicry, and if tendencies for people to be altruistic are self-reinforcing within societies, then it is not remarkable that knowledgeable and well-meaning people sometimes resent the arguments that natural selection is not powerful at group levels, and that humans, as individuals, have evolved to further their own reproduction. Such persons may well believe (or sense) that publicizing or stressing such arguments, even if they are correct, will diminish altrusim and morality by providing an anti-moral model. The indications that humans have regarded moral models as extremely important in achieving societal goals cause such a belief to be completely understandable. Nevertheless, it does not seem useful to allow this attitude to destroy the goal of diminishing human problems through improving self-knowledge. One could argue, for example, that one reason to support the kind of morality that considers it right and good for people to find out about seeming altruism really being selfish is that this revelation might lead to increased efforts at *appearing* to be altruistic, hence (inadvertently), increased altruism rather than increased selfishness. There are also other obvious ways to argue that knowledge of the background of the concept of morality, no matter how distasteful the findings, may actually enhance morality. (For example, such knowledge would heighten awareness of self-interested behaviors posing as costly beneficence and thereby render such awareness costly because of reactions of other self-interested persons to the sham altruist.) This is not to say that the myths and unattained ideals of morality have not contributed to drawing us in the directions they represent. I think it is obvious that they often do so, if for no other reason than by providing illustrations of the degrees and manners by which we may, as individuals, present ourselves to one another as models of beneficence. As I have already suggested, indirect recriprocity and the cost of being identified as less beneficient than others will surely narrow the variance in degrees of beneficence and probably move sociality toward any model of greater beneficence that is taken seriously.

On the other hand, it may be advantageous to recognize that our efforts toward idealized models of morality within societies may also cause, ironically, the most serious threats to humanity. Nationalistic chauvinism, patriotism, and pride in one's own group, society, people, religion, or way of life represent the large-scale cooperative efforts that produce adversaries capable of destroying the world and incapable so far of withdrawing from the brink of disaster. Perhaps we must substitute a different model of morality which admits and accepts the history of individual efforts that philosophers would call egoistic, and which calls for kinds and degrees of altruism falling short of those proposed in the current idealized models from philosophy and religion (and also falling short of what actually occurs under extreme patriotism *within* groups), but which goes considerably beyond what is commonly proposed or expected under the rubric of individualism. I hope that such a model is reasonable and attainable, for we may have no alternative.

*(Conversation overheard between two students leaving a lecture on human behavior and evolution.)*

> Even if these things are true, you shouldn't *tell* people about them or they will just use them to manipulate one another even more!
>
> Oh no, you missed the whole point! Once you find out what it's all about you don't *care* as much about reproduction and deception and all that!

## Summary

The problems that have plagued moral and legal philosphers have tended to involve the dichotomy of egoism versus utilitarianism. Arguments from biology (1) show that egoism has never been appropriately identified by human-oriented investigators; (2) provide reasons for

predicting that moralities based on utilitarianism have been oversimplified, and are only fleetingly likely to be achieved; and (3) explain the
significance of moral systems that are represented in terms of unattained
and probably unattainable goals. Thus, we have evolved to be egoists,
but the "particle of the dove in our makeup" that puzzled Hume is our
evolved tendency to favor relatives, invest in reciprocators, and portray
ourselves favorably to potential reciprocators. Egoism is not simply a
matter of pleasure over pain or "winning" for our own selves. Conflicts
of interest are the source and background of moral systems, and can
only be understood and quantified from a knowledge of rewards
identified ultimately in reproductive terms (or, in modern environments, in terms of novelty in proximate rewards that amount to
surrogates of reproduction). Utilitarianism (in the sense of the greatest
good to the greatest number) is likely only when interests are perceived
as identical throughout societies. Except when external threats cause
individual interests to be the same as group interests, morality as the
pursuit of a goal unrealized is maintained in the expectation that it will
serve its supporters through its effects on others (in both direct and
insubtly indirect fashions).

## Conclusions

The arguments of preceding sections have led us to an additional set
of conclusions:

1. In their efforts to analyze self-interests and altruism, moral
philosophers have usually omitted nepotism, and never included more
than its most obvious aspects (e.g., assistance to one's immediate
family). Inability to deal with nepotism has been a major source of
confusion in efforts to generalize about altruism and morality.

2. Indirect reciprocity is more complex than is usually realized, partly
because of long-term benefits that result from the effects of being viewed
as an altruist, and partly because one must take into account benefits to
the individual that accrue from the success of his group in competition
with other groups. Defining morality as self-sacrificing, failing to
understand all aspects of indirect reciprocity, and injecting the question
of motivation without clarifying how little we understand our own
personal motivations and social acts, have caused crucial points to be
missed.

3. Previous discussions of "value" have commonly referred to the
greatest good (to the greatest number) and in this way tended to
sidestep the problem of conflicts over values or interests. Similarly,
dealing with the "greatest number" has tended to mean "within one

society" and so also sidestepped the problem of within-group amity serving between-group enmity.

4. When these failures are taken into account there do not seem to be any remaining reasons for regarding morality, as normally expressed, as necessarily self-sacrificing, or for invoking anything other than nepotism and reciprocity to account for human societal structure.

5. To the extent that morality is a within-group cooperativeness generated in the context of between-group competition, and with abilities and tendencies to express it in appropriate situations evolved in the same context, consistency requires that we view its original significance as inconsistent with the principles typically associated with modern definitions of moral behavior.

> In brief, I hold that from the very beginning of human evolution the conduct of every local group was regulated by two codes of morality, distinguished by Herbert Spencer as the "code of amity" and the "code of enmity." There were thus exposed to "natural selection" two opposing aspects of man's mental nature. The code of amity favoured the growth and ripening of all those qualities of human nature which find universal approval—friendliness, goodwill, love, altruism, idealism, faith, hope, charity, humility, and self-sacrifice—all the Christian virtues. Under the code of enmity arose those qualities which are condemned by all civilized minds—emulation, envy, the competitive spirit, deceit, intrigue, hate, anger, ferocity, and enmity. How the neural basis of such qualities, both good and bad, came into existence during the progressive development of the human brain, we do not know, but it is clear that the chances of survival of a struggling, evolving group would be strengthened by both sets of qualities: . . . It will thus be seen that I look on the duality of a human nature as an essential part of the machinery of human evolution. (Keith, 1947)

# 4

## APPLYING THE BIOLOGICAL VIEW
## OF MORALITY

### Morality and Openness in the Pursuit of Truth:
### Science, Law, and God as the Models

## INTRODUCTION

Honesty: the truth, the whole truth, and nothing but the truth.

What a difficult set of problems is raised by the above phrase. We associate it with courtrooms. Even though most people may somehow view truth as desirable, even as an ideal, I think we are safe in saying that no one practices the above motto in everyday life. The compulsive truth-teller is as pathological and unhappy as the compulsive liar. Moreover, we do not always want to be told the truth. In the courtroom, presumably, somebody's life, career, or good name is at stake, and there is a sharp conflict of interest that requires special effort by parties external to the dispute to bring about society's version of justice. Even there we are both thrilled and chilled by the prospects of "the whole truth."

What a quagmire we face because we simultaneously seem to seek the truth and to avoid it. In some sense society can never be a completely truthful organization. We proclaim our passion for truth and revere it in *some* situations, despise it and regard it as worse than worthless or harmful in others. Why is this the case, and how do we decide which situations are which? Why do we admonish our children to be truthful yet teach them not to tell Aunt Martha that she is fat or Uncle John that his breath is bad or cousin Jim that his pimples are repulsive; or to reveal to visitors that Mom threw a book at Dad this morning, or what sister Jane looks like with her clothes off, or that what littered the living room was thrown quickly into the closet when they arrived? (Oliver Wendell Holmes is reputed to have said that "Pretty much all the truth-telling there is in the world is done by children.")

Why, if the truth is our goal and motto, do we begin to deceive from

197

the moment we arise from our beds in the morning, with clothes that modify our body shapes flatteringly, makeup and hair arrangements that improve our eyelashes or face shapes or cover a bald spot? Why do we spend our waking hours before and after sleep, and while shaving (shaving?) or showering or dressing, building scenarios by which we may deceive or best in some fashion those with whom we are scheduled to interact during the day? Why do we exclaim enthusiastically upon meeting someone we would rather have avoided; or when we meet another, dear or attractive to us, at a time when the enthusiasm is covering a deep and desolate feeling of despair or boredom or dissatisfaction with the day, ourselves, or the combination of the two? Why do we constantly deceive everyone?

How do individuals, and the collection of individuals that comprise society, make their decisions about what constitute acceptable deviations from "the whole truth and nothing but the truth" in different circumstances?

Piously, perhaps, we assert that one should not do or say anything that hurts another, i.e., "good" people do not do or say such things. How does this premise work out? If one does something that would hurt another if it were discovered, it would only follow that the act should be concealed if and when the additional act of concealment is not likely to lead to further hurt. Does it then follow that one who commits a murder in a moment of passion, quite unlikely to recur, should confess? One might argue that such a moment of passion might in fact recur, and the actor may be the last to know the likelihood, or to assess it accurately. But is this the usual rationale for murder convictions? Or is it revenge? Or a lesson to others? One may ask whether or not it is a "hurt" to others (by being a wrong lesson to some) that a murderer goes undetected. Or detrimental, even, that a case of murder—available as a lesson to others if solved—is not so used by, say, punishing the murderer in a fashion that provides a lesson to all. Gross (1979) says that, ". . . everywhere criminal justice is strangely uncertain in its goals"; and he describes all the above reasons as being invoked by one set of persons or another.

To tell Aunt Martha she is fat, or Uncle John that he has bad breath, hurts. But whom? We discuss such questions, saying that perhaps she will lose the weight, and be happier, if we tell her. Or Uncle John will brush his teeth and people will then like him and he will be happy, if we tell him. But, if we tell them, these may not be our real reasons. Perhaps we were a little angry at Aunt Martha or Uncle John and relished a secret bit of enjoyment at creating discomfort. From another point of view, if we tell them, they may not like us afterward. And if they have resources to distribute they may leave us out. Who then is hurt? Or whose possible or probable hurt is the reason for the truth or the deviation from it? We tend to dislike such questions and analyses. But can we otherwise truly understand ourselves—whether or not it is realistic to take seriously T. H. Huxley's admonition that "The foundation of morality is to have done, once and for all, with lying"?

Earlier I spoke of a circle of secrecy that each person builds around himself—including those items of information about himself, or goals or intentions, that cannot be revealed to others without detrimental effects on the individual's interests. In the United States, where individual initiative and entrepreneurship seem to have been viewed favorably since the arrival of Europeans, this circle of secrecy is rather large, and it is allowed to involve many items that are known to affect others—such as how we fill out our income tax returns or how much we do or do not give to charity. We treasure our right to do these things on our own, and we believe the Constitution gives us many such rights. It is a constitution framed during a time when our population was rapidly expanding into resource-rich regions, and a time when nearly everyone's fortunes were expanding as well. When everyone seems to be gaining—when the economy is rapidly and massively expanding—it seems less important to compare the *rate* of increase in one's fortunes with the rates of increase of the fortunes of others, even though ultimately this is what really counts (or, in evolutionary terms, this is what really counted during the eons across which we were evolving our proximate responses to such things). Perhaps the comparisons were often with the fortunes of relatives and friends left behind in Europe. In any case it seems easy to understand the enthusiasm for individual initiative, and the tendency to overlook blatant exploitations along the way. This is not so true when things level off, and many see themselves as losing ground. Comparisons with neighbors and a closer and more critical eye to exploitation then become the rule.

But we have retained much of our positive feeling about "free enterprise" and the virtues of individual ambition and entrepreneurship. We accept and endorse competitiveness at a level at least as great as anywhere else in the world. We are notorious for our ambition and our efforts to "get ahead"—our "pioneer" spirit.

Consider as a contrast post-World War II China, especially since the advent of socialism. (Perhaps not completely incidentally, unlike the United States, China does not have a history involving victories in a series of prominent international wars. Rather, China has a history of searing internal disputes and devastating civil wars.) From all the glimpses I have been afforded, from television, newspapers, magazines, and talking to both American visitors to China and Chinese visitors to the U.S., I infer that there has been a continual and powerful effort to reduce to some kind of minimum the circle of secrecy that each person is allowed to hold. We refer disparagingly to some of these efforts as encouragement to "snitch." In the U.S. it is common for a parent to be torn between wishing its children to reveal wrongdoing by playmates and not wishing the child to become (known as) a tattletale. Is this indecision not related to the general concern in this society for the rights of individuals (ultimately, ourselves, and others' views of ourselves and our children) with respect to privacy and the seeking of individual interests? In China it appears that there is a strong and continual effort to create in individuals a tendency to subordinate their personal or individual interests to those of the group. In fact, this is brought about by creating punishments for efforts to seek one's own interests at the expense of others at a level that could not currently be accepted in the U.S. Even harboring thoughts about personal ambitions or desires to acquire personal goods or riches is considered wrong. As a biologist I believe that if I were going to try to establish a society in which everyone came as close as possible to the philosophers' ideal of indiscriminate altruism—and to do this independent of external threats or world events—then I would also begin by trying to minimize the individual's "circle of secrecy." Is this not what Thomas Huxley was referring to when he said that the foundation of morality is to have done, once and for all, with lying? Whether or not this is a desirable goal is a question that I am not prepared to resolve, although I believe that the answer given by people involved will depend heavily upon circumstances, such as resource shortages, population pressure, extrinsic enemies, and the specific values they have been taught or learned to revere throughout their lives. Although there are reasons and situations in which it seems innocuous and even desirable to argue for an effort to eliminate deception, the consequences of attempting this in all situations— as Huxley and some moral philosophers seem to have been suggesting should be the object of efforts toward morality—may be somewhat different from what is at first imagined.

## GOD AND SCIENCE AS TRUTH-SEEKING

At least in the modern world, religion is almost synonymous with moral system (but not completely so, because not all moral systems are religious). Many people believe that the concepts of right and wrong, and the rules concerning these concepts, come directly from God. Churches, angels, saints, monks, nuns, priests, rabbis, and ministers are all terms that convey the message of being institutions and agents of morality.

There are also obvious connections between religion and nationalism. Most of the large and long-lasting nations of the world have state religions. In others, two or a few major religions, or denominations, are automatically supported by the taxes of the citizens; although it may be possible to be free of this tax, so to declare one's self may have other deleterious consequences such as social ostracism and inaccessibility of some kinds of employment. Even in countries like the United States, where there are constant highly publicized efforts to maintain separation of particular religions and government, religious beliefs of one sort or another are prevalent, and scarcely anyone would argue that the nation is not in some sense founded on a religious background by religious people, and similarly maintained. Prayers and religious phrases are included in the governmental ceremonies of the United States, as they are in those of virtually every large nation (excepting China and Russia).

There is also a relationship between the two concepts of God and science, if science is defined, as I define it here, as a self-correcting method of seeking the truth. Thus, it seems reasonable to expect the agents of a single just god of all people to seek the truth in all of the *social* matters of *human* life as scientists are expected to do with respect to the physical and nonhuman living universe. Truth-seeking involves openness, and in science the basic criterion of repeatability is maintained through openness. The effectiveness of courtroom procedures, as they seek truth in matters of law and justice, also depends on openness. The widely touted yet rarely realized goal of invoking a single just god for all people cannot by definition refer to a capricious or arbitrary god (as can the notions of multiple gods or tribal gods) but must, I believe, imply an open truth-seeking in respect to *social* matters. To invoke an impartial god is thus a logical trap for those who would then attempt to use the concept to identify and maltreat other people as enemies or subordinates.

The concept of a single just god for all people also implies social unity. This is true, whatever its origin, and leaving aside its essentially universal failure in practice. This concept is one representation of an idealized moral system; and it is just as difficult to adhere to as those generated from moral philosophy. As has been noted by many authors, this kind of god differs from "tribal" gods serving as caretakers or transmitters of group rules explicitly formulated and utilized to serve the interests of the particular tribe or small group.

Whether or not those who originated and promoted the notion of a single god for all people, and an impartial god, really practiced what they preached, the fact remains that the mere concept represented an opposite or a denial of the competitive principles that had governed human existence as a consequence of its evolutionary background. In this sense a universal impartial god represented what Thomas Huxley called "combating" natural selection. The notion of a god of *all* people, who was *impartial*, was the notion of a god who could not condone inequalities such as polygyny, slavery, and caste systems. It was the notion of a god who was, in the modern philosophers' terms, *morally consistent*, and who insisted on, or promoted, moral consistency among humans (I am not talking about any particular individual's or group's view of God, but about consequences that I believe follow necessarily or logically from the concept of a universal and impartial god; see also Keith, 1947, quoted earlier, on the teachings of Jesus). Moral consistency means acknowledging (and acting on) everyone else's rights to do and have whatever one accepts that he himself has a right to. It is the negation of personal selfishness, selfishness for one's family, or favoritism even to one's own group members (tribe, nation) as opposed to others. Institution of such a god represented a formalizing of the moral ideal toward which many humans would like to think they have always been striving. This kind of god would have been from the start the hope of ordinary people—the peasants and the downtrodden and the minorities. Those in power, on the other hand, are not likely to promote the concept of a truly just god unless this promotion becomes a part of a less evident promotion of their own views and interests. MacDonald (1983) notes that "Christianity began as a movement of the lower classes in Roman society, including some slaves" (he cites Case, 1971; Grant, 1977; and Malherbe, 1979). He also remarks that "Christianity is, as Nietzsche (1895/1954) scornfully noted long ago, a leveling ideology" and that "Although Christianity became relatively unconcerned with differences in wealth, there is no evidence that its views on sexual matters ever strayed far from the Pauline ideal in which monogamy and celibacy were viewed as the only acceptable roles for humans."

Once reason (as impartiality or justice through cause–effect seeking) became a recourse, priests or religious leaders had a special role as its agents—and such agents would retain a special place (meaning that not everyone would become one) because of the resistance to the ideal of morality in everyone, due to our evolutionary history.

Religions with either arbitrary gods or plural gods, or religions that did not adhere to the principle of justice through reason and impartiality by an insistence on moral consistency (at least as a principle or goal), would lack the magnificent unifying aspect of these groups deriving from the idea of a single god for everyone, and a god that was rational.

These two concepts in fact go hand in hand, since a rational god would have to be the god of everyone, or God could not be rational, just, and morally consistent. Such a god would tend constantly to reproduce conditions whereby the collective of individually powerless individuals could acquire power through their collective influences; other gods tended continually to erode such directions of cultural and governmental change by reinvesting the already powerful with additional and more permanent power. Law in modern nations can be seen to have the same stated purpose as the concept of a single just god: those who deal in law assert, and probably mostly believe, that they seek to cause it to become, in effect, a "disinterested" third party in every dispute. Surely the connection between a single god and a rational god has been instrumental in the spread of (especially) Christianity through the unity of the nations espousing it and their ability, as a result, to expand through conquest. The idea of a single just god for all people must have become prominent when the downtrodden masses became so unified as well as numerous as to be powerful–and to be able to assert their collective will. In this sense God was presumably a force that unified them and gave hope and strength to their desires.

The concept of a single god for all people is thus a two-edged sword. On the one hand, it implies justice for all (consistency, rationality); on the other hand, it requires or calls for unity in *belief*. This is partly true because the idea cannot persist if others deny it and win. (In science, repeatability cannot be maintained if some flout it and win.) Thus, there is the impetus to evangelism, and even conquest (e.g., Onward Christian Soldiers/Marching as to war . . . ). There is the temptation to enforce, impose, or fight for the concept rather than simply to accept it even in the face of seeming contradictions, which is apparently the response morally consistent with it.

If the "sense of justice," or concern for it, is sharpest—most acute, most conscious, most expressed or discussed—in the *wronged*, this would support the argument that the rise of law was the rise of rule by the collective—by the majority who would be powerless except when united.

The group aspect of religion is a superb unity-producing and maintaining phenomenon. Group religion also sets the stage for individual strategies within the group, in connection with religion. Once humans have evolved so as to accept religion, individuals can manipulate them according to and because of the tendency or ability to accept group religion. If they continue to evolve to accept it, the tendency can be used more widely and more effectively. As leaders become divinized—or as the power of group religion grows and supposed powers magnify—individuals may either seek to, or be told they can, relieve

what many view as the greatest problem of all through religion—
individual mortality. Group religion can also be used by individuals as
a reinforcer of *family* unity, or, more explicitly, personal authority in the
family; and it is so used.

We can wonder whether it was accidental that the commandments
give the appearance of a formula appropriate for running a nation
(Alexander, 1979a, p. 265), and that nations conceived and operated by
groups of people who regarded them as significant became prominent
as cradles of rationality and science; or whether the commandments
contain a rationality in ethics that primed for the development of
long-lasting, huge, and remarkably unified nations (effective in missionary and aggressive expansion and colonization), and for the development of science and law and the concept of a single just god for all
people.

Let me return to the connection between the concept of a rational
god, and those of science and of law as justice. To reason is to seek
causal basis, or the cause–effect connections in any situation. This
operation parallels the tendency or willingness to be impartial, fair, or
morally consistent in respect to all people. To seek impartially to resolve
conflicts or paradoxes is to seek the causes and effects involved in them.
To do this adequately necessarily involves a certain openness. Otherwise, one could not possibly be said to be actually pursuing the truth in
that situation, or the just solution to the problem. George Gaylord
Simpson (1964) referred to science as a self-correcting *method* of finding
out about the universe. The self-correcting aspect of science as the
pursuit of truth is its openness, and its requirement that the route to
every result and conclusion be described well enough to be repeatable,
if possible, by any one who wishes to try. Science in this sense remains
competitive because scientists advance personally by authoring ideas
and results. But the requirement of openness in science is reflected in
the fact that most scientists believe that it is *good* (and I think they mean
this in a moral or normative sense) to dispense knowledge; that it is *good*
for everyone to have access to whatever knowledge is available; that it is
*good* to inform people. I believe most scientists also accept that *not* to
dispense knowledge as widely as possible is *bad*. I do not regard as
accidental the association between (1) openness and the pursuit of truth
within science and (2) the concomitant attitude of scientists toward
openness of information and knowledge as morality in everyday life.
Nor does it necessarily stem from noble motives. Gaining and dispensing knowledge is the scientist's "business"; when all goes well he gains
in direct proportion to the amount and importance of new knowledge
attributed to him. Efforts to suppress knowledge, therefore, can inter-

fere with the career goals of scientists. Regardless of their backgrounds, however, the interests of scientists in respect to dispensing knowledge may coincide with those of the rest of us.

Openness is thus a basic criterion of science, if science is defined as investigation that is repeatable: a scientific investigation is one that can be verified by anyone because the details of its methods are laid out for precisely that purpose. I am suggesting that there are parallels among the efforts toward openness in science, openness in law as impartial justice, and openness of a god argued to be universal and rational. The process of expanding a morality of openness until it characterizes human sociality, on the other hand, is a formidable task. No one can know if we still have the time, let alone the means, to carry it out.

Modern nations promote science, I think, for at least three reasons: First, as cradles of affluence such nations more or less automatically provide the atmosphere and conditions in which the inquiries of science can proceed. Second, such societies are ethical structures permitting and promoting science as a rational pursuit, open enough to acquire and maintain its central attribute of repeatability. Third, in modern, technological nations it is perhaps more obvious how scientific discoveries can be used to benefit the populace generally.

Each step taken in the direction of openness in the pursuit of truth, i.e., in the scientific sense, seems to me likely to better the world situation. None of the partial brakes on the nuclear arms race that I will discuss later can be effective without a degree of openness in society. They depend on the spread of information about the threat that now must hang over the heads of humans for the rest of their time on earth. If this is so, then it would seem that the approach of advocating openness for the purpose of allowing individuals and groups of individuals to make their own cost–benefit analyses is worthwhile, if not imperative. It is also true, I think, that pressure for openness in the matters most relevant to accidental or insane extinction through intergroup strife is directly consistent with the tendencies and goals of individual humans. The intensity of their concern for openness may be expected to increase with their perception of danger to themselves and the usefulness to themselves of others having the same perception. We can best aid the effectiveness of such efforts by recognizing their origins and values and thus pursuing them with more knowledge and more deliberateness. The question is whether the losses to a nation (its people) through openness are greater or less than those resulting from (1) escalation through secrecy and deception, (2) blackmail or advantage-taking as results of defeat or weakness, or (3) nuclear war; and how openness will affect each of these possibilities. There is the additional problem of how a nation's leaders can be induced to ask this question, make such estimates, or reveal the answers. I am not suggesting that all products of technology, or all technological information, ought to be available to all people at all times. Such an argument would require, for example, the supplying of guns and explosives to insane persons, or to individuals openly committed to using these devices in ways contrary to everyone's interests.

As a promoter of one god for all people, and of central rules of morality, a religion is from the start either a part of government or a threat to it. To the extent that any organized religion more stringently insists on unquestioning faith, acceptance of the divinity of leaders, and the absoluteness of the church's dogma, it loses a part of the rationality of the original impartial-god-of-all-people. It loses the aspect that is most conducive to the growth of science. In particular, it loses the aspect of science that involves an interest in seeking our own origins, our background in evolutionary history.

The concept of God also implies continuity of social unity—a long-lasting, intergenerational social contract. If nepotism is our evolved function, then God (in the sense of *vox populi, vox Dei*) really can guarantee a reward "in Heaven," or after our individual deaths—or a kind of "everlasting life" (for our genetic materials via our children and other relatives)—as a reward for moral behavior *during life*. This guarantee is not a matter of everlasting consciousness (although, curiously, one may argue that such an effect may be created, in terms of proximate sensations or beliefs, by certain kinds or degrees of serenity that do not terminate prior to the final loss of consciousness). Rather, it is in the form of a renewable contract in reciprocity which occurs when those who remain after our death use our own life of morality to judge our children and other relatives as suitable risks to continue receiving (and giving, and receiving and giving, and receiving and giving . . . ) the benefits of social reciprocity. The guarantee actually *exists* because, unless those in a position to honor it do so for us, the same possibility will not exist for them. The ceremonies associated with death, and the reverence given to the dead, are surely, in part, ritually related to this guarantee. Similarly, I suggest that much of grief functions to place the grieving person in the role of receiving reassurances that associates will indeed honor obligations and continue reciprocal interactions begun with or previously involving the person over whose demise grief is being expressed. (See Lebra, 1972; Chanley, ms., for parallel views of suicidal behavior and its associated depression.) I am suggesting that the part of religion that deals with the afterlife utilizes the desire of each person to continue his or her influence and to provide for and help relatives. The concept of hereafter as "Heaven" (i.e., as idealized) is also a logical outcome of the use of scenario-building to adjust the future so as to serve one's own interests.

I think that, as with the concept of morality, the concept of *God* must be viewed as originally generated and maintained for the purpose—now seen by many as immoral—of furthering the interests of one group of humans at the expense of one or more other groups. Somehow, as the concept became that of a *universal, impartial* god for *all people*, it converged on the notion of modern moral philosophers that morality means indiscriminate and self-sacrificing altruism by individuals so as to bring about the greatest good to the greatest number. Needless to say, we have not yet been able to develop the concepts of "good," "moral," "god", and "impartiality" in law so as to achieve this elusive goal.

## SUMMARIZING HYPOTHESES

1. Gods are inventions originally developed to extend the notion that some have greater rights than others to design and enforce rules, and that some are more destined to be leaders, others to be followers. This notion, in turn, arose out of prior asymmetries in both power and judgment (e.g., parents manipulating children, husbands manipulating wives, the strong manipulating the weak). It works when (because) leaders are (have been) valuable, especially in the context of intergroup competition.

2. The efforts of moralizers to use gods to serve their own interests caused them to create the concept of a single, just God of all people. (There is probably an inadvertent aspect to this, because actually to apply the concept would not serve the interests of the powerful.)

3. As with the concept of a universal, just God, the effort to develop law that would be acceptable to all (disinterested, or "blind" to irrelevant differences among people) resulted in the concept of "blind" (true, impartial) justice.

4. Similarly, and evidently in parallel, modern moral philosophers created the notion of universal indiscriminate beneficence from the idea of consistency in morality.

5. Science can be related to justice, and to the concept of a truly just God for all people, to the extent that all of these ideas depend on openness and repeatability—the ability to reconstruct (test) cause–effect backgrounds of events and acts.

6. The concept of a hereafter, and the redressing of injustices in it, is a further extension of the social contract because our descendants

continue to interact after we die, and observations of reciprocity overlap generations.

## Modeling Value Systems and Maintaining Indirect Reciprocity

### THE RIGHTS OF EMBRYOS AND THE MORIBUND

Technology and other cultural innovations constantly present humans with novel problems with respect to values. Such new ethical and moral questions are literally thrust at us day after day, and apparently at an ever-increasing rate. What is an acceptable level of pollution? How should scarce resources be distributed? At what point does it become immoral to continue devising and constructing more terrible weapons for the destruction of human life? Is capital punishment proper? Is injection with a lethal drug more or less reasonable than hanging, shooting, or electrocution? When does an embryo acquire rights? What are the rights of children in relation to the interests of their parents? When does a moribund person lose rights?

One may legitimately ask: How would a biologist, making the kinds of arguments I have been making, approach such questions? I suspect the following pages will convey an answer that is disappointingly nonradical and (I hope) commonsense, distinguished only by some aspects of attitude in no way restricted to biologists, and by the weighing in of certain kinds of information, especially about conflicts of interest, that are usually not considered.

The last three questions in the above list are among the most publicized and widely interesting, because they so explicitly concern the rights of helpless individuals, and therefore involve the whole structure of our moral systems. The question of when a dying person should be regarded as available for removal of vital organs for transplant purposes, or when life support systems should be turned off (if the interests of close relatives, or close relatives and society, are deemed to be in conflict with continued life support) seem to be decided, generally speaking, on the basis of the likelihood that the individual has totally lost consciousness, or mental activity, *and* is unlikely ever to gain it back. In other words, though I have never seen it so stated, the condition that is apparently being tested for is one that could be termed *postconsciousness*. The President's Commission for the Study of Ethical Problems in Medicine and Biomedical Behavioral Research (1981) concludes that death "is a unitary phenomenon which can be accurately demonstrated either on the traditional grounds of irreversible cessation of heart and lung functions or on the basis of irreversible loss of all functions of the entire brain" (p. 1). They review studies in this arena, all of which stress *irreversibility* of functions that, ultimately, signify the impossibility of a return to consciousness, and provide criteria that have been found to be reliable. For two reasons it seems to me that this is a reasonable approach. First, many if not most people would care little what happened to their physical selves once it was absolutely certain that they would never again be conscious—especially if this attitude enabled others to benefit (it can be argued that relatives often care but there is the countering argument that dying persons typically have the right to determine how their bodies are treated following their death). Second, the actually postconscious individual cannot care at all, and, assuming that the diagnosis is correct, will never be able again to care. For all practical purposes—or perhaps I should say, from the individual's point of view as well as that of others—he would be dead. Of course, it is unlikely that anyone with careful judgment would profess to be absolutely certain that any living person is totally postconscious, and even if a person of authority were to express absolute certainty he could be wrong. So with this question, as with all significant questions, we can only establish probabilities. Nevertheless, the concept of postconsciousness may represent one reasonable approach to the unavoidable question of the rights of moribund persons.

Without assuming that this way of approaching the question of when to regard a person as deceased gives an actual answer, but instead regarding it as simply a model of how society might proceed in answering such questions, let us take up a second, related problem: When does a developing human embryo acquire rights that should (in the normative sense) cause its interests to be taken seriously when they are regarded as in conflict with those of others—such as its mother, its two parents, its siblings, or others (even society as a whole)?

Generally speaking, this question has not been approached in the same fashion as that of determining when a individual is terminally postconscious. Perhaps this is partly because the developing embryo is progressing *toward greater* consciousness and awareness. Perhaps, too, it is because humans tend to look differently upon helpless offspring or babies than they do upon old or dying individuals. We might have to search a long time to discover all of the historical causes and proximate correlates of this kind of difference in attitude, but such differences do indeed occur. Perhaps the human embryo is even viewed differently by some people partly (and not necessarily consciously) as a vehicle for getting others to view them or their group or creed favorably (or as truly altruistic), due to the general view people have about helping babies. This general view may be a product of a selection favoring beneficence toward babies because (1) they are likely to be relatives if they are in one's vicinity (at least, historically) and (2) the babies of others are almost ideal objects of beneficence in the context of indirect reciprocity because the benefits of aiding utterly helpless individuals are so high and the costs so low. This is especially true because babies also represent enormously important investments to their parents.

Nevertheless, from the point of view of the baby or embryo itself, it would seem that a criterion paralleling that which we have applied to moribund older individuals can also be applied to the decision of when to allow an embryo's interests to prevail over the perceived interests of others. Suppose a parent has decided that an embryo's existence will so conflict with the parent's interests that it simply does not want the child. What reasonable stance can be taken in regard to this wish of the parent? First, we may note that the parent is, curiously, the precise individual who will most frequently have the greatest stake in the success of the embryo, and ordinarily would have the greatest positive effect on its success. Paradoxically, however (and this part of the formula is too frequently left out of modern ethical considerations, though not the considerations of many so-called "primitive" peoples), the parent is also the individual who may stand to gain the most if certain of its offspring or potential offspring are terminated or prevented—i.e., the parent will lose the most if some (or some kinds of) offspring or potential offspring are not terminated or prevented.

With respect to the success of the offspring itself, most other people in society (leaving aside the close relatives of the parents, particularly the parents' parents) are affected less by the offspring's success or failure than are its close relatives. Yet the rest of society acts as though what happens to someone else's offspring is of great concern. I would speculate that this concern has one of the backgrounds suggested earlier, relating to indirect reciprocity, and that the rise of indirect reciprocity in large technological civilizations is what causes the citizenry of such societies—as opposed to those in small, nontechnological societies—to view abortion and infanticide more frequently as a concern of more than the parents alone. The point is that everyone may gain when social beneficence is prevalent. (Laura Betzig has called to my attention an alternative possibility: that disapproval of abortion and infanticide by others may be fueled by a resentment at the use of such practices by others to further their own interests.)

In other words, in different circumstances, the parent's interests—as opposed to those of anyone else— are most likely to conflict with those of the child in some circumstances, as well as most likely to coincide with them in other circumstances. There is the additional fact that conscious control of the fates of embryos and newborns has become increasingly extensive. Thus, it is now possible to abort fetuses more easily and less expensively than ever before. It is also possible to save babies that previously would have died, even though it is not always possible simultaneously to cause the baby to attain the level of *quality* in life that previously characterized all babies (or nearly all) that were able to survive. The question is thus posed, and must be answered by conscious, deliberate decision, whether a child ought to be kept alive if its condition will be, perhaps unprecedentedly, miserable or painful or "vegetable"-like. This increasing degree and consciousness of control by some individuals (doctors, parents) over the life and death of others seems to stir a general uneasiness among people. The rest of society is placed in the position of mediating the conflict of interest between parent and its offspring under the conditions that what is done to one individual, or class of individuals, may affect what is done to other individuals, or other, even totally different classes of individuals in the same society—that is, it may affect the general level of beneficence in society, hence the unity of society as well. (This problem has recently become especially acute with respect to euthanasia in the U.S.—e.g., Rosenblatt, 1985.) I suggest that this is why "when there is a conflict between the demands of utility and the requirements of justice, we usually say that the former must simply yield to the latter" (Arras, 1984). This approach is another way of overriding short-term interests or outcomes in favor of long-term ones of apparently greater significance.

How are decisions involving conflicts of interest between embryos and their parents to be made? If we utilize only the criteria of "life" and "humanness," much publicized in the news media, there seems to be no reasonable way to make a decision about the interests of embryos, even if we adopt the extreme notion that there is no way that a parent's interests can be allowed to hold sway. In that case we are drawn to the problem of when the embryo becomes someone with a future, and there is no way to answer the question: even sperm and eggs are alive and human, and have the potential to produce successful, reproducing, adult individuals. So far as I know, however, no one argues that sperm and eggs have rights equal to those of their producers. Even the Catholic church allows the "rhythm" method of contraception, which, like all methods of contraception, is a deliberate way of maximizing the likelihood of the death of both sperm and eggs. But the criteria of "life" and "humanness" do not allow us to exclude sperm and eggs. No criterion has been advanced that would allow us logically to restrict ourselves to the fertilized egg, and, indeed, arguments about which methods of contraception are moral, and which are not, demonstrate the arbitrariness inherent in currently publicized approaches.

Suppose we now take the same approach as appears to be currently adopted for determining the rights of the moribund—that of postconsciousness. We can ask if the offspring is conscious or preconscious—that is, whether or not it has acquired any kind of self-knowledge equivalent to that we regard as existing in ourselves. Regardless of the difficulty of answering that question, it at least gives us a reasonable starting point. Thus, it can be fairly assumed that sperm and eggs, or even newly fertilized eggs, do not have self-awareness of a conscious sort. There is no way to prove it, but there is also not the slightest evidence that such qualities exist in human gametes or newly formed zygotes.

This is also a reasonable approach because it takes as its criterion a trait that speaks to the feelings of the embryo. If an embryo young enough to be known beyond reasonable doubt to lack conscious self-awareness were never to progress beyond this state, would we regard it as having human interests of its own that could seriously compete with those of individuals who did? In other words, how would we treat such an embryo, knowing that its current state of nonconsciousness is not only preconsciousness but, in effect, also postconsciousness as well? I suggest that we have probably been aiming, more or less unknowingly, at just about what I am talking about, as a criterion, by keeping our protective feelings about embryos' rights directed at such early stages so as to avoid any likelihood that terminated embryos possess any form of consciousness or self-awareness. Or some have been so aiming, while others have been insisting that human life at any and all stages has rights identical to those of any other stage. Once we agree that this last-described stance provides no way to resolve the problems of actual conduct in the real world (indeed, I believe it can be argued that persons making these arguments are in fact defending some perceived rights of their *own* rather than those of embryos), then our problem is that of how to decide when particular kinds of rights come into existence as the individual develops. I suggest that the moment of consciousness is an appropriate focus, even if it is not in any real sense a "moment," and even if it is extremely difficult to determine. My opinion stems not from some kind of direct application of biological knowledge, but from a playing of the question of the interests of one individual (or individuals) against those of another (in this case the embryo). Even if others disagree with how I have done it in this case, I can see no alternative to some kind of balancing of interests. The particular conclusion I reach is not especially important, nor is the fact that I have utilized strongly the notion of consciousness or self-awareness; I present the argument as an illustration of how a biologist with an evolutionary background might generate a tentative proposal. The discussions of Arras (1984) and Strong (1984) are interesting parallels (see also pp. 92ff.). Their arguments are not the same as mine, but they show that biologists and nonbiologists can reach similar conclusions or employ similar arguments. Interestingly, Arras seems always to skirt the issue of *costs* to parents and others.

The *preconscious–postconscious* approach to rights seems to me to be consistent with the aspects of these problems that involve the stake of society as a whole in a viable system of indirect reciprocity. In a society cemented largely by reciprocity it appears to be important that a generally lofty self-view be held by the citizenry with regard to the propensity for beneficence within the society. It does not appear to be beneficent to kill a helpless, developing embryo or a moribund person. If the interests of such embryos and moribund people conflict with those of healthy, conscious, aware people, however, then the question of how to resolve the conflict will not disappear. Just as the postconscious state is by definition beyond the caring of the involved individual, so the preconscious state is by definition one in which the embryo itself can have no regret or sorrow—no ability to experience or express the usual kinds of human sadness and fear—about its terminated opportunities. To focus on a much earlier stage in terms of preconsciousness—that is, to make the decision so as to be absolutely certain that consciousness does not become involved—would be a kind of agreement with this argument.

A problem exacerbating that of deciding how to deal with the rights of embryos is that young, helpless individuals of a highly social species like ourselves are quite likely to have evolved distressing and disturbing responses to danger because of their effects on others available for potential assistance (hence, in part, the effectiveness of the videotape of an abortion—titled *The Silent Scream*—via ultrasound images, used recently by Right-to-Life proponents). Even this film seems to me related to the proposition discussed here, since it seems an effort to show that embryos feel pain in the same way that postembryonic individuals do.

Aged, moribund individuals are less likely to exhibit or elicit the same intensity of distress as young individuals, partly for the reason that their interests are more likely to be realized through death when those interests conflict with the interests of relatives, and such conflicts arise automatically with the onset of irreversible senility or other potentially terminal problems of the aged. Parallel conflicts may be frequent between parents and young offspring, but there they arise in a situation in which the offspring normally benefits itself and its parents (and other relatives) alike by intense, attractive, and emotional calls for assistance. Moreover, the baby or child possesses potential for assisting in its own reproductive success directly by someday producing offspring or helping other relatives; its reproductive value is rising. Such is not the case with the aged, infirm individual whose reproductive value is sinking toward zero. There is also the central and painful factor in dealing with the aged and infirm that an old person who learns (or believes) that his relatives have decided that he will be better off dead may on this account alone make the same decision.

These considerations are involved in the difference between our reactions to helplessness in aged and embryonic individuals, even above and beyond the difference in their respective responses to impending doom: we are surely evolved to be more sensitive about the death of young helpless individuals. This difference in our response carries with it an additional responsibility arising from our self-view, given the significance for everyone of generalized beneficence in any society.

A parallel can be constructed by asking whether one would mind more if individuals in his society routinely and dispassionately put to death old incontinent dogs *or* young healthy puppies, old crippled horses *or* young healthy foals, etc. The mere fact that such comparisons seem cruel and tasteless, or even dangerous, stresses my point that how we treat particular classes of individuals—because of our background of evolved responses to such individuals in the particular circumstances of interest here—may be crucial to the health and unity of society and the mental states of individuals within society.

I think it is fair to ask whether the concern of a U.S. president over abortion may not arise or be intensified by a concern (conscious or unconscious) about the unity of society, hence, society's ability and readiness to defend itself. Thus, Ronald Reagan was quoted in the *Michigan Daily* (4 Aug. 1982) as follows:

> I strongly believe that the protection of innocent life is and has always been a legitimate and indeed the first duty of government. Believing that, I favor human life legislation. . . . This *national tragedy* of abortion on demand must end [emphasis added]. If we don't know when the unborn becomes a human life, then we must opt for life unless and until someone can prove it is not alive. (p. 2)

It is not to be overlooked that the speech was made to a Catholic organization or that the rest of it concerned the international arms race.

If the idea that the "first duty of government" is to protect innocent life is ludicrous, it is not ludicrous to suggest that to make such an argument is a way of using a popular cause to support government, and of using the sacredness both of "innocent life" and of government to restrain the independence of women. In the abortion arguments it is also not irrelevant that abortion "on demand" delivers to women a freedom in respect to sexual life that seems to many to (1) reduce the control of men over women, (2) allow "immoral" or licentious behavior, especially by women, and (3) thus erode the "moral fiber" of the populace—hence the unity, purpose, and strength of the nation. It is not difficult to consider that the entire issue feeds back to the history of the control of resources—hence, control of the lives and reproduction of women—through the defense of the group against other such groups by its adult males.

In all likelihood, the arguments I have just made will seem irrelevant to many whose interest in abortion or its prevention may arise out of motivations entirely different from those discussed here. The possibility of such motivations was expressed succinctly by a young female postdoctoral scholar in anthropology who exclaimed, "Women who have decided to stay home and have babies, and their husbands, are opposed to abortion because women to whom abortions are available are thereby more effective competitors for the jobs of men" (see also Luker, 1984a, b). Such hypotheses link concern about issues like abortion to the system of indirect reciprocity in ways many people may never have suspected, and they do not necessarily refer to conscious motivation. I believe that such hypotheses deserve a great deal more attention than they have received.

As a final note on this topic I return to my earlier contention that moral issues must by definition be resolved by the opinion of the collective. Applied in this instance, one meaning that derives from this realization is that the most logical and reasonable argument may not be able to supercede the effect of a practice—such as aborting embryos—on a society's view of itself. If sufficient horror is generated—from whatever arguments or background—then any such act may be regarded as unequivocally immoral and, indeed, if allowed or promoted, may have a decidedly deleterious effect on the unity of the society and its general level of beneficence. This is one reason that questions about the rights of nonhumans, and helpless humans of particular sorts, must remain somewhat fuzzy, and can never be decided absolutely for all times and places in any one time and place.

## THE RIGHTS OF WOMEN AND MEN

*In men's novels, getting the woman or women goes along with getting the power. It's a perk, not a means. In women's novels you get the power by getting the man. The man is the power.*

Margaret Atwood, 1985

The life efforts of human males and females have evolved to be somewhat different. We can demonstrate this merely by looking at the extensive information on such things as mortality patterns, senescence rates, and length of juvenile life (e.g., Alexander, 1979a; Fries, 1980). As with adults and children, males and females represent a difference in evolutionary background that has typically resulted in an asymmetry of resource control and distribution throughout history. In many societies this situation has recently undergone significant changes. Nevertheless, enormous variations still exist among the societies of the world in regard to the rights of men and women, and the patterns involved are typically deeply embedded in the social structure. The issue is a changing and enormously sensitive one, which makes it particularly appropriate for analysis here. Many people assume, for reasons discussed earlier, that a biological approach to such issues is unlikely to yield insights or assist in the realization of goals judged acceptable on ethical or moral grounds. They have a right to know how a biologist would approach this topic, and I welcome the opportunity to develop it here.

It is not easy to discover precisely what historical differences have shaped current male–female differences. If, however, humans are in a general way similar to other highly parental organisms that live in social groups—as I (and others—e.g., Daly and Wilson, 1983; Symons, 1979) believe they are—then we can hypothesize as follows: for men much of sexual activity has had as a main (ultimate) significance the initiating of pregnancies. It would follow that when a man avoids copulation it is likely to be because (1) there is no likelihood of pregnancy or (2) the costs entailed (venereal disease, danger from competition with other males, lowered status if the event becomes public, or an undesirable commitment) are too great in comparison with the probability that pregnancy will be induced. The man himself may be judging costs against the benefits of immediate sensory pleasures, such as orgasms (i.e., rather than thinking about pregnancy he may say that he was simply uninterested), but I am assuming that selection has tuned such expectations in terms of their probability of leading to actual reproduction (including long-term commitment and success in child rearing).

For women, I hypothesize, sexual activity per se has been more concerned with the securing of resources (again, I am speaking of ultimate and not necessarily conscious concerns) (see also Buss, 1985,

1987; Buss and Barnes, 1986; Daly and Wilson, 1983; Bell and Weinberg, 1978; Bell *et al.*, 1981; Symons, 1979). Ordinarily, when women avoid or resist copulation, I speculate further, the disinterest, aversion, or inhibition may be traceable eventually to one (or more) of three causes: (1) there is no promise of commitment (of resources), (2) there is a likelihood of undesirable commitment (e.g., to a man with inadequate resources), or (3) there is a risk of loss of interest by a man with greater resources, than the one involved in the possible copulation. (I am defining resources in the broadest possible way, I am not necessarily speaking of conscious motivations, and I include physical, mental, social, and all traits of males that might predict both success in resource control *and commitment*).

These speculations are consistent with the widespread impression that women, at least in the past, have tended to be more interested in commitment, more concerned with affection before (and after) sex, and more appreciative of loving conversations that include words like "always" and "forever." It is more typical for men to buy gifts for women in connection with sexual liaisons than vice versa. Fur coats, jewelry, and other such gifts are symbolic in this context. But we cannot ignore the obvious fact that men have lopsidedly controlled resources, thus creating conditions at any and all times that virtually *required*, on a proximate basis, that women be more concerned than men with the resources connected to a liaison. This lopsided male control of resources evidently returns to the original tendencies for males to compete more severely among themselves, leading to men being larger and stronger than women. Whether any of this results partly from genetic differences between males and females, except in the proximate sense of size and strength, is for the moment moot.

These apparent differences between human males and females (see Buss, 1985, 1987; Buss and Barnes, 1986)—which have long been accepted intuitively (by both sexes, I believe) and celebrated in verses, songs, and pithy sayings—may be used to cast light upon attitudes toward issues like prostitution, rape, and equal rights for women, even though they cannot be used to decide what courses ought to have been taken in respect to such moral issues.

To a woman for whom sex is to some significant extent a vehicle for securing resources—the extreme and most desirable case being presumably the promise of commitment by a desired man of his entire lifelong accumulation of resources—there is generally no need to worry directly about how to get pregnant. This end will be achieved more or less automatically. Hence, in part, the absence of advertisement of ovulation in the human female (actually, its concealment), the other aspect being that a female who advertises ovulation may be taken over by other males at ovulation, thereby losing her own male's commitment (re-sources) (Alexander and Noonan, 1979; B.I. Strassmann, 1981). To a man, the problem of securing pregnancies with a particular woman disappears when that woman commits herself to him sexually.

This argument does not predict, for example, that men will *never* wish to use contraceptives or have vasectomies (both evolutionary novelties), but it does predict that most males will be reluctant to do the first and *exceedingly* reluctant to do the second (they may often be more careless or less concerned about contraceptives than their partners, and not necessarily consciously so). It also suggests that men will sometimes be stimulated by contraceptive methods that entail some risk of conception (as opposed to methods that do not), and that they will tend to avoid *certain* contraception or *irreversible* sterility. (Unfortunately, for testing, the same predictions may sometimes hold for women.) For a man use of a contraceptive can actually represent a way of *causing* a pregnancy—either by enabling copulations in which some risk exists when none would occur without contraceptives, or by increasing the likelihood of subsequent copulations (with the same female) without contraceptives.

It will probably be necessary to defend part of the above argument further. Thus, some men will undoubtedly assert that they are *more* interested in sex if there is no possibility of pregnancy, or that they are only interested in sex when contraceptives are used. Although it is not the principal theme of this essay, what is required is a review of the interplay of proximate and ultimate mechanisms. A man behaving so as to avoid pregnancies, and who derives from an evolutionary background of avoiding pregnancies, should be expected to favor copulation with women who are for age or other reasons incapable of pregnancy. A man derived from an evolutionary process in which securing of pregnancies typically was favored, may be expected to be most interested sexually in women most likely to become pregnant and near the height of the re-productive probability curve (see Fig. 1.2). This means that men should usually be expected to anticipate the greatest sexual pleasure with young, healthy, intelligent women who show promise of providing superior parental care. It is likely that young women who are known to be irre-vocably sterile are, even today, somewhat disadvantaged in sexual se-lection, especially in respect to males most inclined to monogamy.

I am suggesting, in part, that the proximate mechanisms of anticipa-tion, excitement, pleasure, and whatever else is relevant, which sur-round human sexual activity, have been tuned somewhat differently in male and female to reflect their different functional (though not neces-sarily and probably not at all conscious) aims or goals in sexual interactions (Daly and Wilson, 1983; Symons, 1979). If such an hypoth esis is supported, we can ponder how such male–female differences have been affecting the moral (and now legal) issue of why women have not been granted equal access to the resources of society (job opportunities, inheritance, ownership of family resources, etc.). How might these differences affect attitudes toward legislation explicitly giving such equal access to women and what do they suggest about its results?

I suggest that men respond in two ways to this issue, both responses reflecting in part their history, evolutionary and otherwise, with respect to male–female interactions. Many men act as though they believe that without lopsided control of resources by males they can expect a remarkable and to them personally detrimental shift in the relations of the sexes. It is true that in a world where women tend to link sexually significant interactions to access to resources, the man who controls few or no resources would seem at a terrible disadvantage. Neither this condition nor any other relationship I am discussing between the sexes is being suggested as a predetermined or inevitable fact: it is my view, for example, that attitudes or actions predicted in people who *lack* knowledge of the human selective background will not necessarily resemble those of people who have such knowledge. Moreover, I am considering a man's "disadvantage" in relation to *other men* and not commenting on how it might compare with the disadvantage to a woman of controlling few or no resources.

In sexual competition, the alternatives of a man without resources are to present himself as a resource (i.e., as a mimic of one with resources or as one able and likely to secure resources because of his personal attributes, for example, through force, persuasion, or intelligence, or by macho, peacock, or otherwise deceptive behavior), to obtain sex by force (rape), or to secure resources through a woman (e.g., allow himself to be kept by a relatively undesired woman, perhaps as a vehicle to secure liaisons with other women). I have little doubt that there is great significance in the descriptions of most rapists as men without wealth, property, or supportive networks of relatives and friends; often with physical appearance and other traits that seem antithetical to successful heterosexual behavior; and, perhaps most importantly, with self-images and past experiences that deny a likelihood of success in ordinary heterosexual experiences (largely through, it must be emphasized, success in resource accumulation and control) (Alexander, 1975, 1978; Thornhill and Thornhill, 1983). Nor do I doubt that, should there be a way to change the rapist's view of himself (and necessarily others' views of him) as a failure in resource control, there would often be a decided diminution of the tendency to take up the miserable "strategy" of rape. It is ironic that prison terms are essentially designed to have precisely the opposite effect. (I have no solution for this problem. One reviewer suggested that I am implying that rapists should be put up in fine hotels; I could just as well be implying, however, that once placed in jail they should never be let out.)

The second expected response of men to the proposition of allowing women equal access to resources may (uncharitably, I suppose) be termed ingratiation. There are two obvious possible rewards, depending on circumstances. If the change is inevitable anyway, then this response places a man in the vanguard of those on the "correct" side, politically; countless politicians and others must have accelerated what they saw— consciously or subconsciously, rightly or wrongly—as an inevitable trend by switching to the previously unpopular side at the appropriate moment to help themselves (there is also the probability, as in women's suffrage, that many men believed that giving their spouses and female relatives the vote would simply increase the number who voted their way). I am arguing that, protestations to the contrary notwithstanding, power tends to be given up in the interests of either gaining more power or of suffering a smaller loss in an inevitable coup.

It is obvious also that women respond in at least two diametrically opposed fashions to the "equal rights" proposition. There are those that seem to throw caution to the winds and aggressively and militantly seek to obtain the rights that by all counts—especially given our general governmental history and structure—are clearly theirs. Others appear just as militantly to ingratiate themselves to the existing power structure by supporting the status quo. We may legitimately ask whether the personal situations and histories of individual women, as with individual men, do not cause their personal strategies and expressed opinions on this issue to reflect the future circumstance that will best fulfill their goals, as women and men, and in the light of the history of male–female interactions in general. In effect, some women accept the strategy of securing resources via one or a few males to whom they are linked (spouses, relatives, etc.), while others seek access to resources in the marketplace at large on their own, necessarily by disrupting the general and historical lopsidedness effected by men acting together.

Now what of the moral issue involved here? As I have warned repeatedly, no solution arises out of evolutionary understanding. But perhaps our view of the issues can be clarified and our collective response as a result altered—and perhaps in a direction likely to be judged by those concerned as positive. Actually there are many moral issues involved, as I hope the previous discussion has shown. There is the general issue of why men have, apparently always, sought to restrict women's rights, and why these restrictions have tended to diminish more in some societies than in others. Knowledge of our evolutionary background may allow us to understand both of these questions better and deal with them more effectively in the future. There is the question of rape and the moral issue of dealing with rapists. My discussion actually seems to predict that with increasing access to resources by women rape might, at least temporarily, become an even more serious problem (that is, unless special measures, such as appropriate increases in penalties or special precautions, are taken). An additional prediction is that rape will occur most frequently in regions populated by women of relatively high status and men of relatively low status. For example, I think it is already widely accepted that rape is more common in university towns with a considerable population of transient males. (Ann Arbor, Michigan, home of the University of Michigan, was described in 1983 as having the highest reported rate of rape in the U.S.) Obviously, all such data are subject to the error of differential reporting. There is also the confusing variable of high proportions of females of high reproductive value in such situations. Thornhill and Thornhill (1983) have shown that women with greater reproductive probability are more likely to be raped.

There is the additional question, disconcerting, perhaps—whether increasing control of resources by women might, at least initially, have a destabilizing effect on the family by diminishing the historical roles of both male and female. It is obvious that, in nonhuman species of higher animals, control of the essential resources of parenthood by females correlates with lack of parental behavior by males, promiscuous polygyny, and absence of long-term pair bonds. There is some evidence of parallel trends within human societies (cf. Flinn, 1981). One wonders if those who express skepticism about Aid to Dependent Children (provided principally to mothers), because of what they see as a deleterious effect on family structure, would be prepared to take the step of providing the access to resources by the (often minority group) males involved that might resolve the situation—that is, to remove the impediments to resource acquisition that plague males of minority groups.

My discussion here obviously deals with only a fraction of the issues surrounding male–female relations. To treat the subject exhaustively would require another essay at least as long as this one.

## THE RIGHTS OF CHILDREN AND PARENTS

Another example illustrating the great difficulty of applying biological information to moral and legal questions can be taken from the effort of Beckstrom (1985) to use evolutionary biology to deal with the problem of child custody (see, also Beckstrom, 1981, on law and intestate wealth transfers). Beckstrom, a professor of law at Northwestern University, begins by asking whether or not the greater confidence of maternity, as compared to paternity, and the history of more intensive parental care by women, ought to be used as a tie-breaker by judges who can find no other grounds for discriminating between father and mother in a custody dispute. He suggests that women, on this basis, would be expected by biologists to be somewhat more parental or caring. In an oral discussion, his early probings (Conference on Law, Biology, and Culture, Monterey, California, September 1981) elicited two questions: First, it was argued that judges who were prepared to use this argument could not easily refrain from allowing it to bias their views early, before they had decided that the custody issue was a toss-up. More seriously, the question was raised whether children might not more severely reduce a woman's than a man's chances to secure another mate. If this were so, then some mothers might in certain circumstances be more likely than fathers to be cruel or neglectful to their children, because they interfered with her ability to obtain a second mate, or they might be more likely to allow cruelty by a prospective mate. (Such things as differences in the sex of a single woman's child might affect both the likelihood of abuse and its nature, as might the woman's intensity of concern about acquiring a new mate—see also, Alexander, 1988.) The important point is not whether or not this is actually true but that the possibility reveals how significant questions of this sort may be in efforts to apply knowledge from evolutionary biology to legal and moral questions. Yet this same issue shows just as clearly that explorations of the type Beckstrom is making may become incredibly important in revealing—perhaps only incidentally in many cases—aspects of our behavior not exposed by any other approach. In any effort to use biological information and theory to contribute to the realization of human desires and preferences, the arguments must be explored in depth. What are their bases and their consequences? How shall we arrive at the "best" procedures?

The reason that evolutionary knowledge has no moral content is made obvious by all of the above examples: morality is a matter of whose interests one should, by conscious and willful behavior, serve, and how much; evolutionary knowledge contains no messages on this issue. The most it can do is provide information about the reasons for current conditions and predict some consequences of alternative courses of action.

## THE PERILS OF ERROR AND UNRECOGNIZED BIASES

When science and morality approach one another, the ideologies of the participants are likely to become increasingly involved in their science. The scientist may not really know what is happening, and he may in all sincerity deny it unequivocally. If accused, he may react with the most righteous and honest indignation. Probably, no one has previously accused him of duplicity in his science, there has never been reason to do so, and, moreover, to make such an accusation constitutes the most serious defamatory attack conceivable; for the essence of science, however far we may be from it at any time, is truth—truth even when what is involved is merely a series of stages in the pursuit of some larger and as yet more elusive truth.

Unfortunately, this situation opens the door for those who may wish to defame by innuendo. This is a problem alien to biology but of long-standing in the social sciences. I have no doubt that it has influenced the directions and rates of change there and the response of social scientists to the current attention from biology. The problem was well summarized by an observer who noted that "In the natural sciences a person is remembered for his best idea, in the social sciences he is remembered for his worst." If a natural scientist were to write a long book in which a single error occurred, most of his peers (except, perhaps, his closest competitors) would probably feel that they could judge the error and the rest of the book independently. Conversely, if a social scientist were to write a long book otherwise of great value in which a sentence such as "Hitler was a good man" appeared, I am sure that everything else in the book would be discarded by most as suspect because of the single preposterous statement. Theoretical revolutions are not common in the social sciences, and they seem to cause even more screaming and hair-pulling there than, for example, George Williams' argument against group selection caused in biology when it appeared in 1966.

Despite skeptics and dissenters, including some biologists (e.g., Lewontin, 1979), introducing the genetic materials into our efforts to understand ourselves does not automatically involve constructing "genetic arguments to establish a kind of biological determinism for human behavior." Nor are the attempts of evolutionary biologists in this area simply " . . . another example of biological determinist arguments, all of which are based on a number of misconceptions about biology and the structure of knowledge [and] . . . on a number of assertions about human genetics that have no factual basis" (Lewontin, 1979). If some biologists and nonbiologists make unfounded assertions into conclusions, or develop pernicious and fallible arguments, then those assertions and arguments should be exposed for what they are. The reason for doing this, however, is not to prevent or discourage any and all analyses of human activities, but to enable us to get on with a proper sort of analysis. Those who malign without being specific; who attack people rather than ideas; who gratuitously translate hypotheses into conclusions and then refer to them as "explanations," "stories," or "just-so-stories"; who parade the worst examples of argument and investigation with the apparent purpose of making all efforts at human self-analysis seem silly and trivial, I see as dangerously close to being ideologues at least as worrisome as those they malign. I cannot avoid the impression that their purpose is not to enlighten, but to play upon the uneasiness of those for whom the approach of evolutionary biology is alien and disquieting, perhaps for political rather than scientific purposes. It is more than a little ironic that the argument of politics rather than science is their own chief accusation with respect to scientists seeking to analyze human behavior in evolutionary terms (e.g. Gould and Lewontin, 1979; for similar opinions, see Bateson, 1985, and Dawkins, 1985).

I do not in any sense regard it as overdramatic to suggest that our survival may depend upon the kind of self-understanding such people seem to be seeking to prevent. At the very least it seems to be their stance that people are not intelligent enough to use fruitfully the knowledge of who they are and how they came to be that way. I do not intend my arguments on this point to be a defense of any conclusions I may reach here, or even of the particular approach I am espousing; these things may be judged on their own merits. Instead my comments are a direct criticism of the particular approach taken by those like Lewontin and Gould, because I see that approach as including claims that mislead, and that capitalize upon fears and ignorance, whether or not for purposes that these authors themselves regard as noble.

In a recent Dahlem Conference volume on "Morality as a Biological Phenomenon" (Stent, 1978), the Cambridge philosopher B.A.O. Williams made a telling point in the final paragraph of the book. He wrote as follows:

> Sociobiology as an ideology, and . . . I wish to emphasize I am not speaking of these writers (Wilson and Dawkins), but of a popular form, combines the features that it is both scientistic and conservative. It combines the notion of being in favor of science and being based on scientific explanation with a fundamentally and literally conservative keeping what is found natural approach to various social institutions. In the present ideological climate, one can predict that is an extraordinarily potent combination of characteristics. Most conservative outlooks are *anti*scientific, and therefore treated with distrust because they seem to leave aside the paradigm of modern knowledge. Many *scientistic* outlooks are deeply *radical*, such as that of B. F. Skinner: Forget everything you ever valued, all's swept away, new world, Walden II . . . we should all be listening to the gramophone all day, people

having their brains cut out in the interest of social conformity. People do not like that either, for various old-fashioned reasons. When you have an outlook which can be at once scientistic and conservative, it can speak to quite a lot of our needs, and therefore, however many disclaimers Dawkins puts in, however many disclaimers Wilson puts in, however many admirable hygienic and analytic observations we have managed to achieve, I still think that, on the whole, we had better watch out. (p. 320)

The reason this paragraph struck me so was that it has been repeatedly demonstrated to me that Williams is correct: the label sociobiology does indeed appeal simultaneously to the politically or socially conservative person and to him who thinks he views science favorably—the "scientistic" person, to use Williams' word. Not infrequently, persons I know to be scientists, physicians, or engineers speak up at lectures, write me notes, or send me tracts, revealing that they are taking a positive view partly because they are also conservatively oriented in their views of social behavior and they think that what they want to call sociobiology supports their politics. Occasionally their comments or support are startling or even immensely embarrassing on this account. On one occasion a highly respected and capable university administrator sent me an essay by another faculty member to show that I had support and sympathy from other fields. In fact the paper was a bit of radical conservative politics, and the man was merely using "sociobiology" in a pernicious way to bolster his own views. I explained to the administrator why I believed this, and he replied immediately, and I am sure in complete honesty, that he was extremely embarrassed that he had not noticed that this in fact appeared to be the case.

I am saying all of this to agree with the philosopher Williams' final sentence, that if we are going to pursue any kind of biological approach to moral issues then, " . . . on the whole, we had better watch out." In spite of all of this, I also believe that, on the whole, we had better *proceed*.

I think that biological and evolutionary approaches to human behavior are unique with respect to how understanding develops among those with sympathy toward such approaches. It seems that such understanding does not continue to grow in all or even most such people but, rather, encounters one or more significant barriers. These barriers are especially troublesome because they seem to inhibit further comprehension and represent misunderstanding from partial knowledge. Perhaps this is the outstanding example of a little knowledge being a dangerous thing. The first barrier to understanding I will call the "Aha! Behavior is either innate or learned" barrier. In its more sophisticated forms this barrier becomes the *"Some* behavior is *biologically* determined!" or "There *are* biological imperatives!" revelation. As such it seems to lead many people to suppose that they have grasped the whole message from biology and now they can return to their everyday dealing with it—whether in psychiatry, politics, academia, or elsewhere. *Nothing could be further from the truth!* My efforts to explain why appear earlier in this book, in *Darwinism and Human Affairs,* and in other publications cited in one or both of these books (see also Irons, 1979). There are at best two other significant barriers to understanding. One is the "hypothesis-to-conclusion leap." It happens when someone speculates or hypothesizes a specific function or causal connection involving human behavior and then, without further ado, transforms the unsupported hypothesis into a conclusion or an "explanation."

The third barrier I will call the "ignorance-of-biology" problem. This is the situation that arises when someone develops hypotheses or derives conclusions that are utterly incompatible with biological facts he has not yet encountered. Here are two such (false) assumptions: "From the point of view of kin selection it is always best to marry the closest possible relative" (Dawkins, 1979, identified the fallacy in this assertion). "The function of outbreeding is to prevent the appearance of deleterious recessive alleles as homozygotes" (Maynard Smith, 1978).

How do we get people past these barriers? As I have already indicated, I doubt that we can ever do so without extensive teaching of evolutionary biology to large proportions of the population, and I believe this may be a project of great significance for the world of the future.

## CONCLUSIONS

I would argue, then, that there is much more to heavily publicized moral and legal questions such as abortion, euthanasia, welfare, and equal rights than meets the eye. And I would argue that many of these "hidden" elements are only likely to be exposed and clarified through a deep understanding of our biological-evolutionary background—specifically, through analyzing the conflicts of interest involved and taking into account the nature and significance of the system of indirect reciprocity involved.

There may be approaches other than the one suggested here which give equally or more consistent or appropriate answers to questions like those involving the rights of embryos and the moribund, women and men, children and parents. I think most people would agree that the search for such approaches should proceed. It seems to me, however, that most of the public arguments on these particular questions could have been enhanced by applying information from biology, as I have done here, even if the approach or conclusions differed from or opposed that suggested here. I cannot imagine actual understanding from biological or other sources (as opposed to misinformation) contributing in any but a beneficial manner.

> I believe . . . it is reasonable to assume that it will become increasingly difficult to be non-moral as a society gains more knowledge about itself and the world. (Nielson, 1978, p. 558)

## Arms Races, Human and Otherwise

> *Justice is helping friends and harming enemies.*
>> Polemarcus, answering Socrates
>> [Cornford, 1941]

> *Civilization begins, because the beginning of civilization is a military advantage.*
>> Walter Bagehot, 1873

> *. . . war prepares the way for civilization . . . civilization prepares the way for war.*
>> Sir Arthur Keith, 1947

> *It is only by means of a standing army that the civilization of any country can be perpetuated, or even preserved for any length of time.*
>> Adam Smith, 1776

I acknowledge at the outset that I have no solution to the international arms race. What is much more important, apparently no one else does either. It is a most curious aspect of the whole topic that virtually no one discusses why solutions should be as difficult as these statements imply, how arms races originate, and whether or not there are precedents for expecting resolution. Perhaps, to people actually seated at the negotiating tables, these things do not seem to matter. But if, as I believe, there is no more significant problem of human existence than the international arms race, and if, as I also believe, the only chance for a solution lies in deep understanding of the human condition by large numbers of thoughtful people, then such background items deserve exposition.

## HUMAN ARMS RACES COMPARED TO NATURAL AND SEXUAL SELECTION

In arms race seminars, I have heard people widely regarded as experts assert that "The Arms Race" began about 35 years ago. The human arms race may have many unique aspects, and it surely underwent some dramatic changes 30 or 40 years ago; but arms races (which include the evolution of teeth, claws, and other structures and behaviors used in combat between competitors) are approximately as old as life itself. They are also an integral part of life's nature, which is to suggest, not that they are inevitable, but that they have occurred more or less continually across the whole spectrum of millions of species and billions of years; there may be some things to learn from expanding our analysis.

Darwin (1859) referred to the causal forces of natural selection as the *Hostile Forces of Nature*. An updated version of Darwin's hostile forces would include parasites, predators, diseases, food shortages, climate, and weather (Alexander, 1979a). What Darwin meant is that these are the forces that normally cause absolute or relative reproductive failure. The human species, however, has placed itself in a unique position with respect to evolutionary history: it has reduced the effects of all of the usual so-called hostile forces of nature, essentially eliminating them as guiding forces in its evolution—especially its behavioral evolution— most of the time. The most pervasive hostile force that remains, for any human individual or group, is other members or groups of the human species itself. Apparently no other species has accomplished this peculiar evolutionary feat, which has led to an unprecedented level of group-against-group *within-species* competition. It is this competition that draws us toward strange and ominous consequences.

Most evolutionary or selective races are tempered to a greater extent than is the human arms race by between-species components. If the swifter or more efficient killers of a predaceous species outreproduce those less efficient or slower, so do the faster or more elusive individuals among their prey also outreproduce slower or less elusive conspecifics. At some point, however, these directions of selection, on both predator and prey, begin to interfere with traits selected in other contexts, so that the original selection becomes less effective: the costs of evolving to, say, run faster become too great because some other trait—such as combat strength or ability to bear babies—is compromised. Every organism can be described as a bundle of such compromises deriving from the composite effects of countless conflicting directions of natural selection; and if a species is still extant this means that all of the selective races involving it, and the species that affect it, are in some kind of cost–benefit balance.

To some extent the intergroup competition of the human species, including the international arms race, is most appropriately compared to sexual selection, which Darwin (1859, 1871) treated separately from natural selection. Sexual selection is a result of the "hostile force" of mate shortages, or relative differences in mating success. Compared to other kinds of selection, it too involves a more direct kind of within-species competition. Even sexual selection, however, is tempered by Darwin's hostile forces whenever its directions conflict sufficiently with relief from these hostile forces to make additional change more costly than beneficial. A male's bright colors or other decorations may secure for him more mates, even if such traits sometimes achieve bizarre extremes. Eventually, however, they begin to cause so many deaths from predation or so much caloric expense that their continued elaboration ceases.

Fisher (1958) aptly termed the most bizarre aspect of sexual selection "runaway sexual selection." Runaway sexual selection is what happens when a trend continues whereby females favor in males the elaboration of traits that reduce the males' likelihood of success in all other life situations. (The converse can occur only if males provide so many resources for offspring that males become limiting for females rather than vice versa.) Runaway sexual selection occurs partly because those females outreproduce who simply choose the most extreme males with respect to some trait that varies. Runaway sexual selection has been considered responsible for such seeming excesses as the outlandish colors and structure of the plumage in many male birds—the peacock, for example. By definition, attributes of males involved in runaway sexual selection have no value except that they lead to the production of more offspring because (and only because) females favor the extreme males in mating. Hamilton and Zuk (1982) have provided evidence that at least some male attributes previously believed to be involved in runaway sexual selection, as just defined, are actually indicators of resistance to diseases and parasites.

Sexual selection is subject to becoming "runaway" because it is largely a within-species process, and because the winners are simply those who are most extreme. Runaway sexual selection may be the closest parallel to the runaway cultural processes of arms accumulation and resource depletion in which humans are engaged. Indeed, it is likely that the two are related: there is evidence that in smaller nontechnological human societies (thus, throughout most of human history) intergroup strife is fueled by sexual competition and the condition of women being limiting factors in the relative reproductive success of men. Chagnon (1979a, b) referred to the connection between intergroup strife and sexual competition as involving "shortages" of women (see also Strate, 1982; Betzig, 1986). The romantic effects of military uniforms in wartime and the deleterious consequences of cowardice or malingering—which may destroy the career or life of the accused—indicate that we have not yet lost this connection. During World War I, in England, women were urged " . . . never to be seen in public with any man who, being in every way fit and free for service, has refused to respond to his country's call," to tell their sons, "My boy, I don't want you to go, but if I were you I should go," and to distribute white feathers to young men not in the service as symbols of cowardice (E.S. Turner, 1980).

But human arms races and intergroup resource competition are even more bizarre and less controlled than runaway sexual selection. These two cultural races are obviously dangerous because together they may lead to irrevocable disasters, up to and including extinction of the human species or all of life on Earth. Part of their danger comes from a kind of synergism or feedback between them. The arms race consumes enormous amounts of resources; competition for these resources is exacerbated by the perceived need to acquire them for weapons manufacture and use; and competition for dwindling resources, in turn, causes increasing friction, reinforcing the whole destructive cycle (For example, the most common reason given for elaborating the capability of waging a nuclear war is to avoid "international blackmail." Even if cast in terms of competing social systems, however, international blackmail ultimately has to do with differential access to resources.)

Perhaps more important, there are no predictable shifts of costs and benefits that can reliably be expected to cause other problems that conflict with the arms race to become more crucial. Unlike all other selective races, evolutionary or cultural, this one does not lead to an inevitable direction change that will rescue us from its dangers. Neither the arms race nor the resource-competition race has any of the usual brakes that eventually slow down and prevent further evolutionary races, whether cultural or noncultural. There are some partial brakes, which I will discuss later, but none that can be expected to be complete.

Because we have so reduced the impact of all other hostile forces on our lives, the weapons and resource races both continue virtually unchecked; indeed, as with other cultural changes, they are accelerating as this aspect of our specialization becomes increasingly bizarre. Because each party to an arms race may be the other party's sole or principal hostile force, not only are there are no effective brakes on the race, but, as well, each response by either party drives the next response in the other. This is true even if the responses are often delayed a few years, and even if, within each of two competing societies, political and economic structures are produced which fuel themselves for several years almost as if the other society did not exist (cf. Nincic, 1982). Thus, the cultural within-species arms race of humans parallels never-ending evolutionary races between species such as those between predators and prey. Even if arms races are as old as life itself, however, there may be no precedent for the kind of *largely unchecked* arms race in which the great powers of the world are currently involved.

In an unchecked arms race, each response by either party, because of the aggression risk the response apparently imposes, seems to lower the cost of a return response by the other party and to raise its benefits: if an enemy builds a better weapon, the cost of doing it one's self suddenly seems more acceptable. I say "seems" because in humans the long-term results of the whole process, as we can now perceive, may be extinction, and that is the highest of all costs. That we have evolved to measure our success in relative terms (because reproductive success is always relative) aggravates the whole situation. It means that people are likely to be satisfied, not by *particular quantities* (of resources, weapons, whatever), but only *in relation* to what those seen as adversaries have. The resulting international attitude is the most pernicious imaginable accompaniment to an arms race.

## ARE THERE PRECEDENTS FOR ARMS RACE RESOLUTIONS?

Several observable outcomes of competitive interactions and "arms races" among nonhuman forms may look like resolution. First, there may be extinction of one or both involved parties. Second, someone may win locally—therefore, necessarily, temporarily—after which another round begins, with somewhat different kinds or arrangements of competitors. Third, there may be a temporary standoff because of a balance of power or effective deterrence by threat. Fourth, two previously competing groups may form an alliance against a third group. Of these examples, only the first is permanent or suggests a precedent for resolution on a global basis; it is probably not, however, the kind of resolution most humans have in mind for their arms race. Nevertheless, *permanent* and *global* resolution is what we seek. Although arms races among all living creatures may be countless in number and diverse in pattern, there is evidently no precedent among them, in either observation or theory, for resolutions that would be acceptable in a human arms race, particularly permanent global resolutions. I believe that such little discussed unusual or unique features of the human arms race are the central reasons for our continuing perplexity in dealing with this cultural cancer that threatens to destroy us.

To comprehend our dilemma a little more starkly, consider these facts: current selective theory indicates that natural selection has never operated to prevent species extinction. Instead it operates by saving the genetic materials of those individuals or families that outreproduce others. Whether species become extinct or not (and most have) is an incidental or accidental effect of natural selection. An inference from this is that the members of no species are equipped, as a direct result of their evolutionary history, with traits designed explicitly to prevent their species from extinction when that possibility looms. (For this reason the widely read essay of Gould, 1982, arguing that adaptation is a concept of limited usefulness because most species have become extinct, is confusing and largely irrelevant.) Humans are no exception: unless their comprehension of the likelihood of extinction is so clear and real that they perceive the threat to themselves as individuals, and to their loved ones, they cannot be expected to take the collective action that will be necessary to reduce the risk of extinction. Infinitely worse, it is not through accidental traits and tendencies, or external forces, that human extinction is threatened. Humans alone have been equipped by their evolutionary history with traits and tendencies that, *as a consequence of their normal functioning,* can bring about human extinction. It is these traits and tendencies (to form exclusive and competitive groups within which loyalty and cooperativeness are fierce and between which hate, loathing, and dehumanization are likely) that have led us into the unique runaway social competition of an arms race involving annihilatory weapons.

Schell (1982) compared our relentless escalation of the arms race to the behavior of "men in a dream, like lemmings heading for the sea." This view is an ironic mistake. Lemmings were long believed to sacrifice themselves, as *individuals,* for the good of the *population* or *species* during times of overpopulation until it was discovered that (1) such behavior is unlikely to persist or be elaborated because its most likely carriers would always be the least likely to reproduce and (2) lemmings live in short-lived habitats separated by fjords and so most probably enter the water not to commit suicide to save their species but to find new habitat and promote the survival of their own genes. (Even if nearly all die, each individual in a nomadic species sooner or later has a better chance by emigrating than by remaining in the exhausted and perhaps disease-ridden old habitat.) The irony of comparing ourselves to lemmings lies in the fact that humans are collectively doing things that enhance the chances of their *populations* or *species* becoming extinct because they have believed, as *individuals,* that it is in their personal interests to support their respective governments in the arms race.

## PROPOSED SOLUTIONS TO THE INTERNATIONAL ARMS RACE

### Universal Brotherhood

Two seemingly opposed strategies have been proposed to prevent global devastation through nuclear war. To some extent they involve opposed views of the nature, history, and future of humans. The first, which I will call the "universal brotherhood" argument, supposes that we can achieve peace and prevent war by expanding the kinds of within-group altruism that gave rise to systems of morality (and by which such systems are maintained and elaborated) so as to include the whole world. This outcome would also result from extending the approach of most philosophers and theologians to morality. It would represent success in the pursuit of an idealized, universally indiscriminate altruism. Such expectations ignore or seek to override the paradox that extreme within-group altruism seems to correlate with and be historically related to between-group strife. They represent the view that, by emphasizing and holding out an ideal model of morality, we can teach people to behave as though they had been group-selected in one large group, even though such selection is evidently a logical impossibility. They suppose that conflicts of interest can either be erased or made so trivial or symbolic as not to threaten world peace. Sometimes the argument seems to take the form that such things can be accomplished merely by thinking about them, or wishing they were so.

In one form or another, the "universal brotherhood" view is espoused by many modern writers, such as Peter Singer (1981) and Jonathan Schell (1982). Its shortcoming is that it is without precedent, and it flies in the face of our history. To many it seems soft-headed and a fantasy. I would not argue that it is impossible to achieve, but I would argue that it is unlikely to be brought about by any means currently supposed adequate, or any likely to be advanced by people who do not understand themselves through knowledge of their biological and evolutionary history. For this reason I am also fearful that there may not be sufficient time to bring about such a profound change in human attitudes.

It is, however, a virtue of the deliberate pursuit of an idealized model of indiscriminate altruism (or universal brotherhood) that, among even partly interdependent parties, no one can afford to lag too far behind the behavior of the most beneficent, or of the majority when most are beneficent. A mere reduction in the variance of expressions of morality, and attitudes toward it, may thus—through the effects of indirect reciprocity—drive us toward conditions within societies that heretofore have only been visualized in the minds of idealists. On the other hand, this virtue, as I am seeing it, disappears whenever such pursuits become mired in *we–they* exclusions contradictory to the model.

It is evidently difficult for those who immerse themselves in the concept of universal brotherhood to believe that their motives may fall short of actual universality. Perhaps in the minds of individuals conscious motivation often does not fall short, and less-than-global ends, such as alliances, may be served by this kind of naivete or self-deception. Nevertheless, it seems clear that universality in outcomes has not yet been achieved as a result of individuals believing in it. The concept of a single, just God for all people everywhere, for example, has always failed. Brotherly love of the most sincere and intense varieties often, if not universally, correlates with the presence of an enemy. This enemy, whose existence by definition precludes universality, may be identified as an object of actual discrimination, ostracism, or efforts at elimination; or it may simply be a greater power to be defeated by passivity until increased numbers or some other change can reverse the power differential. What I am saying is that, for reasons suggested earlier, the concept of brotherly love has all too frequently had its greatest potency in war or its equivalents. In arms race debates I have listened to American peace activists who argue for some form of universal brotherly love yet seem to differ from others chiefly in having designated as their enemy the current administration of the United States government; and I have heard others whose acceptance of their own view of how to resolve the arms race has become so precious to them that anyone with a different view is automatically vilified. Honest disagreement obviously can exist within brotherhoods without inconsistency, but it also seems that universal brotherhood is much easier to believe in than to practice.

## Deterrence

At the other end of the spectrum from the *universal brotherhood* view, that somehow we can extend the amity of kinship to include all humans, there is the view that *deterrence* is the real way to prevent nuclear war. This is the stand taken by all recent administrations of the U.S. government: (Haig, 1982, p. B.1, B.4): "The catastrophic consequences of another world war . . . make deterrence of conflict our highest objective and our only rational military strategy in the modern age . . . " (see also Carnesale *et al.*, 1983; Hardin *et al.*, 1985).

The "mutual deterrence" (or balance-of-power) model for world peace takes a form that is consistent with the assumption that natural selection has been potent at lower levels in the hierarchy of organization of life, and that nations tend to behave like the individuals that comprise them. There is little doubt that this model reflects what has actually happened in the world, perhaps throughout history; unfortunately, this fact in no way implies that deterrence will ultimately rescue us.

(Ironically, what has surfaced in efforts to resolve the international arms race of the late twentieth century is the ancient conundrum of a seeming duality in human nature, the same two aspects of sociality that David Hume, 1750, referred to as the "particle of the dove" and "elements of the wolf and serpent." Selfishness and altruism—in essentially the same forms they have taken throughout the history of humanity's debates about itself—are the two opposed views of how we may best save ourselves from ourselves.)

The spread of nuclear weapons, and the focus on scarce resources owned by third-world entities, promise to complicate dangerously the problem of mutual deterrence. The other difficulty, of course, is that mutual deterrence leaves the world vulnerable to the whims and idiosyncrasies of individuals wielding the power of nations—i.e., the power of extinction of life, the human species, or civilization. Our weaponry is too horrible, its employment too irreversible, and the machinery of its employment too human and too risky to make deterrence in the usual sense a satisfactory insurance. As Fulbright (cited in Frank, 1967) points out, there is no precedent for an absolutely fail-safe deterrence; yet, with our current weaponry, that is what we require. Frank (1967) notes that a preoccupation with deterrence in the negative sense of ever more serious threats, and constant focusing on adversarial relations (rather than what Frank calls "community," or cooperative endeavors), may mean that although the nuclear arms race is motivated by the desire to prevent nuclear war, deterrence actually creates conditions that increasingly favor the outbreak of nuclear war (see Hardin *et al.*, 1985, for some opposing views, especially the chapter by David Gauthier on "Deterrence, maximization, and rationality").

Axelrod and Hamilton (1981) indicate that "tit for tat" (doing what one's opponent did last) is the best (and a stable) strategy in a two-adversary social interaction. But this is only true if the actions of each adversary are quite limited, if certain kinds and degrees of ignorance exist between adversaries, and if sufficient iterations of the interaction can occur (see also Maynard Smith, 1982); Axelrod and Hamilton's games did not deal with the possibility of either or both parties believing they had learned something that would allow them to win; or with the possibility of mutual annihilation by a tat followed by a tit. Two-adversary interactions without relevant third parties, more-over, are probably rare in the real world, although, as Axelrod (1984) points out, the contest between the two superpowers, the U.S. and the U.S.S.R., has for a time approached this condition.

As Martin (1982, p. 36) has also noted in respect to the views of millions of fundamentalist Christians in the U.S. " . . . if the nuclear destruction of Russia is foreordained, as in some pre-millenial schemes, might not a fundamentalist politician or general regard his finger on the button as an instrument of God's eternal purpose?" There are all too many other reasons why the small groups of individuals who control the unthinkable modern weapons of "deterrence" might betray us all and use them to destroy most or all of life as it now exists. Unfortunately there is no lesson from the arms races of nonhuman animals except deterrence, nor is there a precedent for depending on deterrence when the deterred conflict is one that could suddenly extinguish most or all of the species practicing it.

A seeming third possible route toward reduction of the possibility of human self-extinction is suggested by what I will call the "smaller is better" argument. This model says in effect that if we can just do away with huge nations we are unlikely to have stockpiles of weapons large enough to destroy the world. While this may well be so, to suppose that the most powerful nations of the world would submit to partition is not much different from asking all men instantly to observe brotherhood. It does not seem likely that in the near future we can expect the individuals who comprise the populations of great nations to become convinced that their nation imperils them and their loved ones so directly that they would gain by voting its partition into smaller nations. To seek any other method of dismantling large powerful nations would be to invoke directly some version of the international brotherhood model or to imagine that some arm of international government, like the United Nations, might become so powerful as to deny everyone gains from committing armed aggression. Moreover, it has recently become increasingly clear that small nations or groups, or individual deranged leaders, can wield the kind of terror that was once restricted to the superpowers.

Up to this point, then, brotherly love and deterrence have actually been *strategies* in arms races rather than methods of resolving them or causing them to disappear. The aim, when one or another of these strategies has been employed, is the same as with any other strategy— to win or dominate, which means ultimately to secure a disproportionate share of the resources over which the competition exists. Brotherly love seems always to have been less than global, and whether its origins are Marxist, religious, or otherwise, it also seems always to have begun or to have become a means of gaining power, as through alliances.

(Under brotherly love I include not just disarmament but also ending or retarding weapons buildups and research for reasons other than improving one's own status or possibilities—the last including, of course, reducing the risk of unnecessary and catastrophic confrontations or accidents.) Similarly, deterrence has always been a system either for buying time until more power has been gained or for holding off an opponent while power is being exercised with respect to some resource that both desire. At least the evidence suggests that these things have been true in the past. Perhaps someone can bring forth examples to deny it, but none is apparent to me. We are forced to conclude, I believe, that the classes of solutions thus far proposed for the human international arms race—essentially, brotherly love and mutual deterrence—bear no historical relationship whatever to the *resolution* of arms races. Despite the apparent acceptance of each by its proponents as our only salvation, neither seems to have been presented in a *unique* fashion that might suggest a novel prospect of effecting such a resolution in the future. Perhaps their incompatibility with one another, which has placed their proponents in adversarial camps, is partly responsible for leading us to suppose that one or the other must be the answer. Included in the interaction of the U.S. versus the Soviets—and perhaps at the heart of the matter now—is the effort of each to evangelize its own brand of social structure. To those who advocate the particular kind of brotherly love solution that amounts to spreading the word that all people everywhere are equally God's creatures, it must be reinforcing that this "solution" is part of such evangelizing.

## KNOWLEDGE OF THE PHYSICAL UNIVERSE, IGNORANCE OF THE SOCIAL ONE

What we seek, when we think of *world* peace and *world* law, thus has no precedent in the history of life, not to say the history of human life. There seems to be no evidence that humans or any other organisms have ever achieved the species-wide indiscriminate altruism represented in the idealized moral models of philosophy and religion. This means that the problem before us is an absolutely stupendous one: we have created it with our evolved intellects and now we cannot relax until we have used those same evolved intellects to resolve it. How has it all happened? Schell (1982) remarks that:

> . . . the fundamental origin of the peril of human extinction by nuclear arms lies not in any particular social or political circumstance of our time but in the attainment by mankind as a whole, after millenia of scientific progress, of a certain level of knowledge of the physical universe. (p. 48)

Schell's statement is true as written, but it is also incomplete, and therefore misleading. One wishes to add; *while failing to attain a similar level of knowledge about the social universe.* The peril of human extinction arises out of the tendency of humans across history to seek and accept knowledge *more readily* in physical than in social realms. The point is that we have learned how to manipulate the physical universe so as to extinguish ourselves, and we have simultaneously been reluctant about learning how to manipulate the social universe so as to prevent self-extinction. Schell's statement, and his subsequent comments about what to do about the quandary we are in, contain very peculiar and conflicting implications about human nature. The first is that humans are what they are and there is little to do about that: hence, the feeling that our only recourse is somehow to dispose of nuclear arms. The paradox is that to do that, or to create the utopias Schell describes later in which people simply love or respect each other and do not compete dangerously, would require alterations of human behavior so profound as to imply that there is in effect no human "nature" at all. Neither view—of an unchangeable deterministic human behavior or an omnidirectionally plastic one—is realistic. We had better find out very quickly what *is* realistic—how to *use* human nature to save ourselves, rather than assuming either that we cannot, or that we can only save ourselves by proceeding as if there were no such thing as human nature.

In a sense it is indeed the "particular" social and political circumstance of our time that produces the peril that threatens us: the circumstance that we have learned about the physical and not the social things. We have some catching up to do if humans are ever again to relax from the now-permanent peril of self-extinction, and the indications are that we may have to exert remarkably strenuous and creative efforts to bring this about. Given these facts, hostility toward any *bona fide* efforts to unravel the influences that have shaped us is indeed difficult to justify. Schell remarks (p. 58): "'Scientific' progress may yet deliver us from many evils, but there are at least two evils that it cannot deliver us from: its own findings and our own destructive and self-destructive bent. This is a combination that we will have to deal with by some other means." In this curious assertion he implies that science deals only with items other than human behavior. In other statements he makes it clear that he does not understand why the findings of science persist while the results of "social revolutions" do not. Science is a way of locating and demonstrating truths, however trivial or restricted (or at least of *approaching* truth *reliably*) and it is demonstrable correctness that persists. Schell seems to deny that there can be any pursuit of truth in social matters worthy of the label "science." I hope the world is prepared to show that this implication, whether or not I am correct in attributing it to Schell, is wrong.

There may be a general failure to link science, human behavior, and the goals of governments, particularly in dealing with problems such as arms races and international tensions. The international goals of governments call for unity among the governed, and the social scientists, who investigate human behavior, often turn up within-group injustices that look like reasons for disunity. There is a powerful paradox in the facts that (1) science as investigation of the physical universe has created the ultimate problem of human behavior, (2) the problem is widely seen as one of altering or manipulating human "nature" or behavioral tendencies, and (3) those scientists who devote their careers to being expert in dealing with human behavior have been scarcely involved, or have even been actively excluded, from the entire process.

## DECEPTION AND MISINFORMATION

In a game-theoretic analysis of adversarial relations, Parker (1974) argues that combatants (of any sort) assess one another's resource holding power (RHP), and "the stake played for is infliction of loss of RHP, and is determined by the fitness budgets of the opponents (each individual "plays for" the withdrawal of its opponent). This defines a critical probability of winning . . . for each combatant, above which escalation (fighting) is the favourable strategy . . . and below which withdrawal is favorable. . . . Escalation should occur only where [the absolute probability of winning minus the critical probability of winning] is positive for both combatants." He notes that "If assessments [of the adversaries' RHP] are perfect and budget expenditure rates exactly predictable, then there would never seem to be any case for escalation" (see also Maynard Smith and Parker, 1976; Parker, 1984). He means that someone will always lose, and if information is complete the loser-to-be would never attack and would withdraw. For our purposes, however, this also means that the stronger combatant will attack or carry out its own will. Parker also notes that " . . . during a display [for our purpose read "show of strength"], selection should mainly favour presenting an opponent with a maximal impression of one's RHP. Until a 'strategic decision' is reached, no information should be displayed to an opponent concerning withdrawal intentions, since there is the possibility that the opponent may withdraw first. . . . "

Parker's analysis indicates that in an arms race like that of humans, secrecy, deception, and misinformation are necessary; otherwise there would be times (not entirely predictable) when the temporarily more powerful adversary might simply *use* its advantage before it is lost. It is this requirement of secrecy, deception, and misinformation that creates the circumstance whereby government officials oppose citizen concern over international arms negotiations and the development of "peace research" and conflict resolution units outside government or even outside the negotiating terms per se. Thus, in the ABC-TV discussion following the film "The Day After," Secretary of State George Schultz responded to the question (paraphrased): "What can individual citizens do (about the arms race)?" by saying, in effect, "Support the President." When the question was asked again, in the form "What else?" he avoided it entirely. Similarly, Henry Kissinger expressed a vague opposition to support for research on peace and conflict resolution, saying that he did not think it could appropriately be seen as a "separate" topic. One has to wonder how useful it would be for people like Schultz and Kissinger not only to know (as presumably they do) but to state unequivocally the significance of deception, and how this significance relates to citizen participation.

## PARTIAL BRAKES ON THE ARMS RACE

Because I believe that in general people behave as they do because it is (or has been) in their (evolutionary) interests to do so, I also believe that world peace is likely to be achieved only by making it too costly for aggression to proceed. I have here argued that this is how moral systems have always operated; the expense of being selfish is why extreme altruism has prevailed within groups in conjunction with severe extrinsic threats. In a world of awesome nuclear and biological weapons, this is not a comfortable view. It seems to place me in a camp of those who see mutual deterrence as the basis for peace, even though I doubt that either self-extinction or massive destruction can be prevented indefinitely by deterrence alone. I also explicitly decry the assumption that reliance upon mutual deterrence requires acceptance of the levels and kinds of secrecy that now prevail, the restriction of strategizing to a privileged few in government, and the consequent arrogance of those who believe they alone possess the necessary information relevant to alleviating the threat.

The nature of our weaponry now causes the mutual deterrence proposition to become more complicated, for individuals and groups within nations have increasingly begun to perceive the likelihood that aggressive actions by their government are unlikely to be in their self-interest. As a result, I see five partial brakes inhibiting the arms race (see also Hardin *et al.*, 1985—particularly Hardin and Mearscheimer's introduction).

The first, ironically, comes from the perception that the effects of military spending may themselves make the nation more vulnerable to the very threats they are intended to offset. To be effective, even this perception has to come from (1) those who are truly interested first and foremost in national security or (2) those who personally stand to lose by increased military spending. Of course, in either case it must also occur in individuals or groups powerful enough to effect change.

The second brake comes into effect only when the threat of massive destruction becomes so great that individuals begin to see the original source of their security—their own government and its efforts to achieve "national security"—as, rather, the greatest threat to the safety of themselves, their relatives, and their friends. We have recently witnessed an extraordinary rise of just this feeling.

The third brake, which may have been in operation for some time, takes effect when those controlling the use of weaponry come to realize that its use *by only one side* is likely to extinguish or devastate *both* adversaries. My belief that we have already reached this stage rests on two assumptions: (1) under most circumstances, at least, neither side can afford to initiate a nuclear war by unleashing only a small part of its arsenal and (2) any wholesale use of the nuclear arsenal, even if not retaliated in kind, stands likely to devastate much of the planet and alter its climate so significantly as to place all life in jeopardy. This state of affairs cannot prevent accidents or insanity, but it does provide a partial deterrent that will remain in effect until technology solves this problem.

Deterrence as a result of fear, shared by all, that no matter who wins any confrontation will cause all to lose, will not be as easy to maintain as might first be supposed. It will only be successful when *everyone* believes that he will lose *big* (or else some may accept the risk) and approximately *equally* (or else those who think they will lose less may decide that in relative terms they can gain).

It is possible that this "everybody-will-lose-big-and-equally" scenario will turn out to be the only "solution." If so, then a strong element of tragedy will permanently stalk the human species. To survive solely because of a dread that must continually be renewed in consciousness to maintain its effectiveness has to involve a severe diminution of the quality of existence and add an element of desperation to the manner in which individuals plan and pursue their lifetimes. The dread will be unending because there is no clear way to withdraw from such brinksmanship and, universal fear or not, this form of deterrence as a strategy in the kind of arms race we have set into motion has all too great a likelihood of causing a premature and unpredictable—indeed, an accidental—disappearance of the human species, almost certainly in a manner that will be both horrifying and painful for many or most. Recent indications that both the U.S.S.R. and the U.S. embarked (at least briefly) on a strategy anticipating "war-fighting," or protracted nuclear conflict (Powers, 1982; Draper, 1982), suggest that the everyone-will-lose-big-and-equally scenario is not likely to provide continuing security.

The fourth brake, which I have mentioned earlier, takes effect as realization spreads that powerful nations can destroy one another, even when only in retaliation. When this is true there is no longer any virtue in insisting on being first in weapons or strength. Indeed, there is virtue in rejecting such an effort because such rejection will tend to retard the arms race, and it will allow the nation involved to divert resources to other needs of society.

The fifth brake involves increased communication and empathy, and less secrecy and deception, among world powers. It will come into play only as a result of mutual awareness of the threats involved in the first four brakes. But, in that milieu, I believe it will generate and maintain a force of its own that is indispensable in the goal of indefinite postponement of worldwide destruction.

I am impressed by the many positive points listed by different authors writing on this topic, for example, those of Carnesale et al. (1983), Hardin et al. (1985), and Axelrod (1984). It is evidently necessary to accept, with Carnesale et al. (1983) and others, that (1) there is no escape from the nuclear threat and (2) it is imperative that we continue to seek ways to minimize it.

Very recently, two arguments have been made that show how quickly the concepts of both deterrence and some form of deliberate withdrawal can change. Schell (1982) suggests that nuclear weapons may be withdrawn in favor of merely retaining the knowledge and ability to produce and use them quickly. Unfortunately, Schell makes the argument without addressing satisfactorily, in my view, the question of how to induce such withdrawals by governments. I cannot imagine governments taking such steps without an extraordinary change of attitude which most of the material in this book seems to deny is likely.

Jastrow (1984) raises a different kind of possibility, which I hope represents correct reasoning because it does not call for an extraordinary or unprecedented change in human attitudes and behavior. Jastrow notes that the destructive capabilities of warheads are reduced as their accuracy increases. He describes computerized, navigating ("smart") warheads as achieving accuracies of 150 yards and expects even greater accuracy. He believes that the advent of such warheads means that the possibility of massive destruction and "nuclear winter" may be dramatically reduced and even suggests that nuclear warheads may be replaced by conventional explosives like TNT. This seems overly optimistic to me. What is more, he does not adequately discuss the probability that targets will be (1) increased in numbers and (2) increased in invulnerability ("hardness") so that nuclear explosions might be retained, and at a much higher level of potency than he supposes. He does, however, couch his argument in terms of deterrence and the pursuit of self-interest by governments, noting that massive and widespread radiation is detrimental to an invading force. He cites reductions in "average size of nuclear warheads" and "total destructive power" since 1960 as evidence of the trend he thinks will lead to obsolescence in nuclear weapons. Some of the trend in size, however, may have little to do with destructive force in individual warheads, and some of the trend in overall destructive power may not significantly reduce the likelihood of devastation as a result of nuclear war. Jastrow notes that some experts believe that increased accuracy increases the likelihood of "first strikes" being tempting, but he dismisses the notion by arguing that there are far too many hardened sites to attack with the accurate warheads in order to prevent retaliation. I hope he is right, for it appears to me that, at least in the foreseeable future, the safety of civilization and the planet cannot be ensured by exhortations to disarm, rather depending upon changes of the sort he describes. This feeling in no way dismisses the value of concerns about nuclear holocaust that are causing increasing numbers of people to exhort their governments to be conservative in all matters involving international tensions and aggressions.

And so we are returned to the original problem, with no solution from the biologists' studies of adversarial relations in nonhuman species, the political scientists' analyses of the international arms race of humans, or the negotiations of governments. We are only offered the important message that once two nations become capable of destroying one another, and each knows it, there are no penalties for being the weaker adversary, and possibly great benefits, from (1) reducing the likelihood of further arms buildups and (2) the ability to direct more resources to other needs of society. Unfortunately, these conditions continue only so long as both nations remain capable of destroying one another (or *believe* they do).

Many have called for a no-first-use policy on nuclear weapons. Several authors, however, have pointed out serious problems with this policy. First it requires conventional rearmament. Second, it increases the chance of conventional war breaking out, and escalating, between the superpowers. Because no one can guarantee that either side will stick to a no-first-use policy, by making conventional war thinkable it may actually increase the probability of nuclear war.

Given the unique aspects of the nuclear arms race it is worthwhile to consider whether or not situations can be generated in which the initiator of a nuclear war will inevitably suffer even *more* horrible consequences than a defender. This, I believe, would be a unique situation in all kinds of combat and competition. Powers (1982, p.98) makes a relevant comment: "So long as either side's weapons are safe, it can credibly threaten to retaliate, and it can ride out an attack before deciding to do so. This means there is no advantage to be gained by striking first, something the strategists refer to as 'crisis stability.' Weapons that can survive attack help maintain the strategic balance. Accurate missiles threaten to upset the applecart by offering a chance to destroy an enemy's weapons and thereby limit the damage he can do in retaliation." Only in conflicts that may lead to mutual extinction can this be so.

It is astonishing how little is said, even in long complex articles on the status of the arms race and the expected consequences of nuclear war, about the actual consequences of *abandoning* the race (but see Carnesale *et al.*, 1983). Comments on this topic are usually something vague, such as "If they get ahead of us they may start to push us around, or take advantage." I have never seen it admitted by a public official that there could feasibly be anything worse than being subject to such blackmail or "pushing around." Yet this question may become necessary. Is such "pushing around" worse than losing 10% of our population? 20%? Is it worse than having landed in the U.S. the equivalent of ten tons of TNT for every living citizen? Is it worse than extinction of ourselves, or of both nations, or of civilization, or of the human species, or of all life on earth? One or more of these alternatives must be accepted by all reasonable people as worse than being "pushed around." But, of course, the arguments are always available that the development of weapons is not synonymous with their use, and even that a continuing balance in the arms race is the only deterrent to the use of so-called doomsday weapons (e.g., Carnesale *et al.*, 1983). Moreover, it is easy to see why merely accepting questions like the above as reasonable is anathema to those seeking to negotiate to the advantage of their own side.

Perhaps all of the arguments I have just made, about various forms of deterrence, withdrawal, and "universal brotherhood" are wrong or incomplete: I assume they will be subjected to searching skepticism by anyone inclined to take them seriously. If, however, they are accurate and some version of deterrence—modified by a continual effort toward a visualized moral ideal, or universal brotherhood—is indeed our only long-term hope, then certain very significant conclusions follow. The most important is that we should concentrate our efforts and resources on devising ways to make deterrence work, and to penalize moral laggards among nations and their leaders. To protect ourselves we must prevent deterrence from being the sole property of military and political leaders, weapons manufacturers, and other special-interest groups. We must discover a way to do this despite the conflict between the openness necessary for widespread citizen participation and the deception necessary for deterrence and for success in negotiations. We must not allow ourselves the luxury of viewing nuclear war as we view death—as eventually inevitable, therefore too unpleasant to be brought into our consciousness and dwelt upon; we must instead view it as soluble and also view ourselves as participants in its solution.

If my arguments are correct, then all of the efforts of people engaged in what I have called "universal brotherhood" attempts to save us from nuclear holocaust are valuable chiefly or solely because of their effects on *deterrence*, and all of the people so engaged will further their own cause (and ours) by recognizing this fact. We must be *creative* about deterrence—we must control, mold, and shape it so as to reduce both the risk of war and the risk of war destroying us. It is a tricky business. For example, if the most powerful deterrent of all is a general belief that any use of nuclear weapons will lead to the destruction of all of us, then efforts to reduce the risk that war, if initiated, will destroy us, may also reduce the effectiveness of deterrence. Again, knowledge is crucial, and I believe that accurate assessment of the long-term ecological effects of even "limited" nuclear war may be the most potent deterrent available. It is fatal to focus on immediate deaths and the direct effects of the explosions themselves. One thing that follows is that biologists and environmental scientists as well as experts in human behavior must somehow be involved in deterrence teams that currently seem to be made up almost entirely of military and political experts, and physical scientists, whose expertise has to do primarily with weapons and explosions. Recent arguments concerning the probability of nuclear winter following employment of nuclear weapons underscore this argument.

Apparently, then, two sets of items are the hope of the future. First are the weapons freezes, test limitations, control of weapons accumulations, and all activities that tend to maximize and stabilize the deterrent effects of military and political activities. These activities tend to buy time as knowledge grows, and to inform the populace and those in control about deleterious probable effects that they would otherwise pass over. The second is weapon changes that may render large-scale destruction both inefficient and undesirable from the point of view of both adversaries. The two may be employed in concert. Until the second situation occurs, creative efforts at *controlled deterrence* (see Einhorn, Kane, and Nincic, 1984; McNamara and Bethe, 1985) are what we must mount if we are to ensure the future of our children, our species, and our planet. Frank (1967, p. 162) refers to "positive deterrence" and writes as follows: "Some hope can be placed, however, in the fact that nuclear policy is, after all, a mixed-motive game—so there are always opportunities for collaboration, if national leaders are ingenious enough to find and exploit them. . . . it is worth remembering that the concept of deterrence includes not only threats but also implicit assurances that if the nation being deterred refrains from certain acts it will not be punished." Although there are many points on which I would disagree with Frank, his book seems to me one of the most creative and useful in this arena.

McNamara and Bethe (1985) provide one of the best statements about deterrence I have seen (see also Hardin *et al.*, 1985):

> . . . nuclear weapons have only one purpose—that of preventing their use. They must not do less; they cannot do more. Thus, a restructuring of nuclear forces designed to reduce the risk of nuclear war must be our goal. All policies, every existing program, and each new initiative must be judged in that light. (p.47)
>
> . . . all our technological genius and economic prowess cannot make us secure if they leave the Soviet Union insecure. (p.47)
>
> The ultimate goal . . . should be a state of mutual deterrence at the lowest force levels consistent with stability. That requires invulnerable forces that could unquestionably respond to any attack and inflict unacceptable damage. (p.47)
>
> . . . our first duty and obligation [is] to assure the survival of our civilization. *Our descendants could then grapple with the problem that no one yet knows how to attack* (emphasis added). (p.51)

All of the so-called "partial brakes" on the nuclear arms race I have listed develop out of the perceptions of individuals and groups that their own interests would not be served if these "partial brakes" were not applied. In that sense, at least, the discussion is consistent with the general view of morality and moral systems that I have been developing here. There may be some virtue in contrasting this discussion with that in Carnesale *et al.* (1983). These authors take up the issue of morality with respect to nuclear strategies (pp. 243 ff.), and they cite areas of agreement with the Catholic bishops of the U.S. (apparently from the bishops' letter to the President—Anonymous, 1983—although no reference is given).

Carnesale *et al.*'s first point seems consistent with my discussion: They note that "Moral considerations matter in strategic debates primarily because nuclear strategy involves the fates of millions of innocent people." They add, however, that "In addition, in a democracy, public perceptions of the ethical soundness of a government policy or strategy can turn public support away from government actions, in peacetime or in war." Here Carnesale *et al.* give the impression that they are speaking of the concern of people for those in *other* countries who might be endangered by a particular nuclear strategy. Thus, in the next paragraph: "We expect our government to behave morally as much as possible as much of the time as possible. We also expect the government to protect our lives and our property, and if this goal can only be achieved through what we think of as immoral actions, then a dilemma exists."

Carnesale *et al.* then describe three "moral dilemmas" raised by the Catholic bishops (see also Anonymous, 1983; Hardin *et al.*, 1985; Murnion, 1983): (1) ". . . can it ever be moral to initiate the use of nuclear weapons?" (2) "Can it ever be right to have nuclear forces and a targeting doctrine that deliberately aim at civilians?" (3) "Is it justifiable to threaten a nuclear attack that might destroy innocent civilians if the *intention* [my italics] is to deter nuclear war altogether?"

These "dilemmas" are discussed as if they were an issue independent of the consequences of the involved actions to the people whose strategy they are a part of, and Carnesale *et al.* leave essentially no doubt on this point when they write as follows, immediately after listing the three moral dilemmas of nuclear strategy:

> Most people judge the morality of actions on their intentions and their consequences. Moreover, in deterrence our intentions are not to do evil. Our threat is intended to avoid both the horrible outcome of nuclear war and aggressive behavior by the other side. Our intent in making the threat is not immoral, and the consequences depend in part upon the intentions of the other side. On the contrary, to remove the threat altogether—because it is evil to threaten to attack military targets with weapons that are likely to be neither discriminating nor controllable—might indeed have disastrous *moral* [my italics] effects, if it incited one's adversary to take greater risks, and thereby made war more likely. (pp.247–248)

I applaud the effort of Carnesale *et al.* to contribute to the problem of solving the arms race, and I believe that, overall, their book is enormously valuable. But the most charitable thing I can say about the line of argument just described is that it appears as a dangerous kind of self-righteous blindness that confuses the issue, and it does so partly because what is being assumed is precisely the inadequate view of morality that I rejected at the beginning of this volume: that it is a way of helping others at our own expense. How can Carnesale *et al.* imply that their dire concern for the "moral dilemmas" of nuclear strategy only came about because of their desire to be fair to the rest of the world? How can they believe that it is reasonable (or possible) for them to determine by themselves what is *moral* in the strategy of their own government with respect to its effects on the rest of the world? How can they doubt that both sides in any conflict are likely to say just what they have said, and just as sincerely? The Catholic bishops state (see Anonymous, 1983), that "War is permissible only to confront 'a real and certain danger', i.e., to protect innocent life, to preserve conditions necessary for decent human existence, and to secure basic human rights." The arguments of the Catholic bishops have been declared (Tucker, 1985) " . . . a recent and impressive effort in a tradition that has been in Western thought perhaps the principal alternative to the plea of reason of state. The bishops observe that the source of their doctrine is independent of and superior to the state and its necessities." The problem that I am distressed by is that essentially anyone, from Hitler to Attila the Hun, could assert that the above reasons for war were precisely his own, and doubtless secure assent from the populace. The question is: Are we doing something similar when we continue the arms race to serve the interests of our own nation and its allies while asserting that our *intentions* are *merely* to prevent war or promote peace—on our own terms; and when the other side does roughly the same?

One sees no suggestion, at least in Carnesale *et al.'s* section on morality, that the whole question of morality might have been raised because of concern by the Harvard Study Group *for their own* fates, and for the fates of fellow countrymen (who, to the extent that their fates are shared, are likely to agree and accept the definitions of morality they propose). One sees no suggestion that the business of deciding what is moral in our government's strategy might just be self-serving. Therefore, one also sees no suggestion that some aspects of the injection of morality into the question of nuclear strategy might be rationalization for one's view of things or for the actions of one's own government, and just possibly self-deluding in a not particularly conscious way (see also Hardin *et al.*, 1985). There is a persistent tendency, on both sides of any conflict between human groups, to see morality on one's own side and immorality on the other. In conventional confrontations, it is at least not inevitably self-annihilatory to use such feelings to drive one's behavior. The same is not true with respect to international nuclear confrontations. I doubt that a better illustration could be found of the potential significance of informing ourselves in painful detail about our motivations and tendencies, and of understanding the probability that morality was generated, maintained, and elaborated because of its self-serving aspects. We must not lose sight of the fact that we are in the nuclear arms race not first and foremost to deter another nation from initiating a nuclear holocaust but to protect our own interests against what we have for decades seen as their interests. For us to assert now that our motivation *has always been solely* to keep that evil other side from doing something nasty to the rest of the world strikes me as the most dangerous kind of self-delusion.

I have already suggested that, to many people, nuclear war is much like personal death—something the eventual inevitability of which we can do nothing to influence. I believe that we are evolved to keep our awareness of the eventual inevitability of death suppressed nearly all of the time because it is deleterious to dwell upon that which we cannot change. But if we do the same with respect to nuclear war, we surrender too much of our fates to those (particular) weapons lobbyists, military professionals, and government officials who may continue to perceive personal gain for themselves in the escalation of the weapons race, even if only by being able to convince themselves and their constituencies that they are thereby protecting the world. The greater the proportion of a nation's budget spent on the arms race, the more intense and powerful will be the efforts of the weapons and military lobbyists. In other words, what appears as our evolved tendency not to think about the unthinkable coincides perniciously with the evolved tendency of those who believe they can gain personally from brinksmanship to draw us certainly down a path we have no evolved tendencies to avoid: wholesale destruction or extinction. I repeat the prediction that only when our personal lives and those of our relatives and friends seem threatened, in a way we believe we can prevent, are we likely to react in positive and beneficial manners to the imminence of human extinction. The dismal consequence is that only when a very significant proportion of a democratic nation's population is threatened *consciously* by what is known *publicly* about nuclear war (or parallel disasters that may be imminent) will the populace be aroused. To the extent that military and political decisions are in the hands of a small group of people—as is evidently more true of the U.S.S.R. than of the U.S.—the threat, to be effective, must descend directly on those few and their families. An intuitive awareness of this fact may underlie the effort to assure destruction of the refuges of Russia's leaders in the event of nuclear war (Powers, 1982).

If our unique runaway social competition is halted in time, the means used will also have to be unique, and a product of the most serious and imaginative cooperative thinking in history. It is already clear that there will be no easy, simple, or singular solution. Demands for slowdowns or temporary freezes by an aroused populace foreseeing the probability of catastrophe to themselves and their loved ones may delay the inevitable or buy time for a solution, but they will not in themselves solve the problem. Both evolutionary and cultural history indicate that the attitude of the public can be reversed quickly and decisively by either facts or propaganda about gains by the other side. Moreover, the threat of nuclear holocaust can never be erased so long as we contest in the usual ways of history and continue to maintain and elaborate real doomsday weapons—so long as we continue to regard it as natural and inevitable that some other nation(s) are automatically our adversaries. My principal argument is simply that, in the search for real or permanent solutions it will help, and possibly it will be essential, for a great many people to know a great deal more about the background of ourselves, our attitudes, and our actions in respect to morality and ethics, and about the uniqueness of our problem and its relationship to other similar races in evolutionary history.

Einstein is reputed to have said that splitting of the atom has started us on a path of certain destruction unless we change our "modes of thinking." The paradox with which we must deal, and to which I believe Einstein was referring, is that millions of people can go about their daily activities—which are by-and-large peaceful—while accepting in their minds that millions of other people somewhere else are inevitably their mortal adversaries, against whom it is reasonable to plan war and stockpile weapons that one way or another may kill all on both sides. That a life-annihilating nuclear winter resulting from war-induced holocausts in the cities of great nations can even be contemplated, let alone be the essentially inevitable consequence of trillion-dollar planned investments, is bizarre beyond the wildest imagination of anyone considering his or her normal everyday existence. That it is a fact of life in the late twentieth century is, I believe, a flat consequence of the fact that success across all of the several billion years of organic evolution has always been *relative*. And that, somehow, is where the arguments that will alleviate the preposterous conditions, under which we live, must begin, even if the arms control specialists of the world believe that those who seek to discuss it all in such biological terms are beginning with irrelevant impracticalities. That, I believe, is what Einstein meant by "modes of thinking" and what McNamara and Bethe (1985) meant by our descendants grappling with "the problem that no one yet knows how to attack."

It is chilling to observe how immediately and decisively the less-than-global brotherhood of patriotism can be evoked by calls for "defense," and it is also a testimonial to the long history of human intergroup competition. It is the effects of this long history that we must overcome. No one who reads details of plans surrounding current weapons and their deployment, and reflects even for a moment on the question of precisely why the superpowers are adversaries in the first place, can fail to think of the word "madness."

> There are fancy theories about controlled nuclear exchanges and bloodless, chess-like calculations between opponents in the middle of nuclear war. People who think like that do not understand nuclear weapons, and they do not understand war.
>
> Real war is not like these complicated tit-for-tat imaginings. There is little knowledge of what is going on, and less communication. There is blood and terror and agony. We cannot deal with a war a thousand times more terrible than any we have ever seen in some bloodless, analytic fashion.
>
> Admiral Noel Gaylor, 1982

> Strategic planners hesitate to say what the world would be like after a nuclear war. There are too many variables. But they agree—for planning purposes, at any rate—that both sides would "recover," and that the most probable result of a general nuclear war would be a race to prepare for a second general nuclear war.
>
> Powers, 1982, p. 110.

> The discovery of nuclear weapons, like the discovery of fire itself, lies behind us on the trajectory of history; it cannot be undone. Even if all nuclear arsenals were destroyed, the knowledge of how to reinvent them would remain and could be put to use in any of a dozen or more nations. The nuclear fire cannot be extinguished. The fear of its use will remain a part of the human psyche for the rest of human history.
>
> Carnesale *et al.*, 1983, p. 5.

> While the land-, sea-, and air-launched nuclear weapons that compose the United States Nuclear Triad call for different day-to-day job skills, the men who serve them comprise a virtual priesthood, steeped in vitriol and sharing a near-reverence for a world order based on terror. . . . They all profess two articles of faith: Nobody wants nuclear war, but nobody would balk at making his contribution to the unthinkable if it should arise.
>
> Jay B. Lewis, 1984
> UPI (Ann Arbor News; 13 May, p. B1)

But if there is war, nuclear or conventional, you do your job. I'm going to push the button and the bomb's going to fall.

Major Danny Rouse
B–52 Bomber Crew Commander

# 5

## CONCLUSIONS

In examining ourselves we are faced with a multiple paradox: we are forced to use the attributes we wish to analyze to carry out the analysis, while resisting certain aspects of the analysis. At the very same time, we pretend that we are *not* resisting at all but instead giving perfectly legitimate objections; and we use our realization that others will resist the analysis, for reasons as arcane as our own, to enlist *their* support in *our* resistance. And they very likely will give it.

And what are these arcane reasons for resistance? I have argued that the uniqueness of our individual reasons for acting as we do derives from a history of genetic individuality, the apparent fact of our having evolved to act in our individual interests, and the probability of advantage in keeping some of those interests *secret*. I have suggested, for example (initially in *Darwinism and Human Affairs*), that the concept of free will has essentially nothing to do with the philosophical problem of physical causation, with which it is usually associated, but instead represents the freedom and ability to make decisions in our own individual interests as we see fit—to choose on our own among the alternative scenarios we are able by consciousness and foresight to see before us (Searle, 1984, provides a discussion that I think approaches this view but does not elaborate). Similarly, I have argued that consciousness and self-awareness are systems designed largely for seeing ourselves as others see us and then altering others' views of ourselves so as to serve our own rather than their interests when there are conflicts. Conscience, I have hypothesized (1979a), is "the still small voice that tells us how far we can go without incurring intolerable risks. It tells us not to avoid cheating but how we can cheat socially without being caught."

I have also suggested that none of these concepts or motivations is wholly in anyone's consciousness, at least not to the degree that they can be as a result of biological knowledge; and I have argued that they have never been represented accurately in the immense literature about morality and human nature. My discussion will be taken as that of a cynic, and cynics have been prevalent across human history; but no philosophical or political cynic has taken reproduction as the end-all, and none could explain all of the beneficence of nepotism, even though the beneficence of reciprocity has been largely understood by many. Few have envisioned indiscriminate beneficence as potentially self-serving.

If arguments such as those made here have any validity it follows that a problem faced by everyone, in respect to morality, is that of discovering how to subvert or reduce some aspects of individual selfishness that evidently derive from our history of genetic individuality. We cannot live together harmoniously as individuals except when this problem is addressed satisfactorily.

Of inestimably greater importance, however, is the subversion of *group* selfishness—those societal effects, like patriotism and loyalty, that deceptively appear as approaches to an idealized utilitarian or altruistic morality, and that have throughout our history been so effective in binding together large human groups in the context of intergroup competition, strife, and war. These are the effects that make us believe that we are good and the other side evil—that because all of our motivations are noble, because we are disposed to be kindly toward our associates, we are unlikely to do wrong or be immoral. It would appear that, even to survive now, we need to subvert these group-specific, seemingly moral tendencies so that they lead us away from divisions of the world into *we* and *they*, friends and enemies, internally altruistic groups allied against one another. We need them to lead us instead toward some widely or universally favored and nondangerous forms of social compatibility which at least promise to humans as a whole their perpetuation, individually and as a species; and that also promise, perhaps, a degree of comfort and pleasure in the pursuit of happiness. We need to do this because it is *group* activities that threaten to extinguish our species, or civilization, and thus threaten us as individuals.

If I may be granted the analogy, we need to progress toward the kind of minister, priest, or rabbi who prays "God bless everyone everywhere" and means it—as opposed to the kind who prays some version of "God bless everyone in this congregation, and all of those who are too ill to attend" or the kind that sees God as "on our side," or ourselves as God's "chosen people," or others as in the service of the Devil. This is not a call for self-sacrificing or net-cost altruism, and in the end it may not even be compatible with concepts of organized religion or a Supreme Being because such concepts seem to involve nondiscrimination inversely according to the degree to which the group involved is a minority or relatively powerless. Even if we wish only to protect ourselves and our loved ones, we can no longer think only about our "side," our values, our uncertainties. Rather, we must concern ourselves quite directly and profoundly with the feelings and concerns of our adversaries, for our futures also depend on what they do.

The reader who is disappointed at the absence of satisfying resolutions to world problems relating to morality and ethics may now recall that I warned at the outset that this would be the case. As I said in the preface, this is so partly because *by definition* moral issues can only be resolved by the collective opinions and decisions of the populace; otherwise what occurs is either not a resolution or by definition is not moral (this is true even if I, as an individual, disagree with "the populace" and work to change a rule or attitude that I judge to be immoral). If what I have written here changes attitudes and, even if it is wrong, stimulates others to delve into the same problems and develop a more appropriate and effective view—even decades from now—I will suppose that I have succeeded in my original mission.

Three definite conclusions I believe I have substantiated are the following: First, there is no need for the persistence of an aura of mystery with respect to the concept of morality and the understanding of moral systems and the operation of individuals within them. Even indiscriminate beneficence can be compatible with humans having evolved through differential success in reproduction. Second, moral and ethical questions can only be resolved by compromises and contracts among those with different and conflicting interests. Such resolutions require collective opinions and decisions, and rewards and punishments commensurate with the assumption that individuals tend to seek their own self- (reproductive) interests. Third, in the effort to solve humanity's most profound problems, including those with moral and ethical implications, there is potentially great value in continuing to develop a perspective from modern evolutionary biology to be added to those deriving from philosophy, the social sciences, religion, history, and the humanities. This biological perspective is appropriately added, not as an argument for determinism, but, precisely to the contrary, as a possible way to greater freedom, deriving from greater knowledge of the cause–effect patterns that underlie our history and our nature.

Some of my colleagues in biology, and many people outside biology, deny that humans can be understood in such terms. Others cling to the notion that we evolved by an innocuous (and hypothetical) form of group selection, involving true genetic altruism by individuals (as opposed to group selection resulting from consistent confluences of interest among individuals), and that we can somehow return to it. They argue that if this is not the case, we should deny the truth and pretend ourselves toward world peace and human justice; or that it is better to be ignorant with an idealized moral model before us than to know about an immoral history. Or they simply use their ideologies to deny the validity of any and all analytical approaches to questions of morality. I believe that they are wrong. Worse, because of the enormity and uniqueness of the problems that face us today, I think there are good reasons for regarding approaches that deny biology, and sometimes deny reality, as potentially deadly.

If we wish to create some particular kind of society—one that is different from that predicted from evolutionary history—then to know how to do it may well be possible only by understanding that information from biology, and lots of it, must be included. If we have more or less decided that our goal is to create a society in which people can lead long, happy lives, then, unless "happy" requires reproduction as such, in a sense we have not only denied our evolutionary heritage already, but we have done so without even knowing it. I assume that by knowing what we are doing we can go much further in this direction if we wish.

Learning, however, is not a simple disappearance of biases. We cannot necessarily create a generation of exceptionally fine and responsible reciprocators, or eliminate the threat of war, simply by deciding that this is what we want or simply by telling our children to do it. I think that we have no alternative but to know ourselves better, partly through biological knowledge that explicitly includes the manner of operation of natural selection, and to acquire this knowledge and develop its consequences as we are continuing our desperate competitions.

Essentially everyone thinks of himself as well-meaning, but from my viewpoint a society of well-meaning people who understand themselves and their history very well is a better milieu than a society of well-meaning people who do not. The problem is that we may no longer have the time that would be necessary to generate the kind of understanding that could save us from being rendered extinct by our morality.

Having said these things I will add that my one source of optimism about the international arms race is the enormous recent increase in the numbers of people publicizing and pondering the problem. If we are capable of something truly unique in this realm, if anything deserving the label "solution" is possible, then increasing the number and quality of the intellects worrying over the problem can only make such possibilities more likely. On this point, again, the question seems to be whether or not there will be enough time. If current proposals for "resolution" can be identified as nothing more than delayers of the currently inevitable, then they are worth whole-hearted support on that basis alone, and we should perhaps be evaluating all recommendations largely or entirely on that criterion. This may sound like unequivocal support for a constant effort to retard international arms buildups and research, but unfortunately even this issue is probably more complex.

Organisms that live in environments containing deadly snakes evolve to acquire avoidance responses to the snakes before they are ever encountered. As individuals they do not rely upon trial and error learning to react to the danger of the snake's strike; if they did they would be dead. Because we usually do not know how such preprogrammed responses appear in individuals, or even the context of their development, they are commonly given the convenient (but uninformative) label of "innate." As a result of such responses in the members of a prey species, poisonous snakes are no threat to the prey species as a whole, and not as much of a threat to its individuals. But the deadly snake of nuclear warfare was not in our environment as we evolved. It is a novelty that has suddenly assumed the form of the not-so-deadly threat of ordinary arms races and ordinary standoffs by force and threat. Indeed, the deadly snake of nuclear warfare has thrust itself into a role that previously seemed to serve us—to bring us comfort, security, and freedom from oppression. Our evolved responses are those appropriate to its less annihilatory, less deadly counterparts, but they are inappropriate now because they depend upon a kind of experience that will not teach us but kill us. For the first time in our history as a species we have, in our consciousness as individuals, the knowledge of a novel threat that, without efforts on our part that to some extent go against the grain of our history, will extinguish us. There are no moral problems greater than this one. It will be the greatest test of the peculiar and spectacular evolutionary specialization that we call intelligence to see if we can use it somehow to dream up a response appropriate to this sudden pernicious novelty before it is too late.

There is irony in the facts that (1) the process of international deterrence requires that both secrecy and misinformation be directed at the other side (otherwise, as already noted, there will be times—not entirely predictable—when the temporarily more powerful adversary may simply *use* its advantage before it is lost) and (2) the secrecy and misinformation necessarily will reduce the effectiveness of many of the intellects with the greatest likelihood of solving the problem. Secrecy and misinformation will always retard the trends that are most useful in respect to resolution. One cannot but wonder, should some of our intellects hit upon effective routes to resolution, whether those who must agree and implement will even recognize, when it counts, that the security blanket really has turned into a deadly snake.

War is the most general law of the evolution of human societies.

Batault, 1921

Hold, enough! It was dreadful to read such things in obscure and mystic German with its verbs a mile away. It is like a crucifixion to read them in the clear, steel-cut, deadly precise language of a Frenchman. We know he cannot be right, because our hearts tell us so.

Beard, 1921, p. 110 (reviewing Batault)

Let us agree, then, that men desire to lead their lives under conditions of peace. The problem which has to be solved is, What price are they prepared to pay for it?

Sir Arthur Keith, 1947, p. 224.

# Epilogue

I said at the outset that this book would not be concerned with identifying moral and immoral behavior, and so far I have made no effort to
discuss general definitions. On the other hand, it seems appropriate to
show now what form might be taken in criteria of immorality and morality that are at least consistent with the ideas presented here.

It is possible to consider an act immoral to the extent that it represents
interference with the legitimate or rational expectations of another person, particularly in the service of a perpetrator's interests, and most
particularly if the perpetrator carries out the interference with conscious
intent, with knowledge of the legitimacy or rationality of the victim's
expectations, and by employing deliberate deception. I stress that this
view does not arise necessarily or automatically out of considerations
from evolutionary biology. It is not incompatible, however, with the
arguments presented here. Nor is it the only view that such a background
might yield. Moreover, opinions that utilize some of the above factors
obviously are already general (Table 2.5).

This particular definition takes into account variations in situation,
because it refers to legitimacy or rationality of expectations, which will
vary in different circumstances or different social systems. It also allows
for the fact—again with the reference to legitimacy or rationality of
expectations—that interests differ, and not everyone's interests can
always be served or served equally. At least in part, it reinforces the
earlier discussion of indignation, self-righteousness, and moralizing as
efforts to legitimize or parade as rational expectations that might not
have been so perceived. The definition hinges the *degree* of immorality
on six variable items: (1) the legitimacy or rationality of the victim's
interests, (2) the extent of interference with the victim's interests, (3) the
extent to which the perpetrator is by his interfering action serving his
own interests, (4) the extent of the perpetrator's awareness of the
victim's interests and expectations, (5) the extent of conscious intent in
the interference, and (6) the extent to which the perpetrator employs
deliberate deception. According to these criteria, it would also be
immoral either intentionally to create, or even carelessly to allow,
generation of irrational or unreasonable expectations, or to interfere
deliberately with the development of expectations that would normally
be accepted as rational and reasonable.

The question is raised whether or not every social act that is not
immoral is by definition moral. Or are some acts among those that are
not immoral more moral than others? It might be argued that if one does
not search too hard for the most moral thing to do, then his lack of

consciousness about the possibility of that act will to some extent prevent his failure to perform it from being an immoral act. To search for the most moral thing to do, on the other hand, makes it more difficult to be moral, by expanding the universe of possible moral acts of which one is conscious, thereby rendering some acts or some failures to act immoral when they would not have been so identified without the additional knowledge.

To carry this problem to a fine point, one may also notice that to fail to search for the most moral thing to do, when one is conscious of the possibility of such a search, might itself be identified as immoral. One may conclude that, even if it is difficult to identify immorality in any general way, it may be easier than to identify morality; it may be easier to lay claim to not being immoral than to contend that one is moral.

No definition of immorality is easy to apply universally, and this one is no exception. As an example, this definition might seem to imply that adults are immoral who do not provide their parents with grandchildren because they wish to spend their money on personal pleasures, espe-cially if (1) they know that their parents expect and desire grandchildren (and they live in a society in which nearly all people do in fact have grandchildren) and (2) they give reasons other than their desire for personal enjoyment, or otherwise deceive their parents about the rea-sons for not having children. Perhaps some people would agree with the implication of immorality here, but surely most would not. The reason is that we must also take into account the (here conflicting) legitimate and rational expectations of individuals that they are free to lead their own lives as they see fit.

The question might also be raised how an actor could avoid being immoral if he is required to serve the interests of two (or more) parties in conflict, each of which seeks a resource or judgment that the actor is required to arbitrate (e.g., King Solomon's dilemma with the child claimed by two women). Presumably, by the above criteria, a decision by an arbitrator in such a circumstance would be moral so long as it did not thwart legitimate or rational expectations of either party. If both parties expect the same resource that obviously can only be given to one alone, then the expectation of one or both parties is not rational or legitimate. Unless the arbitrator was responsible for generating the expectations of the conflicting parties in such a case, or unless he arbitrates in such a fashion as to thwart legitimate or rational interests when there are al-ternative courses of action available to him, he could not (using the above criteria) be said to be acting immorally. (Note the importance we attach to King Solomon's effort and skill in determining the legitimacy of the interests of the two women who each claimed the baby.)

The above definitions and criteria also bear on the topic of intergroup interactions. There are often few or no legitimate or rational expectations of reciprocity or "fairness" between social groups (especially warring or competing groups such as tribes or nations). Perhaps partly as a consequence, lying, deceit, or otherwise nasty or even heinous acts committed against enemies may sometimes not be regarded as immoral by others within the group of those who commit them. They may even be regarded as highly moral if they seem dramatically to serve the interests of the group whose members commit them.

As already suggested, it seems possible that the subjectivity surrounding definitions of "legitimacy" and "rationality," and the difficulty of determining intent and the presence or absence of deception, are to some large extent responsible for difficulties in being conclusive or absolute about morality and immorality. Aside from pertinacious efforts to resolve these difficulties, perhaps the only alternative is some form of appeal to a presumed higher authority.

The central themes in my thinking—which all the rest of the book has been written to justify or explain—can now be summarized as follows:

As a result of genetic uniqueness caused by sexual reproduction and its recombining effects, the reproductive or life interests of individual humans have typically been separate across all of history. Our interests thus inevitably *seem* separate, at base, regardless of existing situations, because we have evolved to follow genetic interests, and our ancestors' genes tended always to be different from those of their fellows in every time and place of evolution. These things are true of all sexually reproducing organisms. We humans differ only in our ability to comprehend and reflect upon them, and to change how we feel about them.

Uniquely among living beings, however, humans have so controlled their environments that virtually their only significant hostile force of nature now is other humans. Uniquely among living beings, humans have evolved to cooperate extensively in direct intergroup competition. Only humans play competitively, group-against-group. Only in humans are war and other forms of intergroup competition the central aspects and driving forces of social existence. Only humans have embarked upon a virtually unchecked arms race involving cooperative efforts of millions of individuals on the opposing sides.

Only these facts, I believe, can explain why individual people more or less continually treat their fellows as adversaries and competitors, to be manipulated and deceived and used when possible. Only these facts can explain the particular ways in which humans cooperate—within groups of expanding sizes and complexities, and so intensively as to deny even to themselves their manipulations and deceptions. Only these facts can explain the nature and evolution of the peculiar human psyche, which uses self-deception to effect deception of others. Only these facts can account for the inexorable continuation of the international arms race— the inexorable maintenance of hostile and adversarial relations—even when it seems to increasing numbers of the participants a pure and perplexing madness.

These facts constitute the simultaneously trivial and profound reasons for the generation of all moral and ethical questions. If we do not comprehend and deal with them, they may eventually become the simultaneously trivial and horrifying reasons for the disappearance of humans from the face of the earth.

Behold the paradoxical human
By eons of evolution given
The singular skill of introspection
Of consciousness in self-reflection
Himself to see as others do
Precisely when they're human too.

# BIBLIOGRAPHY

Alcock, J.
1984    *Animal behavior: An evolutionary approach.* 3rd. ed. Sunderland, MA: Sinauer.

Alexander, R.D.
1971    The search for an evolutionary philosophy of man. *Proc. Roy. Soc. Victoria, Melbourne* 84:99–120.

1974    The evolution of social behavior. *Ann. Rev. Ecol. Syst.* 5:325–83.

1975    The search for a general theory of behavior. *Behav. Sci.* 20:77–100.

1977a    Evolution, human behavior, and determinism. *Proc. Biennial Meeting Phil. Sci. Assoc. (1976)* 2:3–21.

1977b    Natural selection and the analysis of human sociality. *In* C.E. Goulden (Ed.), *Changing scenes in the natural sciences 1776–1976*, pp. 283–337. Bicentennial Symposium Monograph, Phil. Acad. Nat. Sci., Special Publ. 12.

1978    Natural selection and societal laws. *In* H.T. Engelhardt and D. Callahan (Eds.), *The foundations of ethics and its relationship to science. III. Morals, science, and society*, pp. 249–290. Hastings-on-Hudson, NY: Hastings Institute.

1979a    *Darwinism and human affairs.* Seattle, WA: Univ. Washington Press.

1979b    Evolution, social behavior, and ethics. *In* H.T. Engelhardt and D. Callahan (Eds.), *The foundations of ethics and its relationship to science. IV. Knowing and valuing: The search for common roots.* Hastings-on-Hudson, NY: Hastings Institute, pp. 124–155. [Reprinted in: D. Callahan and H.T. Engelhardt (Eds.), *The roots of ethics: Religion, and values.* NY: Plenum Press, pp. 307–338.]

1979c    Evolution and culture. *In* N.A. Chagnon and W.G. Irons (Eds.), *Evolutionary biology and human social behavior: An Anthropological perspective*, pp. 59–78. North Scituate, MA: Duxbury Press.

1982    Biology and the moral paradoxes. *In* M. Gruter and P. Bohannan (Eds.), *Law, biology, and culture: The evolution of law*, pp. 101–110. Santa Barbara, CA: Ross-Erikson, Inc.

1985a    Genes, consciousness, and behavior theory. *In* S. Koch and D.E. Leary (Eds.), *A Century of Psychology as Science*, pp. 783–802. NY: McGraw-Hill.

1985b    A biological interpretation of moral systems. *Zygon* 20:3–20.

1986a    Biology and law. *Ethol. Sociobiol.* 7:167–173.

1986b    Ostracism and indirect reciprocity: The reproductive significance of humor. *Ethol. Sociobiol.* 7:253–270.

1988    The evolutionary approach to human behavior: What does the future hold? *In* L.L. Betzig, M. Borgerhoff Mulder, and P.W. Turke (Eds.), *Human reproductive behaviour: A Darwinian perspective.* London: Cambridge Univ. Press.

In prep.    Inadvertent selection for early senescence in dairy cattle.

Alexander, R.D., and G. Borgia
1979    On the origin and basis of the male–female phenomenon. *In* M.F. Blum and N. Blum (Eds.), *Sexual selection and reproductive competition in insects*, pp. 417–40. NY: Academic Press.

Alexander, R.D., and K.M. Noonan
  1979      Concealment of ovulation, parental care, and human social evolu-
            tion. *In* N.A. Chagnon and W. Irons (Eds.) *Evolutionary biology and
            human social behavior: An anthropological perspective.* pp. 402–435.
            North Scituate, MA: Duxbury Press.
  In prep.  The evolution of eusociality. *In* P.W. Sherman, J. Jarvis, and R.D.
            Alexander (Eds.), *The natural history and social behavior of naked mole
            rats.*
Alexander, R.D., and P.W. Sherman
  1977      Local mate competition and parental investment in social insects.
            *Science* 196:494–500.
Alexander, R.D., and D.W. Tinkle
  1968      Review of *On Aggression* by Konrad Lorenz and *The Territorial
            Imperative* by Robert Ardrey. *Bioscence* 18:245–248.
  1981      *Natural selection and social behavior: Recent research and new theory.* NY:
            Chiron Press.
Alexander, R.D., J.L. Hoogland, R.D. Howard, K.M. Noonan, and P.W.
  Sherman
  1979      Sexual dimorphisms and breeding systems in pinnipeds, ungulates,
            primates, and humans. *In* N.A. Chagnon and W.G. Irons (Eds.),
            *Evolutionary biology and human social behavior: An anthropological per-
            spective.* North Scituate, MA: Duxbury Press. pp. 402–35.
Altman, P.L. (Ed.)
  1962      *Growth including reproduction and morphological development.* Washing-
            ton, D.C.: Federation of American Societies for Experimental Biol-
            ogy.
Altman, P.L., and D.S. Dittmer (Eds.)
  1964      *Biology data book.* Washington, D.C.: Federation of American Societ-
            ies for Experimental Biology.
Anonymous
  1983      The challenge of peace: God's promise and our response. Na-
            tional Conference of Catholic Bishops, Pastoral Letter. *Origins*
            13:1–32.
Aoki, S., S. Akimoto, and S. Yamane
  1981      Observations on *Pseudoregma alexanderi* (Homoptera; Pemphigidae),
            an aphid species producing pseudoscorpion-like soldiers on bam-
            boos. *Kontyu* 49:355–366.
Arras, J.D.
  1984      Toward an ethic of ambiguity. *Hastings Center Repr.* 14:25–33.
Atwood, M.
  1985      Women's novels. *Open Places* [Spring issue]. Columbia, MO:
            Stephens College.
Axelrod, R.
  1984      *The evolution of cooperation.* NY: Basic Books.
Axelrod, R., and W.D. Hamilton
  1981      The evolution of cooperation. *Science* 211:1390–1396.
Bagehot, W.
  1873      *Physics and politics.* NY: D. Appleton and Co.
Baier, K.
  1958      *The moral point of view: A rational basis of ethics.* Ithaca, NY: Cornell
            Univ. Press.

1965  *The moral point of view: A rational basis of ethics.* Abridged ed. NY: Random House.

Baker, J.R.
1938  The evolution of breeding seasons. *In Evolution: Essays presented to E.S. Goodrich.* pp. 161–177. Oxford: Oxford Univ. Press.

Barash, D.P.
1977  *Sociobiology and behavior.* NY: Elsevier.

Batault, G.
1921  *La Guerre Absolue.* Paris: Payot et Cie.

Bateson, P.
1985  [Review: *Not in our Genes* by Rose *et al.*] *New Sci.* 105:58–59.

Beard, Charles A.
1921  [Review: George Batault, *La Guerre Absolue*, Paris: Payot et Cie, n. d.] *The New Republic* 28:109.

Beckstrom, J.H.
1981  Sociobiology and intestate wealth transfers. *Northwestern Univ. Law Rev.* 76:216–270.

1985  *Sociobiology and the law.* Urbana, IL: Univ. Illinois Press.

Bell, A.P., and M.S. Weinberg
1978  *A study of diversity among men and women.* NY: Simon and Schuster.

Bell, A.P., M.S. Weinberg, and S.K. Hammersmith
1981  *Sexual preference: Its development in men and women.* Bloomington, IN: Indiana Univ. Press.

Bell, G.
1984.  Evolutionary and nonevolutionary theories of senescence. *Amer. Nat.* 124:600–603.

Benshoof, L., and R. Thornhill.
1979  The evolution of monogamy and concealed ovulation in humans. *J. Soc. Biol. Struct.* 2:95–106.

Betzig, L.L.
1982  Despotism and differential reproduction: A cross-cultural correlation of conflict asymmetry, hierarchy, and degree of polygyny. *Ethol. Sociobiol.* 3:209–221.

1986  *Despotism and differential reproduction: A Darwinian view of history.* Hawthorne, NY: Aldine.

Bigelow, R.S.
1969  *The dawn warriors: Man's evolution toward peace.* Boston, MA: Little, Brown.

Boehm, C.
1979  Some problems with altruism in the search for moral universals. *Behav. Sci.* 24:15–24.

Brandt, R.B.
1959  *Ethical theory: The problems of normative and critical ethics.* Englewood Cliffs, NJ: Prentice-Hall.

1979  *A theory of the good and the right.* Oxford: Clarendon Press.

Buss, D.M.
1985  Human mate selection. *Amer. Sci.* 73:47–51.

1987  Sex differences in human mate selection criteria: An evolutionary perspective. *In* C. Crawford, M. Smith, and D. Krebs (Eds.), *Sociobiology and psychology: Ideas, issues, and applications.* Hillsdale, NJ: Erlbaum.

Buss, D.M., and M. Barnes
  1986     Preferences in human mate selection. *J. Personal. Social Psychol.*
           50:559–570.
Callahan, D.
  1985     What do children owe elderly parents? *Hastings Center Rep.* 15:32–37.
Callahan, D., and H.T. Engelhardt (Eds.)
  1981     *The roots of ethics: Science, religion, and values.* NY: Plenum Press.
Campbell, D.T.
  1965     Ethnocentric and other altruistic motives. *Nebr. Symp. Motivation*
           13:283–311.
  1972     On the genetics of altruism and the counter-hedonic components in
           human culture. *J. Social Issues* 28:21–37.
  1975     Conflicts between biological and social evolution and between
           psychology and moral tradition. *Amer. Psychol.* 30:1103–1126.
  1979     Comments on the sociobiology of ethics and moralizing. *Behav. Sci.*
           24:37–45.
  1983     Legal and primary group social controls. *In* M. Gruter and P.
           Bohanan (Eds.), *Law, biology, and culture: The evolution of law,* pp.
           159–171. Santa Barbara, CA: Ross-Erickson, Inc.
Caplan, A.L. (Ed.)
  1978     *The sociobiology debate: Readings on ethical and scientific issues.* NY:
           Harper and Row.
Caplan, A.
  1983     [Review: *Morality as a Biological Phenomenon,* G.S. Stent (ed.),
           Berkeley: Univ. Calif. Press]. *Ethol. Sociobiol.* 4:237–238.
Carneiro, R.L.
  1970     A theory of the origin of the state. *Science* 169:733–38.
Carnesale, A., P. Doty, S. Hoffman, S.P. Huntington, J.S. Nye, Jr., and
S.D. Sagan
  1983     *Living with nuclear weapons.* NY: Bantam Books.
Case, J.
  1971     *The social triumph of the ancient church.* Freeport, NY: Books for
           Libraries Press.
Catholic Bishops, National Conference of
  1983     *The Challenge of peace: God's promise and our response. A pastoral letter on
           war and peace.* U.S. Catholic Conference. 1312 Mass. Ave., Washing-
           ton, D.C. 20005.
Cavalli-Sforza, L.L., and M.W. Feldman
  1981     *Cultural transmission and evolution: A quantitative approach.* Princeton,
           NJ: Princeton Univ. Press.
Chagnon, N.A.
  1968     *Yanomamö: The fierce people.* NY: Holt, Rinehart, and Winston.
  1979a    Mate competition, favoring close kin, and village fissioning among
           the Yanomamö Indians. *In* N.A. Chagnon and W.G. Irons (Eds.),
           *Evolutionary biology and human social behavior: An anthropological per-
           spective,* pp. 86–131. North Scituate, MA: Duxbury Press.
  1979b    Is reproductive success equal in egalitarian societies? *In* N.A.
           Chagnon and W.G. Irons (Eds.), *Evolutionary biology and human social
           behavior: An anthropological perspective,* pp. 374–401. North Scituate,
           MA: Duxbury Press.

Chagnon, N., and W. Irons (Eds).
1979    *Evolutionary biology and human social behavior: An anthropological perspective*. North Scituate, MA: Duxbury Press.

Chanley, J.
In prep.  Suicide: Evolutionary implications.

Charlesworth, B.
1980    *Evolution in age-structured populations*. Cambridge: Cambridge Univ. Press.

Charnov, E.L.
1978    Evolution of eusocial behavior; Offspring choice or parental parasitism? *J. Theoret. Biol.* 75:451–465.

Clare, M.J. and L.S. Luckinbill
1985    The effects of gene-environment interaction on the expression of longevity. *Heredity* 55:19–29.

Clutton-Brock. T.H., and Paul H. Harvey (Eds.)
1978    *Readings in sociobiology*. San Francisco, CA: Freeman.

Comfort, A.
1956    *Ageing: The biology of senescence*. NY: Holt, Rinehart and Winston.

Connor, R.
1986    Pseudo-reciprocity: Investing in mutualism. *Animal Behaviour* 34:1562–1566.

Cornford, F.M.
1941    *The Republic of Plato*. Translated with introduction and notes by F.M. Cornford. Oxford: Clarendon Press.

Curtis, H.J.
1963    Biological mechanisms underlying the aging process. *Science* 141:686–94.

Daly, M. and M. Wilson
1981    Abuse and neglect of children in evolutionary perspective. *In* R.D. Alexander and D.W. Tinkle (Eds), *Natural selection and social behavior: Recent research and new theory*, pp. 405–16. NY: Chiron Press.

1983    *Sex, evolution, and behavior*, 2nd ed. Boston, MA: Willard Grant Press.

Daniels, D.
1983    The evolution of concealed ovulation and self-deception. *Ethol. Sociobiol.* 4:69–87.

Darwin, C.
1859    *On the origin of species*. Facsimile of first edition with introduction by Ernst Mayr, publ. 1967. Cambridge, MA: Harvard Univ. Press.

1871    *The descent of man and selection in relation to sex*, 2 vols. NY: Appleton.

Dawkins, R.
1976    *The selfish gene*. Oxford: Oxford Univ. Press.

1979    Twelve misunderstandings of kin selection. *Zeitschr. Tierpsychol.* 51, 184–200.

1982    *The extended phenotype: The gene as the unit of selection*. San Francisco and Oxford: W.H. Freeman

1985    [Review: *Not in our Genes* by Rose *et al.*]. *New Sci.* 105:59–60..

Dawkins, R., and J.R. Krebs
1978    Animal signals: information or manipulation? *In* J.R. Krebs and N.B. Davies (Eds.), *Behavioural ecology*, pp. 282–309. Oxford: Blackwell Sci. Publ.

de Catanzaro, D.
    1980    Human suicide: A sociobiological perspective. *Behav. Brain Sci.* 3:265–290.
    1981    *Suicide and self-damaging behavior.* NY: Academic Press.

de Waal, F.
    1982    *Chimpanzee politics: power and sex among apes.* NY: Harper & Row.
    1986    The brutal elimination of a rival among captive male chimpanzees. *Ethol. Sociobiol. 7:89-103*

Dickemann, M.
    1975    Demographic consequences of infanticide in man. *Ann. Rev. Ecol. Syst.* 6:107–37.
    1979    The reproductive structure of stratified societies: A preliminary model: *In* N.A. Chagnon and W. Irons (Eds.), *Evolutionary biology and human social organization: An anthropological perspective,* pp. 331–367. North Scituate, MA: Duxbury Press.

Dickstein, E.B.
    1979    Biological and cognitive bases of moral functioning *Hum. Develop.* 22:37–59.

Dobzhansky, T.
    1961    Discussion. *In* J.S. Kennedy (Ed.), *Insect polymorphism,* p. 111. London: Symp. Royal Entomol. Soc. London.

Draper, T.
    1982    Dear Mr. Weinberger: An open reply to an open letter. *N.Y. Rev. Books,* Nov. 4, pp. 26–31.

Ebling, F.J. (Ed.)
    1969    *Biology and ethics.* NY: Academic Press.

Einhorn, M.B., G.L. Kane, and M. Nincic
    1984    Strategic arms control through test restraints. *Intern. Security* 8:108.

Ember, C.R.
    1978    Myths about hunter-gatherers. *Ethnology* 17:439–448.

Engelhardt, H.T., Jr., and D. Callahan (Eds.)
    1976    *Science, ethics, and medicine.* Hastings-on-Hudson, NY: Hastings Center, Inst. of Society, Ethics, and the Life Sciences.
    1978    *Morals, science, and sociality.* Hastings-on-Hudson, NY: Hastings Center, Inst. of Society, Ethics, and the Life Sciences.
    1980    *Knowing and valuing: The search for common roots.* Hastings-on-Hudson, NY: Hastings Center, Inst. of Society, Ethics, and the Life Sciences.

Ewald, P.W.
    1980    Evolutionary biology and the treatment of signs and symptoms of infectious disease. *J. Theoret. Biol.* 86:169–176.

Feinberg, J. (Ed.)
    1970    *Moral concepts.* NY: Oxford Univ. Press.

Fingarette, H.
    1969    *Self-Deception.* London: Routledge and Kegan Paul.

Fisher, R.A.
    1915    The evolution of sexual preference. *Eug. Rev.* 7:184–192.
    1930    (Rev. 1958). *The genetical theory of natural selection,* 2nd ed. NY: Dover.

Flew, A.
    1967    *Evolutionary ethics.* London: Macmillan.

Flinn, M.V.
   1981      Uterine vs. agnatic kinship variablility and associated cousin mar-
             riage preferences: An evolutionary biological analysis. *In* R.D.
             Alexander and D.W. Tinkle (Eds.), *Natural selection and social
             behavior: Recent research and new theory*, pp. 439–475. NY: Chiron
             Press.
Flinn, M.V., and R.D. Alexander
   1982      Culture theory: The developing synthesis from biology. *Hum. Ecol.*
             10:383–400.
Fox, R.
   1971      The cultural animal. *In* J. Eisenberg and Dillon (Eds.), *Man and beast:
             Comparative social behavior*, pp. 273–296. Washington D.C.: Smithson-
             ian Institution Press.
Frank, J.D.
   1967      *Sanity and survival: Psychological aspects of war and peace.* NY: Random
             House.
Frankena, W.K.
   1973      *Ethics*, 2nd. ed. Englewood Cliffs, NJ: Prentice Hall.
   1980      *Thinking about morality.* Ann Arbor, MI: Univ. Michigan Press.
Fries, J.F.
   1980      Aging, natural death, and the compression of morbidity. *New Engl.
             J. Med.* 303:130–135.
Gastil, R.D.
   1985      The past, present, and future of democracy. *J. Intern. Affairs* 38:
             161–179.
Gaylor, N.
   1982      A plan to cut the risk of nuclear war. *Detroit Free Press*, 25 April,
             p. B1.
Georgi, H.
   1981      A unified theory of elementary particle forces. *Sci. Amer.* 244(4):
             48–63.
Goodall, J.
   1986      *The chimpanzees of Gombe.* Cambridge, MA: Belknap Press.
Gould, J.L.
   1976      The dance-language controversy. *Quart. Rev. Biol.* 51: 211–244.
Gould, J.L., M. Henerey, and M.C. Macleod
   1970      Communication of direction by honey bee. *Science* 169:544–554.
Gould, S.J.
   1982      This view of life. *Nat. Hist.* 91:12–16.
   1984      Between you and your genes. *N.Y. Rev.* Aug. 16, pp. 30–32.
Gould, S.J., and R.C. Lewontin
   1979      The spandrels of San Marco and the panglossian paradigm: A
             critique of the adaptationist program. *Proc. Roy. Soc. London*
             B205:581–98.
Grant, G.P.
   1985      *English-speaking justice.* Notre Dame, Ind.: Univ. Notre Dame Press.
Grant, M.
   1977      *Jesus: A historian's review of the gospels.* NY: Charles Scribner's Sons.
Greenberg, L.
   1979      Genetic component of bee odor in kin recognition. *Science*
             206:1095–1097.

Gross, H.
1979    *A theory of criminal justice.* NY: Oxford Univ. Press.
Haig, A.
1982    The administration's stand. *Detroit Free Press,* 25 April, p. B1.
Hailman, J.P.
1982    Ontogeny: Toward a general theoretical framework for ethology.
        *Perspect. Ethol.* 5:133–189.
Hamilton, W.D.
1964    The genetical evolution of social behaviour, I, II. *J. Theoret. Biol.*
        7:1–52.
1966    The moulding of senescence by natural selection. *J. Theoret. Biol.*
        12:12–45.
1967    Extraordinary sex ratios. *Science* 156:477–488.
Hamilton, W.D. and M. Zuk
1982    Heritable true fitness and bright birds: A role for parasites? *Science*
        218:384–387.
Hardin, R., J.J. Mearsheimer, R. Dworkin, and R.E. Goodin (Eds.).
1985    *Nuclear deterrence: Ethics and strategy.* Chicago, IL: Univ. Chicago
        Press.
Harris, M.
1979    *Cultural materialism: The struggle for a science of culture.* NY: Random
        House.
Hill, J.
1984    Prestige and reproductive success in man. *Ethol. Sociobiol.* 5:77–96.
Hirshfield, M.F., and D.W. Tinkle
1975    Natural selection and the evolution of reproductive effort. *Proc. Nat.
        Acad. Sci. U.S.* 72:2227–2231.
Hoffman, M. L.
1981    Is altruism part of human nature? *J. Personal. Social Psychol.*
        40:121–138.
Holmes, Oliver Wendell.
1881    The deacon's masterpiece: or the wonderful "one-hoss-shay." *In The
        autocrat of the breakfast table.* Cambridge, MA: Houghton Mifflin.
Holmes, W.G., and P.W. Sherman
1983    Kin recognition in animals. *Amer. Sci.* 71:46–55.
Hoogland, J.L., and P.W. Sherman
1976    Advantages and disadvantages of bank swallow (*Riparia riparia*)
        coloniality. *Ecol. Monogr.* 46:33–58.
Hrdy, S.B.
1981    *The woman that never evolved.* Cambridge, MA: Harvard Univ. Press.
Hull, D.L.
1978    Altruism in science: a sociobiological model of co-operative behavior
        among scientists. *Animal Behav.* 26:685–97.
Hume D.
1750    *An Enquiry concerning the principles of morals.* LaSalle, IL: Open Court
(1930)  Publ. Co.
1772    *Essays and treatises on several subjects,* Vol. 2. Edinburgh: Bell,
        Bradfute and Blackwood.
Humphrey, N.K.
1976    The social function of intellect. *In* P.P.G. Bateson and R.A. Hinde

(Eds.). *Growing points in ethology*. London: Cambridge University Press.

Hunt, L.
1980    *Selected readings in sociobiology*. NY: McGraw-Hill.

Huxley, T.H.
1894    Speech at the Royal Society Dinner. Orig. publ., *London Times*. Reprinted 1983 *In* G. de Beer (Ed.), *Charles Darwin-Thomas Henry Huxley. Autobiographies*, pp. 110–112. NY: Oxford: Oxford Univ. Press.
1896    *Evolution and ethics and other essays*. NY: Appleton.

Huxley, T.H., and J. Huxley
1947    *Evolution and ethics: 1893–1943*. London: Pilot Press Ltd.

Irons, W.
1979    Natural selection, adaptation, and human social behavior. *In* N.A. Chagnon and W. Irons (Eds.), *Evolutionary biology and human social behavior: An anthropological perspective*, pp. 4–38. North Scituate, MA: Duxbury Press.

Jarvis, J.
1981    Eusociality in a mammal: cooperative breeding in naked mole-rat colonies. *Science* 212:571–573.

Jarvis, J., P.W. Sherman, and R.D. Alexander (Eds.)
In prep.  The natural history and social behavior of the naked mole rat, *Heterocephalus glaber*.

Jastrow, R.
1984    How to make nuclear war obsolete. *Sci. Digest*, June, pp. 39–43, 96–97.

Kaiser, R.B.
1981    The way of the journal. *Psychol. Today* 15:64–76.

Kalin, J.
1957    On ethical egoism. *In* N. Reschet (Ed.), *Studies in moral philosophy*, Amer. Phil. Quart. Monogr. 1. Oxford: Basil Blackwell.

Keith, A., Sir
1947    *Evolution and ethics*. NY: G.P. Putnam's Sons.
1949    *A new theory of human evolution*. NY: Philosophical Library.

Kelsen, H.
1957    *What is justice? Justice, law, and politics in the mirror of science. Collected essays*. Berkeley, CA: Univ. Calif. Press.

Keyfitz, N.
1984    The population of China. *Sci. Amer.* 250:38–47.

Kitcher, P.
1985    *Vaulting ambition*. MA: MIT Press.

Kohlberg, L.L.
1981    *Essays on moral development. I. The Philosophy of moral development*. San Francisco, CA: Harper and Row.
1984    *Essays on moral development. II. The Psychology of moral development*. San Francisco, CA: Harper and Row.

Konner, M.
1982    *The tangled wing: Biological constraints on the human spirit*. NY: Harper Colophon Books.
1984    The politics of biology. *Nat. Hist.* 93:66–69.

Konner, M., and C. Worthman
  1980      Nursing frequency, gonadal function, and birth spacing among
            !Kung hunter-gatherers. *Science* 207:788–791.
Krebs, J.R., and N.B. Davies
  1981      *An introduction to behavioural ecology.* Sunderland, MA: Sinauer.
  1984.     *Behavioral ecology. An evolutionary approach,* 2nd ed. Sunderland, MA:
            Sinauer.
Kupperman, J.J.
  1983      *The foundations of morality.* London, Boston: Allen and Unwin.
Lack, D.L.
  1954      *The natural regulation of animal numbers.* Oxford: Oxford Univ. Press.
  1957      *Evolutionary theory and Christian belief; The unresolved conflict.* London:
            Methuen.
  1965.     Natural selection and human nature. *In* I.T. Ramsey (Ed.), *Biology
            and personality: Frontier problems in science, philosophy and religion,* pp.
            40–48. NY: Barnes and Noble, Inc.
Lacy, R.C., and P.W. Sherman
  1983      Kin recognition by phenotype matching. *Amer. Nat.* 121:489–512.
Lebra, T.S.
  1972      Reciprocity-based moral sanctions and messianic salvation. *Amer.
            Anthropol.* 74:391–407.
Leigh, E.G.
  1977      How does selection reconcile individual advantage with the good of
            the group? *Proc. Natl. Acad. Sci. U.S.* 74:4542–46.
  1983      When does the good of the group override the advantage of the
            individual? *Proc. Natl. Acad. Sci. U.S.* 80:2985–89.
Levins, R. and Lewontin, R.C.
  1985      *The dialectical biologist.* Cambridge, MA: Harvard Univ. Press.
Lewontin, R.C.
  1966      Adaptation and natural selection. *Science* 152:338–339.
  1970      The units of selection. *Ann Rev. Ecol. Syst.* 1:1–18.
  1979      Sociobiology as an adaptationist program. *Behav. Sci.* 24:5–14.
Lewontin, R.C., S. Rose, and L.J. Kamin
  1984      *Not in our genes: Biology, ideology, and human nature.* NY: Pantheon
            Books.
Lindauer, M.
  1961      *Communication among social bees.* Cambridge, MA: Harvard Univ.
            Press.
Lindsey, H.
  1980      *The 1980's: Countdown to Armageddon.* NY: Bantam Books, Inc.
Lipson, L.
  1985      The philosophy of democracy—can its contradictions be reconciled?
            *J. Intern. Affairs* 38:151–160.
Lloyd, J.E.
  1977      Bioluminescence and communication. *In* T.A. Sebeok (Ed.), *How
            animals communicate,* pp. 164–183. Bloomington, IN: Indiana Univ.
            Press.
  1980      Male *photuris* fireflies mimic sexual signals of their females' prey.
            *Science* 210:669–671.
Luckinbill, L.S., and M.J. Clare
  1985      Selection for life span in *Drosophila melangogaster. Heredity* 55:9–18.

Luckinbill, L.S., R. Arking, M.C. Clare, W.C. Cirocco, and S.A. Buck
    1984       Selection for delayed senescence in *Drosophila*. *Evolution* 38:996–1003.
Luker, K.
    1984a     *Abortion and the politics of motherhood*. Berkeley, CA: Univ. California
                Press.
    1984b     The war between the women. *Family Planning Perspect.* 16:105–110.
Lumsden, C.J., and E.O. Wilson
    1981       *Genes, mind and culture: The coevolutionary process*. Cambridge, MA:
                Harvard univ. Press.
Lyons, D.
    1965       *Forms and limits of utilitarianism*. Oxford: Clarendon Press.
MacDonald, K.
    1983       Population, social controls, and ideology: Toward a sociobiology of
                the phenotype. *J. Social Biol. Struct.* 6:297–317.
MacIntyre, A.
    1981a     A crisis in moral philosophy: Why is the search for the foundations
                of ethics so frustrating? *In* D. Callahan and H.T. Engelhardt, Jr.
                (Eds.), *The roots of ethics*, pp. 3–30. New York and London: Plenum
                Press.
    1981b     *After virtue: A study in moral theory. Notre Dame*, IN: Univ. of Notre
                Dame Press.
Mackie, J.L.
    1978       The law of the jungle. *Philosophy* 53:455–464.
    1982       Cooperation, competition, and moral philosophy. *In* A.M. Colman
                (Ed.), *Cooperation, competition, in humans and animals*. pp. 271–294.
                Berkshire, England: Van Nostrand Reinhold (UK) Co., Ltd.
McNamara, R., and H. Bethe
    1985       Reducing the risk of nuclear war. *The Atlantic* 256:43–51 (July).
MacPherson, C.B.
    1979       *The political theory of possessive individualism*. NY: Oxford Univ.
                Press.
Malherbe, J.
    1979       *Social aspects of early Christianity*. Baton Rouge, LA: Louisiana State
                Univ. Press.
Martin, W.
    1982       Waiting for the end. *The Atlantic* 249(6):31–37.
Martin, W.E.
    1954       Learning theory and identification: III. The development of values in
                children. *J. Genet. Psychol.* 84:211–217.
Maynard Smith, J.
    1974       The theory of games and the evolution of animal conflicts. *J. Theoret.
                Biol.* 47:209–221.
    1978       *The evolution of sex*. Cambridge: Cambridge Univ. Press.
    1982       *Evolution and the theory of games*. NY: Cambridge Univ. Press.
Maynard Smith, J., and G. A. Parker
    1976       The logic of asymmetric contests. *Animal Behav.* 24:159–175.
Mayr, E.
    1961       Cause and effect in biology. *Science* 134: 1501–6.
Medawar, P.
    1955       The definition and measurement of senescence. *Ciba Found. Colloq.
                Ageing* 1:14–15.

1957      *The uniqueness of the individual.* London: Methuen.
Miller, D.
1976      *Social justice.* Oxford: Oxford Univ. Press.
Mintzer, A.
1982      Nestmate recognition and incompatibility between colonies of the acacia ant, *Pseudomyrmex ferruginea. Behav. Ecol. Sociobiol.* 10: 165–168.
Murnion, P.J. (Ed.)
1983      Catholics and nuclear war: A commentary on the challenge of peace. The U.S. Catholic Bishops' Pastoral Letter on War and Peace. NY: Crossroad Publ. Co.
Nader, L., and H.F. Todd, Jr. (Eds.)
1978.     *The disputing process—Law in ten societies.* NY: Columbia Univ. Press.
Nielsen, K.
1978      Why should I be moral? *In* P.W. Taylor (Ed.), *Problems of moral philosophy,* 3rd ed., pp. 539–559. Belmont, CA: Wadsworth Publ. Co.
Nietzsche, F.
1895      *The Antichrist.* Republished 1954. *In* W. Kaufmann (Ed.). *The portable Nietsche,* pp. 569–656. NY: Viking.
Nincic, M.
1982      *The arms race: The political economy of military growth.* NY: Praeger.
Noonan, K.M.
1981      Individual strategies of inclusive-fitness-maximizing in *Polistes fuscatus* foundresses. *In* R.D. Alexander and D.W. Tinkle (Eds.), *Natural selection and social behavior: Recent research and new theory,* pp. 18–44. NY: Chiron Press.
Otte, D.
1974      Effects and functions in the evolution of signaling systems. *Ann. Rev. Ecol. Syst.* 5:385–417.
Parker, G.A.
1974      Assessment strategy and the evolution of fighting behavior. *J. Theoret. Biol.* 47:223–243.
1984      Evolutionarily stable strategies. *In* J.R. Krebs and N.B. Davies (Eds.), *Behavioural ecology: An evolutionary approach,* pp. 30–61. Sunderland, MA: Sinauer.
Parker, G.A., R.R. Baker, and V.G.F. Smith
1972      The origin and evolution of gamete dimorphism and the male–female phenomenon. *J. Theoret. Biol.* 36:529–553.
Payne, R.
1983      The social context of song mimicry: song-matching dialects in indigo buntings (*Passerina cyanea*). *Anim. Behav.* 31:788–805.
Perry, R.B.
1954      *Realms of value; A critique of human civilization.* Cambridge, MA: Harvard Univ. Press.
Pitt, R.
1978      Warfare and hominid brain evolution. *J. Theoret. Biol.* 72:551–575.
Pound, R.
1941      My philosophy of law. *Credos of sixteen American scholars.* Boston, MA: Boston Law Book Co.

1959      *Jurisprudence*. St. Paul, MN: West Publ. Co.
Powers, T.
1982      Choosing a strategy for World War III. *Atlantic* 250:82–110 (Nov.).
President's Commission for the Study of Ethical Problems in Medicine and Biomedical and Behavioral Research
1981      *Defining Death. A Report on the Medical, Legal and Ethical Issues in the Determination of Death.* Superintendent of Documents, U.S. Government Printing Office, Washington, D.C. 20402.
Pulliam, H.R., and C. Dunford
1980      *Programmed to learn: An essay on the evolution of culture.* NY: Columbia Univ. Press.
Raymond, J.C.
1982      Rhetoric: The methodology of the humanities. *College Engl.* 44:778–83.
Rawls, J.
1971      *A theory of justice.* Cambridge, MA: Harvard Univ. Press.
Richards, R.
1982      Darwin and the biologizing of moral behavior. *In* W. Woodward and M. Ash (Eds.), *The problematic science: Psychology in nineteen-century thought*, pp. 43–64.
1986a     *Darwin and the emergence of evolutionary theories of mind and behavior.* Chicago: Univ. Chicago Press.
1986b     A defense of evolutionary ethics. *Biol. Phil.* 1, 265–293.
Rose, M.R.
1984      Laboratory evolution of postponed senescence in *Drosophila melanogaster. Evolution* 38:1004–1039.
Rose, M., and B. Charlesworth
1980      A test of evolutionary theories of senescence. *Nature (London)* 287:141–142.
Rosenblatt, R.
1985      The quality of mercy killing. *Time* 126(8):74.
Ross, G.G.
1985      *Grand unified theories.* Menlo Park, CA: Benjamin/Cummins.
Ruse, M.
1979      *Sociobiology: Sense or nonsense.* Dordrecht, Holland: Reidel.
1981      *Is science sexist? And other problems in the biomedical sciences.* Dordrecht, Holland: Reidel.
1982      *Darwinism defended: A guide to the evolution controversies.* Reading, MA: Addison-Wesley.
1986      *Taking Darwin seriously.* Boston, MA: Blackwell.
Russell, B.
1935      *Religion and science.* NY: Henry Holt and Co.
Sahlins, M.D.
1965      On the sociology of primitive exchange. *In* M. Banton (Ed.), *The relevance of models for social anthropology*, pp. 139–236. London: Travistock.
1976      *The use and abuse of biology: An anthropological critique of sociobiology.* Ann Arbor, MI: Univ. Michigan Press.
Sartorius, R.
1975      *Individual conduct and social norms.* Encino, CA: Dickenson.

Schell, J.
1982     *The fate of the Earth.* NY: Knopf.
Schneider, E.L.
1978     *The genetics of ageing.* NY: Plenum Press.
Schwartz, R.D., and J.C. Miller
1964     Legal evolution and societal complexity. *Amer. J. Sociol.* 70:159–169.
Searle, J.
1984     *Minds, brains, and science.* Cambridge, MA: Harvard Univ. Press.
Sherman, P.W., and W.G. Holmes
1985     Kin recognition: Issues and evidence. *In* B. Holldobler and S.
         Lindauer (Eds.), *Experimental behavioral ecology, Fortschritte der
         Zoologie,* Vol. 31, pp. 437–460. NY and Stuttgart: G. Fischer Verlag.
Simpson, G.G.
1964     *This view of life, the world of an evolutionist.* NY: Harcourt, Brace and
         World.
1966     Naturalistic ethics and social sciences. *Amer. Psychol.* 21:27–36.
Singer, P.
1981     *The expanding circle. Ethics and sociobiology.* NY: Farrar, Straus, and
         Giroux.
Smith, A.
1776     (1970). *In* A. Skinner (Ed.), *The wealth of nations.* 1970 ed., Part 1,
         Book v, Chapter 1. Baltimore, MD: Penguin Books.
Sokal, R.R.
1970     Senescence and genetic load: Evidence from *Tribolium. Science*
         167:1733–1734.
Spector, W.S.
1956     *Handbook of biological data.* Philadelphia, PA: Saunders.
Stearns, S.C.
1976     Life-history tactics: A review of the ideas. *Quart. Rev. Biol.* 51:3–47.
1977     The evolution of life history traits: a critique of the theory and a
         review of the data. *Ann. Rev. Ecol. Syst.* 8:145–71.
Stent, G.S. (Ed.)
1978     *Morality as a biological phenomenon. The presuppositions of sociobiological
         research.* Berkeley and Los Angeles: Univ. California Press.
Strassmann, B.I.
1981     Sexual selection, paternal care and concealed ovulation in humans.
         *Ethol. Sociobiol.* 2:31–40.
Strassmann, J.E.
1981     Kin selection and satellite nests in *Polistes exclamans. In* R.D.
         Alexander and D.W. Tinkle (Eds.), *Natural selection and social
         behavior: Recent research and new theory.* pp. 45–58. NY: Chiron Press.
Strate, J.M.
1982     *An evolutionary view of political culture.* Ph.D., Univ. Michigan.
Strong, C.
1984     The neonatologist's duty to patient and parents. *Hastings Center Rep.*
         14:10–16.
Symons, D.
1979     *The evolution of human sexuality.* NY: Oxford Univ. Press.
Thompson, P.R.
1980     And who is my neighbour? An answer from evolutionary genetics.
         *Biol. Social Life* 19:341–384.

Thornhill, R., and J. Alcock
1983    *The evolution of insect mating systems.* Cambridge, MA: Harvard Univ. Press.

Thornhill, R., and N.W. Thornhill
1983    Human rape: An evolutionary analysis. *Ethol. Sociobiol.* 4:137–173.

Tinbergen, N.
1951    *The study of instinct.* Oxford: Clarendon Press.

Titmuss, R.M.
1971    *The gift relationship.* NY: Pantheon Books.

Trivers, R.L.
1971    The evolution of reciprocal altruism. *Quart. Rev. Biol.* 46:35–57.
1972    Parental investment and sexual selection. *In* B. Campbell (Ed.), *Sexual selection and the descent of man,* pp. 136–79. Chicago: Aldine.
1974    Parent-offspring conflict. *Amer. Zool.* 14:249–64.
1985    *Social evolution.* Menlo Park, CA: Benjamin/Cummings.

Trivers, R.L., and H. Hare
1976    Haplodiploidy and the evolution of social insects. *Science* 191:249–263.

Trivers, R.L., and D.E. Willard
1973    Natural selection of parental ability to vary the sex ratio of offspring. *Science* 179:90–92.

Tucker, R.W.
1985    Morality and deterrence. *In* R. Hardin, J.J. Mearsheimer, G. Dworkin, and R.E. Goodin (Eds.), *Nuclear deterrence: Ethics and strategy,* pp. 53–70. Chicago: Univ. Chicago Press.

Turner, E.S.
1980    *Dear old blighty.* Michael Joseph Std.

Vining, D.R.
1986    Social versus reproductive success: the central theoretical problem of human sociobiology. *Behav. Brain Sci.* 9: 167–187.

von, Frisch, K.
1954    *The dancing bees: An account of the life and senses of the honey bee.* Translated by Dora Ilse. London: Methuen.

Waddington, C.H
1941    The relations between science and ethics. *Nature (London)* 148:270–274.

Wade, M.J.
1976    Group selection among laboratory populations of *Tribolium. Proc. Nat. Acad. Sci. U.S.* 73:4604–07.
1978    A critical review of the models of group selection. *Quart. Rev. Biol.* 53:101–114.

Weismann, A.
1891    *Essays upon heredity and kindred biological problems,* 2nd ed. Oxford: Clarendon Press.

West Eberhard, M.J.
1969    The social biology of polistine wasps. *Univ. Mich. Mus. Zool. Misc. Publ.* 140:1–101.
1975    The evolution of social behavior by kin selection. *Quart. Rev. Biol.* 50:1–33.

Whiteley, C.H.
1976      Morality and egoism. *Mind* 85:90–96.
Wickler, W.
1972      *The biology of the ten commandments.* NY: McGraw-Hill.
Williams, B.A.O.
1980      Conclusion. *In* G.S. Stent (Ed.), *Morality as a Biological Phenomenon,*
          pp. 275–285. The Presuppositions of Sociobiological Research.
          Berkeley and Los Angeles: Univ. California Press.
Williams, G.C.
1957      Pleiotropy, natural selection, and the evolution of senescence.
          *Evolution* 11:398–411.
1966a     *Adaptation and natural selection.* Princeton, NY: Princeton Univ.
          Press.
1966b     Natural selection, the costs of reproduction, and a refinement of
          Lack's principle. *Amer. Nat.* 100:687–90.
1975      *Sex and evolution.* Princeton, NJ: Princeton U. Press.
1979      The question of adaptive sex ratio in outcrossed vertebrates. *Proc.
          Royal Soc. London* B205:567–580.
Wilson, D.S.
1975      New model for group selection. *Science* 189:8701.
1980      *The Natural Selection of Populations and Communities.* Menlo Park,
          Calif: Benjamin/Cummings.
Wilson, E.O.
1971      *The insect societies.* Cambridge, MA: Harvard Univ. Press.
1972      On the queerness of social evolution. *Bull. Entomol. Soc. Amer.*
          19:20–22.
1975      *Sociobiology: The new synthesis.* Cambridge, MA: Harvard Univ. Press.
1978      *On Human Nature.* Cambridge, MA: Harvard Univ. Press.
1980      Comparative social theory. *In* S.M. McMurrin (Ed.), *The Tanner
          lectures on human values.* I. pp. 49–130. Salt Lake City, UT: Univ. Utah
          Press.
1981      The relation of science to theology. *Zygon* 15:425–434.
Wilson, J.Q. and R.J. Herrnstein
1985      *Crime and human nature.* NY: Simon and Schuster.
Wittenberger, J.F.
1981      *Animal social behavior.* Boston, MA: Duxbury Press.
Wodinsky, J.
1977      Hormonal inhibition of feeding and death in *Octopus:* control by
          optic gland secretion. *Science* 198:948–951.

# NAME INDEX

## A

Alcock, J., 2, 14, 19
Alexander, R.D., 2, 4–6, 8, 12,
    18, 21, 24–28, 30, 37, 38, 42, 52,
    54–56, 58, 62–69, 71, 72, 79, 80,
    84, 85, 88, 94, 95, 100, 102–105,
    107, 110, 122, 123, 125, 127,
    142, 153, 163, 169, 174, 185,
    204, 216, 218, 219, 222, 228, 253
Altman, P.L., 39
Anonymous, 247–248
Aoki, S., 64–66
Arras, J.D., 211, 213
Atwood, M., 216
Axelrod, R., 85, 95, 235, 242

## B

Bagehot, W., 227
Baier, K., 106, 145, 150, 152, 163,
    180, 182, 183–184
Baker, J.R., 14
Baker, R.R., 64
Barnes, M., 217
Barash, D.P., 4
Batault, G., 258
Bateson, P., 19, 224
Beard, C., 258
Beckstrom, J.H., 221–222
Bell, A.P., 217
Bell, G., 58
Benshoof, L., 153
Bethe, H., 246, 250
Betzig, L.L., 2, 26, 27, 69, 72,
    108, 128, 179, 185, 189, 210, 229
Bierce, A., 126

Bigelow, R.S., xxi, 79, 110, 127,
    163
Boehm, C., 4
Borgia, G., 37, 42, 69, 79
Bradley: 162
Brandt, R.B., 89, 146–150
Bulwer-Lytton, 123
Buss, D.M., 217
Butler, S., 162

## C

Callahan, D., xiv, 89–91
Campbell, D.T., 4, 104, 110, 123
Camus, A., 123
Caplan, A., 4
Carneiro, R.L., 163
Carnesale, A., 234, 242,
    244–245, 246–248, 251
Carpenter, E., 173
Case, J., 202
Catholic Bishops, 247, 248
Cavalli-Sforza, L.L., 2
Chagnon, N.A., 2, 229
Chanley, J., 45, 206
Charlesworth, B., 43, 50, 58
Charnov, E.L., 68
Clare, M.J., 58
Clutton-Brock, T.H., 2
Comfort, A., 45, 46
Condorcet, 173
Connor, R., 87
Cornford, F.M., 143, 227
Curtis, H.J., 44, 45

## D

Daly, M., 2, 14, 179, 216–218
Daniels, D., 115
Darwin, C.R., xvii, 4, 10, 121,

281

# SUBJECT INDEX

## A

Abortion, xiv, 61, 210, 214–216
Act utilitarianism, 120
Adaptation
  *defined*, 17
  as onerous concept, 46
Adaptationist program, 17
Adaptationists, 46
Affirmative action, 185, 186
Afterlife, 206
Aggression, 1
  and mortality of young males,
    61
Aid to Dependent Children, 221
Allele, *defined*, 8
Altruism, 3, 38, 146, 194, 195
  of biologists and philosophers
    compared, 145 ff.
  discriminative, 115
  genetic, 82, 104, 255
  indiscriminate, 192, 233–234
  temporary, of reciprocity, 84
Altruist, kinds of, 118–119
Altruistic tendencies, 86
Amity, within-group, 195
Angels, 200
Ann Arbor News, 72
Anthropology, symbolic, 128
Anticipation, as proximate
    mechanism, 26
Ants, 46, 65, 67
Apes, great, 112
Aphids, as cooperative clones,
    65, 66
Armadillo, monozygotic offspring
    and cooperativeness, 66–67

Armageddon, and nuclear
    holocaust, 129
Armies, 189, 190
Arms races, 23, 214, 227 ff., 256
  brakes on, 205, 230 ff., 240
  resolution of, 231 ff.
Asceticism, 103
Asexual clones, and senescence,
    51
Attila the Hun, 248

## B

Baboons
  cooperation against predators,
    79
  silence of play in, 80
Balance of power, 234 ff.
  hypothesis, 107, 110
  races, 79
Balding, and sexual selection, 56
Bands, 185
Batesian mimicry, and deception,
    74
Bees, 67
Beetles, 56
Behavior
  physiological, psychological,
    social, cultural aspects of,
    7
  purely cultural vs. purely
    genetic, 23
Beneficence
  discriminative, 186
  discriminative and
    nondiscriminative, 97 ff.,
    207
  as evolved, 101–106